SOLDIERS OF THE REVOLUTION

— IN —

BEDFORD COUNTY TN.

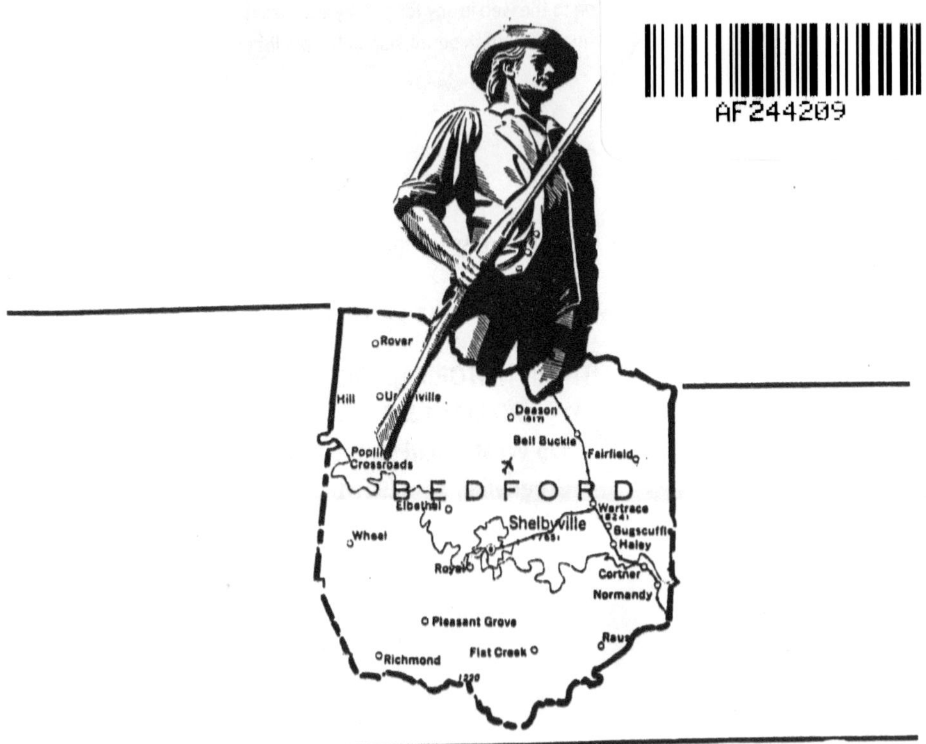

COMPILED BY

HELEN C. & TIMOTHY R. MARSH

SHELBYVILLE TENNESSEE

Please direct all correspondence and orders to:

www.southernhistoricalpress.com
or
SOUTHERN HISTORICAL PRESS, Inc.
PO BOX 1267
375 West Broad Street
Greenville, SC   29601
southernhistoricalpress@gmail.com

ISBN #0-89308-653-3

Printed in the United States of America

PREFACE

Bedford County, Tennessee was organized December 3, 1807 and was taken from the parent County of Rutherford. From October 1799 to October 1803, the western portion of Bedford County, as it exists today, was included in Williamson County. From 1807 to November 1809, Bedford County extended to the southern boundary of the State. Lincoln County was formed out of Bedford in 1809.

A part of Bedford was removed in 1836 to form the western section of Coffee County, Tennessee, another part was removed in 1836 to form the eastern part of Marshall County and finally in 1871, a small strip along the southern boundary was removed in the formation of Moore County, Tennessee.

A number of Revolutionary Soldiers filed for pension while living in the part of Marshall County, Tennessee, that at the time of filing was a part of Bedford County.

Some of the Soldiers and Patriots listed in this publication settled in Bedford County for only a brief time and moved on to other Counties or States, but those that were known to us have been included, because some established "roots" in Bedford County.

This book is not a publication of Genealogical Records of the Revolutionary Soldiers and Patriots of Bedford County, nor was it intended to be such, but rather a documented record with primary reliance on Pension Records obtained from the General Services Administration Records in Washington, D.C. Family records that were in our hands at the time this book was compiled, were included.

Some Patriots, who were in Bedford County, are not included as they died before making application for pension. Some were too proud to apply feeling that "freedom" was pay enough.

Obviously some Soldiers and Patriots were unknown to us and regrettably omitted. Acquiring information on these noble men and women, one hundred and fifty years after the fact, was not an easy tack and had we succumb to the temptation to delay publishing until we found all of them, the book would have never been published.

Helen Crawford Marsh
Timothy Richard Marsh
1988

PATRIOT INDEX

JAMES ANDERSON

Name: Rank: State Served:
James Anderson   Pvt   North Carolina

Born August 18, 1764 in Maryland, died after 1834 (71 years old in 1834 Pension)

In 1850 Census of Bedford County, Tennessee:

       Elizabeth Anderson, aged 73 years, born in Maryland, living near William Carlisle and living with John D. Muse and wife Dienna. (Area of Dyer (Big Spring) Cemetery.

       James Anderson is buried in Bedford County, Tennessee in an unmarked grave.

GSA: James Anderson, S.1786. Served in North Carolina.

6340: West Tennessee, James Anderson, of Bedford County, in the State of Tennessee, who was a Private in the Company by Captain Maxwell of the Regt commanded by Col. Campbell in the Tennessee (North Carolina) Line for Militia Guard from 1776.

       Inscribed on the Roll of Tennessee at the rate of 30 dollars, ___ cents per annum, to commence on the 4th day of March 1831. Certificate of Pension issued 28th day of February 1833 and sent to James K. Polk.

           Arrears the 4th September 1832 $45.00
           Semi-anl allowance ending 4 March 1833   . 15.00
                                                  $60.00

Recorded by Henry H. Sylvester, Clerk   Revolutionary Claim
Book D   Vol 7   page 143   Act June 7, 1832

Declaration:

       Declaration in order to obtain the benefit of the Act of Congress passed 7th June 1832.

       On this 16th day of August in the year of our Lord one, thousand eight hundred and thirty two. Personally appeared in open court, before the Worshipful John L. Neill, Samuel Phillips and John B. Armstrong, Esquire, Gentlemen Justices of the Peace, appointed to hold Court of Pleas and Quarter Sessions of the County of Bedford and State of Tennessee, James Anderson, Sen., aged sixty seven years, eleven months, and twenty nine days, and a resident of Bedford County and State aforesaid, who after being first duly sworn according to law and doth on his oath make the following declaration in order to obtain the benefit of the Act of Congress passed June 7th 1832. That he entered the Service of the United States under the following named officers, and served as herein stated, to wit, that he entered the Service of the United States, as a volunteer under Captain Looney in the Spring of 1776. To assist in guarding a Fort on Holston River, called Looney's. First on the frontiers of the white settlement, he states he entered as one of the guards under Captain Looney and other officers whose names he does not now recollect. In changing to the American Troops previous to the Battle of the Long Island, between the Americans and Indians, he states he was not on the Muster Roll at that time, but by the permission of his father and the promise of Captain Looney, that as he understood and was well acquainted with the use of the rifle, that if he would serve a tour of duty at this time, it would exempt him, when he should be placed on the Muster Roll, and he believes he served on this occasion about two months.

       He further states, that afterwards, he thinks in the year 1778, he volunteered again with one Captain Thomas Caldwell, and was marched to a Fort at the mouth of Big Creek on Holston River, the name of the fort, he does not recollect, and was told by his Captain that the object in going to said Fort was to meet a supposed attack by some white families, that stated they were from North Carolina and intended going down Holston River and was supposed to be friendly with the Cherokee Indians, was enemies at that time to the Americans and he thinks he served on this expedition about two months or upwards. He further states that he volunteered in the year 1779 about the first of December and was attached to Captain George Maxwell's Company of Mounted Gunmen, commanded by Colonel Arthur Campbell and Colonel Joseph Martin.

       On an expedition against the Cherokee Nation of Indians, and was marched into the Cherolee Nation, on what was called Tennessee River, to a little town called the beloved Town, and at that place, was engaged in a skirmish with the Indians, in which engagement or skirmish only one American wounded and several marched on down through the Waxhaw Settlement and from that, to the high hill of Santee, where he states he saw General Green's Army, as he was told, and from that, was marched on and joined Colonel John Sevier's Regiment of Mounted Gunmen from which is now called Washington County, East Tennessee, Nolachucky River, and from that place, was marched on to General Marion's Army, within two or three miles of Santee River where he remained pretty much until he was marched back home. He states while he remained with General Marion's Army, a British hospital was taken by our troops and he thinks about thirty or forty prisoners taken, he thinks he got home sometime after Christmas, after serving a tour of duty as he believes of five (5) months, making in all a term of service of about twelve months. He further states that after he was dismissed, he received an instrument of writing, stating his services, but who it was signed by he does not recollect, but that he sold his claim for his service then to James Campbell and gave him the writing to establish the claim as he now thinks. He hereby relinguishes his claim to any pension or annuity whatever, except the present, and declares that his name is not on the Pension Roll of any agency in the United States. That he had no documentary evidence whatever at this time, and that he knows of no person whose testimony he can procure who can testify as to his service.

Interrogatories by the Court.

Q. 1st: Where and in what year were you born?

A.   I was born in the State of Maryland but I do not recollect the name of the county, on the 18th day of August 1764.

Q. 2nd: Have you any record of your age and if so, where is it?

A.   I have a record of my age taken from my father's Bible, and I have it here with me and it reads thus: "James Anderson born August 18th day 1764."

Q. 3rd: Where were you living when called into service, where have you lived since the Revolutionary War and where do you now live?

A.   I lived in the section of country now called Sullivan County, East Tennessee about twenty six (26) miles from Abington in the State of Virginia, and that was my place of residence during the War of the Revolution and afterwards until the year 1808, in December, when I removed to White County, Tennessee, and from that to Bedford County, Tennessee in the spring of 1812, where I now live.

Q. 4th: How were you called into service, were you a volunteer, were you drafted, or were you a substitute, and if a substitute for whom?

A.   I was a volunteer all the time of my service, except the last tour, and then I was drafted.

Q. 5th: States the names of some of the regular officers who were with you in the troops where you served, such Continental and Militia Regiment as you can recollect, and the general circumstances of your service.

A.   I recollect General Marion and I also recollect there was some officers came to our camp when we were encamped on Santee River and enlisted two men from our troops, one by the name of Moses Webb and a Mr. Baly. I do not recollect the names or numbers of any regiment of Militia or Regulars except what I have given in the foregoing declaration.

Q. 6th: Did you ever receive a discharge and if so, where is it?

A.   I received an instrument in writing which I was told would enable me to get pay, at some time or order which paper I sold to James Campbell and what he done with it, I do not know.

Q. 7th: State the names of persons to whom you are known in your neighborhood who can testify as to your character for veracity and their belief of your service as a Soldier of the Revolution.

A.   The Rev. George Newton, Col. John Warner, John L. Neill, Esquires.

Sworn to in open court this 16th day of August 1832.

Jas. McKisick, Clerk   James Anderson (Seal)

An amendment to the declaration of James Anderson was made at August Term 1832 of Bedford County Court in order to obtain the benefit of the Act of Congress passed 7th June 1832.

2

State of Tennessee]
Bedford County   ]
      Personally appeared before me the undersigned, a Justice of the Peace for said county, James Anderson, who subscribed and was sworn to the declaration above alluded to, who after being sworn according to law, deposeth and said that by reason of old age, and the consequent loss of memory, he cannot swear positively as to the precise length of his service, but according to the best of his recollection, he served not less than the periods below, and in the following grades, to wit, that he served as a private soldier and volunteer under Captain Looney not less than two months in the year 1776 and that he served not less than two months with Captain Thomas Caldwell as a volunteer, private soldier, and that he served not less than three months in a company of Mounted Gunmen commanded by Captain George Maxwell against the hostile Cherokee Indians as a Private Soldier, and that on his last tour, he served as a drafted soldier not less than four months in a company of Mounted Gunmen commanded by Captain Moses Looney and a part of the time by Captain Roger Tapp, making in the whole term of actual service of not less than ten months for which he claims a pension. Sworn to and subscribed this 24th day of December 1832.

William Sharp, J.P.   James Anderson

* * * * * * * * * *

KENNETH ANDERSON

Name:	Rank:	State Served:
Kenneth Anderson	Adj Mil	New Jersey

Born June 8, 1742, died September 15, 1820, buried in the Old City Cemetery, Shelbyville, Tennessee.

No GSA report in Washington, D.C.
        Ref: DAR Patriot Index, page 14
        Ref: Bedford County Tennessee Cemetery Records by Marsh, page 260

* * * * * * * * * *

JAMES ANDES

Name:	Rank:	State Served:
James Andes		

Died in Bedford County, Tennessee
No other information.
        Ref: Susie Gentry's Manuscripts.

* * * * * * * * * *

W.D. ASHBY

Name:	Rank:	State Served:
W.D. Ashby		

Born 1753, died 1818 Bedford County, Tennessee

No GSA report in Washington, D.C.
Cemetery marker was copied in 1938, located in the New Hope Church Cemetery, Fairfield, Tennessee. Marker now gone (1988).
        Ref: Bedford County Tennessee Cemetery Records by Marsh, page 136

AMOS BALCH

Name:	Rank:	State Served:
Amos Balch	Sgt	North Carolina

Born July 20, 1758 in Baltimore County, Maryland, died about 1835 in Bedford County, Tennessee, married in 1782 to Ann Patton who was born December 1, 1760 in Mecklenburg County, North Carolina, died April 4, 1824 in Bedford County, Tennessee. Amos Balch married second to Anna Elizabeth Cosby. Both Amos and

Ann Patton Balch are buried in the Thompson Cemetery which has been destroyed.

Amos Balch was a son of James and Ann (Goodwin) Balch. He removed with his father's family, first to Rockey River Settlement in Mecklenburg County, North Carolina, then to East Tennessee, then to Kentucky and finally to Middle Tennessee. He married in 1784 Ann Patton, daughter of Samuel and Anna Patton of Mecklenburg County, North Carolina. He acquired several grants of land in Bedford County.

Amos Balch was living on part of a grant issued to Samuel Patton, Sr., Balch's father-in-law. Patton having died in 1809 or before, left this portion of his grant to his daughter Ann Balch and her male heirs, wife and sons of Amos Balch.

Ann Patton Balch, wife of Amos Balch, died April 5, 1824 and is probably buried in the Old Patton-Thompson Graveyard that was located some 2000 feet south of the former house and spring. This graveyard included the Pattons, Bradshaws, Thompsons, Balchs, Doaks and others. Amos Balch has no marker.

Children of Amos and Ann Balch:
1. Ann, born November 22, 1785
2. Barbara, born February 6, 1788, married Joseph Alexander.
3. Rhoda, born October 28, 1790, died 1859, married James W. Patton July 5, 1810 Bedford County.
4. Peggy, born March 20, 1793, died 1830
5. John Bloomer, born July 19, 1795, died April 24, 1863(?) near Sardis, Mississippi, married January 1817 to Sarah Cook, born 1801 and died 1852.
6. Alfred Moore, born January 23, 1798 Logan County, Kentucky, died December 2, 1856 Coles County, Illinois, married July 1, 1819 to Elizabeth Gammill, born January 1, 1800 and died December 29, 1858.
7. Samuel Patton, born September 7, 1800 Logan County, Kentucky, died 1877 Tippah County, Mississippi, married 1829 Patricia Hannah Yates, born ca 1801, died ca 1880 in Mississippi.
8. James Calvin, born April 19, 1803 Logan County, Kentucky, died 1857 Sparta, White County, tennessee, married 1st January 10, 1829 to Eliza Jane Hazlett, born November 1803, died 1840. Married 2nd August 26, 1844 to Anna Elizabeth Cosby, born Giles County, Tennessee.

Ref: Balch Genealogy by Thomas W. Balch, 1907.
Ref: Researched by Timothy R. Marsh

Grant for 1000 acres from State of North Carolina, No. 23 to Amos Balch. Cost 10 lbs for every 100 acres. Situation: Middle District. On the north (south) side of Duck River, above the mouth of Sugar Creek, borders William Gilbreath, Jeremiah Chamberlain, Samuel Patton and Robert Hays. Witness: Samuel Johnston, Esq., our Governor, Captain, General and Commander-in-chief at Fairfield, North Carolina. 10th July 1788.

Declaration
State of Tennessee]
Bedford County   ]

On this 11 day of August 1832, personally appeared in open court, before John B. Armstrong, Samuel Phillips and John L. Neill, the court of said county now sitting, Amos Balch, a residence of the county and state aforesaid, aged 74 years, who being first duly sworn according to law, doth on his oath, made the following declaration, in order to obtain the benefit of the Act of Congress passed 7th June 1832, that he entered the service of the United States as a Mounted Volunteer sometime toward the latter end of the year 1779, under the following named officers, to wit, Richard Simmons, Captain, Nathaniel M. Martin, Lieut., and J. Hunter, Ensign and was appointed orderly sergeant for said company and served in that capacity during a tour of three months, the said Captain raised his company in Mecklenburg County, North Carolina, where this deponent lived at that time, and ,arched from thence to the neighborhood of the City of Charleston in the State of South Carolina, where we were put under the command of Colonel Malmadie, by order of General Lincoln and proceeded to Stons in order to watch the British for raging parties, and prevent as far as practicable their depredations on the planters in that section of country. Soon after our arriving at which station, we were joined by Colonel Washington with his troops of Regular Cavalry to whose command we were attached and served during the remainder of the tour, in which time I was engaged in several skirmishes with the British and at the expiration of the three months tour received a discharge, I think signed by Captain Simmons at the town of Dorchester, sometime in the year 1780, from which place I returned home to Mecklenburg, and soon after entered as a volunteer in Captain Spring's Company, which being placed under the command of Colonel Ledbetter, proceeded to and joined the Regular Army under the command of General Gates on Pedee, from which point we marched on through the piney woods to Rugelys Mill, and on the 15th of August at night, left our camp to surprise the British at Camden, and were met by Lord Cornwallis' Army, where I was engaged in the celebrated Battle of Camden, commonly called Gates Defeat, after which defeat and desperation, I was one of those that were collected by the same Captain Springs and continued in the service under the command of General Davidson, watching the notions of the enemy, near the British lines in order to intercept and cut off their foraging parties. At the expiration of three months for which I volunteered. I received a discharge from my commanding officer Captain Springs, but as the particular request of General Davidson, I remained in camp, in the Waxhaw Settlement a number of days but cannot now recollect how many, until other troops should arrive. This deponent also served in three other expeditions after the Tories, one of which was and the command of Captain William Houston, a second commanded by Captain Lapp, and a third under the command of Colonel Alexander, neither of which was for any particularly stipulated time, nor can this deponent now recollect how much service was rendered in this war, but believe that all the services rendered by him during the Revolutionary War would amount to nine months, or thereabouts. The discharges aforementioned in this declaration have been long since lost or destroyed but in what manner or at what precise period of time cannot at this late day be ascertained by the deponent, so that he has no documentary evidence in possession or know of any that can be produced to substantiate the foregoing particulars, neither does he know of . any person or persons at this time whose evidence can be procured to testify to the facts related in this declaration.

Interrogatories by the Court

Q. 1st: Where and in what year were you born?

A.   From the best information this deponent can obtain, he was born in Baltimore County in the State of Maryland, on the 20th day of July 1758.

Q. 2nd: Have you any record of your age and if so where is it?

A.   I have none.

Q. 3rd: Where were you living when called into service, where have you lived since the Revolutionary War, and where do you now live?

A.   I lived at the time of entering the service in Mecklenburg County, North Carolina, from where some years after the war, I removed west of the mountains to the waters of Tennessee River, from which place I removed to Christian County in the State of Kentucky, and in the year 1807, removed my family to Duck River in the present bounds of Bedford County, State of Tennessee in which county is my present residence.

Q. 4th: How were you called into the service, were you drafted, did you volunteer or were you a substitute, and if a substitute for whom?

A.   My services were all voluntarily rendered and here it might be proper to observe that deponent was exempted by law from performing military duty in consequence of being blind in one eye.

Q. 5th: State the names of some of the regular officers who were with the troops where you served, such Continental and Militia Regiments, as you can recollect, and the general circumstances of your services.

A.   In my first tour, General Lincoln was Commander in Chief of the Southern Army, attached to this service was Colonel Malmadie of the Regular Army and Colonel Washington of the Cavalry as this deponent was with the scouting parties, he does not recollect the numbers nor Commanders of the different Regiments of Regular and Militia stationed at Charleston. In my second tour, General Gates had succeeded General Lincoln and with his Army were General Decalb and General Smallwood of the Regular Army and General Rutherford, Colonel Ledbetter and Major White of the Militia. The number of the different regiments is

5

not recollected. The general circumstances of service rendered by deponent are as detailed above.

Q. 6th: Did you ever receive a discharge from the service, and if so, by whom was it given, and what has become of it?

A. I did. One from Captain Simmons and one from Captain Springs but as there was no prospect of their being of any benefit to this deponent, they were long since lost or destroyed.

Q. 7th: State the names of persons to whom you are known in your present neighborhood and who can testify as to your varacity and their belief of your services as a Soldier of the Revolution.

A. James McCarver, Samuel Thompson, Jonathan Mosely, Newcom Thompson, Thomas Greer and William Morton, Jacob Greer and William Hazlett.

This deponent hereby relinguishes every claim whatsoever to a pension or annuity except the present and declares that his name is not on the Pension Roll of the Agency of any state. Sworn to and subscribed, the day and year aforesaid.
Sworn to in open court 11th August 1832   Amos Balch
Jas. McKisick, Clk.

We, William Heazlet, residing in the County of Bedford and State of Tennessee and Jacob Greer, residing in the said County, hereby certify that we are well acquainted with Amos Balch who has subscribed and sworn to the above declaration, that we believe him to be 74 years of age, that he is reputed and believed, in the neighborhood where he resides to have been a Soldier of the Revolution and we concur in that opinion.
Sworn and subscribed the day and year aforesaid.
Sworn to in open court 11th August 1832   Wm. Hazlet
Jas. McKisick, Clk.   Jacob Greer

And the said court do hereby declare their opinion after the investigation of the matter and after putting the interrogatories prescribed by the War Department that the above named applicant was a Revolutionary Soldier, and served as he states, and the court further certifies that it appears to them that William Heazlet of the County of Bedford and State of Tennessee who has signed the above certified and that Jacob Greer, who has also signed the same, are residents in said county and is a creditable person, and that their statement is entitled to credit.

John B. Armstrong
Samuel Phillips
Jno. L. Neill

I, James McKisick, Clerk of the Court of Bedford County, do hereby certify that the foregoing contains the original proceedings of the said court in the matter of the application of Amos Balch for a pension. In testimony whereof I have hereunto set my hand and Seal of Office. This 11th day of August 1832.

Jas. McKisick (Seal)

State of Tennessee]
Bedford County   ]
Personally appeared before me the undersigned Justice of the Peace for said County, Amos Balch, who being duly sworn, deposeth and saith, that by reason of old age, and the consequent loss of memory, he cannot swear positively as to the precise length of his service, but according to the best of his recollection, he served not less than the period mentioned below and in my declaration. I served the whole three months as Orderly Sergeant, in the second tour of three months, I was a foot soldier as also the time I served with General Davidson in the Waxhaw Settlement, which was not less than two months, the first expedition after the Tories under Captain Houston was two weeks, the second under Captain Lapp was two weeks, ranging through the hills of (illegible), after the Tories by day and by night, the third under Colonel Alexander was ten days after the Tories in the counties of Lincoln and Burke.

It is here proper to observe that in making out the original declaration, I had from loss of memory neglected to state one other tour after the Tories under the command of Colonel Phifer, to prevent them burning the public stores at

Salisburg which they had threatened to do, this service lasted eleven days. Another tour I served under the command of Captain Martin Phifer four days after the Tories in the south part of Rowan County and the western part of Anson County and one other tour of three days under the command of Captain James Craig to prevent the British from taking Salisbury.

I was one of a company of Mounted Minute Men who was ordered by Brigadier General Matthew Lock, and in that capacity performed the foregoing services after the Tories. The whole of the services rendered by this deponent during the Revolutionary War was not less than eight months and an half, and for such service I claim a pension.

Sworn to and subscribed before me   Amos Balch
this 4th of April 1833
Jordan C. Holt, J.P

We, George Newton, a clergyman, residing in the County of Bedford and State of Tennessee and residing in the same, hereby certify that we are well acquainted with Amos Balch who has subscribed and sworn to this declaration that we believe him to be seventy-four years of age, that he is reputed and believed in the neighborhood where he resides, to have been a Soldier of the Revolution, and that we concur in that opinion.

Sworn to and subscribed before   . Geo. Newton, V.D.M.
me this 9th day of April 1833   Joseph Thompson
James Brittain, J.P.

I, James Brittain, an acting Justice of the Peace, in and for the County of Bedford and State of Tennessee, do hereby certify that I am personally acquainted with the Rev. George Newton and Joseph Thompson who have signed and sworn to the foregoing certificate and that George Newton is a clergyman of good standing in the Presbyterian Church and that Joseph Thompson is a man of good character for truth and veracity and that they are both citizens of the said County of Bedford.

Given under my hand and seal this 13th of April 1833.

James Brittain, J.P.

I, James McKisick, Clerk of the Court of Pleas and Quarter Sessions for Bedford County in the State of Tennessee, do certify that James Brittain, Esquire, before whom the foregoing certificate was sworn to and who also gives the above certificate is now and was at the time the same bears date, an acting Justice of the Peace for said County, duly commissioned and qualified as such, and that Jordan C. Holt before whom this amended declaration was sworn to is now and was when the same bears date and acting Justice of the Peace for said County. Commissioned and qualified as such and that both the signatures are genuine.

In testimony whereof I have hereunto set my hand ans Seal of Office at Shelbyville, the 13th of April 1833.

Jas. McKisick, Clk.

Ref: GSA S.2943, Washington, D.C.
Ref: Bedford County Tennessee Cemetery Records by Marsh, page 256
Ref: DAR Patriot Index, page 30
Ref: Texas Society DAR Roster Revolutionary Ancestors, Vol. 1, page 88

* * * * * * * * * *

JOHN BEARDEN

Name: Rank: State Served:
John Bearden   Pvt   South Carolina
Born March 11, 1744 in Spottsylvania County, Virginia, died 1836, aged 92 years, buried in Old Flat Creek Cemetery.

GSA John Bearden, S.2991.

John Bearden, Senr., of Bedford County in the State of Tennessee, who was a Private in the Company commanded by Captain Worford of the Regiment commanded by ______ in the South Carolina Line for 19 months.

Inscribed on the Roll of West Tennessee at the rate of $63. and 33 cents per annum, to commence on the 4th day of March 1831. Certificate of Pension issued the 17th day of June 1833 and sent to James McKisick, Shelbyville.

Arrears to the 4th of March $126.66
Semi anl allowance ending 4 Sept   31.66
                                                    $158.32

Recorded by Daniel Boyd, Clerk   Revolutionary Claim
Book e   Vol. 7   page 72   Act June 7, 1832

State of Tennessee]
Bedford County   ]

     Declaration in order to obtain the benefit of the Act of Congress passed the 7th June 1832.

     On this 15th day of May one thousand eight hundred and thirty three, personally appeared before me, William Heaslett, an acting Justice of the Peace for said county, John Bearden, Senr., a resident of the county and state aforesaid, aged eighty nine years, two months, and four days, who after being duly sworn according to law doth on his oath make the following declaration in order to obtain the benefit of the Act of Congress passed 7th June 1832. That he entered the service of the United States under the following named officers and served as herein stated. This applicant says he was born in the County of Spottsylvania and State of Virginia on the 11th of March in the year 1744, agreeable to his father's family record, but has no record of it at this time. He furthur says that he entered the service of the United States as a Private and volunteered in a Company of Rangers or Spies, commanded by Captain Joseph Worford and Lieut. D. Graham in Spartanburg District and State of South Carolina. Some time in the month of April 1777, the precise day he cannot recollect, and was marched to a Fort up on the head of <u>Inman</u>(?) River to Princes Fort and was there stationed but was frequently out on spying and scouting expeditions against the Cherokee Indians and a Torey family by the name of Bates, four in number, to wit, Wm., Harry and Isaac and their father who were skulking about with the Indians and were frequently engaged with the Indians in committing murders on the Frontier Settlers and that he remained in service until some time in January 1778 when he was dismissed after serving not less than nine months in actual service and that he did not receive a discharge in writing but was honorably dismissed, agreeable to orders. Deponent states that about a month afterwards he thinks, in February 1778, he volunteered again and joined a Company of Spies or Rangers under the command of Captain John Gowen, and was marched to a fort on the South Fork of Pacolet River and was frequently out ranging and spying on the frontier settlements on Tigar River. He states that on one of the scouting expeditions he was on, the spies under Captain Gowen assisted and took prisoner, two men, one by the name of Fanning and the other by the name of Smith, that they brought them back into the white settlement and delivered them up to a magistrate, as they were both Tories, and both had a stallion horse each taken from a Mr. James Ford and a Mr. John Patten. Deponent says he was then marched back to the last mentioned fort on the South Fork Pacolet River, near Cowpen Town, where he remained in service until some time in the month of August 1778 and was again dismissed, it being thought and frequently said by the Captain that the Indians had become quiet, and that there was no further use for the troops at that time, he states that he served on this last mentioned tour not less than six months. Deponent further says that he removed shortly after that done into Union District, South Carolina and there entered the service of the United States again about one week before the Seige of Ninety-Six, that he was marched to that place, a drafted soldier and was in the engagement at that place. He says he was then transferred from Captain Blessingames' Company to a Company of Volunteers under the Captain John Putman, and was marched through the country in different directions in search of a band of Tories under the command of a Tory Captain by the name of Jesse Gray, that he continued in service under said last mentioned Captain. A tour of duty of not less than four months when he says he was finally dismissed from service after serving in all a term of actual service of not less than nineteen months for which he claims a pension. This applicant says he remained a citizen of South Carolina until the year 1824 when he removed to Bedford County, Tennessee where he has lived ever since and where he now lives. He further says he was not acquainted with any Regular Officer with the troops where he served nor any Regiment of Regulars whatever.

Deponent hereby relinquishes every claim to a pension or annuity except the present and declares that his name is not on the Pension Roll of any agency in the United States. He further says that he has no documentary evidence whatever and that he knows of no person whose testimony he can procure who can testify as to his service, and that he is known to the Rev. William Martin and Jacob Fuller in his present neighborhood. Subscribed and sworn to the day and year aforesaid before me.

Wm. Heaslet, Acting Justice   John Bearden (Seal)
of the Peace of sd County.

May 15, 1833
2DD237-240 John Bearden. Bedford County, Tennessee. Pension Statement.
        Volunteered in Spartanburg, South Carolina under command of Captain Joseph Worford and Lieut. D. Graham, stationed at Prince's Fort, expedition against Tory family named Bates, entered service of Captain John Gowen, capture of two Tories by name of Fanning and Smith who had taken horses from James Ford and John Patten, under command of Captain John Blessingame and Captain John Putman in Seige of Ninety-Six, in pursuit of Tory Captain Jesse Gray. Copy 4 pp.

1835 Bedford County, aged 89 years, states he was a Private in the South Carolina Line.

He is buried in the Old Flat Creek Cemetery, Flat Creek.

Known children: Wm., b. Oct 3, 1786, mrd Patience Powers.   Eli mrd Nancy
Sons, Eli Bearden and William Bearden.   Langston.

> Ref: GSA Record, Washington, D.C.
> Ref: Tennessee and King's Mountain Papers by Lyman C. Draper
>   Collection, Madison, Wisc.
> Ref: Marsh Collection.
> Ref: Mr. J. Jack Keller, Madison, Tennessee

* * * * * * * * * *

SAMUEL BIGHAM

Name: Rank: State Served:
Samuel Bigham
        Samuel Bigham may be buried in an unmarked grave in Clark Cemetery, near Liberty Gap, Bedford County.

        Samuel Bigham of Mecklenburg County, North Carolina, left North Carolina about 1816 and settled on a farm near Bell Buckle, Tennessee, situated on the line of Bedford and Rutherford County, still in the hands of Bigham Families (1966). Samuel Bigham is believed to buried on the old farm.
Children: Samuel Bigham, born ca 1785 in Mecklenburg County, North Carolina.
        His daughter, Anna Bigham married Robert Wilson.
        William Bigham married Isabella Wilson.

Ref: Mrs. Edwin S. Brewster, a descendant of Anna Bigham and Robert Wilson.

* * * * * * * * * *

JACOB BLEDSOE (BLETCHER)

Name: Rank: State Served:
Jacob Bledsoe, Jr.   Cook   North Carolina
Born March 28, 1762 wake County, North Carolina, died 1848 Bedford County. His marker was copied in the Moores Chapel Cemetery in 1960 in Bedford County, died 1848. (Death date by Mr. Tom Muse, Belfast, Tennessee).
He was married to Ruth _____.

GSA: Jacob Bletcher, Jr. S.3012
Declaration
State of Tennessee]
Bedford COunty   ]

9

This day personally appeared before me, John O'Neal, an acting Justice of the Peace of said County, Jacob Bledsoe, a resident citizen of said County of Bedford and having been first duly sworn according to law, depose and says that he, the deponent, is about seventy years of age, that he was born in Wake County, North Carolina. His father's name was Aaron Bledsoe. Jacob Bledsoe, who is now and has for the last eight or ten years been a resident of Carroll COunty in this State, is a first cousin of this deponent. The said Jacob of Carroll County was also born in Wake County, North Carolina. The name of the father of said Jacob of Carroll County was also Jacob Bledsoe. This deponent was brought up from infancy in the same neighborhood with said Jacob of Carroll County, if this deponent knows anything with certainty in this uncertain world, he knows that himself and this said Jacob Bledsoe of Carroll County are two distinct persons altho they happen to be brothers, children of the same name, and of about the same age.

This deponent states that in the year 1780 in the month of July as well he recollects, this deponent and the said Jacob Bledsoe, both entered the service of the United States in a company which was drafted from Wake County, North Carolina. This deponent was commanded during the whole term of its service, which was three months, by Captain Lewis Bledsoe, the older brother of said Jacob of Carroll County, the said Jacob Bledsoe of Carroll County as Lieutenant P. Andrew Muckelroy, Ensign _____ Moore was Colonel of the Regiment to which we belonged and _____ Nalls our Major. The given names of Colonel Moore and Major Nalls, this applicant does not recollect but this deponent well remembers that said Jacob Bledsoe of Carroll County was the Lieutenant and the only Lieutenant of said company and that he served the said tour of three months in that capacity in the service of the United States during the War of the Revolution.

On this tour, the different Companies of Militia fell in at different points on the route of the main body, as best suited convenience or as circumstances would permit. Applicant does not remember or believe that there was any particular place of rendezvous for said Companies, after were organized, we marched about in different counties in North Carolina. I remember that we were marched through Chatham County, by Moore Court House and at length to Bergesly (?) Mills, during this tour we were at Gales Defeat, I think in August 1780. Here we were scattered and put to flight. Further particulars this deponent does not recollect except that this deponent served during the said three months as one of the cooks to the officers of said company, to wit, Captain Lewis Bledsoe, Lieutenant Jacob Bledsoe now of Carroll County, Tennessee and Ensign Muckleroy.
Sworn to and subscribed before me   Jacob (X) Bledsoe
this 17th day of February 1834
John O'Neal, Justice of the Peace.

Children of Jacob Bledsoe: (see later)

JACOB BLETCHER

Name: Rank: State Served:
Jacob Bletcher   Pvt   North Carolina
Born 1760 , died after 1834 Bedford County, Tennessee.

GSA: Jacob Bletcher, S.39198
Declaration
West Tennessee/North Carolina
Jacob Bletcher of Orange County, in the State of North Carolina, who was a Private in the company commanded by Captain Armstrong of the Regiment commanded by Colonel Shepperd in the State of North Carolina Line for the term of one year, from 1781 to December 1782.
Inscribed on the Roll of North Carolina at the rate of eight dollars per month, to commence on the 30 day of May 1828.
Certificate of Pension issued the 7 of June 1828 and sent to Willie P. Monguin, Secy. Hillsboro, North Carolina.
Arrears to 4th of Sept. 1828 $25.57
Revolutionary Claim, Acts March 18, 1818, and May 1, 1820.
8th July 1834 transferred to West Tennessee, from 4th Sept 1832 and notice sent to him at Shelbyville, Tennessee on the 13.

State of North Carolina
        Be it remembered that at a Court of Pleas and Quarter Sessions began and held for the County of Orange at the Court House in Hillsborough on the fourth Monday in February in the year of our Lord one thousand eight hundred and twenty eight, the following declaration was filed, which said declaration is in these words... to wit, State of North Carolina, Orange County, on this the 2nd day of February 1828, personally appeared in open court in the Court of Pleas and Quarter Sessions for the said county, the same being a Court of Record, having first being duly sworn according to law doth on his oath, make the following declaration, Jacob Bletcher, residing in said county, aged sixty eight years, who being first duly sworn according to law, doth on his oath make the following declaration in order to obtain the benefit made by the Act of Congress of the 15th May 1818 and 1st of May 1820. That is the said Jacob Bletcher entered a few weeks before the Battle of Eutaw Springs in the Continental Service by A. Bugg, a recruiting officer, that he was a Private, placed in Captain Armstrong's Company for 12 months service. Then he remained in service until the 23 December 1782 when he was honorable discharged at Wilmington, North Carolina.   That during his service on the Continental Establishment, he was in no battle, but that in the Militia of the State of North Carolina, he had served three tours and was in the Battle of Pate's Defeat.... Of Colonel Pates in Orange County by Colonel Lee and Pickins and then served under Captain M. George White on the Continental Line.

Amendment of a Declaration made in Orange Court of Pleas and Quarter Sessions Feby Term 1828 by Jacob Bletcher for a pension.
State of North Carolina
Orange County
        Jacob Bletcher personally appeared in open court, being the May Term of the Court of Pleas and Quarter Sessions 1828, and being duly sworn saith that in the declaration heretofore made and to which this is appended, he omitted to state that Regiment Captain Armstrong Company was attached and by whom said regiment and was omitted on account of being unable to remember further the regiment ot the name of the Colonel who commanded the same, that he since applied at the office of the Secretary of State, and by reference to the Record or Rolls of the same, he is unable to remember, now states that Captain Armstrong's Company belonged to the 10th Regiment and that Colonel Abraham Shepperd commanded the same.   That the said declarant oftained a memorandum of the Secretary of State in the proper hand writing of the Secretary, stating the fact, which is appended to a former certificate made by the Secretary.
Sworn to and subscribed in open Court   Jacob (★) Bletcher
the 30th day of May 1828
J. Taylor, Clk.

Pension Office: That he relinguishes every claim whatever to a pension except the present. The following are the reasons that he has not made earlier application for a pension, that until within a few days, he has been able to labor for subsistance, aided by some of his children who have all married and removed from his service except one daughter about 17 years old. That upon his poor land with labor and economy, he was unabled to support himself and family, that his family now consists of his wife, an old and very weakly woman and the aged and helpless mother of this deponent and said daughter. That this declarant by reason of age and infirmity as well as disease that has rapidly increased upon him within the last 5 or 6 years, has become unable by his labor and the economy to get along without permitting his debts for necessities constantly to increase. That he has hoped for the best and struggled unremittingly and had with the strictest economy and notwithstanding, his debts have increased so as to threaten his entire ruin and beggary. That his creditors are pushing their claims, several of the largest have judgement, to wit, G. Barba for $60, James Gooch for $61, and Sampson Moore for $38. and that a sale of his property is forced the whole of it will be likely to be sacrificed, that he applied nearly 2 years ago, but by unfortunately his papers were returned to him.
        And in persuance of the Act of the 1st May 1820. I do solemnly swear that I was a resident citizen of the United States on the 18th March 1818, and that I have not since that time by gift, sale or in any manner dispersed of my property or any part thereof with intent hereby so to deminish it as to being myself within

the provisions of an Act of Congress entitled "An Act provide for certain persons engaged in the land and naval Service of the United States in the Revolutionary War, passed the 18th March 1818" and that I have not nor has any person in trust for me any property or securities, contracts or debts, due to him, nor have I any income other than what is contained in the schedule, hereto annexed abd by me subscribed, that since the year 1818 the 18th March, no changes have been made in my property except a gradual decay, resulting from an increasing age, debility and infirmity.

Sworn to and declare in open court the day and date above written.

Jacob (★) Bletcher

A true schedule of all the estate real or personal of and belonging to Jacob Bletcher of the County of Orange and the State of North Carolina, together with the value of each article or item:

1 tract of land in Orange County, 109½ acres of poor, pine and black jack land, stript of timber more than half. Nearly two thirds cleared and much worn.	$150.00
1 other tract in Wake County of poor and barren land unoccupied	$ 50.00
2 heads of horses, 1 worth $30., the other worth scarcely anything being old and lame, say	$ 10.00
6 heads of cattle consisting of 2 cows and yearlings and calves	$ 24.00
26 heads of hogs, 6 grown and 20 pigs	$ 15.00
8 sheep, old and young	$ 6.00
10 geese	$ 2.00
2 pine chest or boxes $1. 2 pine tables $1.	$ 2.00
10 common chairs	$ 2.50
2 pots and hooks, one broken	$ 1.50
1 oven $1. 1 skillet, 40¢	$ 1.40
1 pair smoothing or sad irons	$ 1.00
6 pewter plates, old and worn	$ 1.00
2 dishes, 60¢ 6 spoons, 60¢	$ 1.20
6 earthenware plates, 30¢ 1 set cups & saucers, $2.70	$ 3.00
1 pair fire tongs, 25¢ and 3 wheels (spinning) $1.20	$ 1.45
2 w. tubs, 1 pail & 2 piggins	$ 1.00
2 bread tray and 1 ----	$ .40
1 loom, $1. 3 barrels, old, 45¢ & 4 open barrels, 40¢	$ 1.85
1 open stand, 80 ¢	$ .80
Also some bacon and corn insufficient to serve the family for half the year.	
8 grindstones	$ 4.00
Total	$310.10

<u>Court of Pleas and Quarter Sessions</u>]
February Term A.D. 1828   ]

Jacob Bletcher in open court being duly sworn, saith the above schedule he delivered to be true, both as to property he has and its value and that it is the whole of his property to the best of his knowledge and recollection except two beds and wearing apparel.

Jacob (★) Bletcher

Application for transfer:
State of Tennessee]
Bedford County   ]

On this thirty first day of May 1834 before me, the subscriber, a Justice of the Peace, for the said County of Bedford, personally appeared, Jacob Bletcher, who on his oath declares that he is the same person who formerly belonged to the Company commanded by Captain Armstrong in the Regiment commanded by Colonel Shepperd in the service of the United States, that his name was placed on the Pension Roll of the State of North Carolina from whence he has lately removed, that he now resides in the State of Tennessee where he intends to remain and wishes his pension to be there payable in future. The following are his reasons for removing from the State of North Carolina to Bedford County and State of Tennessee to get to a newer country, and to live near his children who had previously removed to Bedford County, Tennessee.

Sworn and subscribed to before me,   Jacob (✳) Bletcher
the day and year aforesaid.
John O'Neal, J.P.

State of Tennessee]
Bedford County   ]
        On the 31st day of May 1834 before me, the subscriber, a Justice of the Peace for the said County of Bedford, personally appeared, William Holly, and made oath in due form of law that Jacob Bletcher, who has taken the above oath is the identical person described in the foregoing afidavit.
Sworn and subscribed to before me the day and year   William Holley
last above mentioned before me.
John O'Neal, J.P.

State of Tennessee]
Bedford County   ]
        I, John O'Neal, a Magistrate in the County above named, do hereby certify that I am personally acquainted with William Holley who appeared before me and made the last foregoing afidavit and that he is a person of veracity and entitled to full credit.
        Given under my hand and Seal of Office, this 31st day of May 1834.
                                 John O'Neal, J.P.

State of Tennessee]
Bedford County   ]
        I, James McKisick, Clerk of the COurt of Pleas and Quarter Sessions for the County of bedford in the State aforesaid, do hereby certify that John O'Neal, Esq., whose name appears to the foregoing certificate is now and was at the time of signing, the name, an Acting Justice of the Peace in the County aforesaid and that the signature to be his, are genuine.
        In testimony whereof I have here unto set my hand and affixed the Seal of Bedford County Court at Office this 9th day of June 1834.
                                 James McKisick, Clerk
                                 by his deputy,
                                 Danl. McKisick

Article from North Carolina Genealogical Journal, August 1984 issue.
        Jacob Bledsoe, on 27 October 1828, Jacob Bledsoe, resident in North Carolina, Orange County, and 68 years, made the following declaration in open court in the Court of Pleas and Quarter Sessions to obtain the benefits in the Acts of Congress of 18 March 1818 and 1 May 1820. He was enlisted by Sherod Bugg, a recruiting officer, a few weeks before the Battle of Eutaw Springs in the Continental Service and was in Captain Armstrong's Company for 12 months service, being honorably discharged on 23 December 1782 at Wilmington, North Carolina. He was in no battles and served under Captain Hall and Captain Armstrong. He also served three tours in the North Carolina Militia and "was in the Battle of Gates Defeat" and at the memorable surprise of Colonel Piles in Orange County by Lieutenant Colonel Lee and Pickins. He then serving under Captain McLeary". He had not made earlier application for a pension because until a few years ago he was able to labor for subsistance aided by some of his children, all of whom have either married or removed from his service, except one daughter about 17 years old. His family now consists of his wife, old and very weakly woman, and the aged and helpless mother of this deponent and said daughter. That by reason of age and infirmity as well as disease that has rapidly increased within the last 5 or 6 years, has become unable by his labor and the strictest economy to get along without permitting his debts for necessaries constantly to increase. That his creditors are pressing their claims. Several of the largest have judgements, &c.
                                 Jacob (   ) Bledsoe)

Sworn to before John Taylor, Clerk of the County Court for Orange County, North Carolina, who certifies that to the satisfaction of the Court, the said Jacob Bledsoe did serve in the Revolutionary War as stated... That the total amount of the property exhibited in said schedule is $310.10... That Jacob Bledsoe is an illeterate man, and that <u>his name and family name is and always been pronounced in their neighborhood and by themselves as if written :BLETCHER"</u>.

Children of Jacob Bledsoe:
1. Aaron, born 5 Feb 1781/2 North Carolina, died 27 July 1867, married 6 July
        1815 Elizabeth Hall.
2. David, born ca 1800 North Carolina, married 7 Feb 1823 Susannah Hall.
3. Henry, married 19 May 1825 Temperance Robards.
4. Lewis, died 1848, married Fanny ____.
5. Jacob, Jr., married Polly Robards.
6. Amy, married 26 Nov 1816 John Hall, Jr.
7. Martha, married William Thompson.
8. Sarah Margaret, married J.J. Wise
9. Yancey, born 1806 North Carolina, died 1842, married 1823 Martha Thorne.
10. Mary, born ca 1811 North Carolina, died Orange County, North Carolina,
        married 7 May 1828 James Husk.*
8 Mary is guess work as we couldn't find another place for her and she fits the 17
        year old daughter Jacob mentions in his pension application.

Editor's Note: There is debate and argumentation even today as to whether Jacob
        Bledsoe and Jacob Bletcher is the same man but both are included here
        for the record.

* * * * * * * * * *

CHARLES BRANDON

Name: Rank: State Served:
Charles Brandon   Pvt   South Carolina
Born 7th April 1750 in York County, Pennsylvania, died 1834.
In 1835, aged 85 years. Bedford County, Tennessee

GSA: Charles Brandon, S.3086
Pay Voucher No. 1355.
        West Tennessee, of Bedford County, State of Tennessee, who was a
Private in the Company commanded by Captain Duff of the Regt commanded by
Col. Sumpter of the South Carolina Line for 10 months from 1776.
        Recorded by Nathan Rice, Clerk
        Book D   Vol 9   page 144

        Inscribed on the Roll of West Tennessee at the rate of 33 dollars, 33
cents per annum to commence on the 4th day of March 1831.
        Certificate of Pension issued the 2nd day of J___ 1832 and sent to Chas.
Ready, Murfreesboro, Tennessee.
Arrears to 4th of Sept 1832 $49.99
Semi-anl allowance ending 4 March 1833 $16.67
        Revolutionary Claim, Act June 7, 1832.
Order to pay 23 Oct 183_.   Letter to E.H. Brandon, ____

Affidavit
State of Tennessee
County Court, Bedford County
        County Court, Bedford County, August Term 1832. On the 14th day of
August 1832, personally appearing in open court before Samuel Phillips, John B.
Armstrong and John L. Neill, Esq. Justices of said Court. Charles Brandon, a
resident of the County of Bedford and State of Tennessee aforesaid, aged eighty
three years or there abouts, who being first duly sworn according to law, doth on
his oath, make the following declaration, in order to obtain the benefits of the
provision made by the Act of Congress passed June the 7th 1832. That he enlisted
in the Army of the United States in the latter part of February 1776, with Captain
James Duff and served in the 2nd Regiment of Riflemen of the Continental Line,
under the following named officers, he served in the Company of Captain James
Duff under whom he enlisted, in whose Company George Duff, a brother to the
Captain, was Lieutenant and Joshua Lacy was Ensign. The aforesaid 2nd Regiment
of Riflemen, to which he belonged and in which he served, was commanded by
Colonel Thomas Sumpter, afterwards General Sumpter, and he belonged to the
division of said Regiment commanded by Major William Anderson who also

14

afterwards became a General in the Continental Line during the war. The term for which he enlisted was twelve months and he served about the term of eight months during said enlistments, at the end of eight months, he returned home under a furlough and did not again return into service during the period of his enlistment but provided one Thomas Rhea to take his place as a substitute and to serve under an enlistment during the war. At the time he entered the service, he resided in Union County in South Carolina, on the waters of Pawlet River. During this enlistment he was at the Battle at Fort Mouterie which was attacked by Lord Parker or Sir Peter Parker who commanded the British, for the American forces in the Fort were commanded by Colonel O'Rea and Francis Marian who held some commission but he is not positive what was then his rank. The regiment to which he belonged under the command of Colonel Sumpter was stationed some distance from the Fort to watch and counteract the movement of the British forces under General Clinton who it was expected would land his forces at Bottom's Landing on Sullivan's Island to assist the forces who made the attack upon the Fort. He, however, did not land his forces as was expected during the engagement at the Fort which lasted about ten hours, the British Commander Parker was wounded and his vessel, a fifty gun frigate was shattered and much injured by the shot from the cannon in the Fort. One of the enemy vessels called the "Action" was abandoned by them and burned the next morning after the engagement. This engagement occured in the month of June 1776, as well as the applicant can now remember. During this term of service or enlistment, this applicant well remembers that he was under arms when the Declaration of Independence was made. He was at that time stationed in the barracks at Charleston and the troops was all paraded, and the Declaration read to them, as he believes, and as well as he can remember, by Edward Rutledge, the then Governor of South Carolina.

Longtime after the aforesaid term of service, declarant states that he volunteered and entered General Green's Army and was at Seige of Ninety-Six, the precise period at which he volunteered and entered the service in Green's Army, he cannot remember, but thinks it was sometime in the year of 1777. He belonged to Captain James Moore's Company, but he does not remember the names of any of his field officers. During this term of service, he was engaged in procuring provisions for the army about the span of four weeks. The army after the Seige of Ninety-Six, which ...(illegible)... to raise by the approach of the troops under Francis Lord Random, who had landed at Charleston and marched to the relief of the beseiged troops who was under the command of Colonel Croger. This applicant with the army under the command of General Green, situated on Sandy River. A distance, as he thinks of about one hundred miles and struck his camp at the plantation of an old Mr. Celey. From this place, declarant was sent with a small detachment, he thinks of twenty or thirty in number under the command of General Henderson, to scour the country and spy out the situation of the enemy. He marched with this detachment on the back route til they reached Mud Lick, a branch of the Saluda River, and about the distance of fifteen miles from Ninety-Six. Having made no discoveries of the enemy at this point, declarant volunteered his services to go on alone, as a spy, to the British Camp, and crossing over the Saluda River, proceeded on his route until he discovered that the enemy had left their encampment and marched towards the Eutaw, this intelligence, he carried back to the balance of the detachment under General Henderson and having then performed all the duties which were required of him, he was verbally discharged by General Henderson and returned home to Pendleton where he resided when he entered into service, having been on duty in this campaign about six weeks as a volunteer. After this declarant performed no other service except upon Scouting Parties who was engaged for a few days at a time in persuit of the Tories, when declarant was in regular service, he knew Captain Taylor, Jackson and Marygold who were all officers in the Regular Service. Declarant had a written discharge from the Regular Service, but he has lost or mislaid it so that it cannot now be found. This discharge which he received was from General Henderson, and stated the fact that Thomas Rhea had been received as a substitute in his place and had entered the service during the war. Declarant was born in the State of Pennsylvania, in York County. There was a record of his age made by his father in his Family Bible, but he does not now know where it is. He states that according to that record, he was born on the 7th day of April 1750. Old Styles. Declarant has now no documentary evidence and knows of no person whose testimony he can procure to testify to his service. He hereby relinquishes every claim whatever to a pension or annuity except the present, and declares that his name is not on the Pension Roll of the agency of any state.

Sworn and subscribed the day and year   Charles Brandon
aforesaid.
J. McKisick, Clk.

        We, Kimbro Allison and Job Cooper and T. Wilson, residing in the County of Bedford and State of Tennessee, hereby certify that we are well acquainted with Charles Brandon who has subscribed and sworn to the foregoing declaration, that we believe him to be about 83 years of age, that he is reputed and believed in the neighborhood where he resides to have been a Soldier of the Revolution, that we concure in that opinion.

Sworn to and subscribed this day   T._. Wilson
and year aforesaid   Job Cooper
Jas. McKisick, Clk.

Charles Brandon lived and died on his farm located between Rover and Unionville, Bedford County, Tennessee.

        Ref: GSA Report, Washington, D.C.
        Ref: Marsh Collection.

* * * * * * * * * *

WILLIAM BRECHEN

Name: Rank: State Served:
William Brechen   Pvt   North Carolina
Born 25 April 1754 Hanover County, Virginia, died 10 March 1834, married prior to January 1, 1794 to Elizabeth _____.
In 1835, aged 79 states he was a Private in the North Carolina Line.

GSA: William Brechen, R.1170.
13114: West Tennessee, William Brechen, Senr., of Bedford County in the State of Tennessee who was a Private in the company commanded by Captain Douglass of the Regiment commanded by Colonel Moore in the North Carolina Line for 5 months and 3 days.

        Inscribed on the Roll of West Tennessee at the rate of 27 dollars, 21 cents per annum, to commence on the 4th day of March 1831.

        Certificate of Pension issued the __ day of June 1833 and sent to James McKisick, Shelbyville.

Arrears to the 4th March $54.42
Semi-anl allowance ending 4 Sept $13.60
                                                    $67.82

Recorded: Book O Vol 7 page 92

Declaration:
        Declaration in order to obtain the benefits of the Act of Congress passed the 7th June 1832.
State of Tennessee]
Bedford County   ]
        On this 25th day of April in the year of our Lord one thousand eight hundred and thirty three, personally appeared before me, Thos. Coffey, one of the acting Justices of the Peace in aforesaid county, William Brechen, Senr., a resident of Bedford County and aged seventy eight years, seven months and 28 days, who first being duly sworn according to law doth on his oath make the following declaration to obtain the benefit of the Act of Congress passed 7 June 1832. That he entered the service of the United States under the following named officers, to wit, as herein stated to wit, that he entered the service of the United States as a drafted soldier of Person County and State of North Carolina, entered service October 7, 1779 as well as he now recalled and was placed in a company commanded by a Captain John Douglas who was under the command of Colonel William Moore and was marched from Person County into Orange County, North

Carolina to ________ where he says he was kept for about 20 days, there his Captain was ordered to march his men home and dismiss them. Deponant says he was marched back home and dismissed accordingly. His tour of service on this not less than five weeks. This applicant states that he was called into service again in the same County (Person), where he says he entered the service of the United States as a drafted soldier and was placed in a company commanded by Captain McFarland and was marched to Ramsour's Mill in Chatham County, North Carolina, the 18th of March 1780. There he says he was stationed until ____ the last of May in the same year, where he was ordered to the part of the county when he was attacked with the flux, to _____ that he was not able to return, but that he received a discharge for his three months tour in writing by his Captain of said tour, and that he entered the service of the United States again in about the 15th of September in the same year 1781, as well as he now recollects and in the same county (Person). As a volunteer for the Mounted Gunmen, he was placed under command of Captain Henrick Hargis who was under the command of General Fuller and Colonel William Moore and was marched on down the country across Peedee River at a Colonel Lann's and from there he was marched on towards Wilmington to a bridge and watercourse, the name of which he cannot at this time recollect. Deponant states he was told that the object of this expedition was to retake the Govr. of the State of North Carolina, who he says he understood was taken prisoner with the British and from there he states he was marched through the country for sometime but from the great number of years since it took place, he cannot recollect the names or places he was at until he was marched back home and dismissed after serving not less than two months. According to the best of his recollection at this time. This applicant further says he entered the service of the United States in the same county (Person) as a drafted soldier on or about the 15 of September 1781 and was placed in a company commanded by a Captain but cannot at this time recollect his name, his Colonel's name was O'Neal and that he was marched through the counties of Orange, Chatham and Moore in order to disperse the Tories who were very numerous and frequently embodied in different parts of the last mentioned counties where he says he continued in service not less than two months, when he says he was dismissed and returned home, making in the whole a term of active service of not less than six months and one week for which he claims a pension.

Deponant states that he was born in Handover (Hanover) County in the State of Virginia on the 25th of April in the year 1754 agreeable to the best information he could from his parents, but has no record of his age whatever. That he was a citizen of Person County and State of North Carolina during all the time he was in service and after the close of the Revolution until 1815 when he removed to Wilson County in the State of Tennessee and two years afterwards he removed to Bedford COunty, Tennessee where he has lived ever since and where he now lives. Deponant says he did secure one discharge in writing but what has become of it he cannot tell. This deponant states he was not acquainted with any regular officers where he served and that the foregoing declaration is the most precise history of the general circumstances of his service that he is able at this advanced stage of his life to give. He further says that he is known to the Rev. W. Hopwood, John Dysart, Esq., and Archibald Adams, Jas. Edmiston, Thomas Davidson and William Williams in his present neighborhood. He further states that he has no documentary evidence whatever and that he knows of no person whose testimony he can procure who can testify as to his service and declares that his name is not on the Pension Roll of any agency in the United States.

Subscribed and sworn to before me   William Brechen
this 25 day of April 1833
Thos. Coffey, J.P.

We, Rev. W. Hopwood, a clergyman residing in Bedford County in the State of Tennessee and three Justices of the Peace, residing in the same, do hereby certify that we are well acquainted with William Brechen who has subscribed and sworn to the foregoing declaration that we believe him to be seventy eight years, seven months and 28 days of age. That he is reputed and believed in the neighborhood where he resides to have been a Soldier of the Revolution and that we concure in that opinion. We further certify that his character for veracity is unimpeachable, that he is a man of good morals and strict

and honesty.
Sworn to the 15 day of April 1833
Rev. W. Hopwood

Declaration:

Declaration in order to obtain the benefits of the Act of Congress of the 7th of July 1838, entitled "An Act granting half pay and pension to certain widows.

State of Tennessee]
Marshall County   ] S.S.

On the 14th of February in the year of our Lord eighteen hundred and forty three, personally appeared before me, Jeremiah C. Briant, one of the acting Justices of the Peace in and said county, Mrs. Elizabeth Brechen, a resident of said county but formerly a resident of Bedford County, Tennessee, and upwards of ninety years, at the dwelling house of Josiah Brechen, her son, who being sworn according to law, doth on her oath make the following declaration in order to obtain the benefit of the provisions made by the Act of Congress passed July 7th, 1838. Entitled an act granting half pay and pensions to certain widows, that she is the widow of William Brechen who departed this life on the 10th day of March in the year of our Lord one thousand eight hundred and thirty four in Bedford County, Tennessee. She further states that her said husband, William Brechen, Senr., obtained a pension certificate which is now in her possession, the following is a copy of the same. "War Department, Revolutionary Claim, I certify that in confirmity with the law of the United States of the tenth of June 1832, William Brechen, Senr., of the State of Tennessee, he was a private in the army of the Revolution is entitled to receive twenty seven dollars and twenty one cents per annum, during his natural life, commencing on the 4th of March 1831 and payable semi-annually on the 4th of March and 4th of September in every year. Given at the War Office of the United States this seventeenth day of June one thousand eight hundred and thirty three. John Robb, Acting Secretary of War examined and countersigned, J.L. Edwards, Commissioner of Pension, payment to be made at Nashville, Tennessee by the Pres. of the United States. Rank Agency for paying pension in the agency of West Tennessee. Recorded in Pension Office in Book E, Vol 7, page 72, by Dan'l Boyd, Clerk. She further states that her husband, William Brechen impowered his son, Josiah Brechen to draw the amount of his pension previous to his death but owing to some informity of the Clerk's Certificate,   he was unable to draw the money from the agency of the United States, at Nashville, and that the money is still unpaid. She states further that she was married to her husband some years previous to the 1st of January 1794 and that she has not since the death of her said husband, William Brechen, intermarried with any other person whatever.

Sworn and subscribed to before me the day and   Elizabeth (X) Brechen
month above written.
Benj. H. Brantley
Justice of the Peace for Marshall County, Tennessee

* * * * * * * * * *

PHILIP BRITTAIN

Name:	Rank:	State Served:
Philip Brittain	Pvt	North Carolina

Born 1760, died after 1834

GSA: Philip Brittain, S.39243, Claim # 9450

West Tennessee, Philip Brittain, of Bedford County in the State of Tennessee who was a Private in the Regiment commanded by Colonel Williams of the North Carolina Line for the term of four years.

Inscribed on the Roll of West Tennessee at the rate of 8 dollars per month, to commence on the 15 of June, 1818.

Certificate of Pension issued the 16 of April '19 (1819) and sent to John McNairy, Dist. Judge, Nashville, West Tennessee.

Arrears to 4th of March, 1819	$68.30
Semi-anl all'nce ending 4 Sept 1819	$48.00
Notification sent 5 Oct 1822	$116.30

to S.R. Rucker, Murfreesboro, Tennessee

Declaration:
West Tennessee
          On this 15th day of June, 1818, before me the subscribers, one of the Judges of the Circuit Court of the United States for the said District, personally appears, Philip Brittain, aged fifty eight years and some few months, resident in the State of Tennessee, and in Bedford County, in said District, who by me first duly sworn according to law, doth on his oath make the following declaration in order to obtain the provisions made by the last Act of Congress entitled "An Act to provide for certain persons engaged in the Land and Naval Service of the United States in the Revolutionary War", that he the said Philip Brittain enlisted in Orange County in the State of North Carolina in the company commanded by Captain John Rochel of the 9th Regiment of _____ Continental Soldiers commanded by Colonel John Williams. There he continued to serve in said Corps or in the service of the United States until or about the 1st day of February, 1780. When he was discharged from service in Halifax Town, State of North Carolina, that he was in the Battle of Monmouth and one or two small skirmishes, and that he is in dire circumstances and stands in need of the assistance of his country for support, and that he has no other evidence now in his power for his said service. He further states that he has not _____ discharg that delivered it up at Hillsboro in North Carolina, when an adjustment of the Soldiers Claims was made and has never seen it since. That he never had any pension from the United States or any state.
Sworn to and subscribed before me   Philip Brittain
John McNairy, District Judge
          The applicant further made oath that he enlisted in, a aforesaid service in December 1776 and served until the time mentioned in the foregoing affidavit.
Sworn to before me, John McNairy, District Judge

          His occupation is that of a farmer and due to his bodily and mental infirmities, he is not able to prosecute his business and assure a certain maintenance. He has no wife now living with him. he has two sons living with him, Samuel and Philip. The first aged thirteen, the second about eleven years and two daughters, Nancy aged fifteen and Mary aged fourteen and they are not able to support themselves.
Sworn to in open court   Philip Brittain
11th June 1822
Danl. McKisick, Clk.

State of Tennessee]
Bedford County   ]
          I, Daniel McKisick, clerk of the Circuit Court of Bedford County, do hereby certify that the foregoing declaration and schedule thereto annexed are truly copied from the records of said court, and that it is the opinion of the said court that the property mentioned in the schedule thereto annexed is worth one hundred and ninety seven dollars and fifty cents. In testimony whereof I have herewith set my hand and affixed my private seal (there being no Seal of Office) this 14th day of ___ A.D. 1822 of the Independence of the United States. (Seal)

          States on the 18th day of March 1818 and that I have not since that time by gift, sale or in any manner disposed of any property or any part thereof (illegible) written the provision of an Act of Congress entitled, An Act to provide for certain persons engaged in the Land and Naval Service of the United States in the Revolutionary War passed on the 11th of March 1818, and that I have no property what ever besides my wearing apparel nor has any persons in (illegible) for me any property or securities contracts or debts due me nor have I any income whatever other than what is contained in the schedule hereto annexed and by me subscribed.
          Schedule of real and personal property of Philip Brittain:
2 mares, 1 colt, 2 cows, 1 calf, 4 heifers, 1 year old steer, 2 sows, 8 shoats, 6 pigs, 1 pot, 1 oven, 1 skillet, 1 frying pan, 1 rifle gun old, 1 bed, 1 chest, ½ dozen pewter plates, 1 pewter basin, 2 shovel ploughs, 2 pair chains, 1 axe, 1 meat axe, 3 hoes, 2 pair pot-hooks, and 1 loom.
Sworn to in open court   Philip Brittain

11th June 1822
Daniel McKisick, Clk.
District of West Tennessee

On this 11th day of June 1822, personally appeared in open court in the Circuit Court of Bedford County, State of Tennessee, the same being a Court of Record, before the Honorable Robert Mack, one of the Circuit Judge of said State, Philip Brittain, resident in said county, aged sixty two years, who first being first duly sworn according to law doth on his oath, make the following declaration in order to obtain the provisions made by the Act of Congress of the 18th of March 1818 and the 1st of May 1820, that the said Philip Brittain enlisted for the term of three years in the month of December 1776 in the State of North Carolina, in the company commanded by Captain John Rochelle, in the 9th Regiment in the North Carolina Line on the Continental Establishment, he continued to serve in said company of seven or eight months, when he was transferred to Captain McCrory Company in the same Regiment. He served in said company for three or four months, when he was transferred to the 1st Regiment commanded by Colonel Clark in the North Carolina Line, he continued to serve in said regiment about two years and one month, when he was discharged in January 1780, in the town of Halifax, North Carolina. He was in the Battle of Monmouth and other skirmishes. He made a forward declaration on the sixteenth day of April 1819 upon which he obtained a Pension Certificate. And in persuance of the Act of the __ of May 1820. I do solemnly swear I was a resident citizen of the state.

> Ref: GSA Record, Washington, D.C.
> Ref: Pension List, Served in North Carolina Line
>   Transferred from Orange County, North Carolina
> Ref: Roster of North Carolina

* * * * * * * * * *

WILLIAM BROWN

Name:	Rank:	State Served:
William Brown	Pvt	New Jersey

Born about 1750, died after 1834

GSA: Bounty Land Warrent Record Card

Brown, William	Grade "Private:	Line "New Jersey"
Warrent No. 8136	Acreage 100	issued April 27, 1798
		to: __ not shown__

William Brown (the father of Captain E.W. Brown).
"William Brown was eventually put on the Pension Rolls under an Act passed by Congress in June 1832. At the bottom of this letter, Polk wrote that the papers were probably in the War Department and might already be in the Pension Department. He noted that he would check in Washington and then would write Brown in Shelbyville.

> Ref: James K. Polk's Papers, "Correspondence of James K. Polk"
> Vol. 1, page 419. Letter dated Shelbyville September the 4th 1831.

In 1835, aged 82, Private   New Jersey Militia

> Ref: GSA Record, Washington, D.C.
> Ref: 1835 Pension Accounts of Bedford County, Tennessee

* * * * * * * * * *

THOMAS BUCHANAN

Name:	Rank:	State Served:
Thomas Buchanan	Pvt	North Carolina

Born 1764 Pennsylvania

GSA Record: Thomas Buchanan S.2105
State of Tennessee]
Bedford County   ]

On the 10th day of August 1832, personally appeared before the Judge of the Circuit Court of Bedford County, in open court, the same being a Court of Record, Thomas Buchanan, a resident of the County of Bedford and State of Tennessee, aged about seventy three or four, who being first duly sworn according to law doth on his oath make the following declaration in order to obtain the benefit of the Act of Congress passed June 7, 1832. That he entered the service of the United States under the following named officers and served as hereinafter stated.

In the beginning of the year 1781 in the County of Orange in the State of North Carolina, I entered the service as a volunteer to assist in guarding the town of Hillsborough in said stateand in reconnoitering the surrounding county after the Tories. I was attached to a company commanded by Captain Williams whose christian name I do not recollect, and under whom I served about a month and a half. I then substituted in place of Thomas Hunt who was a drafted militia man and his Captain as well as I now recollect was by the name of Covington. In this company I served three months as a sergeant in said company. I then substituted in the place of a man by the name of John Williams who was a Militia Man in what was called the eighteen months service. I served the balance of his time which was about two months. I cannot now recollect the name of the Captain. Major Dickson was attached to this service, there was also one Taylor whose christian name I believe was John but whether he was a Colonel or Major I now cannot recollect. He was also connected with this service in some way but in what particular I cannot now say. In this service I served about two months.

I then substituted in place of a man whose name I cannot now recollect, he was in the Militia Service for twelve months, I served the balance of his time, about one month and a half and the only officers that I can now recollect is Colonel or Major Taylor, my former officer. In the above service where performed in guarding the town of Hillsborough and in guarding prisoners, except some excursions I was engaged in the pursuit of the Tories in North Carolina and in the others to Haw River in said State. I then volunteered with three others to guard some wagons from Hillsborough to Deep River, about fifty miles. In this service I was engaged about half a month. In all the above tours, I served about ten months and a half all of which service was performed as well as I now recollect in the year 1781. There may be other incidents connected with said service which I have not detailed but from lapse of time I have forgotten them. I have no documentary evidence by which to prove the above services nor do I know of any witnesses as such by whom can testify as to my having performed them. I hereby relinguish every claim whatever to a pension or annuity except the present and declare that my name is not on the Pension Roll of any agency of any State in the United States.Sworn to and subscribed the day and year   Thos. (X) Buchanan
aforesaid in open court.
John T. Neill, Clerk of Bedford County Circuit Court

Questions by the Court as prescribed by the War Department:
Q. 1st: When and in what year were you born?
A.   I was born in Pennsylvania in 1764.
Q. 2nd: Have you any record of your age and if so where is it?
A.   I have. It is at home in my Bible.
Q. 3rd: Where were you living when called into service, where have you lived
           since the Revolutionary War?
A.   I lived in Orange County, North Carolina when called into the service
           after the war I went to South Carolina, Pendleton District and lived
           there for some twelve or fifteen years. I then moved to Kentucky where
           I lived some three or four years when I moved to Bedford County,
           Tennessee where I have lived ever since.
Q. 4th: How were you called into the service, were you drafted, did you
           volunteer or were you a substitute, and if a substitute for whom?
A.   I was a substitute for three months in the place of Thomas Hunt and
           volunteered when I first entered the service. I also substituted for some
           two or three others, names of whom was by the name of John Williams,
           the others not recollected.
Q. 5th: State the names of some of the regular officers who were with the
           troops where you served, such Continental and Militia Regiments as you

can recollect and the general circumstances of your service.

A.   Major Dickson was attached to the regular army and was with the troops where I served, there were some more but their names not now recollected. There were some Militia Regiments and of which was under the command of Colonel O'Neal and General Butler. I cannot state the circumstances of my service better than they are named above to which I again refer.

Q. 6th: Did you receive a discharge from the service and if so by whom was it given and what has become of it?

A.   I received two discharges, one for THomas Hunt for whom I was a substitute, and also John Williams for whom I was also a substitute and do not recollect to have received any other discharge and then I delivered to Hunt and Williams expeditiously.

Q. 7th: State the names of the persons to whom you are known in your present neighborhood and who can testify as to your character for veracity and their belief in your services as a Soldier of the Revolution.

A.   I am known to Thomas Hopper, Martin Sims, John Robertson, and the Rev. George Newton who lives in Shelbyville, also Joseph McCord another clergyman living in Marshall County of Tennessee of whom can testify to my character &c.

We, George Newton, a clergyman, residing in Shelbyville, Bedford County and Martin Sims residing in said County of Bedford, hereby certify that we are well acquainted with Thomas Buchanan who has signed and sworn to the above declaration that we believe him to be about seventy three or four years of age, that he is reputed and believed in the neighborhood where he resides to have been a Soldier of the Revolution and that we concur in that opinion.

Sworn to in open Court   Geo. Newton
John T. Neill, Clerk   Martin Sims
of the Circuit Court of Bedford County   Joseph McCord

No. 31268 - West Tennessee - Thomas Buchanan of bedford County in State of Tennessee who was a Private in the company of Captain Williams of the Regiment commanded by Colonel _____ in North Carolina for six months.

Thomas Buchanan
        Inscribed of the Roll of West Tennessee at the rate of 20 dollars per annum to commence on the 4th day of March 1831.

Certificate of Pension issued 23rd day of Nov 1837 and sent to Pension, Farmington, Tennessee.

Arrears to the 4th of Sept 1837 $120.00
Semi-anl allowance ending 4 Mar '38 $ 10.00
                                        $130.00
                                        Revolutionary Claim
                                        Act June 7, 1832

Recorded by Wm. S. Allison, Clerk
Book 62   Vol 7   page 82

        Ref: GSA Report, Washington, D.C.

* * * * * * * * * *

JOHN BURNS, SR.

Name:	Rank:	State Served:
John Burns, Sr.	Pvt	North Carolina

Born 10 February 1753 in Baltimore COunty, Maryland, died about 1836 in Bedford County, Tennessee. Probably buried in the Burns Cemetery, Bedford County, no marker for his grave.

GSA: John Burns, Sr.   S.1944   Certificate of Pension No. 7295.
        West Tennessee, John Burns, of Bedford County in the State of West Tennessee who was a Private in the Company commanded by Captain Nelson of the Regiment commanded by Colonel Martin in the North Carolina Line for 7 months and 21 days.

Inscribed on the Roll of West Tennessee at the rate of 25 dollars 66 cents per annum to commence on the 4th day of March 1831.

Certificate of Pension issued the 27 day of March 1833 and sent to J. McKisick, Shelbyville, Tennessee.

Arrears to the 4th of March $51.32
Semi-anl allowance ending 2 Sept $12.83
                                               $64.15

Recorded by Daniel Boyd   Revolutionary Claim
Book E   Vol 7   page 2__   Act June 7, 1832

Declaration in order to obtain the benefits of the Act of Congress passed 7th June 1832.

On this 10th day of August in the year of our Lord one thousand eight hundred and thirty two, personally appeared in open court before Samuel Phillips, John P. Neill and John B. Armstrong, Esquires, Gentlemen Justices of the Peace, appointed to hold the Court of Pleas and Quarter Sessions for Bedford County in the State of Tennessee, now sitting. John Burns, Senr., a resident of the County and State aforesaid, aged seventy nine years and six months, who first duly sworn according to law doth on his oath, make the following declaration, in order to obtain the benefit of the Act of Congress passed June 7th 1832, that he entered the service of the United States under the following named officers and served as herein stated.

That he entered the service of the United States as a Volunteer in the County of Guilford and State of North Carolina, in Captain John Nelson's Company, attached to a Regiment commanded by Colonel James Martin. He states his Lieutenant was by the name of Josiah Gates and that he volunteered and was mustered into service in the Spring or Summer of 1776. He thinks about 1st June. He states he was marched from Guilford Court House in North Carolina to Salisbury, from there to Cathey's Fort on Catawba River from thence into the Cherokee Nation to Catawba Town, at which place one of our men killed one Indian, our troops destroyed Catawba Town and a great many other towns that he cannot recollect the names and he recollected "Turkey Town", the Americans destroyed the _____ that deponant further states that he remained in the Nation for some time and was then marched back home and discharged or dismissed at Robert Nelson's in Guilford County, North Carolina, he thinks and was believed about the first of November in the same year. He also states that afterwards, he was numbered where every ten men had to furnish one man for the Continental Service and in the (illegible) at different times does not recollect the year. He further states that the Governor of North Carolina called for troops guard the Legislature of the State convened at Salem, he does not recollect the year, but he thinks he served about one month as a volunteer on this occasion under John Nelson as Captain. He afterwards volunteered under Captain John Nelson in Guilford County aforesaid to go against the Tories who were embodied on the Yadkin River about a mile from Shallow Ford on said river, but they were driven from that place as he was informed by Colonel Campbell from Halston before Captain Nelson and his men reached that place. He states that Captain Nelson returned home with his men in about six or seven days afterwards they were dismissed. He states that afterwards he volunteered with the same Captain John Nelson, his Lieutenant was Josiah Gates, his Colonel was James Martin, he thinks he volunteered about the first of February in the year 1781. He states he was mustered into service at Arthur Manganues' about six miles below Guilford Court House in the State of North Carolina in General Green's Army. He states the troops remained for some (illegible) then were mustered into service but he states that he was ordered from that place to pilot some baggage wagons to the Rockey Springs, was in Rockingham County, North Carolina and after some days, was ordered to have said wagons moved across Dan River into Henry County, Virginia, which he performed agreeable order. He states that afterward he was marched to the Battle Ground of the Guilford Battle to bury some of the Americans who fell in that battle and were left on the ground. They found ten men and buried them. He thinks he served on this tour of duty about one month and a half and was dismissed, making in all about seven months and twenty one days. He states he knew Major John Nelson of the Continental Line but day not known, what regiment he was attached to (illegible). He further states he has no documentary evidence and that he knows of no person whose testimony he can procure except the testimony of William Cunningham whose affidavit is hereto annexed, who can prove a part of one tour, who can testify to his service. He hereby relinquishes every claim whatever to a pension or annuity except the present and declares that his name is not on any pension roll of any agency in the United States.

Interrogation by the Court

Q. 1st: Where and in what year were you born?
A.   I was born in Baltimore County in the State of Maryland on the 10th day of February 1753, as I was informed by my parents.
Q. 2nd: Have you any record of your age and if so where is it?
A.   (illegible).
Q. 3rd: Where were you living when called into service, where have you lived since the Revolutionary War and where do you now live?
A.   I lived in Guilford County, State of North Carolina, I then entered in the service of the United States and I remained there until after the Revolutionary War and moved from that county in the year 1807 to Bedford County, State of Tennessee.
Q. 4th: How were you called into service, were you a volunteer, were you drafted, or were you a substitute, and if a substitute for whom?
A.   I was a volunteer all the time I served.
Q. 5th: State the names of some of the regular officers who were with the troops where you served, such Continental and Militia Regiment as you can recollect and the general circumstances of your service.
A.   I recollect Major John Nelson who was a Regular Officer. I cannot recollect any particular regiment except those under Colonel Martin and the Militia and Volunteer Regiment under General Green. The numbers of which if I ever knew, I have forgotten.
Q. 6th: Did you ever receive a discharge from the service?
A.   I never did.
Q. 7th: State the names of persons to whom you are known in your present neighborhood and who can testify as to your character for veracity and their belief as to your service as a Revolutionary Soldier.
A.   The Rev. John Brooks, John A. Moore, Thos. Davis, Benjamin Strickler, John Eakin and John C. Coldwell.

In 1835, aged 81. Pvt in North Carolina Line.

Benton County, Arkansas

John H. and James P. Burns, merchants of Bentonville, Arkansas, were born in Bedford County, Tennessee in 1830 and 1838, respectively, sons of Thomas P. and Mary Ann (Knott) Burns and grandsons of John Burns who was a native of Ireland came to the United States when a young man (this statement conflicts from GSA Report) was a Soldier in the Revolution and drew a pension. He located in North Carolina but afterward located in Bedford County, Tennessee, where he died about 1836. Thomas P. was born in North Carolina in 1793, died in 1838. Mary Ann Knott was born in Bedford County, Tennessee and died in 1870 at the age of 63, mother of five children. They moved to Benton County, Arkansas in 1860.

> Ref: GSA Report, Washington, D.C.
> Ref: Goodspeed History of Benton County, Arkansas.
> Ref: Tennessee DAR 1941-1942 yearbook, page 97.

* * * * * * * * * *

"DADDY" CALL

Name:	Rank:	State Served:
"Daddy" Call	---	---------------

Born about 1765 South Carolina, died before 1850
Married to Mary A.E., who was living with Thomas Call in 1850.
Thomas Call was born about 1812 in South Carolina.

No GSA Report in Washington, D.C.
No proof of this man being in the Revolutionary War.

* * * * * * * * * *

SOLOMON CAMPBELL

Name: Rank: State Served:
Solomon Campbell   Pvt   North Carolina
Born ca 1755, died 24 August 1849

GSA: Solomon Campbell, S.39287, Certificate No. 20390.

West Tennessee, Solomon Campbell of Bedford County, State of Tennessee, who was a Private in the company commanded by Captain Jarvis of the Regiment commanded by Colonel _____ in the North Carolina Line for the term of _____ from _____ 1777 to _____ 1777.

Inscribed on the Roll of West Tennessee at the rate of eight dollars per month to commence the 16th of January 1832.

Certificate of Pension issued 16 of January 1832 and sent to James K. Polk, Hon.

Arrears to 4th of March $13.15
Semi-anl all'nce ending $13.15
Recorded   Revolutionary Claim
Book D   Vol 3(5)   page 145   Acts March 18, 1818 &
                                                  May 1, 1820

Declaration:
District of Eastern Kentucky

On this 22nd day of August 1820, personally appeared in open court in the Garrard County Court, being a Court of Record, that the aforesaid Solomon Campbell, aged 65 years, who being first duly sworn according to law, doth on his oath make the following declaration in order to obtain the provision made by the Act of Congress of the 18th of March 1818 and the 1st of May 1820, that he the said Campbell, enlisted for the term of four months in the Spring of 1777 or the Fall of 1776 in the State of North Carolina in the company commanded by Captain Guess in the regiment commanded by the Colonel Mayum in the line of the State of North Carolina. North Carolina Continental Establishment, that he continued to serve in the Corps until 1780 where he was discharged from the said term and at Santee Hill in the State of South Carolina.

He was in the battle of the Seige of Charleston and was in the Battle of Eutaw Springs. And that he has no other now in his power, of his said services. And in pursuance of the Act of the 1st of May 1820, I do solemnly swear that I was a resident citizen of the United States on the 18th day of March 1818 and that I have not since that time, by gift or in any manner dispersed of my property or any part thereof with intent thereby so to diminish it as to bring myself within the provisions of an Act of Congress, enacted by an Act of Congress for certain persons engaged in the Land and Naval Service of the United States in the Revolutionary War, and the Act of Congress passed 18th day of March 1820, and that I have not -------(illegible)------.

Two cows of the value of $20. and no more $20.
One mare and colt, worth $50. and no more $50.
40 head of young hogs, worth $30. and no more $30.
                                                    $100.

His wife about 60 years old, two children living with him, one son and a daughter, both over 21 years of age. And not under his control. His occupation is Agriculture.

Solomon Campbell

Sworn to and declared, this 22nd day of August 1820,
before _____.

I, Benjamin Letcher, Clerk of the County Court of Gerrard, do hereby certify that the aforesaid, doth in this declaration _______(illegible)_____, 22nd day of August 1820.

Ben Letcher
Clerk of this Gerrard
County Court

From Letter:
It appears that Solomon Campbell enlisted in the fall of 1776 or spring of 1777 and served in Captain Jarvis' North Carolina Company, he was at the Seige and Battle of Charleston, Monck Corner, was wounded four times at Battle of

Camden, was in the Battle of King's Mountain and Eutaw Springs. He also served under Captain Guess at the capture of Cornwallis. He was allowed pension on his application executed in Gerrard County, Kentucky, August 22, 1830, at which time he was sixty-five years old, he referred to his wife aged about sisty years, and a son and one daughter, both over twenty one years, no names are stated.

In 1827, Soldier was living in Bedford County, Tennessee. He died August 24, 1849.

The above noted Solomon Campbell is the only soldier of that name found on the Revolutionary War Records in the Washington Bureau.

by Wilder S. Metcalf,
Commissioner

Ref: GSA Report, Washington, D.C.
Ref: Declaration made in Eastern Kentucky.
Ref: Letter from Wilder S. Metcalf, Washington, D.C., Commissioner

* * * * * * * * * *

WILLIAM CAMPBELL

Name:	Rank:	State Served:
William Campbell		
Born		
Died		

William Campbell served in Revolution, an early settler in Bedford County, Tennessee.

No GSA Report in Washington, D.C.

Ref: James K. Polk Papers, Vol 1, page 344.

* * * * * * * * * *

ROBERT CARUTHERS

Name:	Rank:	State Served:
Robert Caruthers	Pvt	North Carolina

Born 14th February 1750 Lancaster County, Pennsylvania, died after 1834 (Pension List).

GSA: Robert Caruthers, S.2416, Certificate No. 7578, West Tennessee.

Robert Caruthers of Bedford County, in the State of West Tennessee, who was a Private in the company commanded by Captain Brumfield of the Regiment commanded by Colonel Ewing in the North Carolina Line for 8 months.

Inscribed on the Roll of West Tennessee at the rate of $26 dollars 66 cents per annum, to commence on the 4th day of March 1831.

Certificate of Pension issued the 3 day of May 1833 and sent to James McKisick, Shelbyville.

Arrears to the 4th of March	$53.32
Semi-anl allowance ending Sept	$13.33
	$66.65

Recorded by Daniel Boyd, Clerk	Revolutionary Claim
Book e Vol 7 page __(97?)	Act June 7, 1832

Letter to Robt. J. Moore in compliance with request of James Caruthers April 4, 1837.   Let. to _____ Nashville April 4, 1837

Declaration:

Declaration in order to obtain the benefit of the Act of Congress passed the 7th June 1832.
State of Tennessee]
Bedford County   ]

On this 9th day of February 1833, personally appeared in open court, now sitting, for said county before the worshipful Samuel Phillips, William McClure and (illegible), Esquires, Gentlemen Justices of the Peace, appointed a Quorum to hold Court.

Robert Caruthers, Senr., a resident of said county, aged eighty-two years, eleven months and twenty six days, who after being sworn according to law doth on his oath make the following declaration in order to obtain the benefit of the Act of Congress passed the 7th June 1832, that he entered the service of the United States under the following named officers and served as herein stated, to wit, That he entered the service of the United States as a drafted soldier in the County of Mecklenburg and State of North Carolina some time the thinks in the monthabout the first of June in the year 1780 and was placed in a company commanded by Captain John Brumfield who was attached to a regiment under the command of Colonel Robert Erwin and was marched to General Sumpter's headquarters and thence on to what was called Hanging Rock, in the State of South Carolina where he says they had an engagement with the British and Tories. Sometime in July but the....(line of declaration was deleted)...

He states that he remained in service under the foregoing officers until his term of three months expired when he was dismissed and returned home, and was ordered out immediately again about the time the British was in Charlotte in Mecklenburg County, as a Militiaman, his Captain, he thinks, perhaps was Porter but is not certain and his Colonel was Robert Erwin and he thinks General Lock was along, and was marched to Salisbury in Rowan County, North Carolina and thence up the county and across back to Charlotte Crossing "Curdle Creek" and Rocky River and after serving two months he was dismissed.

Deponant says that afterwards, he joined Colonel Davy's Regiment of Mounted Gunmen, in order to suppress the Tories who were numerous and frequently committing depredations on the property of the Whigs, but from old age and the consequent loss of memory he cannot swear positively to the precise length of this last mentioned tour of duty. It being performed at different periods of two or three weeks at a time but to the best of his recollection, he served not less than three months, making in all a term of service of not less than eight months for which he claims a pension and that he has no documentary evidence whatever and that he knows of no person whose testimony he can procure who can testify as to his service, except what he can prove by the oath of James Wilson, and declares that his name is not on the Pension Roll of any agency in the United States.

Interrogatories by the Court

Q. 1st: Where and in what year were you born?
A.   I was born in Lancaster County in the State of Pennsylvania on the 14th day of February in the year 1750, agreeable to what my parents informed me.
Q. 2nd: Have you any record of your age?
A.   I have no record of my age whatever.
Q. 3rd: Where were you living when called into service, where have you lived since the Revolutionary War and where do you now live?
A.   I was a citizen of Mecklenburg County in the State of North Carolina all the time I was in service and after the close of the war, when I removed in the year 1791 to Davidson County, Tennessee where I resided for six years, and from there I removed to Williamson County where I resided until the 1st day of January 1831 when I removed to Bedford County, Tennessee where I now reside.
Q. 4th: How were you called into service, were you drafted, did you volunteer or were you a substitute and if a substitute for whom?
A.   I was a drafted soldier my two first tour and my last tour I was a volunteer.
Q. 5th: State the names of some of the Regular Officers who were with the troops where you served, such Continental and Militia Regiments, as you can recollect, and the general circumstance of your service.
A.   I did not form an acquaintance with any Regular Officers that was with the troops where I served nor do I recollect the names of members of any regiment whatever, and believe I given as near the general circumstances of my service as I am able to do at this advanced age.
Q. 6th: Did you ever receive a discharge from the service, and if so, by whom was it given, and what has become of it?
A.   I never did receive a written discharge, only dismissed from service or mustered out of service.
Q. 7th: State the names of persons to whom you are known in your present

neighborhood who can testify as to your veracity and their opinion of your service as a Soldier of the Revolution.

A.   I have not lived a sufficient length of time in my present neighborhood and not being able to travel about much, I have not formed an acquaintance with many persons and have not formed an acquaintance with any clergyman. I am acquainted with Samuel Haggard, Abraham Mayfield, William _____, John S. Marion and James Wilson. And I hereby relinguish all claims to a pension or annuity except the present.

Sworn to and subscribed the day and year   Robert Caruthers
aforesaid.
Jas. McKisick, Clk.

State of Tennessee
On this 9th day of February 1833, personally appeared in open court, James Wilson, Senr.* a resident of Bedford County in the State of aforesaid, aged seventy six years, who after being duly sworn according to law, deposith and saith that he was himself a Soldier in the Revolutionary War, where and when he knew Robert Caruthers who was then a Private Soldier in Captain Brumfield's Company and that said Caruthers was in the Battle of the Hanging Rock, in South Carolina, between the British and the Americans, and that he has been acquainted with the said Robert Caruthers who subscribed and was qualified to the foregoing declaration, both in the State of North Carolina and Tennessee...

War Department Pension
Office, 1833

In 1835, aged 84, Pvt in North Carolina Line.

Children: Son, Robert Caruthers (1791-1829) married 1812 to Elizabeth Brown Porter (1795-1881).

Ref: GSA Report, Washington, D.C.   *James Wilson of Marshall Co.,
Ref: 1835 Bedford County Pensioners List.   Tennessee.
Ref: DAR Lineage, Vol 67, page 139-140.

Children of Robert Caruthers and Elizabeth Patillo:
1. Susanna married John Draper Love
2. Mary married George Patton
3. Samuel
4. John
5. Robert, Jr. married Elizabeth Porter
6. Elizabeth married John Dillard Love

Ref: Mississippi Daughters and their Ancestors by Lela Taylor, 1965

* * * * * * * * * *

ABNER CHAPPELL

Name:	Rank:	State Served:
Abner Chappell	---	Virginia

Born 13 April 1763 Amelia County, Virginia
Died

Abner Chappell, S.16707.
4 February 1833 Howard County, Missouri. Abner Chappell declares that agreeable to his register he was born 13 April 1763 in Amelia County, Virginia, where he lived until 1807 when he moved to Bedford County, Tennessee, where he remained until 1820 and then moved to Howard County, Missouri, where he now lives.

In the fall of 1780 his state was invaded by a British force under the traitor Arnold and he was called to defend his country. He served a tour of six months terminating in April 1781 under General Steuben, Generals Lawson and Mead. Rawley Dowlman commanded the regiment. They marched out of their county under Captain William Crawley, a militia officer, who resigned his command and went home. He was then put under Captain Holmes, a regular officer. His company soon after was broke and he was attached to Captain Allen's company from Cumberland County from whom he received his discharge. He was stationed about two months near the Great Bridge where the British had a fort. No engagement took place except scouting parties.

After his return he volunteered under Captain Pleasant Roberts, a Militia Soldier, to collect and pasture horses for the service of the United States. The first collection they delivered at Satunton and the second and last one they delivered in Goochland County. His term of service terminated at the time Cornwallis and Tarleton appeared in Virginia.

Abner Chappell of Howard County, Missouri, a Private in the company of Captain Pleasants in the brigade of General Steuben in the Virginia Line for six months, was placed on the Missouri Pension Roll at $20. per annum under the Act of 1832. Certificate No. 13104 was issued 13 May 1833.

Ref: Virginia Revolutionary Pension Applications Vol 17 by John F. Dorman.

* * * * * * * * * *

JOSHUA CHERRY

Name:	Rank:	State Served:
Joshua Cherry	Pvt	North Carolina

Born 15 February 1761 in Martin County, North Cárolina, died after 1840 in Marengo County, Alabama.

GSA: Joshua Cherry, S.32.174
Claim No. 13.997 West Tennessee, Joshua Cherry, of Bedford County in the State of Tennessee who was a Private in the company commanded by Captain Chiles of the Regiment commanded by Colonel Hogan in the North Carolina Line for one year and six months.

Inscribed on the Roll of West Tennessee at the rate of 60 dollars __ cents per annum to commence on the 4th day of March 1831.

Certificate of Pension issued the 20th day of July 1833 and sent to Jas. McKisisk, Shelbyville.

Arrears to the 4th of March	$120.
Semi-anl allowance ending 4 Sept	$ 30.
	$150.

Recorded by Dan'l Boyd, C;l.   Revolutionary Claim
Book E Vol 7 page 74   Act June 7, 1832

Transferred to Mobile, Alabama from March 1838 - 11 Jany 1839.

Declaration:
State of Tennessee]
Bedford County   ]

This 6th day of August 1832, personally appeared before me, James Billington, one of the acting Justices of the Peace in and for said county, Joshua Cherry, a resident of said county and state aforesaid, aged seventy one years, being first duly sworn and according to law, doth on his oath, make the following declaration in order to obtain the benefit of the Act of Congress passed June the 7th 1832.

That he entered the service of the United States under the following named officers and served as herein stated. This deponent states that according to the document he received from his father's family record, he was born in the year 1761, February 15, in the State of North Carolina, Martin County and in the same county, about the age of seventeen, he enlisted in the United States as a soldier and served under Captain Francis Chiles and Lieutenant James Tatum, Regular Officers in the Third North Carolina Regiment commanded by Colonel James Hogan. They rendezvoused at Petersburg in Virginia. They marched through the States of New York, went up North River and built a fort at West Point called Putman's. Rode out from thence to Philadelphia where we wintered and where his time expired. He was then placed on board a vessel, brought back to Virginia, Suffolk, then to North Carolina, Halifax, where he was discharged but states that his discharge, he cannot produce, but knows he enlisted for nine months but served twelve before he was discharged, which he thinks will be found on the roll. This deponent further declares that in the year 1780, he entered the service again as a substitute in the Militia Line in the place of a certain James Cattenhead of Pitt

County, North Carolina for the term of three months, he was first under Captain Shoot then under Captain Samuel Dudley and under his three months tour under Captain White and received his discharge which he cannot produce. The above Militia Companies belonged to the Third Regiment of North Carolina Militia commanded by Colonel Allen under General Caswell in this tour we were marched for Charlestown but it was said we got within forty miles of that place when it was taken.

This deponent further states that in the same year, the fall season, he entered the service as a substitute for Benjamin Russels who was drafted in the same County of Martin, North Carolina, for three months and served the said tour of three months under Captain John Bullard and Lieutenant Isiah Kennedy in a regiment commanded by Colonel Branch, under General A. Jones, in this tour he states we marched to the upper part of the State of North Carolina and ended this tour in the State and obtained his discharge which the wrecks of time as in the other tours has placed out of his power to produce.

But further declares that some few years past, he thinks he could have obtained witnesses to have proven his actual service for the above tours but now believes they are all dead. One particular witness was Major James Tatum who died a few years ago in the town of Nashville, Tennessee.

He hereby relinguishes every claim whatever to a pension or annuity except the present and declares that his name is not on the Pension Roll of the agency of any State.

Sworn to and subscribed the day and year aforesaid.
J. Billington, J.P.   Joshus (X) Cherry

We, James Y. Green, a clergyman residing in the County of Bedford and State of Tennessee and Hugh McClelin (McClellan) residing in the same, hereby certify that we are well acquainted with....(incomplete)...

Application by Joshua Cherry for a transfer of his pension from Tennessee to North Alabama.

The State of Alabama]
County of Marengo   ]

On this sixth day of September in the year 1838, before me, the subscriber, a Justice of the Peace for the said County of Marengo, personally appeared Joshua Cherry, who on his oath declares that he is the same person who formerly belonged to the company commanded by Captain Francis Chiles in the regiment commanded by Colonel Hogan (he believes, James Hogan) in the service of the United States, that his name was placed on the Pension Roll of Tennessee from whence he has lately removed, that he now resides in the State of Alabama where he intends to remain and he wishes his pension to be made payable in future. The following are his reasons for removing from Bedford County, Tennessee to Marengo County in the State of Alabama, his son Jared W. Cherry had previously removed to Alabama and with a view of living with or near his son and of bettering his condition and improving his health by living in a southern climate, he removed to Alabama in the Summer of 1835.

Sworn and subscribed to before me   Joshua (X) Cherry
the day and year aforesaid.
T.J. McFarland, J.P.

Witnesses: John W. Napier
           T.J. McFarland

* * * * * * * * * *

ANTHONY CLARK

Name:	Rank:	State Served:
Anthony Clark	---	-------------

Born 1759, died July 14, 1827 Bedford County, Tennessee, buried in the Clark Cemetery.

No GSA.

Tombstone in Clark Cemetery, Bedford County:

30

In Memory of Anthony Clark
who died July 14, 1827
Aged: 78 years
(Epitaph illegible)

Across the top of his tombstone was an American Eagle with spread wings.

No proof of his service in the Revolutionary War.

Ref: Cemetery Records of Bedford County, Tennessee by Marsh

* * * * * * * * * *

RACHEL CLAY

(Mrs. Barkley Martin)

Name:	Rank:	State Served:
Rachel Clay	Patriot	South Carolina

Born

Died _____, buried beside her husband, Barkley Martin, in the Martin Cemetery near Fairfield, Bedford County, Tennessee. Grave not marked. No children.

Rachel Clay, daughter of Henry Clay, Jr. of Mecklenburg, Virginia. She was the wife of Barkley Martin (1756-1815).

Rachel Clay Martin served as a Patriot with her sister Sallie. During the Revolution, while Rachel was living with her in-laws, the Abram Martin's of Edgefield County, South Carolina, she with her sister-in-law Grace, dressed in their husband's clothing, waylayed a party of British Officers and Courier bearing important papers, they took the officers by surprise, took the documents and sent them on to General Green's Headquarters. The British never knowing that their capturers were women.

Ref: Reminiscences and Indian Legends.

* * * * * * * * * *

SALLIE CLAY

(Mrs. Matt Martin)

Name:	Rank:	State Served:
Sallie Clay	Patriot	Virginia

Born November 16, 1765 in Cumberland County, Virginia, died January 2, 1842 Bedford County, Tennessee, buried in Martin Cemetery. She married March 8, 1787 to Matt Martin in Charlotte County, Virginia.

Served as Patriot. Married to Matt Martin who was born December 26, 1763 and died October 16, 1846.

Children:
1. Mary, born January 7, 1788, married John Marshall
2. Rachel, born May 16, 1789, married John Tillman
3. Rebecca, born July 11, 1791, married Thomas Bedford Mosely
4. Lucy Green, born August 6, 1793, married Theodore Bradford
5. Letitia, born April 6, 1795
6. Henrietta, born May 7, 1797
7. Sally C., born November 4, 1798, married John L. Neil
8. Abram, born November 12, 1800, married Betty Lane
9. Barclay, born December 17, 1802
10. Betty, born December 13, 1804, married Edmond Archer Mosely
11. Henry, born November 26, 1806, married Amanda Davenport
12. Mattie B., born December 2, 1808, married Samuel Rucker
13. Matt, born June 18, 1812, married Sarah Williams

Ref: DAR Roster
Ref: Ellet's "Women of the Revolution" Vol 1, page 311
Ref: Patriotic Service, Virginia
Ref: Roster and Soldiers of DAR (Blue Book) Vol 1, page 457

NICHOLAS COBLE

Name:	Rank:	State Served:
Nicholas Coble	---	North Carolina

Born 1759, died 1838 Bedford County, Tennessee, buried in the Three Forks Church Cemetery, Bedford County. He has a Military Grave Marker that reads:

> Nicholas Coble
> N. Carolina
> Rev. War
> 1759-1838

Nicholas Coble was born 1759 in Guilford County, Salisbury District, North Carolina, son of John Jacob and Catherine (Glass) Coble. His first wife was Margaret Deveney, a daughter of Samuel Deveney who was a Regulator. After her death, he moved to Bedford County, Tennessee where he had North Carolina Land Grant No. 4620, issued September 9, 1783, here he married _____ Lowe and died 1838 and is buried at Three Forks Cumberland Presbyterian Church Cemetery in Bedford County, Tennessee.

> Ref: Susie Gentry, Nashville Monument
> Ref: Government Marker, October 27, 1948
> Ref: Cemetery Records of Bedford County, Tennessee by Marsh

* * * * * * * * * *

JOHN CONNELLY

Name:	Rank:	State Served:
John Connelly	Pvt	Virginia

Born 27 January 1760 in Bruinswick County, Virginia, died 29 June 1835 in Bedford County, Tennessee, burial place unknown, married Mary _____, 2nd March 1790 in Mecklenburg County, North Carolina.

GSA: John Connelly, W 74, Wife Mary. Pension Claim No. 7460

West Tennessee, John Connelly, County of Bedford in the State of Tennessee, who was a Private in the company commanded by Captain Harrison of the _______ commanded by _____ in the Virginia Line for 6 months.

Inscribed on the Roll of West Tennessee at the rate of 20 dollars ___ cents per annum to commence on the 4th day of March 1831.

Certificate of Pension issued the 16 day of April, 1833 and sent to J. McKisick, Shelbyville.

Arrears to the 4th of March	$40.00
Semi-anl Allowance ending 4 Sept	$10.00
	$50.00

Recorded by Daniel Boyd, Clerk	Revolutionary Claim
Book E Vol 7 page 74	Act June 7, 1832

Declaration:
State of Tennessee

Declaration in order to obtain the benefit of the Act of Congress passed the 7th June 1832.

On this 10th day of November in the year of our Lord one thousand eight hundred and thirty two, personally appeared in open court before the Worshipful John L. Neill, Samuel Phillips and John B. Armstrong, Gentlemen Justices of the Peace appointed to hold the Court of Pleas and Quarter Sessions in and for the County of Bedford and State of Tennessee. John Connelly, aged seventy two years, nine months and fourteen days, who being first duly sworn according to law doth on his oath make the following declaration in order to obtain the benefit of the Act of Congress passed 7th June 1832.

That he entered the service of the United States under the following named officers and served as herein stated. That he entered the service of the United States as a drafted Militiaman in the County of Bruinswick, in the State of Virginia. Sometime, he thinks, in the year 1778 and he thinks the Captain, that he was placed under was by the name of Harrison but is not certain, and was marched from that to General Mulingburg's Headquarters at Cabbin Point, in the County of Prince George in the State of last aforesaid, where he states he was stationed for the term of three months, when he was discharged and returned home, deponent states that some time after returned home, Colonel John Jones, the Colonel of Brunswick County in the State of Virginia, proposed to each young blacksmith in said regiment that would repair and put in complete order, twelve muskets each and should be exempt from the next tour of duty, and deponent says that himself, an elder brother, and an apprentice boy repaired and put in good order thirty six guns and delivered them to Colonel Jones, the time he was engaged in repairing said guns, was a month or more. He further states that afterwards in the spring of the year 1779, he was again called out as one of the drafted Militia in the same county, to wit, Brunswick and State of Virginia, and placed in Mark Stead or William Blalock's Company but he is not positive which, and was marched from that place under the command of Colonels Halkhams and St. George Tucker to the fork of James River called Paintly Fork, to General Steuben's Headquarters, he states that on the same evening that the troops that he was with, joined General Steuben that the British commenced a discharge of cannon across the river at the American Army and General Steuben retreated or marched his army about twelve miles from that place and encamped, he says he was then marched to Cumberland Court House, Prince Edward Court House, and here he was discharged, making in the whole a term of actual service of seven months in the Army of the Revolution.

Interrogatories by the Court

Q. 1st: Where and in what year were you born?
A.   I was born in the County of Brunswick and State of Virginia, on the 27th day of January in the year 1760, agreeable to the information I have secured from my parents.
Q. 2nd: Have you any record of your age and if so, where is it?
A.   I have a record of my age at my house in this county, in my Bible taken from my father's family record.
Q. 3rd: Where were you living when called into service, where have you lived since the Revolutionary War, and where do you now live?
A.   I was a citizen of Brunswick County in the State of Virginia, when called into service and from there I removed to the State of North Carolina about two years after the close of the Revolutionary War and remained there in the County of Mecklenburg on Catawba River where I remained forty four years and that I then removed in the year of 1831· to Bedford County, Tennessee, where I have lived every since and where I now live.
Q. 4th: How were you called into service, were you drafted, did you volunteer, or were you a substitute and if a substitute for whom?
A.   I was a drafted soldier during all my service.
Q. 5th: State the names of some of the regular officers who were with the troops where you served, such as, Continental and Militia Regiments as you can recollect and the general circumstances of your service.
A.   I recollect General Steuben, personally, and I was also recollect to have seen a number of his officers but cannot now remember the names of any of them except Adjutant Abner Grissom and I believe I have given the most prominent circumstances of my service in the foregoing declaration.
Q. 6th: State the names of persons to whom you are known in your present neighborhood and who can testify as to your character for veracity and good behavior, your service as a Soldier of the Revolution.
A.   I have not been living long enough in my present neighborhood to form an acquaintance with many persons, but I was well acquainted with Doctor William Houston and William Means, Esqrs., in Mecklenburg, Iredell and Cabarrus Counties in the State of North Carolina who are now citizens of Bedford County, Tennessee, but have not formed any acquaintances.

Declaration:
    In order to obtain the benefit of the Act of Congress of the 7th July 1838 entitled "An Act Granting half pay and Pensions to certain Widows".
State of Tennessee
Maury County
    On this 1 day of June 1846, personally appeared before me, Isaac N.

33

Bills, one of the Justices of the Peace in and for Maury County in the State aforesaid and one of the members of Maury County Court of the County of Maury in the State aforesaid, aged seventy-nine years who being first duly sworn according to law doth on her oath make the following declaration in order to obtain the benefit of the provisions made by the Act of Congress passed July 7th, 1838 entitled an act granting half pay and pensions to certain widows, that she is the widow of John Connelly who was a Soldier of the Revolution. That in July or August 1780, her husband, John Connelly entered the service of the United States in the Virginia Line, was a Private, that he was drafted and was _____ _____, that he resided in Brunswick County in the State of Virginia at the time he went into service. That owing to the great lapse of time and the consequent loss of memory, she does not at this time recollect any of his officers names. That after he joined the army of the United States, he marched to the town of Hillsborough in the State of North Carolina in Scouring against the British and continued there but a very short time. He then left Hillsborough and marched through different parts of the United States till the expiration of his first tour. That his first tour was nine months and at the expiration of said nine months, she does not know whether he received a written or verbal discharge and at the expiration of said first tour, he returned home to Brunswick County in Virginia and continued there a few days then went into the service again as a Private in the Militia, that he was drafted. Thereafter, he joined the Army of the United States, the second time, he marched to a point near Hillsborough in North Carolina at which place he was taken very sick and was compelled to go to the hospital and continued at said hospital two weeks, at the expiration of which time he left the hospital and marched through different parts of North Carolina, against the British and Tories till his second tour ended, that his second tour was three months. At the expiration of his second tour, she does not recollect whether he received any written discharge or not. At the expiration of service second tour, he returned home to Brunswick County in Virginia, and continued there but a short time and then went into the service again. That he went into service, the third time as a Private in the Militia. That he was drafted, that after he joined the Army of the United States, the third time, she does not know what part of the county he marched through, but his third tour was six months but she does not know whether he received a written or verbal discharge, that he served, in all, eighteen months. That sometime after the year 1830, her husband, the said John Connelly, applied for and obtained a pension from the government of the United States, that said pension was twenty dollars per annum. That her husband, the said John Connelly, left the service of the United States sometime in the year 1782. That in Mecklenburg County in the State of North Carolina, on the second day of March 1790, she married the said John Connelly, that but a very short time after she married the said John Connelly, that their said marriage was put down in a book called Brown's Dictionary of the Bible by the said John Connelly himself in his own hand writing, and afterwards said book and record was kept in the possession of the said John Connelly himself till his death and afterwards returned and kept in the possession of this declarant herself, sworn to this to me, declarant states that after they married, the said John Connelly, she continued to live with him as his wife till the 29th day of June 1835 at which time he died in Bedford County in the State of Tennessee, and but a very short time after he died, his death was set down by one James M. Connelly, in his own hand writing in the said book, called Brown's Dictionary of the said Bible which record of the said John Connelly's death and book has been kept and returned by this declarant herself to this time. And the record of said death and marriage aforesaid were marked as documents in this cause. Declarant states after the death of said John Connelly, she delivered the Pension Certificate which he obtained to a gentleman who resides in Bedford County in Tennessee to get a pension for her. But she has not yet obtained said pension and said Certificate is at this time in the possession of said gentleman, but she will endeavor to get the same from said gentleman, and if she can obtain the same, she will send it on with the other papers in this cause, declarant states that she has no documentary evidence whatever in support of her claim except that which has been transmitted with the papers in this cause. She further states that she was married to the said John Connelly on the 2 day of March 1790, and that her husband the aforesaid John Connelly died on the 29th day of June 1835. That she was not married prior to his

leaving the service but the marriage took place previous to the first of January seventeen hundred and ninety four, viz, at the time ____ stated, declarant further states that after the death of her husband, the said John Connelly, she remained single and never had married any person whatever.
Sworn to and subscribed on the day and year   Mary (X) Connelly
aforesaid written before me.
Isaac N. Bills
Justice of the Peace, M.C.

State of Tennessee]
Maury County   ]
      On this 1st day of June 1846, personally appeared before me, Isaac N. Bills, one of the Justices of the Peace in and for the County Court of Maury County and State of said, John B. Connelly of the COunty of Maury in the State aforesaid, aged fifty two years, who being first duly sworn according to law states as follows, that he was well acquainted with John Connelly in his life time and that he died on the 29th day of June 1835 in Bedford County, in the State of Tennessee, and that he resided in bedford County in the State aforesaid at the time of his death. Applicant further states that the copy of the marriage of the said John Connelly married and is in the handwriting of the said John Connelly.

Bible Record of John Connelly

"Be fruitful and multiply, and replenish the earth," Gen:1
Births:
      Milton H. Connelly was born January 22nd, 1810
      James M.C. Connelly was born December 21st, 1811
      Jefferson Connelly was born November 3rd, 1803
      Charles L. Connell was born August 10th, 1807
Marriages:
      "This is now bone of my bones...therefore shall a man leave his father and his mother, and shall cleave unto his wife and they shall be one flesh." Gen. 11: 23-24
      John Connelly was born January 27th, 1760
      maried March 2nd 1790, died June 29th, 1835
      John Connelly married March 2, 1790 in Mecklenburg County, North Carolina, Mary Stanford.

The widow, Mary Connelly, was allowed pension on her application executed June 1, 1848, at which time she was seventy nine years of age and living in Maury County, Tennessee. She was living in 1850 in Giles County, Tennessee.

      In 1846, James M. Connelly was a Missionary in Africa, and John B. Connelly was fifty two years of age and a resident of Maury County, Tennessee. One Robert Stanford was in Mecklenburg County, North Carolina in 1790. (The relationship of these people is not known)

West Tennessee, Mary Connelly, widow of John Connelly, under Captain Harrison, Virginia, who served in the Revolutionary War as a Private.
      Inscribed on the roll at the rate of $20 dollars and ____ cents per annum, to commence on the 4th day of March 1848.
      Certificate of Pension issued the 5 day of November, 1850 and sent to Milton A. Magnes, Cornersville, Giles County, Tennessee.
      Recorded on Roll of Pensioners under _____February 2, 1848
Vol 8(?) page 287
H.E. Robinson

1835 , aged 76, Bedford County Pension List.

      Ref: GSA Report, Washington, D.C.
      Ref: Widow's Pension

* * * * * * * * * *

Name:	Rank:	State Served:
Horatio Coop	Pvt	Maryland

Born 1758 Baltimore County, Maryland, died 1843 Bedford County, Tennessee, buried in Cross Church Cemetery with a Military marker.

GSA: Horatio Coop, S.3193, Pension Claim No. 14457
    West Tennessee, Horatio Coop of Bedford County in the State of Tennessee, who was a Private in the company commanded by Col. _____ in the Maryland Militia Line for 18 months from 1777.
    Inscribed on the Roll of West Tennessee at the rate of $60 dollars ____ cents per annum, to commence on the 4th day of March 1831.
    Certificate of Pension issued the 11 day of September 1833, and sent to Hon. J.K. Polk, Columbia, Tennessee.

Arrears to the 4th of Sept '33	$150.
Semi-anl allowance ending 4 March	$ 30.
	$180.00

Recorded by William Allison, Clerk	Revolutionary Claim
Book E Vol 7 page 75	Act June 7, 1832

Declaration:
State of Tennessee]
Bedford County   ]
    On this 14th day of August in the year 1832, personally appeared before John B. Armstrong, John Neill and Samuel Phillips, Esquires, Justices appointed to hold the Court of Pleas and Quarter Sessions for the County and State aforesaid for the year 1832. Horatio Coop, a citizen of and resident in the County aforesaid and State of Tennessee, aged seventy four years, who being first duly sworn according to law doth on his oath make the following declaration in order to obtain the benefit of the provision made by the Act of Congress passed June 7th 1832. Deponent states he volunteered in the Service of his country in the year _____, under Captain Robert Harris, of the Maryland Line, for the term of nine months which he served, at the time he entered the service of his country, he was living in the County of Baltimore and State of Maryland at which place he entered the service.   After entering the service as aforesaid they were marched to Philadelphia, and thence to Brunswick, at the latter place, we had an engagement with the enemies, after the battle, we were stationed at Brunswick until my term of service expired. I was discharged at the expiration of said nine months and returned home. The officers who commanded the Americans, General George Washington and Robert Harris my Captain. I do not recollect any others. I _________ join short time after my ____ ____ drafted for the term of 4 months and was marched from Maryland where I lived at that time to Plumb Point where I was stationed during this term of service.
    The officers who commanded at Plumb Point as well as I recollect were, Captain Cole, Lieutenant William Davis, being the Captain and Lieutenant under whom I was placed and served during this tour.   Having received my second discharge, I again returned home to Baltimore County, State of Maryland where I remained until the year ____, when I enlisted for three years in the Regular of Continental Line of the Maryland Troops. I enlisted under John Kane. We were then marched and stationed at the city of Baltimore where we remained until deponent was selected as driver of one of the forage wagons. He continued during the term of his said enlistment to discharge this duty. During the discharge of his duties, he was appointed to drive the forage wagon as aforesaid. He states he was at Philadelphia and at the White Plains. He had his headquarters at Middlebrook in the State of New Jersey the first year. He then went to Valley Forge and continued there for ______, we were marched from Valley Forge to Morristown where I remained until my term of enlistment expired, when I was discharged and returned home.   He does not recollect the precise date or year when he volunteered, the different times above mentioned. ____ he states with any precision the date he enlisted for the three years aforesaid. He is confident that during the first term of service as aforesaid for nine months, the battle or engagement aforesaid at Brunswick in New Jersey took place. He was stationed during the four months tour at Plumb Point and for that period, he was in no

battle or engagement. Before any engagement after the period on his enlistment, he was taken from the company and placed with the Wagon Department and was during his service as Wagon Driver, in no engagement. While I was engaged in the wagon business as aforesaid, I was under the immediate direction of McDaniel who as I suppose and believed was under the control of John Caton, the business of this latter person was to ascertain when the forage and _____ could be had and the other was to go with the wagons. I have the same lodge at the forage yard. From the forage yard it was carried to the army under the direction and control of Colonel John Thompson and Major Fossett, I suppose the two latter persons were called Commissioners, but of this I cannot speak. Certainly, he further states that during this term of service, he recollects that the Battle of Brandywine, when the Americans were defeated, also the battle between General Gates and Burgoyne in which the latter capitulated, were fought and he was in hearing of the artillery at the time this action took place, he saw a great many of the British after they had surrendered and as they were marched from the battle ground. He states he received his discharge from Major Fossett at Morristown in the State of New Jersey. After ____ ____ another call was made for men, and I was then drafted for the term of five months. This took place in the County of Hartford, State of Maryland. He states that he was sent to the city of Baltimore and I was there, put under the command of Joseph Webster as Captain who carried us on to Annapolis in Maryland, on our way to join the American Forces against Lord Cornwallis, who understood was in York Town. He states that on the night, the company arrived at Annapolis, he happened with the misfortune to have his wrist put out of joint, in consequence of which he was left the next day in the hoslital, where he remained until his tour of service expired, which was sometime after the surrender of Lord Cornwallis. He states he was finally discharged from the service at Annapolis by General Smallwood. He states he received written discharge for each and every tour of service above mentioned and as he believes had all of them in his pocket book, the three years discharge. He is confident it was in his pocket book some considerable time after the war ceased. His pocket book and many other papers as well as his discharge were stolen out of his house and has never since been seen by him. He believes this is the way his discharge have been all lost. He states the different periods of service above mentioned and which he served made four years and six months which he served his country, all of which he did faithfully perform except the last tour of 5 months, the performance of which he presented on account of having his wrist put out of place. He states he knows of no person now living whom he can prove the fact of his service in any or all of the foregoing tours of duty, except Richard Coop and Barachias Coop, both brothers, by them he expects he could prove many facts which are stated above, and which would be material. Those persons live in different parts of the State of Tennessee, one in Blount County near Maryville and is now as deponent is informed, a pensioner under the former law, though I have not seen him for the space of twenty seven or eight years, and about 200 miles from my residence, the other, Richard Coop lives in Sumner County, Tennessee, about 100 miles from my residence in Bedford County. I have not seen him upwards of 18 years. Deponent states he is old infirm and unable to go about and that it is with much difficulty he was unable to ride to Shelbyville to have this declaration made out. That each of his brothers, aforesaid, are old infirm and as he is informed, they could not attend to this business or to make an affidavit of the above facts before any Court of Record in this State. He has no documentary evidence in his possession and he knows of no person except as aforesaid by whom he can prove or can testify to his service. He hereby relinquishes any claim whatever to a pension or annuity except the present and declares that his name is not on the Pension Roll of the agency of any State in the United States.

Sworn to in open Court and subscribed   Horatio (X) Coop
this 1st of August 1832
J. McKisick, Clerk

Where upon the Court preponded to said applicant, Horatio Coop, the following:

Interrogatories

Q. 1st: Where and in what year were you born?
A.   I was born in Baltimore County, State of Maryland in the year 1758.

Q. 2nd: Have you any record of your age and if so where is it?
A.   I have a record of my age, it is at my house in the Family Bible, it is transcribed from the record kept by my father into my own Family Bible, and still remains on the leaf upon which it was transcribed.
Q. 3rd: Where were you living when called into service, where have you lived since then?
A.   I was living in Baltimore County, State of Maryland when first called into service, I lived in North Carolina in the counties of Orange and Caswell, for about seven years, since the war, I then moved to Smith County, Tennessee and from there I moved to Bedford County, State of Tennessee where I now live, and have lived for more than 22 years.
Q. 4th: How were you called into service, were you drafted, did you volunteer or were you a substitute and if a substitute for whom?
A.   I was a volunteer in the first place for nine months, next was drafted for four months, next enlisted for three years and finally was drafted for five months.
Q. 5th: State the names of some of the Regular Officers who were with the troops where you served such Continental and Militia Regiments as you can recollect and the general circumstance of your service.
A.   General George Washington was at the Battle of Brunswick. My other campaigns and services being either at Plumb Point or with the wagons, I know but little of the officers marched to the army or their names. I have no recollection of the manner or numbers of the Continental or Militia Regiments.
Q. 6th: Did you ever receive a discharge from the service, if so, by whom was it given and what has become of it?
A.   I did receive a discharge for every tour of duty I performed, the first was given by Robert Harris, I received it at Philadelphia although I was discharged at Brunswick. The next was given by William Cole at Plumb Point. The third was given by Major Fossett at Morristown in the State of New Jersey and the fourth by Smallwood at Annapolis, Maryland. They were all lost or stolen as above stated.
Q. 7th: State the names of persons who are acquainted with you in your neighborhood and who can testify as to your character for veracity and truth and their belief of your services in the Revolution.
A.   Many persons are well acquainted with me in my neighborhood and can state what my character is. I know of none who can say anything of my services in the Revolution, as to their own knowledge. Rev'd John Mash, William Norvill, Esq., Captain John Davis and many others can speak, I presume as to my general reputation in this respect.

Sworn to and subscribed in open court   Horatio (X) Coop
14th of August 1832
Jas. McKisick, Clerk

We, John Mash, a clergyman residing in the County of Bedford and State of Tennessee and William Norvill residing in the same County and State, hereby can testify, that we are well acquainted with Horatio Coop, who has subscribed and sworn to the above and forgoing declaration and interrogatories, that we believe him to be seventy four years of age. That he is reputed and believed in the neighborhood where he resides, to have been a Soldier of the Revolution, that the same has never been doubted and that we concur in that opinion.

Revolutionary War Records Section 3-525
Department of the Interior, Bureau of Pensions, Washington, D.C.
A statement of the Military history of Horatio Coop, a Soldier of the Revolutionary War, you will find below the desired information as contained in his application for pension on file in this bureau.

Dates of enlistments or appointments	Length of service	Rank	Officers under whom served		State
			Capt.	Col.	
Feb 1, 1777	8 months	Pvt	Robt. Harris		
			Jas. Thompson		MD
May 1777 to 1778	4 months	Wagoner	McDaniel & Cole		
May 17-18, 1778	3 years	"	John Kane		

Battles engaged in--- Brunswick
Residence of Soldier at enlistment ---------------------- Baltimore, MD
Date of application for pension --------------------------- August 14, 1832
Residence at date of application -------------------------- Bedford County, TN
Age at date of application -------------------------------- Born 1758 in Baltimore
                                                            County, MD

No. 179: Oaths of Fidelity, Horatio Coop
1840 Census of Bedford County, Tennessee, he is in the house of James Coop.

> Ref: GSA Report, Washington, D.C.
> Ref: Cemetery Records of Bedford County, Tennessee by Marsh.
> Ref: Maryland Records by Brumbaugh, page 16
> Ref: DAR Patriot Index
> Ref: Oaths of Fidelity, Maryland Records by Brumbaugh, page 247

* * * * * * * * * *

ABRAHAM COOPER

Name: Rank: State Served:
Abraham Cooper   ----   --------------
Born _____, died _____

No GSA on Abraham Cooper in Washington, D.C.

The Abraham Cooper Family

The manuscript presented below was contributed by Mr. Biffle Owen, Clarksdale, Mississippi. It is signed by John S. Cooper May 9, 1917 from Trenton, Tennessee. Mr. Cooper concluded the sketch by commenting that the statements were dictated to a sister, Tempie E. Cooper, by their father John Linzapher Cooper, Bedford County, Tennessee in December 1886. John L. Cooper was 79 years of age at that time and died in May 1895. All statements were made by him from memory. Mr. Biffle Owen states that he has obtained proof of part of the data.

The father of Abraham Cooper came from England and settled in Culpepper County, Virginia, most probably between the dates 1750 and 1760. He had five sons, among whom was Abraham, the direct ancestor of our branch of the family. The names of the other four sons are unknown or not remembered. One of these four sons went from Virginia to South Carolina, one to Georgia, another to Kentucky, and the fourth remained in Virginia.
Abraham Cooper, our ancestor, married a Miss Browning in Virginia about the year 1775. They removed from Virginia to Tennessee soon afterward and settled in Carter County (Carter County was taken from Washington County in 1796), where they brought up a family of five sons and two daughters, in order of birth, John, James, Sarah, William, Jane, Robert and Charles. Abraham Cooper's wife died at their home in Carter County. Abraham Cooper and his family moved from Carter County and settled in Smith County on the Caney Fork River, about three miles above Carthage, about 1805. His son, Robert Cooper, did not come to Smith County until two years later in 1807. John L. Cooper, the eldest child of Robert Cooper, was born prematurely upon this journey. About the year 1812, Abraham Cooper, with his daughters and three sons, William, Robert and Charles, came from Smith County and settled in Bedford County. In 1820, Abraham's son, James, came to Bedford, leaving only one member of the family, the eldest son John, in Smith County where he lived and died. This John Cooper, in early life, while yet in Carter County, married a Miss Moffitt, and brought up a family of two sons and five daughters. His son, Abram, married a Miss Hale. His son, Bluford, removed to West Tennessee and while hunting, was thrown from his horse and killed. This was the supposition concernting his death. He married in West Tennessee. The oldest daughter of John Cooper, Lavina, married a Mr. Jones. Jane, the second daughter, was the second wife of William Sharp of Bedford County. Sarah, the third daughter, married Green Moore of Bedford County. He was a brother of Colonel John A. Moore, long a well-known citizen of the county.

The fourth daughter, Letha, married John Sharp, the son of William Sharp, her sister's husband. Thomas Sharp and his sister, Mrs. T.F. Bates of Shelbyville, are children of Jane Cooper Sharp. I have lost sight of the fifth daughter and do not remember whether she was ever married or not.

James Cooper, familiarly called "Uncle Jimmy", the second son of Abraham Cooper, hwile a young man in Carter County, Tennessee, married Elizabeth Bogart. As has been stated, he settled in Bedford County in 1820. His children were all born in Smith County, the oldest of whom at this time (1820) had reached manhood and womanhood. His oldest child, Polly, married John Tune, and was the mother of a large family of sons and daughters. Of these, John B. Tune, K.L. Tune, Mrs. Mat Williams and Mrs. Mary Boman reside in Bedford County. The second daughter, Sally, married Dennis Springer. They had several children, all of whom went to Hickman and Dickson Counties. The third daughters, Jane, married Alsea, otherwise known as "York" Harris, and died without children. The fourth daughters, Elizabeth, married Price Cooper Steele. The fifth daughter, Catherine, married Carlos D. Steele. The sixth daughter, Malinda, married Caswell Puckett of Rutherford County. Of Elizabeth Steele's children, only four survive, Rev. Marion Steele of Arkansas, Hon. John W. Steele, Miss Fanny Steele, and Mrs. T.N. McCord of Bedford County. Of Catherine Steele's children, only two remain, Captain B.P. Steele of Tullahoma, and John Bell Steele of Arkansas. Mrs. Puckett left three sons and five daughters, all living in Rutherford County.

Washington Bogart Cooper, the oldest son of James Cooper is an artist by profession. He has long been a resident of Nashville, Tennessee, and is now about 84 years of age. He married in 1842 Miss Ann Litton, a native of Dublin, Ireland. They have three children, James Litton, Kate Litton and Joe Litton.

Jonathan J., the second son of James Cooper married Mary Ann Young, a Kentuckian by birth and a schoolmistress. In 1860, he removed from Bedford County to Arkansas, first to Benton County and then to White COunty, where he died. His widow and two daughters reside in Fayetteville, Arkansas, while the three sons, as I am informed, are in Benton County, Arkansas.

William Browning, the third son of James Cooper, is also an artist of distinction and reside in Nashville. His wife was first a Miss Berkley of Williamson County, then Mrs. Reedy, then Mrs. Breckenridge, and as Mrs. Cooper, is the mother of two children, John L. and Mrs. Slaughter of Louisville, Kentucky. The two brothers, Washington B. and William B., are the only survivors of James Cooper's family.

The third son of Abraham Cooper was William H., who married Sarah Jamison of Dixon Springs, Smith County. They reared five daughters and one son. The oldest daughter, Betsy, was the second wife of John Woods of Bedford County. Her five children are all dead except Jesse. She died in August 1883. The second daughter, Clarissa, died while young. The third daughter, Jane, married Robert Brooks of Giles County, a first cousin of Bishop Pain of the Southern Methodist Church. Brooks removed from Giles County to Yalobusha County, Mississippi, where he reared his family. The fourth daughter, Mary, died unmarried atMrs. Wood's. The fifth daughter, Nancy, married Mr. Dodson of Mississippi, and is the only surviving member of the family. Thomas Jamison, the only son, married in Giles County, went to Leake County, Mississippi, and settled there and died in 1882. He left some children, all of whom live in Mississippi.

Robert Cooper, the fourth son of Abraham Cooper, married Rebecca McInturf in Carter County, Tennessee. They were borh born in Carter County in 1784. They had nine children, eight sons and one daughter, the daughter having died when six months old. All of the sons grew to manhood except Abram, who died at three years of age.

John Linzapher Cooper, the oldest son of Robert Cooper, was born November 20, 1807, as had been stated, upon the trip from Carter County, and, therefore cannot claim any county as the place of his nativity, but has been a citizen of Bedford County since 1812. He was married May 15, 1834, to Frances G. Lindsey of Rutherford County. She was the daughter of Caleb and Temperance (House) Lindsey, and was born June 28, 1813, in Granville County, North Carolina. They were the parents of five children, Caleb Lindsey, Adalaide Rebecca, John Summerford, Temperance Elizabeth and Robert Browning. Caleb L. married Miss Isabella Smith of Rutherford County, November 14, 1860. They have no children. Adalaide R. was married August 17, 1858 to Rev. J.S. Malone of the Southern

Methodist Church, and died December 24, 1876, leaving no children. John S. was married October 15, 1879 to Miss Anna Hess, a daughter of Dr. Nelson _. Hess, long a prominent physician of Trenton, Tennessee. They have two children, Arthur F. and Gussie Lee. Frances Green, wife of John L. Cooper and mother of his children died March 25, 1874. He married Sarah W. Jamison of Rutherford County in December 1875.

The second son of Robert Cooper was Abner James. He was born in 1810 and died in '28 or '29. William Browning was the third son. He was born 1812 and died of dropsy in 1834. The fourth son, Abram, died in childhood.

The fifth son, Charles Dickson, was born in 1814 and died in Tallahatchie County, Mississippi in 1862. He first married Elizabeth Lindsey, a sister of his brother John's wife, in June 1835. She died in June 1840. He next married Elizabeth Rogers of Bedford County, and after her death, he married Mrs. Crenshaw of Mississippi who survivied him, but is now dead. Elizabeth Lindsey left three children, William H., Sally T.E. and Wise A. Cooper. William H. became a surgeon of distinction in the Confederate Army and died unmarried July 10, 1866. Sally T.E. married Lewis Sims of Rutherford County and died October 1881 leaving one child, Bessie Sims. Wise A. Cooper married in September 1866, Miss Senie Shaw of Gibson County, Tennessee. They have a large family of children and now reside in Fort Smith, Arkansas. The second wife of C.D. Cooper left a son John F., whose whereabouts are unknown.

Bedford Campbell was the sixth son of Robert Cooper. He was born about 1816. (I am not positive as to dates, not having a record). His first wife was Elizabeth Tinnin. She died, leaving three children, and then he married her sister Laura Tinnin. He and his wife are both living near Bloomfield, Missouri. His oldest son, William, was a Confederate Soldier, and was killed at Tupelo, Mississippi. Robert, the second son, received a wound in the same battle from the effects of which he died a year or two afterward.

Robert Caldwell was the seventh son of Robert Cooper. He was born about 1820 and is still living, unmarried.

Thomas Price was the eighth and youngest son. He was born in 1827 and died February 3, 1877. He married Lucretia W. Rogers, and they had seven children, all sons. Their names were, Samuel, Morgan, Robert Linzapher, William, John Harris, Thomas Oliver, George Franklin, and "Rob". All are dead except John H. who is a resident of Nashville.

Robert Cooper, the son of Abraham, died suddenly of heart disease in June 1833 and is buried at the old home in Rutherford County, Tennessee. His wife Rebecca died in December 1862.

Charles Cooper was the fifth son of Abraham Cooper. He married Sarah Brooks of Bedford County and died in 1822, leaving three sons and five daughters. John B., the oldest of these, first married Miss Sivley of Alabama, and after her death, he married Miss Jane McGuffin of Middletown, Rutherford County. They reared a family of children, one of whom, Mrs. James L. Goodrum, resides in Bedford County. John B. died at his home in Alabama in '82 or '83.

Abram was the second son of Charles Cooper. His first wife was Miss Martha Sample of Bedford County. His second wife was a lady of Giles County, Tennessee. They removed to Crawley's Ridge, Arkansas, where he died.

William Franklin was the third son of Charles Cooper. His first wife was Mary Morton who left three children, Sarah (Mrs. Claxton), Mary (Mrs. Hunter), and W.C. Cooper of Bell Buckle, Tennessee. His second wife was Miss McCrory. His third wife was Miss HUnter of Marshall County who is the mother of four children, Sue (Mrs. Claxton), John T., Virgil E., and Maggie Cooper. "Frank" Cooper, as he was called, was killed instantly by the accidental discharge of a soldier's gun, in camp, near Shelbyville, Tennessee, in March 1862. He had gone to camp to visit his son, W.C. Cooper, who was one of the daring of Confederate Soldiers.

Charles Cooper's oldest daughter was Maria B. who is still living in Nashville, Tennessee. She was born in 1814, and was married while young to Learner Knott who died in 1871. They were the parents of eleven children, only three of whom survive, Mrs. R.D. Reed and Mrs. Landon Hollowell of Nashville, and W.C. Knott. Their oldest son, Rufus, was a Confederate Soldier and was killed at the Battle of Shiloh, 1862.

Matilda was Charles Cooper's second daughter. She was married while young to Anderson J. Goodrum of Williamson County, Tennessee. They made their home in Bedford COunty where they brought up a large family of sons and daughters, all of whom are living except son Charles who was killed by lightning at his home in Kentucky. The second son, James L., was a gallant Confederate Soldier, and left a leg on the field of Chickamauga. He has three times filled the office of Trustee of Bedford County.

Malinda and Adeline were the third and fourth daughters of Charles Cooper. They married brothers, William and Sam Phillips and removed to Illinois. I know nothing of their families.

Elizabeth was the fifth daughter of Charles Cooper, and was born after her father's death. She married William Holt and they reside near Wartrace, Tennessee. They have several children.

The oldest daughter of Abraham Cooper was Sarah. She married Richard Coop of Bedford County. In 1828, they removed to Gibson County and settled near Katon. I remember the names of only the four oldest children, Jane, William, Elizabeth and Henderson. And I also remember Mrs. Yahs, another daughter, who once visited us. Richard Coop and his wife both died in West Tennessee.

Jane was the second daughter of Abraham Cooper. She married John Montgomery of Rutherford County, Tennessee. They removed to Gibson County in company with Richard Coop's family and settled in the same neighborhood. There John Montgomery died and after his death his widow and children removed to Arkansas.

John Cooper, the eldest son of Abraham, outlived all his brothers and died about 1840. I omitted to mention in the proper connection that he married the second time. I do not remember the lady's name. She had two children, Timothy Walton and a daughter who married a Walton. They both reside in Smith County, Tennessee.

James Cooper, the second son of Abraham, died in 1823 in Bedford County and is buried on what is known as the Steele Farm, where he lived for some years.

William, the third son of Abraham, died about 1818, at his home in the northeast part of Bedford County, three or four miles from Bell Buckle, and was buried there. His father Abraham Cooper was also buried there.

Charles, the fifth son of Abraham, as stated, died in 1822 and was buried on his home place five miles from Shelbyville, on the Fairfield Pike.

NOTE: The cemetery in which Abraham Cooper is buried is known as the Clark Cemetery and there is no marker for his grave. - eds.

Ref: The Abraham Cooper Family by Mr. Biffle Owen of Mississippi.
Ref: Cemetery Records of Bedford County, Tennessee by Marsh
Ref: Index to Revolutionary Application (Pension)
Abraham Cooper, Conn., S36468, Pvt, Conn., BLWt. 5576 issued
May 15, 1795 to E. Munson, Jr. & Kneeland Townsend, assignees.

NOTE: We have no proof that this Abraham Cooper was in the Revolutionary War. -
eds.

* * * * * * * * * *

JAMES COURSEY

Name: Rank: State Served:
James Coursey   Pvt   Virginia
Born 16th January 1748/9 in Granville County, North Carolina, died 8th of May 1840 in Bedford County, Tennessee, married 1777 to Susannah _____.

GSA: James Coursey, R.2308, Virginia, Indian Disturbances of 1774.
State of Tennessee]
Bedford County   ]

On this 6th day of August 1833, personally appeared in open court before the Justice of the Court of Pleas and Quarter Sessions for Bedford County being a Court of Records now sitting, James Coursey, a resident of Bedford County in the State of Tennessee, aged about 84 years, who being first duly sworn according to law, doth on his oath make the following declaration in order to obtain the benefit of the provision of an Act of Congress passed June 7th 1832.

That he entered the service of the United States as a Revolutionary Soldier in the year 1774 as volunteer for a tour of three months under Captain Abram Penn in Henry County, Virginia. Colonel Garden of the Militia in Henry County, sent Captain Penn's Company consisting of 45 or 50 men to Botetourt COunty, Virginia to be commanded by Colonel Christy, when Penn's Company to which this applicant belonged arrived there, Colonel Christy sent them on to Fort Kenasaw with a view of their proceeding further on to the Indian Settlements on the Ohio, but when Captain Penn's Company arrived at the Fort, they found that the Company which had been stationed to guard the Fort had already proceeded to the Indian Settlements on the Ohio. Captain Penn then remained at the Fort for the purpose of guarding it until the three months for which this applicant had volunteered, expired. The Company then returned home and were verbally dismissed or discharged by Captain Penn.

In the Spring of 1775 or 1776, this applicant from the failure of memory cannot recollect which but to the best of his recollection, it was in the Spring of 1776, he again volunteered under Captain Abram Penn, in Henry County, Virginia, for a term of three months service and his company marched down the James River to Jamestown to guard the magazine and breastworks at that place against the British where the applicant remained until his three months expired or probably a little longer. During this tour of service, Lieutenant Harvy Lyons was the Lieutenant of his Company. At the expiration of this tour this applicant was verbally dismissed or discharged by Captain Penn.

After this applicant's return from James Town, the Militia COmpany to which he belonged in Henry County, Virginia, drew Numbers to serve according to the numbers drawn. This applicant drew number 10 and his time to serve did not arrive until shortly before the surrender of Lord Cornwallis at Yorktown when he was with some of his neighbors sent to Yorktown to fight the Brittish. But before they arrived there this applicant was taken sick and furloughed by a Lieutenant Clay who had charge of him and some others. His Captain whose name he does not recollect having gone on before, he then returned home and never served any more as the war ended about this time.

This applicant states that during his first term of service under Captain Penn, Joseph Martin was his Lieutenant and Brice Martin his Ensign. This applicant further states that he was acquainted with no other Regular of Militia Officers during the Revolutionary War but those mentioned. In this declaration except Colonel Tunstall, Major Wells and Major Redd and some other Militia Officers in the county where he resided, this applicant further states that he has no documentary evidence of his service and he knows of no person now living by whom he can make any proof of his services. At the time he was furloughed by Lieutenant Clay he received a written furlough which he will enclose with this declaration if he has not lost it during the different tours of service above mentioned. He served as a Private Soldier. This applicant was born in Granville County, North Carolina. His father left his mother when he was a child and his mother married John Couch who removed and carried him to Virginia. He was born the 16th day of January 1748 or 1749. He does not recollect which, this he learned from his mother but he has no record of his age. He was about 24 or 25 years of age when he first entered the service of his country in the Revolutionary War at which time he was living in Henry County, Virginia, where he also resided at the close of the war. This applicant is acquainted in his present neighborhood with the Rev'd John Rushing, Barney B. Haley, William Sims, William Smotherman and others, all of whom will testify as to his character for veracity and their belief of his service as a Revolutionary Soldier.

This applicant states that he removed from Henry County, Virginia, to Maury County, Tennessee, almost twenty years ago and from thence to Williamson County, from thence to Rutherford County and from thence to Bedford County, Tennessee, where he has resided for about nine years and now resides. He states that he only claims a pension for six months altho he served something longer than that time.

He hereby relinguishes every claim to a pension or annuity except the present and declares that his name is not on the Pension Roll of any agency of any state.

Sworn to and subscribed the day and year aforesaid   Jas. (X) Coursey
George Davidson, J.P. and Jas. McKisick, Clk.

State of Tennessee]
Bedford County   ]
        On this 9th day of September 1843, personally appeared before me, James Foster, an acting Justice of the Peace for the county aforesaid, Susannah Coursey, a resident of bedford County in the State of Tennessee, aged between eighty six or eighty seven years, who being first duly sworn according to law, doth on her oath make the following declaration in order to obtain the benefit of the provision made by the Act of Congress passed July 4th, 1836. That she is the widow of James Coursey who was a Private in the Army of the Revolution, that her said husband served three tours in the Militia of the State of Virginia, that his first term of service was three months, which was performed in 1777 or 1778 as well as she remembers. He served in Captain George Penn's Company, but she does not know the names of any of his other Company or Field Officers. He served a second term of three months in Captain Joseph Martin's Company, which term of service was shortly after his first term. She does not remember the names of his other Company Officers or of his Field Officers in this tour. He also entered the service for another three months term in 1778 or 1779, in Captain Clay's Company. She thinks he was discharged from this term after he had served between two or three months. She does not remember his other Company or his Field Officers in this last tour, nor does she knows to what Brigade or Division he belonged, in any one of his terms of service. A part of his service was rendered on Smith's River and she thinks that in each instance, he rendezvoused at Henry Court House, Virginia, and he resided in Henry County, Virginia, when he entered the service each time.

        She cannot state the day or month in which he entered the service either time nor does she know whether he was drafted or was a volunteer, but he entered the service each time in one of these ways. She further states that she has no documentary evidence in support of her claim. She further declares that she was married to the same James Coursey in 1777, but does not remember the day and month, that her husband, the said James Coursey died on the 8th day of May 1840 and that she has remained a widow ever since that period, as will more fully apply reference to the proof unto annexed.

Sworn to and subscribed on the day and   Susannah (X) Coursey
year above written before me.
James Foster, J.P. (Seal)
for said County.

State of Tennessee]
Bedford County   ]
        Personally appeared, Barnaba Haley and James Haley, before me, James Foster, an Acting Justice of the Peace for the County aforesaid, and made oath in due form that they were personally acquainted with James Coursey, late of said county, that they believe he died on 8th day of May 1840 and old age was the cause of his death, that Susannah Coursey is his widow and has remained a widow ever since his death. They further swear that the said James Coursey was reputed and believed in the neighborhood where he resided to have been a Soldier of the Revolution.

Sworn to and subscribed before me this   James Haley
4th day of September 1843   Barnaba Haley
James Foster, J.P. (Seal)
for the County.

State of Tennessee]
Bedford County   ]
        Personally appeared Nancy Haley, formerly Nancy Coursey, and Charles Coursey, citizens of said County, before me, James Foster, an Acting Justice of the Peace for said County, and made oath in due form of law, that they are the two oldest children of James Coursey and Susannah Coursey, and according to the information received from their parents, the said Nancy was born on the 26th day of January 1778 and the said Charles was born on the 4th day of June 1780 which information they believe to be correct.

Sworn to and subscribed before me   Nancy (X) Haley
this 18th day of October 1843
James Foster, J.P. (Seal) for Bedford County   .   Charles (X) Coursey

Ref: GSA Report, Washington, D.C.
Ref: Tennessee DAR 1940 Yearbook, page 81.

* * * * * * * * * *

JOHN CULVER

Name: Rank: State Served:
John Culver   Pvt   New Jersey
Born 1762 in Morris County, New Jersey, died November 23, 1836 in Bedford
County, Tennessee, married 1786/7 in Guilford County, North Carolina to Sarah
Bailey who died October 23, 1843 in Bedford County, Tennessee.
Children of John and Sarah (Bailey) Culver:
1. George, born ca 1788
2. Nathan
3. Charity Cook
4. John
5. Sarah Anglin, born ca 1801
6. Benjamin
7. Susan Jones
8. Haymond
9. Samuel
10. Edith Anglin
11. Simeon
12. Fanny Campbell

GSA: John Culver, R.2573, wife Sarah, Service in New Jersey.
Claim No. 13.680 West Tennessee, John Culver, of Bedford County in the State of
Tennessee, who was a Private in the company commanded by Captain Reynolds of
the Regiment commanded by Colonel Butler and others in the New Jersey Line for
two years.

Inscribed on the Roll of West Tennessee at the rate of 80 dollars __
cents per annum, to commence on the 4th day of March 1831.

Certificate of Pension issued the 1 day of June 1833, and sent to J.K.
Polk, Columbia.

Arrears to the 4th March 1833 $160.00
Semi-anl Allowance ending 4 Sept $ 40.00
                                                   $200.00

Recorded by Wm. L. Allison, Clerk   Revolutionary Claim
Book E   Vol 7   page 74   Act June 7, 1832

State of Tennessee]
Bedford County   ]
On this 7th day of August in the year one thousand eight hundred and
thirty two, personally appeared in open court before John B. Armstrong, John L.
Neill and Samuel Phillips, Gentlemen, Justices of the Peace, appointed to hold the
Court of Pleas and Quarter Sessions for Bedford County in the State of Tennessee
for the year 1832. John Culver, a citizen of and now residing in the County of
Bedford and State aforesaid, aged between sixty nine and seventy years and being
duly sworn in open Court, doth on his oath make the following declaration, in order
to obtain the benefit of the provision, made by the Act of Congress passed June 7,
1832. That he entered in the Army of the United States in October 177_ for the
term of two years under William Reynolds who also commanded the company as
Captain for the said two years. He served in the Fourth Regiment of the
Pennsylvania Line of Regular or Continental Troops under the following named
officers, viz, General Anthony Wayne, as principal officer, General Sterling, Colonel
Lee. The names of the other officers, I do not distinctly recollect. My Captain
during this term of two years was William Reynolds. My Lieutenant was named
___.
I lived at the time of my first enlistment in Sussex County in the State
of New Jersey. He states he enlisted at the Court House in said County, Hills of
Morristown and Spring Field, all in the State of New Jersey, at the White Plains.
Generals George Washington, Anthony Wayne and Sterling and I think
General Lee commanded as Officers of this grade, Colonel Butler commanded the

Regiment to which I belonged, and William Reynolds commanded the Company to which I was attached, in the battle, the American were successful, and the enemy were defeated. The Battle of Morristown and Springfield were commanded by the same officers at the White Plains and fought by the same Troops, in all of the foregoing battles the Americans were successful and kept the ground. He states it is his belief that the distance from the White Plains to Morristown is about sixty miles, and from the latter place to Springfield, he thinks, is twenty or thereabouts. He states that during his two years service, he was stationed in New Jersey, at the above named places and at Elizabethtown, sometimes at one and sometimes at another but that no battle was fought by him of any note except as aforesaid. He was in many skirmishes unnecessary to mention. He states that at the expiration of his term of service of two years, he was stationed at the White Plains in New Jersey, at which time and place, he enlisted for three years or during the war under Captain Chapman in the Fifth Regiment of the Connecticut Troops, or Continental Line. Colonel Lee was commander of the Regiment to which he was attached or belonged during the balance of the war. The General who commanded that part of the army to which he belonged during the rest of the war were General Washington, Anthony Wayne and during his second enlistment in the State of COnnecticut, from whence he was ordered to the White Plains in New Jersey, where he was finally discharged, at the close of the Revolutionary War. He was in the Battle of Fairfield in the State of Connecticut. General Lafayette was the principal Commander of the Americans at this battle, Colonel Lee and Captain Chapman were both at this battle. Chapman was wounded in this battle being occasioned by a grape shot which struck him in the right shoulder. He has no recollection of any other officers, they were mostly Militia Officers except Lafayette, Lee and Chapman.

He states he was discharged fromt he service of the United States at the White Plains in the State of New Jersey, on the 14th day of November next after the surrender of Lord Cornwallis. When he suppose to be November 1781. I received a regular discharge from Colonel Lee by order of General Washington. This discharge I have long since lost in the State of North Carolina. I took very little care of it, not believing it would ever be of any service or advantage to me. He states that the periods and dates when the different battles spoken of above took place, he does not recollect nor can he speak of these with any kind of certainty. He supposes they are recorded in the history of the Revolutionary War. He hereby relinguishes every claims whatever to a pension or annuity except the present State in the United States. He states he has applied for a pension under the former law, but owing as he supposes to the death of the person who was preparing his evidence and papers for the same, he never obtained one, and he has been advised his name is to be placed on the Muster Roll now in the War Department.

He states that after he was discharged as aforesaid, he moved to the State of Maryland, in which State he spent one summer, that he moved from that State to the State of North Carolina, Guilford County, as he believes in the year 1786. He lived in North Carolina until he moved to Sevier County in the State of Tennessee as he believes in the year 1796. Since he settled in Sevier County, he has moved and lived in different Counties in Tennessee, viz, Overton, Rutherford and Bedford , in which last county he has lived for about four years and is now a resident in the same. He does not know that there is living any person by whom he can procure the particular facts of his service and the battles he was in. He was born in the State of New Jersey, Morris County, in the year 1762. He has seen it on the Family Register of his father's family, but has no recollection of what has become of it at this time.

Sworn to and subscribed in open court   John (X) Culver
7th August 1832

State of Tennessee]
                   J.P.
Bedford County   ]

In open Court of Record, held in and for said County, on the 6th day of October 1851, personally appeared, Sarah Anglin, aged fifty five years, resident in said County, who being first duly sworn according to law, make the following declaration under the Act of Congress passes 7 July 1838, 3rd March 1843.

This declarant states that she is the lawful child of John and Sarah

Culver of Bedford County in the State of Tennessee. That her said father was a Revolutionary Pensioner of the United States at the rate of $80.00 per annum and that he died on the 23rd day of November eighteen hundred and thirty six, leaving a widow who survived him several years and who was the mother of this declarant, and whose maiden name was Sarah Bailey, and who died on the twenty third day of October in the year eighteen hundred and forty three. This declarant further states that the said John and Sarah Culver were lawfully married (as this declarant believes from what she had heard her parents say) about the year seventeen hundred and eighty six, and that the ceremony of said marriage took place in the State of North Carolina. Declarant states that she has no knowledge of the existance of any record of said marriage, either public or private. Declarant states that the said John and Sarah lived in lawful wedlock as man and wife from the time of their said marriage up to the present when the said John died, and that they had 3 children born as the fruits of their said marriage prior to the year 1794, whose names are: George Culver, Nathan Culver and Charity Cook. That the said Sarah Culver did not again marry after the death of her said husband, that she and her husband, John Culver, had the following surviving, George Culver, Nathan Culver, Charity Cook, John Culver, Sarah Anglin, Benjamin Culver, Susan Culver, Haymond Culver, Samuel Culver, Edith Anglin, Simeon Culver and Fanny Campbell.

Sworn to and subscribed on this 6th day of   Sarah (X) Anglin
October, before me,
Andrew Vannoy, Clerk

State of Tennessee]
Bedford County   ]

       I, Andrew Vannoy, a clerk of the County Court of the said county, certify that, at a Court of Record, held in and for said County, satisfactory proof was made in open court that, John Culver, late a Pensioner of the United States in the County of Bedford in the State of Tennessee at the rate of $80.00 per annum, died on the 23rd day of November 1836, leaving a widow named Sarah Culver, who did not again marry, but died being his widow, that her death occured on the 23rd day of October in the year eighteen hundred and forty three (1843) and that she left twelve children, only surviving her whose names are, George Culver, Nathan Culver, Charity Cook, John Culver, Sarah Anglin, Benjamin Culver, Susan Jones, Haymond Culver, Samuel Culver, Edith Anglin, Simeon Culver and Fanny Campbell.

       In testimony whereof I have hereunto set my hand and the Seal of said Court and County this 6th day of October 1851.

Andrew Vannoy, Clerk

       John Culver, a resident of Bedford County, Culver had served in the Pennsylvania Line during the Revolution. He was granted a pension under the Congressional Act of June 1832, and it was retroactive to March 1831.

       1835, aged 71 years, Bedford County pension list.

       Ref: GSA Report, Washington, D.C.
       Ref: Correspondance of James K. Polk, Vol I, page 450
       Ref: 1835 Pension List of Bedford County, Tennessee

* * * * * * * * * * * *

GEORGE CUNNINGHAM

Name:	Rank:	State Served:
George Cunningham	---	South Carolina

Born 7 April 1753 Rowan County, North Carolina
Aged 79 years in 1832.

GSA: George Cunningham, War Records File W-2071

Declaration:
State of Tennessee]
Bedford County   ]

       On this 13th day of August 1832, personally appeared in open court before Samuel Phillips, John L. Neill and John B. Armstrong, Justices of the Court of Pleas and Quarter Sessions in the County of Bedford County and the State of

Tennessee now sitting George Cunningham, a resident of said County and State, aged seventy nine, who first being duly sworn according to law doth on his oath make the following declaration in order to obtain the benefit of the Act of Congress passed June 7, 1832.

That he entered the service of the United States under the following officers and served as herein stated.

That he was born on the 7th day of April 1753 as appears by a record kept by his father which is now in the possession of George W. Cunningham of this County, that he was born in Rowan County, North Carolina, that he was living in York County, South Carolina when he entered the service and lived there until the close of the war when he moved to Buncombe County, North Carolina where he resided until the year 1815 when he removed to the said County of Bedford where he resided until 1824 when he removed back to Buncombe where he resided until December last when he returned to Bedford County where he has since resided and still resides.

That sometime in the latter part of the Winter of 1779, as he believes, he entered the service as a volunteer in York County, South Carolina under Captain Robert Thompson, John Cunningham (brother of affiant) was Lieutenant, the Ensign he does not recollect, Frank Ross was Major, that there was about one hundred volunteers at the same time, that shortly after they volunteered they marched to Augusta, George and joined Colonel Hammond who was stationed there, that they then marched down the country to the aid of General Ashe and joined him at Brier Creek the evening he was defeated, that on the next morning after he joined Ashe, he was sent out on a scouting party and took 4 or 5 Tories prisoners and when they returned to camp they found that Ashe had been defeated and that the British had possession of the ground and the British fired upon then as they returned to camp after night. They then returned to Augusta and remained there some time. When he returned home and remained there a few weeks during harvest, that whilst at home he and a man by the name of Duncan were taken prisoners by a party of Tories under Colonel Floyd and made their escape in about 24 hours, that a few weeks before the Battle of Hanging Rock, he and Duncan joined Sumpter in the Waxas, who shortly afterwards moved to Fishing Creek, when he joined Sumpter, he attached himself to Captain Robert Thompson's Company again with Joseph Howie, his Colonel he thinks. Shortly afterwards Sumpter marched them to Hanging Rock where they defeated a party of Tories under Brian and also whilst engaged with the Tories a party of British attacked them and they had a warm engagement that Sumpter took as he thinks 48 prisoners, that his Captain Thompson left the army after that battle and Lieutenant Cunningham (John) took the command of his company, that shortly after that he was in Sumpter's defeat at Fishing Creek, that he was standing guard at the time and his brother-in-law Matthew Patton (son of Thomas) was dangerlously wounded, that he was also in the Battle in Williams plantation where Huck, a Tory, was defeated and killed, his Colonel was Archie Neill in that engagement who was afterwards killed at Rocky Mount, that he was also in the Battle of Kings Mountain, that he was under the command of his brother Captain John Cunningham, that he was in Mecklenburg County, North Carolina with some relatives when he heard there was likely to be a battle between the mountaineers and Ferguson, that himself and a man named Robert Cunningham crossed the country in the direction of the mountains and joined Williams' Army at the Cowpens where he resumed his place in his company that at about 10 o'clock that night they left the Cowpens for the mountains and that the next evening met with the enemy, that he fought on the right wing under Williams, that the battle lasted until sunset or after, that Williams was killed in said battle.

That the next service, he was called on to perform except scouting was during the Winter of 1780 and 1781 when his wagon was pressed and sent to Newborn, North Carolina, after Military Tories, and he was sent with it, that as he was returning from Newborn, when within 13 miles of the Yadkin, he left the wagons and started for home and when he reached the Yadkin he found Cornwallis and his army on the opposite side about to cross. He immediately turned about and gave the alarm to the wagons and they retreated towards Virginia and they all would have been captured had not Morgan interposed between them and the British. He remained with the wagons some time in Virginia at Henry Old Court House. They finally deposited their Tories at Henry New Court House and returned home with their wagons and on the way heard the cannons firing at the Battle of Guilford, that he returned home and performed no other service. That he did not volunteer for any particular time but that from the time of first entering the service until his return from Newborn with the wagons embracing a period about two years and three months, he was constantly in some way or other engaged in the service without ever remaining home more than two or three weeks at a time. That he never received any formal discharge. He does not recollect the names of any regular officers with whom he served, he was with Ashe too short a time as not to learn these facts. He recollectes there were some regulars in Sumpter's Army at the time of his defeat. For he saw them when the British charged and routed them but he does not recollect the number of their regiment or the names of their officers. That he has no documentary evidence by which he can prove his service and he knows of no person by whom he can positively prove his service except John and Moses McWhirter who lives in Lawrence County, Alabama and William McCarter who lives in York County, South Carolina and that affiant is old and infirm and unable to procure their evidence as to his character for veracity and the reputation of the neighborhood that he was a Soldier of the Revolution. He has only been in this County a few months since 1824 but he can refer to the Rev. Humphrey C. Ferguson, Thomas Couch, the Rev. George Newton, John Davidson and also Colonel Samuel Davidson of Buncombe County, North Carolina and Colonel Robert Love of Haywood County, North Carolina. He is not sure that in stating the events of the Revolutionary War he has been entirely correct in chronology or consequence of the failure of memory.

He hereby relinguishes every claim whatever to a pension or annuity except the present and declares that his name is not on the Pension Roll of any agency of the Nation.

Sworn and subscribed in open court 13th
of August 1832.   George (X) Cunningham
Jas. McKisick

In the declaration for a widow's pension by Mary (McCarty) Cunningham, names the following children:

1. Magdalen, born 10 November 1799, married William H. Bryson
2. Kathy, born 4 June 1802, married _____ Moore
3. Sally, born 19 August 1808
4. Elizabeth (date of birth unknown)

Mary (McCarty) was the daughter of William McCarty, executed her pension application in 1851, age 77, and died 1 February 1852 in Macon County, North Carolina.

George Cunningham was a son of Humphrey and Rhoda (Simeral, some accounts say Summerville) Cunningham. He and his wife Mary had a sizable family, one known son, George Cunningham. George Cunningham, Sr. probably died in Macon County, North Carolina 3 August 1837. His father Humphrey died in Buncombe County, North Carolina in 1806. His mother Rhoda died in Bedford County, Tennessee in 1831.

Ref: GSA Record, Washington, D.C.
Ref: Widow's Pension, Washington, D.C.
Ref: Cemetery Records of Bedford County, Tennessee by Marsh
Ref: Family information by Mr. Joseph H. Duncan, Dunwoody, Georgia

* * * * * * * * *

MATTHEW CUNNINGHAM

Name:	Rank:	State Served:
Matthew Cunningham	Pvt	North Carolina

Born ____, died 14 May 1840 in Bedford County, Tennessee, married in 1791 or 1792 in Orange County, North Carolina to Elizabeth _____.

GSA: Matthew Cunningham (Elizabeth) R.2582.

30 January 1852 of Bedford County, Tennessee, Elizabeth Cunningham of said county, aged 84, declares she is the widow of Matthew Cunningham who was a Private in the Revolution. She thinks he entered service in 1776. He was at the

the Battle of Camden 12 August 1779 and served one tour of three months and one of six months (or two others of three months). She thinks he was under Captain Leeper in Colonel Porterfield's Regiment in North Carolina or South Carolina Militia.

She was married in 1791 or 1972 in Orange County, North Carolina by William Hodges, a Preacher of the Gospel. Her first child was born in 1793. Her husband died in Bedford County, Tennessee 14 May 1840.

20 March 1852. J. Allison, Clerk of Orange County, North Carolina, reports no record of the marriage of Matthew Cunningham to Elizabeth _____. The files of Marriage Bonds in my office, give abundant proof of having been kept in a very loose and careless manner.

J. Allison, Clerk

Bedford County, Tennessee Deed Books DD, page 494 and Deed Book U, page 231 lists Children of Matthew and Elizabeth Cunningham as, Jeremiah, Mathew, Jr., Mary wife of William Word, Elizabeth wife of Samuel Neely, Katherine Cunningham and Jane Cunningham. Land on Big Flat Creek, adjoining John and Andrew Reed (near) Shelbyville, Tennessee). May 1, 1834.

Ref: GSA Report, Washington, D.C.
Bedford County Deed Book DD and U.

* * * * * * * * * *

WILLIAM CUNNINGHAM

Name: Rank: State Served:
William Cunningham   Pvt   North Carolina
Born 2nd February 1748 in Donnegal, Ireland, died April 15, 1842 near Hickory Level, Alabama, married Martha Blair who died in March 1838 in Bedford County, Tennessee.

GSA: William Cunningham, S.3249, born in Ireland.
Claim No. 13777, West Tennessee, William Cunningham, of Bedford County, in the State of Tennessee, who was a Private in the company commanded by Captain Nelson of the Regiment commanded by Colonel Martin in the North Carolina Line for 6 months.

Inscribed on the Roll of West Tennessee at the rate of 20 dollars ___ cents per annum to commence on the 4th day of March, 1831.

Certificate of Pension issued the __ day of June 1833 and sent to James McKisick, Shelbyville.

Arrears to the 4th of March $40.--
Semi-anl allowance ending 4 Sept $10.--
                                               $50.--

Recorded by Daniel Boyd, Clerk   Revolutionary Claim
Book E   Vol 7   page 74   Act June 7, 1832
         Dead
         halted to Wm. Cunningham, 20 Sep '4- (184-)
              Wm. R. Chapman, Jan 24 '4- (184-)

Declaration:
State of Tennessee]
Bedford County   ]
Declaration in order to obtain the benefit of the Act of Congress passed the 7th June 1832.

On this 9th day of May in the year of our Lord, one thousand eight hundred and thirty three, personally appeared in open court before the Worship Samuel Phillips, John B. Armstrong and William McClure, Esquires, Gentlemen, Justices of the Peace, appointed the Quarum to hold the Court of Pleas and Quarter Sessions for Bedford COunty in the State of aforesaid, now sitting, William Cunningham, a resident of said county, aged eighty five years, three months and seven days, who after being first sworn according to law, doth on his oath made the following declaration in order to obtain the benefit of the Act of Congress passed the 7th June 1832.

That he enteres the service of the United States under the following named officers and served as herein states, that he entered the service of the United States as a drafted soldier in Guilford County and State of North Carolina, sometime about the last of July 1776, and was placed in a company commanded by Captain John Nelson and Lieutenant Josiah Gates who was under the command of General Rutherford, Colonels James Martin and John Paistley. He states he was marched to Salisbury and from there to Cathey's Fort on the head of the Catawba River, and from there he was marched into the Cherokee Nation, passing through several small Indian Towns, the names of which he does not now recollect, on to the town of Watawga, where an engagement was expected, but the Indians had left the town and the Americans set it on fire and destroyed it. Deponant states that the troops under General Rutherford remained near that place for some days for the arrival of the troops from South Carolina under the command of General Williamson, and from there he was marched back into Guilford County again and dismissed in the month of November in the same year, after serving not less than three months.

Deponant says that some time after that he thinks year 1780, he removed to that part of the country now called Washington County in the State of Tennessee and settled on Nolachucky River, and that he volunteered and entered the service again as a Private Soldier in Captain Adam Sherril's Company of Volunteers, who were under the command of General John Sevier, and was marched upon the French Broad River about the middle of June 1780 and was stationed there for three months, during which time he was frequently out on scouting parties against the Cherokee Indians, who were at that time very troublesome and frequently committed depredations on the whites, and as well as he now recollects, he was dismissed from service about the middle of September 1780, after serving not less than three months, making in all a term of service of not less than six months actual service in the War of the Revolution for which he claims a pension, although he states he was on several scouting expeditions against the Tories, previous to his removal from North Carolina from some eight or ten days at a time, but for that service he does not claim a pension. He further says that he never did receive a discharge in writing. This applicant says he was born in the County Donnagal in the North Ireland on the 2nd day of February 1748. Agreeable to information of his parents and that he has no record of his age whatever. He further says that he has no acquaintance with any Regular Officers with the troops where he served, he says he saw General Williamson in the Cherokee Nation who he was told was a Regular Officer. That he has no recollection of the name or number of any Regiment that was with the troops where he served at this time, and believes the foregoing declaration exhibits a history of the most prominent circumstances of the service. Aplicant says he is known to James B. Lowery, Esquire, Colonel John Blackwell, Thomas Coffey, Esquire, and James D. Anderson in his present neighborhood, but on account of old age and being very infirm, he has not been able to travel about so as to form an acquaintance with a Clergyman, nor does he know of one in the immediate neighborhood where he now lives. He says he was a citizen of Guilford County, North Carolina when he first entered the service and resided in Washington County, East Tennessee when he was last in service and from there he removed to South Carolina and in the year 1817 he removed to the State of Alabama where he remained until the year 1829 when he removed to Bedford County, Tennessee where he has resided ever since and where he now resides, and that he hereby relinguishes all and every claim to a pension or annuity except the present and declares that his name is not on the Pension Roll of any agency in the United States. He further states that he has no documentary evidence whatever and declares that there is no person whose testimony he can procure who can testify as to his service except what he can prove by the affidavit of John Burns, Senr., who testify as sworn to and subscribed in open court the day and year aforesaid.

Jas. McKisick, Clk   Wm. Cunningham (Seal)

To: Mr. J.L. Edwards   7th Sept. 1844
Dear Sir,

in writing for poor old Graham, I have learned to whom to write for myself. My father, William Cunningham was a Revolutionary Soldier, resided in Middle Tennessee at the passage of the Law and drew a small pension up to March '38 (1838) if mistaken not at which time my mother died, my father wrote me that

if I would go to Tennessee and know him better he would spend the balance of his days with me, I done so, he lived till the 15 April '42 (1842). He frequently requested me to apply for his pension as an annuintant for the troubles I had with him, being near 100 years of age, my sitting in the woods, the same year '38 (1838) placed me in a whirlwind of business and neglected to apply the old man left me forever. Now being hard run and the claim just, I want it. Its a small matter not being able to prove all his services. Be so good as to instruct me how I am to proceed in this matter and I shall ever feel under obligation to you.
Mr. J.L. Edwards   William Cunningham

1835, aged 85, Pvt in North Carolina Line.

>   Ref: GSA Report, Washington, D.C.
>   1835 Bedford County Pension List.

* * * * * * * * * *

TIGNEY DAMRON

Name:	Rank:	State Served:
Tigney Damron	-----	---------------

Born ____, died ____. Tigney Damron is buried on James Garrett farm near Shelbyville, Tennessee. No marker for his grave.

No GSA Report in Washington, D.C.

>   Ref: Nashville Monument, Susie Gentry, State Historian

* * * * * * * * * *

ANDREW DAVIDSON

Name:	Rank:	State Served:
Andrew Davidson	-----	---------------

Born ca 1760 Virginia, died after 1850, aged 90 years. married Sarah _____, born ca 1777 Virginia, died after 1850, aged 73.

In 1850 Census of Bedford County, Tennessee, 20th District, area of Richmond and Moores Chapel. In the house with them were, Richard Davidson, born ca 1805 Virginia and Thomas Davidson, born ca 1820 in Tennessee.

No GSA in Washington, D.C.

>   Ref: 1850 Census of Bedford County, Tennessee.

* * * * * * * * * *

JOHN DAVIDSON

Name:	Rank:	State Served:
John Davidson	Pvt	North Carolina

Born 15 February 1764 Rowan County, North Carolina, died 17 September 1842 in Bedford County, Tennessee, married Lydia Wood. Both are buried on Union Ridge in the Davidson Cemetery, both graves are marked.

GSA: John Davidson, S.1758, Claim No. 13584
West Tennessee, John Davidson of Bedford County in the State of Tennessee who was a Private in the company commanded by Captain Davidson of the Regiment commanded by Colonel Dowel in the North Carolina Line for 9 months.
Inscribed on the Roll of West Tennessee at the rate of 30 dollars ___ cents per annum to commence on the 4th day of March 1831.
Certificate of Pension issued the 23rd day of May 1833 and sent to James McKisick, Shelbyville.

Arrears to the 4th of March	$60.00
Semi-anl allowance ending 4 Sept	$15.00
	$75.00

Recorded by Daniel Boyd, Clerk   Revolutionary Claim
Book E   Vol 7   page 76   Act June 7, 1832

Letter to Pension and Pension Agent, Sept 28, 1835
_____ to Pension Agent, Dec 14, 1835
_____ 29 May 1837, Pension Agent
_____ 15 May 1838

Paid at the Treasury under Act of 1 April 1838 from 4th March to 4th Sept 18_7,
Agent notified 31 May 1838.

Declaration:
       Declaration in order to obtain the benefit of the Act of Congress passed
the 7th June 1832.

State of Tennessee]
Bedford County   ]   February Term, 1833

       On this 8th day of February in the year of our Lord, one thousand eight
hundred and thirty three, personally appeared in open court before the Worshipful
Samuel Phillips, John B. Armstrong and William McClure, Esquires, Gentlemen
Justices of the Peace, appopinted to hold the Court of Pleas and Quarter Sessions
of said County, now sitting, John Davidson, a resident of said county, aged sixty
eight years, eleven months and twenty four days, who after being sworn according
to law, doth on his oath make the following declaration in order to obtain the
benefit of the Act of Congress passed the 7th June 1832. That he entered the
service of the United States under the following officers and served as herein
stated, to wit, that he entered the service of the United States in the County of
Burke and State of North Carolina in the month of April in the year 1781 as a
substitute in the room and stead of one William McGonnigal, who was at that time
drafted in said County of Burke, and placed in a company commanded by Captain
Samuel Davidson and was marched to a Fort on the Catawba River then called the
Upper Fort. Where he was stationed until sometime in the month of July in the
same year when he says he was discharged for a tour of duty of three months
actual service. Deponant says that soon after he entered the service again in the
same County as a volunteer in a Company of Volunteers commanded by Captain
Daniel Smith, he said deponant thinks the first of August in the same year 1781,
and was marched to the same Fort before mentioned and was stationed there and
at another Fort on Broad River on the frontier of the State of North Carolina and
was frequently out on scouting and spying expeditions to assertain the movement of
the hostile Indians, who were often committing murders and other outrages upon
the white settlements on Broad River, and the Catawba River he says he was
marched back into Burke County again about the first of November, when he was
dismissed after serving a tour of three months. Deponant further says that he
volunteered again in the month of March 1782 under the same Captain Daniel Smith
who was attached to a Regiment under the command of Colonel Joseph McDowel of
said County of Burke and State of North Carolina, and was marched against the
hostile Cherokee Indians, into their Nation, across the Blue Ridge. He says he was
marched in the first place to Watawga Town, on Tennessee River and from there he
was marched to a small town called <u>Canes</u> where the Americans and Indians had an
engagement in which there was but little damage on their side, he says on this
expedition, the American Troops under Colonel McDowel in several little skirmishes
with the Indians at different towns, and on the way from one town to another,
killed and took Indian prisoners to the number of fifty, though some of the
prisoners made their escape, there was eleven of them marched to the Upper Fort
on the Catawba where deponant says he remained until his term of three months
which he volunteered to serve expired which took place in the month of June 1782,
which he says he was dismissed from further service making in the whole a term of
service of not less than nine months for which he claims a pension. He further
states that he has no documentary evidence and that he knows of no person who
can testify as to his service, except what he expects to prove by the testimony of
Robert Brown of Warren County, Tennessee, who is a very old man, and at the time
is blind and unable to travel from home, and he hereby relinguishes every claim to
a pension or annuity except the present and declares that his name is not on the
Pension Roll of any agency in the United States.

Interrogatories by Court

Q. 1st: Where and in what year were you born?
A.   I was born in Rowan County in the State of North Carolina on the 15th day of February in the year 1764, agreeable to my father's Family Records.
Q. 2nd: Have you any record of your age and if so where is it?
A.   I have a record of my age at my dwelling house in this County, in my father's Old Bible.
Q. 3rd: Where were you living when called into service, where have you lived since the Revolutionary War and where do you now live?
A.   I was a citizen of Burke County in the State of North Carolina during all the time I was in service, and continued to be so for sometime after the war, I then removed to that part of the State of North Carolina now called Buncombe County in said State, where I remained until the year 1809 or 10 when I removed to Bedford County, Tennessee where I have lived ever since and where I now live.
Q. 4th: How were you called into service, were you drafted, did you volunteer or were you a substitute and if a substitute, for whom?
A.   I served my first tour of three months as a substitute for William McGonnigal, and my other two tours for three months each, I served as a volunteer.
Q. 5th: State the names of the Regular Officers who were with the troops where you served, such as Continental and Militia Regiments, as you can recollect, and the general circumstances of your service.
A.   I was not acquainted with any Regular Officers where I served, nor do I recollect the names or number of any Regiment whatever. And I believe my declaration gives the most prominent and general history of my service that I am able to give at this time.
Q. 6th: Did you ever receive a discharge and if so what has become of it?
A.   I did receive a discharge in writing, signed by Captain Samuel Davidson, for a tour of three months but what has become of it, I cannot tell.
Q. 7th: State the names of persons to whom you are known in your present neighborhood who can testify as to your character and veracity and their opinion of your service as a Soldier of the Revolution.
A.   The Rev. George Newton, Colonel A. Erwin and Humphrey Cunningham.
Sworn to and subscribed the day and year aforesaid.
Jas. McKisick, Clerk   John (X) Davidson (Seal)

We, George Newton, a clergyman, residing in Bedford County and State of Tennessee, and Humphrey Cunningham of the same County and State, do hereby certify that we are now and have been for the last forty years, in the County of Buncombe, North Carolina and Bedford County, Tennessee, well acquainted with John Davidson, Esquire, who has subscribed and sworn to the foregoing declaration in order to obtain the benefit of the Act of Congress passed the 7th June 1832, that we believe him to be sixty eight years, eleven months and twenty four days old, as he has stated in his declaration, that he is reputed and believed in the neighborhood where he now resides to have been a Soldier of the Revolution and that we concur in that opinion and we further certify that during the great length of time since first acquaintance with said applicant, we never heard his character for veracity questioned by any person whatever and we believe him to be strictly honest in every particular. This 8th February 1833.
Jas. McKisick, Clk.   Geo. Newton
                                      Humphrey Cunningham

Feb 8, 1833
2DD53-56   John Davidson, Bedford County, Tennessee. Pension Statement.
      Entered service in Burke County, North Carolina as a substitute for William McDonnigal, under command of Captain Samuel Davidson, stationed at Upper Fort on Catawba River, North Carolina, volunteered in Captain Daniel Smith's Company under command of Colonel Joseph McDowell, fifty prisoners taken in skirmishes with Cherokee Indians. (copy 4 pages)

John Davidson, born Feb 15, 1764 in Rowan County, North Carolina, died September

9, 1845 (Sept 13, 1845) in Bedford County, Tennessee, married Martha Davidson (his cousin, daughter of James Davidson) in Buncombe County, North Carolina in 1794. She was born 1760/70 and died after 1845.
Service: Enlisted in Burke County, North Carolina, as a substitute for William McGonnigal under Captain Samuel Davidson. Also under Captain Daniel Smith and Colonel Joseph McDowel.
Children:

    1. Hugh, born January 29, 1795, married _____ Caldwell
    2. James, born September 12, 1796
    3. William, born July 8, 1798, unmarried
    4. George, born March 11, 1800, married 1st Caroline D. _____. married
        2nd Mrs. Sophia E. Peacock
    5. Lorenzo, born June 29, 1804
    6. Margaret, born December 26, 1807, married Frank Smartt
    7. Andrew M., born October 22, 1811
    8. Mary, born October 4, 1814

Ref: GSA Report, Washington, D.C.
Ref: Tennessee and King's Mountain Papers by Lyman C. Draper, Collection, Madison, Wisc.
Ref: Texas Society DAR Roster Revolutionary Soldiers, Vol II, page 571

Ref: 1835 Bedford County, Tennessee Pension Lists.

* * * * * * * * * *

JESSE DAVIS

Name:	Rank:	State Served:
Jesse Davis	Pvt	North Carolina

Born March 14, 1766 in Butte County (now Warren), North Carolina, died July 18, 1833 Bedford COunty, Tennessee. Lived in the area of Rev. John Brooks, Rev. Richard W. Cardwell, William Norvill, Stephen Murphree, Baxter Ragsdale and William McGrew.

GSA: Jesse Davis, S.2497   Claim No. 7581, West Tennessee, Jesse Davis, of Bedford County in the State of Tennessee who was a Private in the company commanded by Captain Wells of the Regiment commanded by Major Crawford in the North Carolina Line for 7 months.

Inscribed on the Roll of West Tennessee at the rate of 23 dollars 33 cents per annum, to commence on the 4th day of March, 1831.

Certificate of Pension issued the 5 day of May 1833 and sent to James McKisick, Shelbyville.

Arrears to the 4th of March	$46.66
Semi-anl allowance ending 4 Sept	$11.66
	$58.32

Recorded by Daniel Boyd, Clerk   Revolutionary Claim
Book E   Vol 7   page 76   Act June 7, 1832

Declaration:
State of Tennessee]
Bedford County   ]

Declaration in order to obtain the benefit of the Act of Congress passed June the 7th 1832.

On this 8th day of November in the year of our Lord, one thousand eight hundred and thirty two, personally appeared in open court before the Worshipful John B. Armstrong, Samuel Phillips and Jno. L. Neill, Esquires, Gentlemen Justices of the Peace of the Court of Pleas and Quarter Sessions appointed to hold the present term of said court, now sitting, Jesse Davis, aged sixty six years, seven months and twenty four days, who being first sworn according to law, doth on his oath, making the following declaration in order to obtain the benefit of the Act of Congress passes 7th June 1832. That he entered the service of the United States under the following named officers and served as herein stated, to wit, That he entered the service of the United States as a drafted soldier in the County of Franklin and State of North Carolina, sometime in the month of June 1781 and was placed under the command of a Captain Wells Milner and was stationed at a place then called Partrage in said County of Franklin and was employed in cleaning the weavel from public corn deposited there for the term of about two months. He says that he was transferred to a Company of Light Horse commanded by Captain William Rush who was engaged in chasing the Tories and _____ which were then very numerous in that part of the country, and remained with said company reconnoitering through that county until about the first of November following, when he was transferred to a Captain Swan Trantton who was stationed at Durham Halls to guard the public munitions and provisions for the army of nine months. Men who were stationed at that place where he says he remained in service until sometime about the first of February 1782. Making in all a term of service of about seven months and upwards, that he only claims a pension for seven months, when he was discharged. And that he has no documentary evidence whatever and that he knows of no person whose testimony he can produce who can testify as to his service, and he hereby relinguishes all and every claim whatever to a pension as annuity except the present and declares that his name is not on the Pension Roll of any agency in the United States.

Sworn to and subscribed the day and year aforesaid   Jesse Davis (Seal)
Jas. McKisick, Clk.

Interrogatories by the Court

Q. 1st: Where and in what year were you born?
A.   I was born in what was then called Butte County in the State of North Carolina on the 14th of March in the year 1766, as I was informed by my parents.
Q. 2nd: Have you any record of your age and if so where is it?
A.   I have no record of my age whatever.
Q. 3rd: Where were you living when called into service?
A.   I was a citizen of Franklin County in the State of North Carolina all the time I was in service.
Q. 4th: Where have you lived since the Revolutionary War and where do you now live?
A.   I was a citizen of Franklin County in the State of North Carolina during the War of the Revolution and afterwards, until the year 1807 when I removed to Bedford COunty, Tennessee, where I have resided ever since and where I now reside.
Q. 5th: How were you called into service, were you drafted, were you a volunteer or were you a substitute, and if a substitute for whom?
A.   I was a drafted soldier the whole time of my service.
Q. 6th: State the names of some of the regular officers who were with the troops where you served such Continental and Militia Regiments as you can recollect, and the general circumstances of your service.
A.   I recollect General Jethro Sumner at Durham Halls where I was stationed the last time and I think a Major Crawford but I am not certain, I do not recollect the name or number of any Continental or Militia Regiments whatever and I believe my declaration sworn to this day in Court here contains the general circumstances of my service as much so at least as can give at this period of my age.
Q. 7th: Did you ever receive a discharge and if so what has become of it?
A.   I never received a discharge in writing.
Q. 8th: State the names of persons to whom you are known in your present neighborhood who can testify as to your character for veracity and their opinion of your service as a Soldier of the Revolution.
A.   The Rev. John Brooks, the Rev. Rich'd W. Cardwell, William Norvill, Esq., Stephen Murphree, Esq., Baxter Ragsdale and William McGrew.

State of Tennessee]
Bedford County   ]

     We, John Brooks, a clergyman, residing in the County and State aforesaid, and William Norvill, residing in the same, do hereby certify that we are well acquainted with Jesse Davis, who has subscribed and sworn to the foregoing declaration, and has been for many years, that they believe him to be sixty six years, seven months, and twenty four days of age. That he is reputed and believed in the neighborhood where he now resides to have been a Soldier of the Revolution, and that they concur in that opinion, and the said William Norvill further states upon his oath that the said Jesse Davis, the above applicant, was in the service of the United States as a Soldier, but how long he does not know. Sworn to and subscribed this 8th day of November 1832.

Jas. McKisick, Clk.   Jno. Brooks
                                                        Wm. Norvill

   And the said Court do hereby declare their opinion. After the investigation of the matter and after putting the interrogatories prescribed by the War Department, that the above named applicant was a Revolutionary Soldier, and served as he states, and the Court further certifies that it appears to them that the Rev. John Brooks, who has signed the preceding certificate, is a clergyman of good standing in the Methodist Church and a resident of this County, and that William Norvell, Esq., who has also signed the same, is a Deputy Sheriff in this County at this time, and has heretofore been the High Sheriff of said County, that he is a credible person and that his statements are entitled to full faith and credit.

                                        Jno. L. Neill
                                        Samuel Phillips
                                        John B. Armstrong

   I, James McKisick, Clerk of the Court of Pleas and Quarter Sessions for Bedford County in the State of Tennessee, do certify that the foregoing contains the original proceedings of the said Court in the matter of the application of Jesse Davis for a pension. In testimony whereof I have set my hand and Seal of Office, at Office in Shelbyville, the 15th of February A.D. 1833.

                                        Jas. McKisick, Clk.

Revolutionary War Invalid File No. 2497, Jesse Davis, Private, Rev. War.
Act June 7, 1832   Index: Vol A   page 88

In 1835, Jesse Davis, Pvt, North Carolina Line, died July 18, 1833.

   Ref: GSA Report, Washington, D.C.
   Ref: 1835 Bedford County Pension List

* * * * * * * * * *

JEREMIAH DIAL

Name: Rank: State Served:
Jeremiah Dial   Pvt   South Carolina

Born 1758 in Ireland, died September 22, 1834 in Bedford County, Tennessee, buried in the Dial Cemetery which has now been destroyed. He married December 13, 1788 to Nancy Anna McDaniel.

Known children: Anna, born September 26, 1796, married Alexander Freeman.

GSA: Jeremiah Dial, W.914, wife Ann, born in Ireland, Service in North Carolina. Claim No. 3817

   West Tennessee, Jeremiah Dial, of Bedford County, in the State of Tennessee, who was a Private in the Company commanded by Captain Kersey of the Regiment commanded by Colonel Williams in the South Carolina Line for 2 years from 1778.

   Inscribed on the Roll of West Tennessee at the rate of 80 dollars _____ cents per annum to commence on the 4th day of March, 1831.

   Certificate of Pension issued the 3rd day of January 4, 1833 and sent to Hon. J.K. Polk, House of Reps.

Arrears to 4th of Sept $120.00
Semi-anl allowance ending 4 Mar '33 (1833) $ 40.00
                                                $160.00

Recorded by Nathan Rice, Clerk   Revolutionary Claim
Book D   Vol 9   page 146   Act June 7, 1832

Declaration:
State of Tennessee]
Bedford County   ]

Court of Pleas & Quarter Sessions, August Term 1832.

On this 15th day of August 1832, personally appeared in open Court before John L. Neill, Samuel Phillips and John B. Armstrong, Esquires, Justices of the Peace, appointed to hold the COurt of Pleas and Quarter Sessions, now sitting, Jeremiah Dial, a resident of Bedford County and State of Tennessee, aged about seventy four years, who being duly sworn according to law doth on his oath make the following declaration in order to obtain the benefit of the provisions of an Act of Congress passed the 7th June 1832 for the relief of Revolutionary Soldiers.

He states that he entered the service of the United States in the Militia of South Carolina in the year 1778 or early in 1779, he does not recollect which, and served under Captain Levi Kersey who belonged to Colonel Williams' Regiment, as a substitute for his father who was drafted to serve a tour of three months in Kersey's Company, which was to go to Georgia to serve under the command of General Lincoln when they joined General Lincoln, he was stationed on the Savannah River, Georgia, watching the movements of the British after Kersey's Companyremained with Lincoln a short time, he sent a detachment consisting of this company and probably others to the mouth of Briar Creek on the Savannah River, some distance below Lincoln encampment to assist General Ash against the British but when they arrived at or near the place where Ash was, they found that he was defeated. This applicant states that this detachment in which he was then retreated back to Lincoln's. They were persued a short distance by the enemy who fired at them as they crossed Briar Creek. Captain Kersey's Company was then sent out by Lincoln in persuit of the Tories with whom they had a skirmish at S------ Creek, Georgia in which they killed a good many men. This skirmish took place near the end of the three months which this applicant served for his father. At the expiration of which he was discharged by Captain Kersey.

Shortly afterwards, he was drafted for three months in the Militia of South Carolina and served in Captain Kersey's Company under the command of Colonel Purvis during the whole of this three months tour. We were engaged principally in scouting and endeavoring to subdue the Tories lying between in that part of Georgia, lying between the Oconee River and Augusta. at the expitation of this tour of service this applicant was again discharged by Captain Kersey.

This applicant states that shortly after this, he volunteered under Captain Kersey for nine months, who was then raising a Company of Volunteers in Newberry County or District, South Carolina, to fight the British and Tories, during this term of service, Kersey's Company was frequently engaged in the persuit of the Tories and scouting in different parts of South Carolina. They had many skirmishes with the Tories, one of which this applicant recollects was at Captain Dougan's in Newberry County within five miles of the place where his father lived. Here this applicant states, we killed a great many Tories and took about twenty of them prisoners during this term of service, the Company to which this applicant belonged, had many other little skirmishes with the Tories, and at the expiration of nine months, he was verbally discharged by Captain Kersey. At the time he was discharged, he received Certificate of his service which he oresented to the auditors at Charleston sometime afterwards from whence he received an indented certificate of the pay due him for his services. This Certificate, he bartered away, for little or nothing.

Soon after his nine months volunteer service expired in the year 1780, a short time after the surrender of Charleston, this applicant enlisted with Captain Daniel McDuff in Colonel Henderson's Regiment of the South Carolina Continental Line for and during the remaining period of the war. He states that he enlisted under said McDuff as a Light Horseman and was immediately after his enlistment put under the command of Major John Hampton who commanded a Company of Light Horsemen attached to Henderson's Regiment, as well as this applicant recollects. The Tories were at this time troublesome in South Carolina and Hampton's Company was generally engaged in persuits of them endeavoring to suppress them and subdue their foraging parties as well as those of the British, whileHampton's Company were out scouting or a part of them, this applicant does not recollect whether the whole Company was together or sent. They were persued by a party of British and Tories and compelled to retreat to General

Sumpter for refuge who was only a short distance from them at Black Stocks on or near Tyger River. They served at this place but a few minutes before Sumpter was attacked by the British and Tories and assisted him in the battle. In this battle, Sumpter was wounded in the shoulder and while the Company of Light Horsemen to which this applicant belonged were advancing up to being on the attack against the enemy. His horse was shot dead but as he had got off him. The battle continued until sometime in the night, when both armies retreated from the battleground. This applicant states that when his horse was shot he mounted another which belonged to one of his party or Company who had been killed. In this battle the British suffered more than the Americans under Sumpter. This applicant states that when Sumpter retreated, he crossed Tyger River and while crossing the river, this applicant assisted in crossing the brin, on which Sumpter was placed. General Sumpter's forces made a halt at Woford's Iron Works, when the Company to which this applicant belonged, left these and went in persuit of a party of Tories on the Encore River, but when they arrived there the Tories were gone, from this until the arrival of Colonel William Washington in South Carolina, Hampton's Company or at least part of them among whom was this applicant were engaged in scouting and in the persuits of Tories on Encore River, Broad and Tyger Rivers, but when Colonel Washington came out South Carolina with a number of Light Horse Troops, this applicant was with several others, taken from under the command of Major Hampton and attached to Washington's Company to pistol him through some parts of South Carolina in persuits of the Tories, as this applicant and the others taken with him were well acquainted with the country. This was in the beginning of the Winter of 1780. This applicant went with Washington to Hammond's Store when they overtook and put to flight a large number of Tories, some of whom they killed and wounded, this store was in Newberry County. Washington then sent one of his Lieutenant or Ensigns with a small party of them to take Williamson's Fort on Little River in Newberry County not more than eight or ten miles from Hammond's Store. This applicant was one of the party sent when they arrived in sight of the Fort, which was occupied by Tories as well as this applicant recollects, they were stationed by _____ Lieutenant who then took a flag and went up to the Fort and demanded its surrender, the commander of the Fortasked a few minutes for consideration, which were granted, during which time he and the Tories deserted the Fort and it was then burnt by this applicant's party. After this, they returned and rejoined Washington who then went back towards the borders of North Carolina to join General Morgan. This applicant states that as well as he recollects, Washington joined Morgan a few days before the Battle of the Cowpens and as well as he remembers when Washington's Company in which he was joined Morgan, he was retreating before Colonel Tarlton and his forces. At all events, Tarltons was in persuits of him, when Morgan, Washington and Colonel or General Pickens who commanded the Militia _____ at the place called Cowpens, they stopped to fight the British under Tarlton. This battle was fought on the 17th day of January 1781. This applicant particularly recollects this battle because it was the greatest he was ever in. This applicant states Tarlton commanded this battle early in the morning by firing his field pieces at Morgan's Army but he does not remember how long the battle lasted. Washington's Cavalry with whom this applicant fought during the engagement were stationed in the rear of Morgan's Forces and when the British broke through the left wing of the Militia, Washington's Cavalry made an attack upon them and repelled them with considerable loss. After this battle was over, in which the Americans gained a triumphant victory. This applicant states that Morgan, Washington and Pickens with their prisoners in order to prevent Lord Cornwallis' Army from retaking them. An express was sent about this time, sent from South Carolina for aid and General Pickens returned into South Carolina with his troops. This applicant went along with him, they had several skirmishes with the Tories in different parts of South Carolina after their return and before, General Green came unto South Carolina, but when Green cause General Pickens along with whom this applicant still continued joined him about thirty or forty miles from a place called Ninety-Six, when the British had a garrison or fort. Greene with his Army then marched to that place for the purpose of taking it. Greene's Army in which this applicant then was lay before the Garrison of Ninety-Six for several weeks as well as this applicant recollect endeavoring to take it, but before he could succeed, a reinforcement of the British came to its assistance and Greene's Army was compelled to retreat. He retreated across Encore and Broad Rivers and having met a supply of ammunition and a reinforcement of men, the then turned and went to the Eutaw Springs, but before he got to the Springs, this applicant was ordered out in a detachment after a party of Tories and was not in the battle at that place. This detachment was under the command of Captain George Auberry. This applicant served under Auberry and was engaged in scouting and skirmishing with the Tories in South Carolina with him from the time his detachment left Greene's Army until the close of the war or until he went under General Pickens in an expedition against the Cherokee Indians, but this applicant cannot recollect whether or not this expedition took place before he was dismissed from the regular service or afterwards. If it was afterwards, he went with Pickens as a volunteer, however, he was in the service of the United States until regularly discharged from the regular service, at the end of the war when the whole American Army was discharged. He was verbally discharged but he cannot recollect by whom. This applicant states that to the best of his recollection, he served the United States during the war nearly three years, if not altogether then, including his service as a substitute for his father, a drafted Soldier, on his own account, a volunteer, and regular soldier. He is not certain that he has detailed the events and circumstances of his service in the exact time and order in which they occured in consequence of the failure of his memory when he first enlisted as a regular soldier he received a Certificate for the reward of eighty dollars from Captain McDuff as well as he recalls this certificate he lost many years ago.

He states that he has no documentary evidence of his service. This applicant also states that Captain McDuff was captured shortly after he enlisted under him and lost as he understood and believes the roll of names of those who enlisted under him could not make any return of them to the Department of War. This applicant further states that he knows of no person now living by whom he can make any proof of his services, except what he has made by the affidavits of those hereunto annexed. He states that two or three years ago, probably in 1829, he applied for a pension under the Act of Congress passed in May 1828, at that time he procured the testimony of Captain Daniel McDuff who was then alive but has since died, as well as the following of two or three others, but before his claim was acted upon by the War Department. He was informed by the Hon. J.K. Polk, Representative in Congress from his District, that all the testimony which he had sent or relative to his claim, was lost. He states that he again, this last Spring, made application for a pension under the Act of 1828 and transmitted his declaration together with all the testimony of his services which he could possibly procure to the Hon. Secretary of War thru the hands of the Hon. James K. Polk. He has not learned what disposition has been made of this latter application but if it has not been granted, he would now beg to transfer the Secretary of War to the testimony then transmitted to him, in support of the present application. He does not now recollect whether the testimony above mentioned was transmitted to the Treasury on the War Department. This applicant states that he never received any written discharges at the expiration of any tour of his service, except the one already mentioned above. He states that he was born in Ireland in the year 1759, as he was informed by his father. He emigrated with his father from Ireland to South Carolina and landed in Charleston in that State in the year 1772, shortly afterwards in the same year, his father settled in Newberry County or District in said State where this applicant resided when called into service. He states that he has no record of his age, but he was about nineteen or twenty years of age when he entered the service of the United States. At the close of the war, he still resided in Newberry County for several years. He then removed to Fairfield County where he lived a year or two, then he removed to Edisto River, South Carolina. He does not recollect the County. From thence he removed to Wilkes County in the State of Georgia where he lived two years, then he moved back to Pendleton County, South Carolina and after living there several years, he removed to the State of Kentucky, Warren County, where he resided about four years. He then removed to Wilson County in Tennessee and from thence to Bedford County, Tennessee where he has resided for nearly twenty three years and still continues to reside. This applicant states that he was acquainted particularly with no other Regular or Militia Officers than those already named in this declaration. He saw General Francis Marion several times before the close of the war in South Carolina.

This applicant states that he is well acquainted with and has been for many years, Colonel James McKisick, Daniel McKisick, William Gilchrist, Esquires, Colonel Robert Cannon, Colonel K.L. Anderson, William Murphy, Cook Anderson, William Norvell, Stephen Murphy(Murphree), Horatio Coop, all citizens of Bedford County, Tennessee, some of whom are his immediate neighbors, all of whom will testify as to his character for veracity and their belief of his services. He would refer to many others highly respectable citizens of his County, was required to do so.

This applicant hereby relinguishes every claim whatever to a pension or annuity except the present and declares that his name is not on the Pension Roll of any agency of any State.

Sworn and subscribed the day and year aforesaid   Jeremiah Dial
Jas. McKisick, Clk.

This day personally appeared in open court, Eli Cook Anderson, a resident of Bedford County, State of Tennessee, and made oath in due form that he lived with his father in Newberry County, South Carolina at the commencement of and during the Revolutionary War, and altho this affiant was then a small boy, he recollects of having seen and known Jeremiah Dial who has subscribed and sworn to the foregoing declaration, in Newberry County, South Carolina. This affiant states that he has frequently heard his father who was in the Revolutionary War, say that Dial served in that war and was occassionally with him during part of his service. This he heard from his father at the close of the war. This affiant states that he had been acquainted with said Dial about twenty years since his removal to this County and State, and he never heard his services as Revolutionary Soldier doubted, either here or in South Carolina, but he had always been reputed and believed to have been a Revolutionary Soldier both there and where he now lives and from the information of his father he believes said Dail to be a Soldier of the Revolution.

State of Tennessee]
Bedford County   ]
Before me, Kindred Pearson, a Justice of the Peace in and for the County of Bedford aforesaid, this day personally appeared, Jesse Scott, who after being duly sworn deposith and saith that he was personally acwuainted with Jeremiah Dial and Nancy, his wife, that from the annexed paper. They were married on the thirteenth day of December in the year of our Lord seventeen hundred and eighty eight.

MARRIAGES FROM BIBLE RECORD

Jeremiah Dial and Nancy, his wife, was married December the 13th, 1788.

That said paper is in the hand writing of said Jeremiah Dial, deceased, that the same may be taken from the Bible of Jesse Scott and that the same was written, not less than fourteen years ago, that said Bible has never been out of the possession of said Scott since that time. Said Jeremiah Dial departed this life on the twenty second day of September A.D. eighteen hundred and thirty four.

Subscribed and sworn to before me this second day of April 1839 and I do certify that said deponant is a respectable person and worthy of credit.

Kindred Pearson (Seal)   Jesse Scott
Justice of the Peace.

State of Tennessee]
Bedford County   ] February Term
On the fourth day of February in the year of our Lord, eighteen hundred and thirty nine, personally appeared in open court, opened and held for said County, Ann Dial, aged seventy six years, who being duly sworn according to law doth on his oath, make the following declaration in order to obtain the benefit of the provision made by an Act of Congress passed July 7th, 1838, entitled "An Act Granting half pay and Pensions to Certain Widows." That she is the widow of

61

Jeremiah Dial who was a Private in the Revolutionary War and whose services were proven upon an application heretofore made to the War Department by him for a pension which said pension he obtained as may be seen by the Certificate (dated January 3rd, 1833) herewith filed marked "A". She further declares that she was married to the said Jeremiah Dial on the thirteenth day of December in the year seventeen hundred and eighty seven, that her husband the aforesaid Jeremiah Dial died on the twenty second day of September eighteen hundred and thirty four, that she was not married to him prior to his leaving the service but the marriage took place prior to the first day of January seventeen hundred and ninety four, viz, at the time above stated.

Ann (X) Dial

I, William D. Orr, Clerk of the County Court of Bedford County aforesaid, do certify that the above declaration was duly sworn to and subscribed in our said Court, the said being in open court, on this day and in the manner stated in said declaration.

Anna died January 1849.

BIBLE RECORD OF ALEXANDER FREEMAN

Jeremiah Dial (1758-1834) married Dec 13, 1788 to Nancy Anna McDaniel (1763-1848) had a daughter Anna Dial (1798-1886) who married Alexander Freeman (1789-1859).

Alexander Freeman and Anna Dial Freeman had a son, Joseph Henry Freeman who married 1st Harriet Johnson and married 2nd Jennie Coop Oct 9, 1876. Harriet was born Apr 12, 1825, died July 12, 1873.

Children: 1st wife, Harriet:

1. William Rucker Freeman, born Jan 5, 1848, married Dec 10, 1881 to Della Braden, died Jan 1, 1903.
2. James Marshall Freeman, born July 26, 1850, died July 26, 1888, married 1st Dec 25, 1872 to Annie Peacock and had three children. Married 2nd Nov 30, 1886 to Emma Elizabeth Braden (sister to Della) and had one child.
3. Margaret Elizabeth Freeman, born Nov 9, 1852, married Feb 29, 1872 to William Richard Bomar, Sr. of Bell Buckle, Tennessee.
4. Andrew JOhnson Freeman, born June 1, 1855, married Dec 8, 1879 to Mattie Ivy.
5. Anna Eliza Jane Freeman, born Jan 5, 1858, married Aug 9, 1876 to Benjamin A. Fugitt.
6. Fannie Florence Freeman, born April 27, 1860, married Feb 6, 1881 to Wm. Hamilton Jameson.
7. Joseph Christopher Freeman, born Aug 11, 1863, died Jan 23, 1881.
8. Hattie Letitia Freeman, born April 7, 1870, died Nov 10, 1887.

Index to Revolutionary War Applications to Pension, (RG15) Ann W914.

No. 2829

Tennessee, Nashville, Ann Dial, widow of Jeremiah Dial, who was a Private in the South Carolina Line, for 2 years.

Inscribed on the Roll at the rate of 80 dollars, ____ cents per annum, to commence on the 4th day of March, 1843.

Certificate of Pension issued the 23rd day of ___ (Nov), 1843 and sent to H. Hockam, Murfreesborough, Tennessee.

Recorded in Book "A"   Act of March 3, 1843
Vol _(?) page 218

Ref: GSA Report, Washington, D.C.
Ref: 1835 Bedford County Pension List
Ref: Bedford County, Tennessee Cemetery Records by Marsh
Ref: Bible Record taken from The Millers of Millersburg by John B. Nicklin, Jr., 1923
Ref: Widow's Pension, No. 2829, Washington, D.C.
Ref: Tennessee DAR Yearbook, page 98

THOMAS DRAKE

Name: Rank: State Served:
Thomas Drake   Pvt   Virginia
Born ca 1750 in Virginia, died 13th day of August 1834 in Bedford County,
Tennessee, wife Catharine. Burial place unknown.

Newspaper Obit:
>   "Thomas Drake, died 24th March 1835, leaving a desolate widow and a
>   large family of children and relatives. Aged 85 years." He had been
>   drawing a pension for a number of years from the General Government.

GSA: Thomas Drake, wife Catharine, W.5264, born in Virginia
>   A statement of the military history of Thomas Drake, a Soldier of the
Revolutionary War, you will find below the desired information as contained in
the widow's application for pension on file in this Bureau. Ind. F.5264.

Length of Service: Enlisted from during the war and served until its close.
Rank: Private.
Officers: Captains Parson and Johnson.
>   Colonels White, Wm. Washington, Lee and Mathews.
State: Virginia.
Age at date of application: 76 years.
Remarks: Soldier was born in Virginia. He married August 12, 1802 in Brunswick
>   County, Virginia to Catharine Vaughn (Caty). He died 13th day of
>   August 1834 in Bedford County, Tennessee.
>   He had children by a former wife, names of wife and children not
>   stated. Children by wife Catharine: Nancy age 49 years, James age 48
>   years, Susan age 45 years, Polly age 42 years, George age 40 years, and
>   Susan (Sarah) age 38 years in 1853.
The heirs probably entitled to Bounty Land which was never drawn by Thomas
Drake, the Commissioners will draw ... for in ...

>   W.F. Bradford
>   Shelbyville, Tennessee

State of Tennessee]
Bedford County   ]
>   On this the 15th day of April 1852, personally appeared before me, John
L. Davidson, an Acting Justice of the Peace in and for the County and State
aforesaid, Catharine Drake, aged about seventy six years, who being duly sworn
according to law, doth on her oath make the following declaration in order to
obtain the benefit of the Act of Congress passed 7th July 1838, 3rd of March
1843, 17th June 1844 and 2nd Feby 1848, also 29th July 1848, to wit, That she is
the widow of Thomas Drake, deceased, who was a Private in the Army of the
Revolution for the State of Virginia and the widow of said Thomas Drake,
deceased, pensioned under Act of Congress passed 7th June 1832, or some Act
and who received a pension till the time of his death. She was married to her
aforesaid husband in 1793 in Brunswick County, Virginia, and he died 13th day of
August 1834. She most respectfully ask that the aforesaid claim may be allowed
under the aforesaid Acts of COngress 7th July 1838, 3rd of March 1843, 17th of
June 1844, 2nd of July 1848, also 29 July 1848, and the certificates evidencing
the same may be sent to Mr. Maney Aleney(?).
>   She hereby makes all other authority heretofore given to prosecute her
aforesaid claim. That she is still a widow.

Sworn to and subscribed before me   Catharine (X) Drake
on the day and year aforesaid
John L. Davidson (J.P.)
for Bedford County, Justice Peace

State of Tennessee]
Bedford County   ]
>   On this the fourth day of May in the year of our Lord eighteen hundred
and fifty three, personally appeared before me a Justice of the Peace of the
County Court, written and for the State and County aforesaid, Catharine Drake,
aged seventy seven years, who being duly sworn according to law, doth on her
oath make the following declaration in order to obtain the benefit of the

provision made by an Act of Congress passed the third day of February in the year of our Lord eighteen hundred and thirty three, that she is a resident of Bedford County, Tennessee. That she is the widow of Thomas Drake, deceased, who was Pensioner and Revolutionary Soldier, and commenced drawing a pension at Nashville, Tennessee, as well as she recollects about the __ day of ___ in the year of our Lord, eighteen hundred and ____ and drew ___ dollars. A year that he resided in Bedford County, Tennessee during the time he drew and resided in _____ Virginia when he entered the service of the United States and served during the war and was in the Battles _____ _____ _____ through the States.

She further states that she was married to the same Thomas Drake on the twelveth day of August in the year of our Lord eighteen hundred and two in Brunswick County, Virginia by one Aaron Brown, a preacher of the Gospel, that her husband the aforesaid Thomas Drake died on the twenty four day of March in the year of our Lord eighteen hundred and thirty five, at his home in Bedford County, Tennessee, and that she was a widow the third day of February A.D. eighteen hundred and fifty threeand is a widow and have never been married ... or received a pension, that she had by the said Thomas Drake the following named Children: Nancy aged 49 years, James aged forty eight years, Susan aged forty five years, Polly aged about 42 years, George about 40, and Sarah 38 years, all of whom were over sixteen years of age at the passage of this act, there with by aforesaid wife, are all his children.

Catharine (X) Drake

Sworn to and subscribed on the day and year above written before me a Justice of the County Court of the State and County aforesaid. I certify that I am well acquainted with Mrs. Catharine Drake and believe her to be the widow of said Soldier and that I have no interest in her claim for a pension and am not concerned in its prosecution and from old age and infirmity, unable to attend Court.

Squire Haggard, J.P. BC

State of Tennessee]
Bedford County   ] appeared

On this the fourth day of May A.D., eighteen hundred and fifty three, personally appeared before me, a Justice of the County Court, written and for said County and State who being duly sworn according to laws, declares that Mrs. Drake who makes the foregoing declaration is the widow of Thomas Drake who was reputed during his life to be a Revolutionary Soldier and drew a pension at Nashville, Tennessee, that she had by said Thomas Drake the following children all of whom were over the age of sixteen years. The third of February A.D. eighteen hundred and fifty three.

Inscribed and sworn to before me the day and year above written and I certify that they are credible and disinterested person.

(E.C.)

Know all men by these present that Catharine Drake of this County and State aforesaid do hereby _____ make constitute and appoint Wm. F. Bradford of Shelbyville, Tennessee, my Agent and Attorney for me and in my name to prosecute and receive any and all land, etc, that may be due, run or become due on transfer from general government and the Commissioners is authorized and requested to direct the Certificate of Pension, etc to him, my said Attorney, given under my hand and seal, this the fourth day of May A.D. eighteen hundred and fifty three.

Witness: John _____   Catharine (X) Drake

Acknowledge in my presence, day and date above written.

Squire Haggard (J.C.C.)

State of Tennessee]
Bedford County   ]

I, John H. O'Neal, Clerk of the County Court of the County and State aforesaid, do hereby certify that Squire Haggard before whom the foregoing declaration and acknowledgements was made is and was at the time of so doing, a Justice of the County Court of the County and State aforesaid, duly commissioned and sworn and that his signature hereto is genuine and in Court is a Court of Record in testimony whereof I have here unto set my hand and affixed the seal of my office as Clerk of the County Court of the County said

64

office and on this the nineth day of August in the year of our Lord, eighteen
hundred and fifty three.

John H. O'Neal, Clk.

BIBLE RECORD

List of marriages solemnized by Aaron Brown
Eighteen hundred & two, August, twelveth
Thomas Drake to Caty Vaughan.

Aaron Brown, M.G., M.E. Church

Returned sixth February, eighteen hundred & eight,
in the office and registered according to law by

Hubert Hill, C.B.C.

State of Virginia]
Brunswick County]

    I, E.R. Turnbull, Clerk of the County Court of Brunswick, in the State
of Virginia, hereby certify that the above is an exact copy of the Record of
Marriage, with the exception, that the dates appear on the record in fair legible
figures alone.

    In testimony whereof I hereto set my hand, Court this 28th July 1853,
in the 77th year of our Indepencence.

E.R. Turnbull

No. 3331: Tennessee, Nashville, Catharine Drake, widow of Thomas Drake,
Virginia, who served in the Revolutionary War, as a Private.

    Inscribed on the Roll at the rate of 80 dollars, 00 cents per annum, to
commence on the 3rd February 1853.

    Certificate of Pension issued the 24th day of December '53 (1853) and
sent to W.F. Bradford, Shelbyville, Tennessee.

Recorded on Roll of Pensioners under Act February 3, 1853.
Page 181   Vol A

Drake, Thomas et als

    Thomas Drake and Catharine his wife of Bedford County, Tennessee to
Merritt Davis, Brunswick County, State of Virginia.... Consists $380.00 paid to me
by Henry Davis the next friend of Merrit Davis... conveys all rights and interests
the said Thomas Drake and Catharine, his wife, have to certain lands and
tenements as heirs, or legatees, of George Vaughn, deceased, late of Brunswick
County, Virginia.

Dated 18 August 1815   Recorded 28 November 1815

Marriage Bond: 12 August 1802, Thomas Drake and Caty Vaughan, age 21
Security: Joshua Vaughan
Married by the Rev. Aaron Brown, Methodist Minister.

    Ref: GSA Report, Washington, D.C.
    Ref: Brunswick County, Virginia Marriage Records, page 134
    Ref: Brunswick County, Virginia Deed Book 23, page 30
    Ref: Emigration to other States from Southside Virginia by Elliott
    Ref: Western Freeman, Friday March 27, 1835, Bedford County,
        Tennessee.

* * * * * * * * *

WILLIAM EAKIN

Name:	Rank:	State Served:
William Eakin	Pvt	South Carolina

Born October 8, 1765 in York District, South Carolina, died July 11, 1840 in San
Augustine County, Texas, married to Elizabeth _____.

GSA: William Eakin, W.3530, wife Elizabeth, served in South Carolina.
Claim No. 13778 West Tennessee, William Eakin, of Bedford County in the State
of Tennessee, who was a Private in the company commanded by Captain Howe of
the Regiment commanded by Colonel Hawthorn in the South Carolina Line for six
months.

65

months.

Inscribed on the Roll of West Tennessee at the rate of 20 dollars, ____ cents per annum, to commence on the 4th day of March 1831.

Certificate of Pension issued the 17th day of June 1833 and sent to James McKisick, Shelbyville

Arrears to the 4th of March $40.--
Semi-anl allowance ending 4 Sept $10.--
              $50.--

Recorded by Daniel Boyd, Clerk   Revolutionary Claim
Book E   Vol 7   page 77   Act June 7, 1832

Declaration:

In order to obtain the benefit of the Act of Congress passed the 7th June 1832.

State of Tennessee]
Bedford County] Court of Pleas and Quarter Sessions, May Term 1833

On this 7th day of May one thousand eight hundred and thirty three, personally appeared in open court, William Eakin, a resident of Bedford County, aforesaid, aged sixty seven years and seven months, who being first duly sworn according to law, doth on his oath make the following declaration in order to obtain the benefit of the Act of Congress passed the 7th of June 1832. That he entered the service of the United States under the following named officers and served as herein stated, to wit, That he entered the service of the United States, in York District, South Carolina on the 6th of November, 1780, as a volunteer and Private Soldier in a Company of Volunteers commanded by Captain Joseph Howe and Lieutenant Benjamin Rowan, who were under the command of Colonel James Hawthorn, and was marched to Brandon's Mill upon the Fairforrest River in the Union District, South Carolina, where he was kept for some time, applicant says he was then marched to Ninety-Six where he was kept for six or seven weeks and from there he was marched to the Fishdam Ford on Broad River, Fairfield District, where he remained some time and from there to Waynesborough where he says he was stationed upwards of two months and from that place he was marched to Lands-Ford on the Catawba River, and from there to what was then called the Old Nation-Ford where he says the volunteers under Colonel Hawthorn, were emcamped for sometime and from there he was marched to the mouth of Pacolet River, where it intersects Broad River and from that to Bigger's Ferry on the Catawba, where he remained in service until the latter part of May or first of June 1781. Where he says he was discharged in writing, signed by Colonel Hawthorn for a tour of six months for which he claims a pension. Deponant states that he has long since lost his discharge, not knowing it would ever be of service to him, he took very little care of it. Applicant states he was born in York District, Rockhill, State of South Carolina on the 8th day of October in the year 1765, agreeable to his father's Family Record, and that he has a copy of the same in his possession at this time. He further says that there was not any Regular Troops with the Army where he served and that he was not acquainted with any Regular Officer of the name or number of Regiments, except the Regiment he belonged to, which was called Colonel Hawthorn's Regiment of Volunteer Mounted Gunman and that he understood that the troops under Colonel Hawthorn was ordered into service by General Sumpter. This applicant says that he was a citizen and resident in York District, South Carolina, when he entered the service and continued to be a citizen of said District until the year 1810, when he removed to the State of Illinois and in 1812, he removed to Bedford County, Tennessee, where he has lived ever since, and where he now lives. Deponant states that the foregoing declaration contains the most history of the general circumstances of his service that, that he is able at this stage of his life to give. And that he has no documentary evidence whatever and that he knows of no person whose testimony he can produce who can testify as to his service. This applicant hereby relinguishes all and every claim to a pension or annuity except the present and declares that his name is not on the Pension Roll of any agency in the United States. He further says that he is known to the Rev. Richard W. Morris, Allen Perry, Esq., and Edward Whitworth, in his present neighborhood. Sworn to and subscribed the day and year aforesaid.

Jas. McKisick, Clk.   William Eakin   (Seal)

No. 1131   Louisiana, Elizabeth Eakin, widow of William Eakin who served in the Revolutionary War, South Carolina, as a Private.

Inscribed on the Roll at the rate of 20 dollars, ___ cents per annum to commence on the 4th day of March, 1848.

Certificate of Pension issued the 26th day of April 1852, and sent to Hon. G.W. Smythe, House of Reps.

Recorded on Roll of Pensions under Act July 29, 1848.
Page 457(9)   Vol A   1832

The State of Texas]
County of Shelby]

Before the undersigned, E. Sanford, an Acting Justice of the Peace in and for the County, personally came Mrs. Elizabeth Eakin, a resident of Shelby County, aged about 81 years, who being first duly sworn according to law, doth on her oath make the following declaration in order to benefit of the Act of COngress granting provisions to the widows of Revolutionary Soldiers. That she is the widow of William Eakin who was a Soldier in the service of the United States in the Revolutionary War, that he served, she thinks, in the South Carolina State Troops. That about the year A.D. 1834, while her husband was a resident of Bedford County, Tennessee, he made application to the Pension Office of the United States for a pension, and a pension was granted to him for life. The Certificate bearing the date about the year 1834. Her said husband was placed on the Pension List Roll of the Nashville, Tennessee Agency where his name remains. Until the date of his death which occured about the 11th day of July A.D., 1840. That in drawing the arrears of Oension due her said husband, the Pension Certificate was returned to the proper office at Washington City, all of which facts in reference to the granting of a pension to William Eakin, his name being on the Roll of the Nashville, Tennessee Agency, his Certificate having been returned to the proper Office at the Washington City and etc... She presumes are Battle of Record, and she would by leave to refer to and make said record a part of this declaration. She further says that she was married to the said William Eakin on the 5th day of February to the best of her recollection in the year 1793 or 1794 in York District and State of South Carolina, that she is informed and believes that there is no record of said marriage in evidence, nor is there any persons now alive who was present at said marriage so far as known or declares. She would therefore by service to refer to the accompanying proof as the best she can furnish of the fact of her marriage to said William Eakin. She further says she and her said husband lived together from the date of their marriage until the 11th day of July 1840, when the said William Eakin died in the County San Augustine and State of Texas. That she has not intermarried but still remains the widow of the above named William Eakin and that she now resides in Shelby County, Texas, where she has resided ever since her said husband's death.

Elizabeth (X) Eakin

Sworn to and subscribed before me this 8th day of March, one thousand eight hundred and fifty four. I further certify that I have personally known Mrs. Elizabeth Eakin, above named for about fourteen years and that I believe her statements above were to be true and correct. I further certify that from age and bodily infirmity, she is unable to go before a Court of Records, therefore this declaration is sworn to before me at her residence.
Witness my hand this 8th day of March, A.D., 1854.

E. Sanford, J.P.

1835, age 68, Pvt in South Carolina Line.

Ref: GSA Report, Washington, D.C.
Ref: 1835 Bedford Co unty, Tennessee Pension List.
Ref: Pension for widows of Revolutionary Soldiers

* * * * * * * * * *

RICHARD ELKINS

Name: Rank: State Served:
Richard Elkins   Pvt   South Carolina
Born 1761 in King George County, Virginia, died ____ .

GSA: Richard Elkins, S.2535, Claim No. 7582

    West Tennessee, Richard Elkins of Bedford County in the State of West Tennessee, who was a Private in the Company commanded by Captain Oliver of the Regiment commanded by Colonel Tate in the South Carolina Line for 13 months.

    Inscribed on the Roll of West Tennessee at the rate of 43 dollars, 33 cents per annum, to commence on the 4th day of March 1831.

    Certificate of Pension issued the 3 day of May 1833 and sent to James McKisick, Shelbyville.

Arrears to the 4th of Mar	$ 86.66
Semi-anl allowance ending 4 Sept	$ 21.66
	$108.32

Recorded by Daniel Boyd, Clerk   Revolutionary Claim
Book E   Vol 7   page 77   Act June 7, 1832

Order to pay and letter to Pension 4th April 1838 - to P. Agt. May 21, 1838. Same May 26, 1838.
Paid at ____ Treasury under the Act of the 4 April 1838, from 4 March 1837 to 4 Sept 1837. Agt notified 28 July 1838.

State of Tennessee]
Bedford County   ]

    Declaration in order to obtain the benefit of an Act of Congress passed 7th June 1832.

    On this 8th day of November in the year of our Lord, one thousand eight hundred and thirty two, personally appeared in open court before the Worshipful Samuel Phillips, John L. Neill and Jno. B. Armstrong, Esquires, Gentlemen Justices of the Peace in and for said County, appointed to hold the Court of Pleas and Quarter Sessions of Bedford County and State aforesaid, now sitting, Richard Elkins, aged seventy years, eleven months and thirty days, who being first duly sworn according to law, doth on his oath make the following declaration in order to obtain the benefit of the Act of Congress passed 7th June 1832.

    That he entered the service of the United States under the following named officers and served as herein states, to wit, That he entered the service of the United States in the County of Marion and State of South Carolina, as a volunteer in a Company of Volunteers under the command of Captain Olliver and was attached to a Regiment commanded by Colonel Tate and Major M. Sabb. Sometime he thinks in the Spring or Summer of the year 1780, he was mustered into service at Orangeburg, South Carolina and was marched from that place with a detachment under the command of General Montrey to what was then called Purysburg in the last mentioned State, and at that place he says the Americans was attacked by the British, under the command, as he was informed, General Provost and that the Americans were compelled to retreat from that place to Charlestown in the same State where he says he was kept until his term of three months service expired, where he was discharged, he thinks in writing but is not certain. He further states that shortly after he returned home, he was drafted in the same County (Marion) and was placed under the command of Captain Aaron Little as Captain in a regiment under the command of Colonel Grifett and Major Olliver who were attached to the troops under the command of General Lincoln as Chief Commander and Generals Mutry, McIntosh, Sumpter and General Marion was there part of the time at Monks Corner where he says he was marched to, and where he says he saw General Woodford and Scott of the Regular Army and from that place was marched to what was called the Quarter House and remained there for sometime, and was then marched into the City of Charlestown and after serving a tour of about four months, a month longer than his proper time, and his Captain having liberty to return home with his men if his men could pass the British, which at that time had surrendered the Town, by land and water but he says his Captain passes the British in a small skiff up Ashly River in the night and was then discharged. Deponant further says that in a short time after he returned home, he was in company with some of General Marion's men, who was then stationed in a swamp near where he said deponant lived, when he was taken prisoner together with two of General Marion's men and marched to Nelson's Ferry on Santee River where the British men conveying prisoners across that they said were taken at General Gates Defeat and at that place he made his escape from them, and went immediately and joined General Marion and continued with him until after the Battle of Eutaw Springs. He says that on that day he was in a detachment reserved as he was informed to prevent the escape of the enemy. He says he thinks he served with General Marion about six months or upwards and was then dismissed. Making a term of service in the whole about thirteen months and more but that he claims a pension for thirteen months only. He says that he has no documentary evidence and that he knows of no person who can testify as to his service whose testimony he can procure and that he hereby relinguishes every claim whatever to a pension or annuity whatever except the present and declares that his name is not on the Pension Roll of any agency in the United States.

Interrogatories by the Court:

Q. 1st: Where and in what year were you born?

A. I was born in King George County in the State of Virginia on the 9th day of December in the year 1761 agreeable to my father's Family Record.

Q. 2nd: Have you any record of your age and if so where is it?

A. I have no record of my age in my possession at this time.

Q. 3rd: Where were you living when called into service? Where have you lived since the Revolutionary War and where do you now live? .

A. I was a citizen of Marion County in the State of South Carolina when I entered the service of the United States and remained there until the close of the Revolution and from there I moved into Franklin County, State of North Carolina and then I removed to Lancaster County in the State of South Carolina, on Hanging Rock Creek, where I remained until the year 1812, when I removed to Bedford County in the State of Tennessee where I have lived ever since and where I now live.

Q. 4th: How were you called into service? Were you drafted? Were you a volunteer or were you a substitute and if a substitute for whom?

A. I volunteered in the first place, and the next time I was drafted and the last tour I was a volunteer under General Marion.

Q. 5th: Did you ever receive a discharge and if so, what has become of it?

A. I think I did receive a discharge for my first tour of duty, but what has become of it, I cannot tell.

Q. 6th: State the names of some of the Regular Officers that were with the troops where you served, such Continental and Militia Regiments as you can recollect, and the general circumstances of your service.

A. I recollected General Woodford and Scott at Charlestown and General Lincoln, I also saw a great many other officers but do not recollect the names of any except General Pulaski of the Lighthorse. I do not recollect the names or numbers of any Regiments either _____ the Regular or Militia at this time. And believe I have given the most prominent history of the circumstances of my service that I can at this period of my age, in my declaration.

Q. 7th: State the names of persons in your present neighborhood who can testify as to your character for veracity and their opinion of your services as a Soldier of the Revolution.

A. William Bawden, Hugh Davidson, Esq., Joseph Johnson and several Clergymen but have not been able to procure their attendance at Court at this time.

Sworn to and subscribed, the day and year aforesaid.

Richard (X) Elkins

1835, age 73 years, Pvt, South Caroline Line.

Ref: GSA Report, Washington, D.C. and 1815 Bedford County Pen. List.

Name: Rank: State Served:
Alexander Ewing   PVT   North Carolina
Born 1762 in Mecklenburg County, North Carolina, married Sarah _____.

GSA: Alexander Ewing, wife Sarah (Chappel), W.1584
     B.L.Wt. 36637-160-55
Claim No. 14.000   West Tennessee, Alexander Ewing of Bedford County in the State of Tennessee who was a Private in the Company commanded by Captain Osburn of the Regiment commanded by Major White in the North Carolina Line for 2 years.

Inscribed on the Roll of West Tennessee at the rate of 80 dollars, ___ cents per annum, to commence on the 4th day of March 1831.

Certificate of Pension issued the 20 day of July 1833 and sent to Jas. McKisick, Clerk.

Arrears to the 4th of March $160.00
Semi-anl allowance ending 4 Sept $ 40.00
                                                   $200.00

Recorded by Daniel Boyd, Clerk   Revolutionary Claim
Book E   Vol 7   page 77   Act June 7, 1832

237.600   Act Mar 3, '33 (1833)
          Mar 10, '36 (1836)

Sarah Ewing, wife   Alexander Ewing, Pen. Rev. War.
No. 36637 of Aug 7/50
            Aug 4/56

State of Tennessee]
Bedford County   ]
In order to obtain the benefit of Act of 7th June 1832.

On this 30th day October 1832, personally appeared before me Robert McCrory, an Acting Justice, Justice of said County, Alexander Ewing, a resident of the County and State aforesaid, aged about seventy years, being first duly sworn upon whole Evangelist of all Mighty God, doth on his oath corporal oath, answer the following interrogatories to him propounded by the said Robert McCrory in order to obtain the benefit of the Act of Congress passed on the 7th day of June 1832, entitled, "An Act supplementary to an Act for the relief of the surviving Officers and Soldiers of the Revolution."

Interrogatories by the Court:

Q. 1st: Where and in what year were you born?
A.   I was born in Mecklenburg County, North Carolina about the year of 1762, the precise date I cannot remember having no record of my age and being unable to read or write.
Q. 2nd: Where were you living when called into service?
A.   In Mecklenburg County, North Carolina.
Q. 3rd: Where have you since lived and where do you now live?
A.   A part of my time in Mecklenburg, North Carolina and part of my time in Bedford County, Tennessee, at which latter place, I now live.
Q. 4th: How were you called into service and when?
A.   I volunteered for 12 months and was afterwards drafted for 12 months more, I served the first 12 months under General Green and the other 12 months under General Rutherford. When I was called in service, I cannot remember keeping the dates.
Q. 5th: How many Battles were you in?
A.   None but the Battle of the Town of Camden, South Carolina.
Q 6th: By what Officers were you commanded and discharged?
A.   In the first Company by General Green and discharged by Major Gilford Dudley and in the last I was commanded by General Rutherford and discharged by Major White. I do not remember the names of any of the Regular Officers but it appears to me that my last Captain's name was Cole, of the Drafted Militia. And that my first of the volunteers were James Osburn.

Q. 7th: Through what Countries did you march?
A.   Through North Carolina.
Q. 8th: Did you receive honorable discharge from each tour of service?
A.   I did.
Q. 9th: What has become of your discharges?
A.   They have been either lost or destroyed.
Q. 10th: Do you know of any person or persons who have seen your discharges?
A.   My brother Robert Ewing has read one of or both of them.
Q. 11th: Do you know of any person now living who served with you?
A.   I do not.
Q. 12th: Have you any property?
A.   Not enough for a comfortable support.
Q. 13th: What is your present state of health?
A.   I'm very weakly and infirm being almost unable to get about and
           intensely unable to get to our County Court to prove up this claim a
           distance of 22 or 23 miles off.
Q. 14th: What is the nature of your disease?
A.   I have been laboring for some time under rheumatism and have for
           many years passed, but very much troubled constantly more or less with
           a weakly bowel complaint which has been produced by my exposure
           while in the service of the United States.
Q. 15th: Did you receive any pay for your services of time or before you were
           discharged?
A.   I did for my last tour bbut not for the first.
Q. 16th: Have you ever received any pension from the Government of U.S.A.?
A.   I have neither applied for or received any, I also hereby relinguish every
           claim whatever to any pension or annuity except the present and
           declare that my name is not on the Pension Roll of the Agency of any
           State.
Sworn to and subscribed the day and date above written.
Robert McCrory, (J.P.)   Alexander (X) Ewing

We, John Paxton of Bedford and John Vincent of Maury County, both Clergymen
of the Counties and State aforesaid and in the neighborhood of the above
applicant, Alexander Ewing do certify that we are well acquainted with him and
weere present when he swore to and subscribed the above declaration and that
we believe him to be about seventy years of age and that he is reputed and
believed to have been a Soldier of the Revolution and that we are confident of
that fact as above stated. Sworn to and subscribed the day and year above
written.

                                        John Paxton
                                        John Vincent
And I the aforesaid Robert McCrory, Justice as aforesaid do heretofore declare
that the investigation of the matter and after putting the interrogatories
prescribed by the War Department that I do _____ believe the above named
applicant was a Revolutionary Soldier and served as he states. I also further
declare that it appears to me that John Paxton and John Vincent who has
assigned the preceeding Certificate as Clergymen, are residents as aforesaid and
are creditable witnesses and that their statements are entitled to credit.

        In testimony whereof I have hereunto set my hand and seal, the day and
year above written.
                                        Robert McCrory, (J.P.)

State of Tennessee]
Bedford County   ]
        Robert Ewing of State and County aforesaid, this day, personally
appeared before me the aforesaid Robert McCrory, an Acting Justice of the
Peace for the County and State aforesaid and being duly sworn on the wholey
Evangelist of All Mighty God, deposeth and sayeth that he has seen and read both
the discharges given to his brother Alexander Ewing and that one was dated a
few days after the Battle of _____ town at Camden, South Carolina and that it
was assigned by Colonel Guilford Dudley to the best of his knowledge and belief
and the other was assigned by Major White of North Carolina.

Given under my hand ans seal, this 29th Oct 1832.

Robert Ewing

Sworn to and subscribed before me,
Robert McCrory, (J.P.)

Declaration:
  In order to obtain the benefit of the Act of Congress of the 7th July 1838, entitled "An Act granting half pay and pensions to certain widows."
State of Tennessee]
Marion County]

  On this 9th day of January 1845, personally appeared before John K. Tate, an Acting Justice of the Peace and County aforesaid and Commissioner, appointed by the County Court of said County as by the Commission hereto attached will more fully appear, Sarah Ewing, aged about sixty nine years, who being first duly sworn according to law, doth on her oath make the following declaration in order to obtain the benefit of the provision made by the Act of Congress passed July 7, 1838, entitled "An Act granting half pay and pensions to certain widows", that she is the widow of Alexander Ewing who was a volunteer Private in the Company of Captain Falls and Regiment commanded by Colonel Read, in the Army of the Revolution, that applicant's husband joined the company aforesaid or Captain Osburn but believe the latter in Charlotte, Mecklenburg County, North Carolina in the year 17-- as believed tho the precise time cannot be certain, nor certain as to the term of service. The second tour, applicant believes her said husband was drafted in the company commanded by Captain Osburn or Captain Falls but believe the former, applicant thus unites the two Captains having heard her husband say he was with both in the Army and believes she has heard him say that Captain Falls at the engagement with the British and Tories at Ramsour's Mill or Camden was killed, and in said engagement, applicant's husband shot bag strop was shot in two. Applicant does not know the time her husband entered the service, or their lengths of time neither does she know the Country through which applicant's husband passed nor other Officers under which he served except hearing him repeatedly speak of being with General Greene, coupling that with Camden. Applicant has no documentary evidence of the service of her said husband unless on file in the Pension Office of the United States. Her said husband, Alexander Ewing being placed on the Pension Roll of the United States in the year 1833 or 1834 at eighty dollars per annum. Applicant's husband, Alexander Ewing and herself was married in Mecklenburg County, North Carolina in the month of _____ 1791, and her said husband departed this life in Marshall County, formerly Bedford County, Tennessee, on the 20th day of April 1843. That applicant drew the arrearage of pension due from the semi-annual payment before, to the day of his death. Applicant has heard her said husband say he received his discharge from Major Dudley. His term of service, applicant believes expired with the termination of the War, that she was not married to him prior to his leaving the service (the reason of her indistinct knowledge of the period he entered and continuation of his service and only know from his statements made frequently) but the marriage took place previous to the first of January, Seventeen hundred and ninety four, viz, at the time above stated. Applicant further states since the death of her husband, Alexander Ewing, she has remained a widow ever since that period as will more fully appear by reference to the proof hereto annexed. Applicant further states she has no children. Applicant further states she has no documentary evidence of her marriage.
Sworn to and subscribed on the day and year above written, before

John K. Tate, Justice of the Peace,   Sarah (X) Ewing
and Commissioner, aforesaid.

State of Tennessee]
Marion County]

  On this 9th day of January 1844, the said Sarah Ewing, personally appeared before me, John K. Tate, an Acting Justice of the Peace in and for the County aforesaid and Commissioner by authority of the County Court of the County aforesaid hereto attached, do certify that the said Sarah Ewing, with whom I am personally acquainted subscribed and sworn according to law to the foregoing declaration in order to obtain the benefit of the provisions of an Act

granting half pay and pensions to widows and that the same was true to the best of her knowledge and belief. I further certify that I am personally acquainted with the said Sarah Ewing who is respectable person and that her statement is entitled to credit. I further certify that said Sarah Ewing from bodily infirmity is unable to appear in open court.
Given under my hand and seal this date above written.

John K. Tate   (Seal)
Justice of the Peace &
Commissioner, aforesaid.

State of Tennessee]
Marion County   ]
On this 9th day of January 1845, personally appeared before me, John K. Tate, an acting Justice of the Peace in and for the County aforesaid and Commissioner aforesaid, Jane Caughran, a respectable person with whom I am personally acquainted, aged about sixty six years, who being sworn according to law, deposes and says that in this month of September 1791, she was present at the infair given to Alexander Ewing and Sarah Chappell, now Sarah Ewing, that affiant was at the time of the return of the said Alexander & Sarah from the Justice before whom the marriage was celebrated at the house where said infair was had, that she heard the said Alexander Ewing and said Sarah Chappell say they were married on that day. Affiant further states she was well acquainted with the said Alexander Ewing and Sarah Chappell,now Sarah Ewing, before their marriage and was acquainted with them from their marriage to the death of the said Alexander Ewing on the 20th April 1843, during the time of coveture. They lived in the greatest harmony and peace and they the only husband and wife either had during that time, that since the death of her said husband Alexander Ewing, she has remained unmarried, and that the said Sarah Ewing who has made the foregoing declaration to the identical Sarah Chappell, now Sarah Ewing, the wife of a Pensioner of the United States placed on the Pension Roll in 1833 or 1834 as affiant believes. He then exited in Bedford now made Marshall County, Tennessee. Affiant further states she has examined the declaration of Sarah Ewing and believe her statement true. Affiant further states that said Sarah Ewing is a respectable person and entitled to credit.
Sworn to and subscribed the day above written before
John K. Tate   Jane (X) Caughran
Justice of the Peace &
Commissioner, aforesaid

No. 12653
State of Tennessee]
Marion County   ]
On this 9th day of January 1845, personally appeared before me, John K. Tate, an acting Justice of the Peace for the County aforesaid and Commissioner aforesaid, Edward Garner, a respectable person with whom I am personally acquainted, aged about fifty one years, who being sworn according to law deposes that he is well acquainted with Sarah Ewing who made the foregoing declaration and that her statement is entitled to full credit. Affiant further states said Sarah Ewing is an orderly and acceptable member of the Methodist Church.
Sworn to and subscribed before me the date above.
John K. Tate   Edward Garner
Justice of the Peace &
Commissioner, aforesaid

State of Tennessee]
Marion County   ]
On this 22nd day of February A.D. 1856, personally appeared before me an acting Justice of the Peace within and for the County and State aforesaid, Sarah Ewing, aged eighty years past, a resident of Marion County in the State of Tennessee, who after first being duly sworn according to law, declare that she is the widow of Alexander Ewing, deceased, who was a Soldier of the War of the Revolution and served in the North Carolina or South Carolina and drew a Pension for said service and belonged to the Middle Tennessee Division, and was

paid at Nashville, Tennessee, $80. per annum. And since his death, she has been inscribed upon the Pension List at the same rate as his widow and placed upon the Tennessee Roll, and is paid at Knoxville, Tennessee, which Certificate is now in her possession, and which is recorded in the Pension Office on the Roll of Pensioners under Act July 29th, 1848. Page 181, Vol A, to which reference is hereby given. She also refers to the application proof and records produced and adduced, and now on file in the Pension Office Department, which was made by herself and her husband, and upon which their Pension Certificate was issued. As proof of the services and death of her husband, as well as their marriage. She further declared that she is now and have continued to live a widow ever since the death of her husband, as well appear by reference to the accompanying proof. She makes this declaration for the purpose of obtaining the Bounty Land to which she may be entitled under the provision of the Acy of Congress approved the 3rd of March 1855. She further declares that she has never received Bounty Land under any Act of Congress whatever, and that this is her first application for the same.

R.B. Roberts of Altamont, Tennessee, is hereby authorized to prosecute this my claim and to receive any Warrant that may issue hereon.
Elijah D. Tate   Sarah (X) Ewing

We, Elijah D. Tate and James Fults, residents of Marion County in the State of Tennessee, upon our oaths declare that the foregoing declaration was signed and acknowledged by the above named, Sarah Ewing, in our presence, that we know the applicant to be a person she represents herself to be. That she is now the widow of Alexander Ewing, a Pensioner of the War of the Revolution and that she also draws a pension as his widow, and that we have no interest in the results of this application.

E.D. Tate
James Fults

The foregoing declaration and affidavit were sworn to and subscribed before me the day and year above written, and I so certify that I know the affiant's to be credible persons, the claimant to be the widow of Alexander Ewing, deceased, and to be a Revolutionary Pensioner, as his widow, that she is now a widow, and that I have no interest in the claim, nor any connection with its prosecution.

J.M. Tate, J.P.

State of Tennessee]
Marion County   ]
I do hereby certify J.M. Tate, Esq., before whom the foregoing declaration and affidavit was taken, was at the date thereof, an acting Justice of the Peace in and for said County duly commissioned and qualified and his oath as such are entitled to credit.

In testimony whereof I have here unto subscribed my name and affixed the Seal of said County at Office, this 23rd day of February A.D., 1856.

J.H. Canaster, Clerk

1835, age 72, Private, South Carolina. Bedford County, Tennessee.

Ref: GSA Report, Washington, D.C.
Ref: Widow's Pension Application.
Ref: 1835 Bedford County, Tennessee Pension List.

* * * * * * * * * *

CHARLES FANE

Name: Rank: State Served:
Charles Fane   PVT   North Carolina
Born August 1742 in Chesterfield County, Virginia, died after 1834.

1835, age 91, Private, North Carolina.

GSA: Charles Fane, S.3343   War Record 3762
State of Tennessee]
Bedford County   ]

On this 14th day of August 1832, personally appeared in open court before the Justices of the Court of Pleas and Quarter Sessions for Bedford County now sitting, being a Court of Records, Charles Fane, aged ninety years, a resident of Bedford County, Tennessee, who being first duly sworn according to law, doth on his oath make the following declaration in order to obtain the benefit of the Act of Congress passed June 7th, 1832.

He was an orphan boy and was informed, he believes, after he grew up by his mother, one of his uncles, that he was born in Chesterfield County, Virginia in the month of August 1742. He has no register of his age, he does not know whether there is any in existance or was ever any in existance.

He was also informed and believes it to be true, he was an illegitimate child and when he was about three years of age, his mother put him out to learn the trade of a gun-smith with one Philip Mathews, who lived in Albemarle County, Virginia, who removed him at that early age to the County but when the Revolutionary War was declared, he lived in Halifax County, Virginia. Before he entered the service, however, he had removed to Surry County in North Carolina after the Revolutionary War, he removed to Georgia, afterwards he removed to Blount County, East Tennessee, then to Sevier County, adjoining Blount, from there he removed to Bedford County, West Tennessee, where he has lived since 1806 or 1807. Soon after he removed to Surry County, North Carolina, he was drafted on a tour of six months and entered into a company commanded by Captain Reed of the Militia and attached to a Regiment of Militia commanded by Colonel Joseph Williams but the name of the Regiment he does not recollect. He cannot recollect at this time at what time particularly when he was drafted but thinks it was some time in the Fall of 1779. They marched to the assistance of Charleston and at Monks Corner, was informed by Colonel Washington, the route to Charleston was so guarded by the British, they could not pass to Charleston on that route. They changed their route and went by Hedley's Point at which point they took shipping and entered Charleston after night. Most of the men commanded by Captain Reed, when they first left home, deserted and abondoned him so that when they got to Charleston there was but six of his men entered with him into Charleston. This applicant was then placed under the command of Captain Collins in Charleston and his former Captain Reed returned home. He thinks they got into Charleston about the 1st of March before it was captured which he believes was in April 1780. He remained there under the command of Captain Collins until Charleston was captured by the British and he was taken prisoner. He does not recollect the names of any of the Regular Officers except the American Forces at Charleston was commanded by General Lincoln nor does he recollect the names of his own Regiment or that of any other.

About nine days after the recapture, he was sent home on his parole of honor which read as well as he can recollect as follows: I, Charles Fane, do acknowledge myself a prisoner of war to his Excellency, My Lord Clinton, till I am exchanged or released.

This applicant states from that time until the end of the war, he never was in any regular tour of service, but he was almost constantly upon scouting parties against the Tories until the conclusion of the war under Captain Speers and Captain Bruce headed by Colonel Joseph Williams. He never received a discharge owing to his being taken prisoner by the British. The written parole of honor above __________ out and destroyed. He has no documentary evidence and he knows of no person whose testimony he can procure who can testify to his service.

He is known to John Rushing, Job Cooper, George C. Cooper, Thompson Fulks and a number of others in his present neighborhood who he believes can testify to his character for veracity and their belief of his service as a Soldier of the Revolution. He hereby relinguishes any claim to a pension or annuity whatever except the present and declares that his name is not on the Pension Rolls of the agency of any State whatever.

Sworn to and subscribed this 14th of August 1832.

Charles (X) Fane

We, John Rushing, a clergyman, residing in the County of Bedford and State of Tennessee, and George C. Cooper, residing in said County and State, do hereby certify that we are well acquainted with Charles Fane who has subscribed and sworn to the above declaration. That we believe him to be ninety years of age. That he is reputed and believed in the neighborhood where he resides to have been a Soldier of the Revolution and we concur in that opinion.

Sworn to in open Court   John Rushing
14th August 1832   Geo. C. Cooper
Jas. McKisick, Clk.

An amendment to the Declaration of Charles Fane made at August Term 1832 of Bedford County Court, in order to obtain the benefit of the Act of Congress, the 7th June 1832.

State of Tennessee]
Bedford County   ]

On this 11th day of April in the year of our Lord one thousand eight hundred and thirty three, personally appeared before me, James H. Lile, an Acting Justice of the Peace in and for said County, Charles Fane, Senr., who subscribed and was qualified to the declaration above alluded to, who after being sworn according to law deposity and saith that by reason of old age and the subsequent loss of memory, he cannot swear positively to the precise time when he first entered the service of the United States but according to the best of his recollection at this time, it was on the first of January 1780. Deponant further says that one of the tours mentioned in his former declaration, as a scouting expedition, he now recollects was performed by order of Captain Sam'l Moseley, when he says he was marched to Salem in North Carolina and was placed there as one of the guards to enable the General Assembly of that State to convene as he was told, where he served not less than two weeks, when he was discharged. He further states, the other scouting mentioned in his former declaration, he does not wish a pension pay. But that he absolutely did serve not less than six months and two weeks as a Private Soldier in the American Army during War of the Revolution. At the period above mentioned for which he claims a pension, subscribed and sworn to the day and year aforesaid.

Jas. H. Lile, J.P.   Charles (X) Fane
Bedford County

Pay Voucher No. 13991
Book E   Vol 7   page 88

Ref: GSA Report, Washington, D.C.
Ref: 1835 Bedford County, Tennessee Pension List.

* * * * * * * * * *

MICHAEL FISHER

Name: Rank: State Served:
Michael Fisher   PVT   Pennsylvania

Born May 20, 1766 in Pennsylvania, died December 18, 1833 in Bedford County, Tennessee, married Christina Earnhart on November 23, 1786 in Germantown, Pennsylvania. Both are buried in Crowell's Chapel Church Cemetery, Bedford County, Tennessee. Michael Fisher has a Military Marker and has been marked by the Shelby Chapter DAR. His Marker:

Mich'l Fisher

Pa. Mil.

Rev. War

NOTE: Christina Earnhart Fisher's grave is unmarked.

No GSA on Michael Fisher in Washington, D.C.

Served as Private under Captain Henrick Mach, Berks County, Pennsylvania Militia, 1782. (May have been two Michael Fishers)

Michael Fisher Bible

In possession of Mrs. W. Nowlin Taylor, Shelbyville, Tennessee.

MARRIAGES:

Michael Fisher was married to Christiana Earnhart, November the 14, 1786

Jacob, son of Michael and Christiana Fisher was married to Sarah Smith,
        July 9th, 1813.

Philip Fisher was married to Phoebe Dice, April 1813.
Elizabeth Fisher was married to Edward Wade, Feby 26th, 1807.
Christiana Fisher was married to Thompson Thompson, June 13th, 1811.
Margaret Fisher was married to George Parsons, July 18th, 1811.
Thomas T. Parsons was married to Mary F. Clardy, Sept 14, 1852.
Mary Fisher was married to Michael Fisher, January 2d, 1812.
Martin Fisher was married to Margaret Earnhart, June 24th, 1813.
Anna Fisher was married to Jacob Morton, August 31st., 1815.
George Fisher was married to Permelia Parsons, November 14th, 1817.
Sarah Fisher was married to Samuel Sloan, Aug 29th, 1816.
Amy Fisher was married to Newcomb Thompson, July 6th, 1820.
Mary Ann Fisher was married to Silas Tilgman, Sept 28th, 1820.
Michael Fisher was married to Elizabeth Turrentine, July 5th, 1822.
John Fisher was married
BIRTHS;
Michael Fisher was born May 20, 1766
Christiana Fisher was born February 19th, 1764
            Children of the above:
Jacob Fisher was born July 10th, 1787.
Philip Fisher was born July 15th, 1788.
Elizabeth Fisher was born September 29th, 1789.
Christiana Fisher was born November 6th, 1790.
Martin Fisher was born January 6th, 1792.
Margaret Fisher was born July 23rd, 1793.
Mary Fisher was born February 19th, 1795.
George Fisher was born May , 1796.
Anna Fisher was born April 27th, 1798.
Michael Fisher was born October 13th, 1799.
Sarah Fisher was born August 5th, 1801.
Mary Ann Fisher was born March 22nd, 1803.
Amy Fisher was born May 22nd, 1805.
John Fisher was born July 23, 1808.
            Finis
                illegible   was born January 18th, 1823.
John F. Thompson was born November 24th, 1813.
George W. Tilmon was born January the 25, 1821.
Cristena A. Tilmon was born 14 day of April, 1824.
Nicholas Harris was born december the 23, 1815 and was married to Mary Ann
            Parson July the 12, 1838.
Silas M. Tilmon was born May the 15, 1829.

M.F. Parsons was married to Y(Z). W. Thomas in April the 22, 1836.
A.C. Parsons was mared to Eliza More, August the 3, 1834.
J.M. Parsons was mared to Lisinda Crowell, August 16, 1841.

DEATHS:
Martin Fisher exit December 10th, 1828.
Charley Fisher exit November 13th, 1828.
Christiana Fisher exit the 9th day of April 1830.
Michael Fisher exit December 18th, 1833.
Mary An Clardy exit April the 30, 1839 3 O'Clock in the morning.
George Parsons departed this life 16th November, 1842 at 9 O'Clock night.
Michael F. Parson departed this life April 2nd, 1849 3 O'CLock in New Orleans.
Amey Thompson departed this life March 20, 18__.

George Parsons was born December 27, 1787.

Michael F. Parsons was born June the 30, ____.
A.B. Parsons was born the 10 of September, 1815.

Mary An Parsons was born March the 1, 1816.
Amie Parsons was born November 1st, 1817.
Martha T. Tilman was born April 13th, 1825, dau of Silas Tilman.

DEATHS;
Jacob M. Parsons was born August 29th, 1819.

George W. Parsons was born April 19th, 1821.

John W. Parsons was born January 3rd, 1824.
Elizabeth J. Parsons was born April 14th, 1825.

Newton B. Parsons born October 23rd, 1826.
Thomas T. Parsons was born February 16th, 1827.

Benjamin S. PArsons was born February 3rd, 1831.
Margaret C. Parsons was born December 17th, 1832.
Philip A. Parsons was born April 12th, 1835.
   (Copied by Helen C. Marsh, 1977)

     Ref: Roster and Soldiers, Tennessee Society DAR 1960-1970, Vol 2,
         page 348
     Ref: Pennsylvania Arch. 5th Series Vol 5, page 188
     Ref: Fisher Family Bible.
     Ref: Bedford County, Tennessee Cemetery Records by Marsh.

* * * * * * * * * *

DAVID FLOYD, SR.

Name: Rank: State Served:
David Floyd, Sr.   ---   ---------------
Born in Union District, South Carolina, died Bedford County, Tennessee, married
a Miss Norman, Jane (Elizabeth Jane). Both are buried in the Old Flat Creek
Cemetery, Flat Creek, Tennessee, withour gravemarkers.

No GSA Report from the National Archives, Washington, D.C.

    WILLIAM FLOYD FAMILY RECORDS
Original in possession of Mr. James Gore, Shelbyville, Tennessee.

Family Records of William Floyd as given to Charles E. Gowen in the Summer of
1904, when in his 84th year.
   Dave (David) FLoyd and wife, my great grandparents, came from Union
District, South Carolina, settled at what is now known as the Boyer's place about
one mile south of Flat Creek, Bedford County, Tennessee. Wife was a Norman, a
sister to Edward Gore's wife. Hence the Gore relationship. He raised a large
family and died (he and his wife) on the same day and were buried in one grave
at Flat Creek. Children are as follows: Johnathan, George, David, Enoch, Elijah,
Hosea Halcum, Peggy, Priscilla and Jane.
   Mr. Klyne Jack Keller, Madison, Tennessee, has a letter that states that
David Floyd, Sr.'s, parents were Enoch Floyd and Margaret Milton Floyd.
Family of William FLoyd:
   Jonathan married _____ Finney, went to Illinois.
   George married Annie Cox, daughter of Thomas Cox who died in 1860 in
       Mississippi and Peggy Allison who died in 1831 in
       Bedford County, Tennessee.
   David, born 1786, married Mary Magdaline Reagor, daughter of Anthony
       Reagor. David died 1856, both buried in Shook
       Cemetery, Bedford County, Tennessee.
   Enoch, married Ann Waters Shook who was born 1794 in Knox County,
       Tennessee. Enoch made a M.E. Preacher, went
       to Jackson County, Alabama. Ann was daughter
       of Wm. and Elender Waters Shook.
   Elijah, married Sallie Watson.
   Hosea Holcum, married Elizabeth Ann Couser. Hosea was killed by
       Yankee in Fayetteville, Tennessee, about 1864.
   Peggy (Margaret), married Jim Beavers. Buried on Cane Creek, Lincoln
       County, Tennessee, Will Book, page 110.
   Prescilla married John Davis.
   Jane married Norman Finney.
Jonathan, George and David, all in Battle of New Orleans, 1812.

Newton and Clemment Cannon to David Floyd, $500., Deed. Land situated on

78

head waters of Flat Creek of south side of Duck River, bordering Thomas Cox and John Allison.
David Floyd: 26 June 1809.

Ref: Records by Mr. Klyne Jack Keller, Madison, Tennessee.
Ref: Bedford County Court House, Deed Book B, page 20.

* * * * * * * * * *

NATHAN FRIZEL or FRIZZELL

Name:	Rank:	State Served:
Nathan Frizel or Frizzell	PVT	South Carolina

Born August 7, 1759 in Baltimore County, Maryland, died December 17, 1843 in Calloway County, Kentucky, married 1783 in North Carolina to Ruhama, born Feb 3, 1765, died March 29, 1840.

GSA: Nathan Frizzell, S.3380, South Carolina
Claim No. 7298: West Tennessee, Nathan Frizzell of Bedford County in the State of West Tennessee, who was a Private in the Company commanded by Captain Deason of the Regiment commanded by Colonel Marshall in the South Carolina Line for 1 year.

Nathan Frizel Records OK.

Inscribed on the Roll of West Tennessee Feby. 25, '_4, at the rate of 40 dollars, cents per annum, to commence on the 4th day of March 1831.

Certificate of Pension issued the 27 day of March 1833 and sent to J. McKisick, Shelbyville, Tennessee.

Arrears to the 4th of March 1833	$ 80.00
Semi-anl allowance ending 4 Sept	$ 20.00
	$100.00

Recorded by Daniel Boyd, Clerk   Revolutionary Claim
Book E Vol 7 page 28(78)   Act June 7, 1832.

Declaration:
Declaration in order to obtain the benefit of the Act of Congress passes 7th June 1832.

On this 14th day of August in the year of our Lord, one thousand eight hundred and thirty two, personally appeared in open court before John L. Neill, Samuel Phillips and John B. Armstrong, Esquires, gentlemen Justices of the Peace appointed to hold the Court of Pleas and Quarter Sessions for the County of Bedford in the State of Tennessee, now sitting, Nathan Frizzell, a resident of Bedford County and State aforesaid, aged seventy three years, and seven days, who being first duly sworn according to law, doth on his oath make the following declaration in order to obtain the benefit of the Act of Congress passed the 7th of June 1832.

That he entered the service of the United States under the following named Officers and served as herein stated, to wit, that he entered the service of the United States as a volunteer under Captain William Deason in what is now called Chesterfield District in the State of South Carolina, sometime in the month of October 1780 and was attached to a Regiment commanded by Colonel John Marshall, of General Sumpter's Brigade. He states they were not marched from that County or District any distance but was engaged in reconnoitring and acted as Rangers, and watching the movements of the Tories, until the following May, when he states Colonel Marshall's Regiment was attached to General Green's Army. He states he was marched with General Green's Army from Camden, South Carolina to the high hills of Santee by way of a little town called Statesville, from that on to the Eutaw Springs, where he states he was in an engagement against the British, who was under the command of Lord Roddin. He states that Colonel William Washington was taken prisoner at that engagement by the British. He states that the Company he belonged to was permitted to return after the Battle of the Eutaw Springs, after serving about eight months. He states that he was attached to General Sumpter's Brigade again and continued with him until Cornwallis was taken. He states he was engaged in several small skirmishes with the Tories, one at Regeley's Mill on Granney's Quarter Creek, one other at Rockey Mount on Catawba River and one other skirmish at Black

79

Creek with the Tories in Chesterfield District, South Carolina. And one small engagement, which should have been mentioned previously in this declaration, at the High Hill, two miles from Camden about the 1st of May 1781. Making in all a term of service of twelve months or there abouts. He further states that he has no documentary evidence whatever, and knows of no person whose testimony he can procure who can testify as to his service. And relinguishes all claims to a pension or annuity whatever except the present, and he declares that his name is not on the Pension Roll of any agency in the United States.

Interrogatories by the Court:

Q. 1st: When and in what year were you born?

A. I was born in Baltimore County in the State of Maryland, agreeable to my father's record on the 7th day of August 1759.

Q. 2nd: Have you any record of your age and if so, where is it?

A. I have a record of my age at my dwelling in this County, wrote in my Family Bible which record was taken from my father's Bible.

Q. 3rd: Where were you living when called into service? Where have you lived since the Revolutionary War? And where do you now live?

A. I was a citizen of Chesterfield District in the State of South Carolina when I volunteered under Captain William Deason. And after the Revolutionary War I moved to Anson County in the State of North Carolina, from that to Robeson (Robertson) County in the State of Tennessee about 1802, and from that I moved to Rutherford County in the same State and from there I removed to the County of Bedford in same State sometime in the year 1808 or 1809 where I have lived ever since, and where I now live.

Q. 4th: How were you called into service? Were you drafted? Were you a volunteer or were you a substitute, and id a substitute for whom?

A. I was a volunteer during the whole time I served.

Q. 5th: State the names of some of the Regular Officers, who were with you or the Troops where you served, such Continental and Militia Regiments as you can recollect.

A. I do not recollect the names of any Regular Officers, except Colonel William Washington. I saw Colonels Lee and Washington's Troops frequently.

Q. 6th: Did you ever receive a discharge and if so what has become of it?

A. I did receive a discharge in writing, signed by Colonel John Marshall, but I have lost or mislaid it many years ago and cannot produce it at this time.

Q. 7th: State the names of persons to whom you are known in your present neighborhood who can testify as to your character for veracity and their belief of your services as a Soldier of the Revolution.

A. The Rev. John Rushing, Captain John Deason, William Norvell, Esq., John C. Coldwell, Charles Taylor, Senr., and nathan Chaffin, Esq.

Sworn to in open court the day and year aforesaid.
Sworn in open Court 14th August 1832   Nathan Frizel
Jas. McKisick, Clk.

1835, age 75, Private, South Carolina.

Nathan Frizzell, 5-3- ----, Certificate No. 7298 3-7-1833 Pension.
Children:

1. Margaret, born Jan 17, 1783
2. Hester, born Dec 23, 1785, married Nathan Rushing
3. James, born Sept 21, 1787
4. Abraham, born Mar 15, 1790
5. William, born Feb 19, 1793, married Nancy Wilson
6. Isaac, born June 19, 1796, married Susannah Arnold
7. Martha, born Mar 27, 1799
8. Elizabeth, born Jan 4, 1802
9. Rebecca, born June 5, 1805
10. Jacob, born Jan 18, 1808, married Amelia (Millie) Morgan

Ref: GSA Report, Washington, D.C.

Ref: 1835 Bedford County, Tennessee Pension List.
Ref: Roster and Soldiers of DAR, Tennessee Blue Book, Vol 1, page 683.

* * * * * * * * * *

CHARLES GARMON

Name: Rank: State Served:
Charles Garmon   -----   ---------------
Born _____, died _____, married to Mary _____.

No GSA Report in Washington, D.C.

Ref: Susie Gentry, Nashville Monument

* * * * * * * * * *

JOHN GIBBEY

Name: Rank: State Served:
John Gibbey   PVT   Virginia
Born _____, died after 1834.

No GSA Report in Washington, D.C.

1834 P.L.W. Pension List
1835, age 78, PVT, Virginia Line.

Ref: 1834 P.L.W. Pension List.
Ref: 1835 Bedford County, Tennessee Pension List.

* * * * * * * * * *

THOMAS GORE

Name: Rank: State Served:
Thomas Gore   PVT   South Carolina
Born 1763, died after 1834

GSA: Thomas Gore, S.38746, South Carolina
Claim No. 18.056, West Tennessee, Thomas Gore, (aged 58) of Bedford County in the State of Tennessee, who was a Private in the Regiment commanded by Colonel Thompson of the South Carolina Line, for the term of 3 years, (from 1777).

Inscribed on the Roll of West Tennessee, at the rate of 8 dollars per month, to commence on the 2nd of April 1821.

Certificate of Pension issued the 18 of June 1822 and sent to John Mims, Esq., Shelbyville, Tennessee.

Arrears to 4th of March 1822 $ 88.76
Semi-anl allowance ending 4 Sept '22 (1822) $ 48.--
                                                $136.76

Recorded: Vol 10, page 195   Revolutionary Claim
                                                Act 18th March, 1818

District of West Tennessee
On this second day of April in the year of our Lord 1821, personally appeared in open court in the Court of Pleas and Quarter Sessions of Bedford County, being a Court of Record for the said County of Bedford, Thomas Gore, aged fifty eight years, and resident in said County, who being first duly sworn according to law, doth on his oath, make the following declaration, in order to obtain the provision made by the Acts of Congress of the 18th of March 1818 and the 1st May 1820, that he, said Thomas Gore, enlisted for the term of three years on the __ day of ___ in the year of our Lord 1777, in the State of South Carolina in the Company of Cavalry commanded by Captain David Hopkins in the 3rd Regiment commanded by Colonel William Thompson in the South Carolina Line on the Continental establishment, that he continued to serve in the said Corps for the term of three years, when he was discharged in the State of South Carolina in the year 1780.

That he was in the Battle of Sullivan's Island and of S_____ and that he has no other evidence was in his power of his said services excepting his own oath and the accompanying Certificate of Captain David Hopkins and Colonel Thompson. And in persuance of the Act of the first of May 1820 and do solemnly swear that I was a resident citizen of the United States on the 18th day of March 1818 and that I have not since that time, by gift, sale or in any manner disposed of any property or any part thereof, with intent thereby so to deminish it, as to bring myself with in the provisions of Act of Congress, entitled "An Act provided for certain persons, engaged in the Land and Naval Service of the United States during the Revolutionary War, passed on the 18th day of March 1818", and that I have not any property whatever besides my necessary wearing apparel, nor has any person in trust for me, any property of Securities or debts, not have I any income whatever.

His occupation is that of a farmer but having no land and on account of his age and consequent infirmities of body and mind, he cannot pursue his business so as to provide a necessary support, he has no family living with him, but has to depend upon the precarious bounty of his friends for the means of substance.

Sworn to and subscribed in open Court this day of ____ 1821.

Thomas (X) Gore

G.3. South Carolina
Thomas Gore
3rd South Carolina Regiment
commanded by Col. Wm. Thompson
Revolutionary War
Appears in a Book*
Copied from Rolls
of the Organization names above.
Date of enlistment Aug 23, 1776
Remarks: Omited Aug '79
Vol 9, page 119

* Original Roll, Office of
  Army Accounts.

Amt. of Continental and State Pay:
Days: 120
Amt.: 80 lbs.
Casualties: Prisoner of War or Parole
Remarks: Next Pay Roll on file
         Aug 1779.

G. 3. South Carolina
Thos. Gore
PVT (Capt. David Hopkins'
Co., 3rd Regiment, South
Carolina Continental Troops,
commanded by Col. Wm. Thompson)
Revolutionary War
Appears on Company Pay Roll
of the Organization named
above, for the month of _____
to 1 July 1779, commencement
to pay 1 March to what
time 1 July Amt. of time
for pay 4 months.
Amt of pay: $26.60

Ref: GSA Report, Washington, D.C.

* * * * * * * * * *

JOHN GIBBS

Name: Rank: State Served:
John Gibbs   PVT   Virginia
Born December --, 1765 in Pittsylvania County, Virginia, died September 28, 1843 in Breathitt, Kentucky, married 22 day of January 1782 to Hannah _____.

GSA: John Gibbs, W.2729, wife Hannah, Service Virginia.
Claim No. 19.191   West Tennessee, John Gibbs of Bedford County in the State of Tennessee, who was a Private in the Company commanded by Captain Farmer of the Regiment commanded by Colonel Rogers in the Virginia Line for 16 months and 12 days.

Inscribed on the Roll of West Tennessee at the rate of 54 dollars, 66 cents per annum, to commence on the 4th day of March, 1831.

Certificate of Pension issued the 14 day of August 1833 and sent to Thos. C. Whiteside, Shelbyville.

Arrears to the 4th of March $109.32
Semi-anl allowance ending 4 Sept $ 27.33
                                                     $136.65

Recorded by Dan'l Boyd, Clerk   Revolutionary Claim
Book E   Vol 7   page 79   Act June 7, 1832

Note on reverse side of Claim:
        Letter to A.B. Patrick Mar 31, 1843
        To paid Agt.   11 July 1842
        To Kentucky from 4 Sept 1842, 28 Sept 1843
Notification to Pension, Breathitt, KY.

No. 18810, John Gibbs, Bedford County, Tennessee
        From 1777, Private, 16 months and 12 days.
        $154.66 Farmer   Rogers, Virginia   Thomas C. Whiteside
                                                     Shelbyville, Tennessee

Declaration:
State of Tennessee]
                   ] Court of Pleas and Quarter Sessions.
Bedford County   ]

        On this 12th day of November 1832, personally appeared in open Court
before Samuel Phillips, John L. Neill and John B. Armstrong, Esqrs., Justices
appointed to hold the Court of Pleas and Quarter Sessions for the County
aforesaid, now sitting, John Gibbs, a resident of Bedford County in the State of
Tennessee, aged about seventy six years, who being first duly sworn according to
law, doth on his oath make the following declaration in order to obtain the
benefit of the Act of Congress passed the 7th June 1832. That he entered the
service of the United States under the following named Officers and served as
herein stated. He was born in Pittsylvania County, State of Virginia but the year
of his birth he cannot recollect positively but he is certain that he will be
seventy six years of age sometime in December (1832). His parents died when he
was very young and he was at the age of fifteen, boarded out as an apprentice in
Halifax County, Virginia. States that he entered the service of the United States
in the Revolutionary War sometime in the Spring or Summer of the year 1777 but
the particular month he cannot now recollect. As a volunteer under Colonel
Peter Rogers in Halifax County, Virginia for a term of three months, the name
of his Captain he does not remember. As soon as he volunteered, his Company
marched to Portsmouth, Virginia to guard and defend that place against the
British. He remained stationed at that place until the expiration of his three
months term of service when he was verbally discharged by his Captain. He
states that he remained at home until the latter part of August or first of
September 1778, when he again entered the service as a substitute for a man by
the name of Edmond Kelly, for nine months, in the Militia in Granville County,
North Carolina but before they serve any service, his Company was discharged
for a few months on furlough, but in a few weeks after they were dismissed upon
their furlough, an express came for them to meet at Hillsboro, North Carolina
and offering all of those who would agree to serve before their furlough express
pay for what time they had been on furlough agreeable to this express.

        This applicant and a large number of the Company to which he
belonged, which was commanded by Captain John Farrar, met at Hillsboro about
the first of October 1778, as well as he recollects when after remaining there a
short time probably a week or two for the purpose of organizing themselves and
making the necessary preparations for marching. They marched under the
command of Captain Farrar and Colonel Henry Dixon and Colonel Lytle to a
place called the Ten Mill Spring or the Mill House, within ten miles of
Charleston, South Carolina. They arrived at this place shortly before Christmas
and spent their Christmas there. They then took up their line of march to go to
the assistance of General Lincoln on the Savannah River between South Carolina
and Georgia. They arrived at a place called Perryville, sometime in January
1779, at which place Lincoln's Army was then stationed. Shortly after their
arrival at this place, this applicant with others of his Company were placed under
the command of Captain High, Major Thomas Donahoe and Major Armstrong,
Officers of General Lincoln's Army and sent in a detachment up the Savannah
River to Black Swamps where General Lincoln had an encampment, at the same

time some of Captain Farrar's Company were sent to Briar Creek to assist General Ash against the British, after remaining at Black Swamp a short time, this applicant was sent in a detachment under the above named Officers, still higher up the Savannah to Galfon's Mills, from this place the detachment to which he belonged was ordered to march under the same Officers to Charleston, South Carolina, to defend that place against the British, they arrived at Charleston sometime in the latter part of the Spring as well as this applicant recollects, it was in the month of May, shortly after they got into Charleston, they had a little engagement with the British under General Prevost, this was the first engagement that this applicant ... (page missing)... about ten weeks.

Several months afterwards, he entered the service of the Militia in Halifax County under Captain Long for three months as a substitute for a man by the name of Ervin Brannon. He marched under Captain Long to Yorktown to said General Washington against the British under the command of Lord Cornwallis. This applicant's Company arrived at Yorktown some two or three weeks as well as he recollects before the surrender of Cornwallis, when they arrived they found General Washington there and they were immediately set at work digging and throwing up entrenchments for the purpose of beseiging Cornwallis' Army, then in possession of the town. This applicant states that he saw General Washington frequently at this place and on one occasion while he was at work, he recollects that General Washington took his axe and worked a little while with it. He states that he was in the Battle of Yorktown but he took sick and left that place the day after the battle was fought and before the British marched out of town.

Shortly after the surrender of Cornwallis, this applicant's three months term of service expired and he was verbally discharged by Captain Long. This applicant states that he served his country in the Revolutionary War, including the different tours above stated about seventeen months. He further states that he has no documentary evidence of his service nor does he know any persons now living by whom he can make any proof of it. He never received any written discharge but the above mentioned from Major Armstrong which is lost or mislaid.

He was acquainted with all the American Officers mentioned in this declaration except General Green. He cannot now recollect the names of any Regular or Militia Regiments that he was in or acquainted with during his service. He states that he has no record of his age. He recollects that he was ...(illegible)... that... fifteen when bound out as before stated and he has kept his age from memory ever since. After the Revolutionary War, he moved from Virginia to North Carolina, from North Carolina to York County, South Carolina, then he removed back to the waters of the Yadkin, North Carolina, from thence to Kentucky, from thence to Bedford County, State of Tennessee where he has lived upwards of seven years and now lived. He is acquainted with Major William Guy, Major Murphree, Robert Clark and William Van Cleave, said ____ acquainted with said declarant states he ________ one certificate he cannot this time procure, all of whom will testify as to discharge and their belief of his services as a Revolutionary Soldier. He hereby relinguishes every claim to a pension or annuity whatever except the present and declares that his name is not on the Pension Roll of the agency of any State.
Sworn to in open court and subscribed 12 November 1832.
Jas. McKisick, Clk.   John (X) Gibbs

We, William Murphree, Robert Clark and William Van Cleave, residing in Bedford County, Tennessee, hereby certify that we are well acquainted with (and which has known a number of years), John Gibbs, who was subscribed and sworn to the above declaration, we believe him to be seventy six years of age or near that age as he states. He is a man of strict honesty and veracity and has always sustained that character since we became acquainted with him. He is reputed and believed to have been in the neighborhood where he resides, a Revolutionary Soldier and we fully concur in that opinion.
Sworn to and subscribed the day and year aforesaid.
Jas. McKisick, Clk.
                                                          William Murphree
                                                          Robt. Clark
                                                          Wm. Van Cleave

No. 943: Kentucky, Hannah Gibbs, dec'd, widow of John Gibbs, who served in the Revolutionary War in Virginia, was as a Private.

Inscribed on the Roll at the rate of 54 dollars, 66 cents per annum, to commence on the 18th of October 1848.

Certificate of Pension issued the 20 day of May 1852 and sent to Hon. J.C. Mason, House of Reps.

Ending 17th September 1850.

Recorded on Roll of Pensioners under Act passes July 29, 1848, page 174, Vol A.

State of Kentucky]
Morgan County   ] April, County Court, 1851

It was this day proven to the satisfaction of the Court, Hannah Gibbs, who has personally made application to the War Department for a pension, departed this life on the 7th day of September 1850 and that the said Hannah Gibbs left the following heirs as her legal and representatives, to wit, John Gibbs, Sally Weaver (late Sally Gibbs) and Nathan Gibbs, and it was also proven by John Gibbs and John Rose that they have been acquainted with John Gibbs and Hannah Gibbs for sixty years and that they knew them as man and wife up to the day of the death of said John Gibbs and that the said Hannah Gibbs, deceased, his widow up to the day of her death, all of which in order to be certified to the War Department.

Given under my hand and Seal of Office, this 8th day of May 1852.

F. Garnett, Clerk Cty Ct.

State of Kentucky]
Morgan County   ]

On this 29th day of March, one thousand eight hundred and fifty, personally appeared before the undersigned, Caleb Kash, a Justice of the Peace, in and for the County and State aforesaid, Hannah Gibbs, a resident of Morgan County, Kentucky, aged ninety five years, who being duly sworn according to law, doth on her oath make the following declaration, in order to obtain the benefit of the provisions made by the Act of Congress passed the 29th day of July 1848.

John Gibbs (formerly of the State of Tennessee) who was a Private of Infantry in the Army of the Revolution was entitled to receive a Pension of fifty four dollars and sixty six cents per annum during his natural life commencing on the 4th day of March 1831, according to an Original Certificate given at the Office of the United States on the 14th day of August 1833 and recorded in the Pension Office, Book E   Vol 7   page 79.

She further declares that she was married to the said John Gibbs on the 22 day of January, seventeen hundred and eighty two, that her husband the said John Gibbs died on the 18th day of October 1848, that she was not married to him prior to his leaving the service but the marriage took place previous to the second of January eighteen hundred, viz: At the time above stated. She further swears that she is now and said widow and that she has never before made any application for a pension.

Sworn to and subscribed on the day and year above written before.

Caleb Kosh, J.P.M.C.   Hannah (X) Gibbs

In 1840, he was in house of Ebenezer F. Gibbs.

> Ref: GSA Report, Washington, D.C.
> Ref: Widow's Pension Application.
> Ref: 1840 Bedford County, Tennessee Pension List.
> Ref: A1

* * * * * * * * * *

SAMUEL GRAY

Name:	Rank:	State Served:
Samuel Gray	PVT	North Carolina

Born April 22, 1752, died March 23, 1837 in Lincoln County, Tennessee, married on 19th August 1773 to Rachel (Scales).

GSA: Samuel Gray, W.7574, North Carolina, wife Rachel.

Claim No. 13536: West Tennessee, Samuel Gray of bedford County in the State of

Tennessee, who was a Private in the Company commanded by Captain Walton of the Regiment commanded by Colonel Cleg---- in the North Carolina Line for 13 months.

Inscribed on the Roll of W. Tennessee, at the rate of 43 dollars, 33 cents per annum, to commence on the 4th day of March, 1831.

Certificate of Pension issued the 16th day of May 1835 and sent to A. Yell, Shelbyville.

Arrears to the 4th of March $ 86.66
Semi-anl allowance ending 4 Sept $ 21.00
                                         $108.32

Recorded by Daniel Boyd, Clerk   Revolutionary Claim
Book E   Vol 7   page 79   Act June 7, 1832

State of Tennessee]   November Term, 1832
Bedford County   ]

This the 6th day of November 1832, personally appeared in open court before the Justices of the Court of Pleas and Quarter Sessions for the County of Bedford, not sitting, Samuel Gray, a resident of the County of Bedford and State of Tennessee, aged about 81 years of age, who being first duly sworn according to law, doth on his oath make the following declaration in order to obtain the benefit of the Act of Congress passed June the 7th 1832.

I entered the service of the United States as a volunteer for the term of six months under Captain Jesse Walton cometime in the month of November 1778, as well as now recollected in the County of Wilkes in the State of North Carolina, soon after my enlistment, we all marched to the frontier to guard the settlements against the Cherokees. Captain Walton's Company was marched into the Cherokee Nation, or most of them, myself with a few others, was attached to Captain Joseph Herndon's Company of Rangers or Spies, who were on constant duty in guarding the frontier Settlement of Wilkes and Burke County on the yadkin River. After my time of service had expired, we were permitted to return home, for this term of service, I received no written discharges.

My next term of service was in the year ____ as well as I now recollect, I was drafted for three months and was attached to Captain Richard Allen's Company. We were attached to Colonel Cleveland's Regiment, we were ordered to take up the line of march for King's Mountain, we were joined at the Pleasant Gardens on our route to King's Mountain, of the command of Colonel Campbell, from the head of Halston from which place we marched direct to meet Colonel Fergason. My Company was in the engagement, but I was on the morning of the engagement, detained with a few others at Camp, and did not join a Company until the engagement was ended. From this place we were ordered to guard the prisoners that was taken at the Battle of King's Mountain. We took them to Salem or the Maravian Tavern, where I remained as guard until the expiration of my time of service, when I was discharged.

Soon after my return, we were ordered to join General Rutherford for a term of thirty days, under Captain Beverly, we joined the Commanding Guard near Salisburg at the mouth of Little Rocky River, we remained herein on duty until the expiration of one term of service. When we were permitted to return to our homes in Wilkes County.

Sometime in the Summer of the year 1778 or 79, as well as now recollected, I was drafted for a term of three months. I was attached to Captain Joel Lewis' Company, who was attached to the command of Major Hartgroves who marched through Salem and to Cross Creek, when we remained in that section of the country, guarding against the Tories who were extremely troublesome, this service in that section of the State and in the edge of South Carolina. I was discharged at the end of my term of service from Major Hartgrove, which is lost or mislaid, so that I cannot have now the benefit of it.

Sometime after I volunteered under Captain Richard Allen who was commanded by Colonel Cleveland, they marched to New River, against some Tories and horse thieves, under the command of a certain Captain Cagle, we drove him out of that part of the country, he was ____ afterwards taken by one party and hung. This expedition lasted about ten or fifteen days. I was on duty, one or two other short trips but the time or particular service, I can not now recollect the whole term of service, which I can distinctly recollect was upward of thirteen months.

I know of no Regular Officers except those mentioned and I am now unable to say that they _____, I mean I was different times under Colonel Cleveland Campbell, Major Hartgrove and General Rutherford, I have no written discharges of my services. My John Gray and Old Captain Smith of Franklin County. They give them certificates, as to my service, my brother testified to all my service having been with me, and further to and or two campaigns.

I hereby relinguish every claim whatever to a pension or annuity except the present and declare that my name is not on the Pension Roll of the agency of any State or Territory.
Sworn and subscribed the day and year aforesaid.
Jas. McKisick, Clk.   Samuel Gray

No. 4327, Tennessee, Rachel Gray, widow of Samuel Gray, N.C., who was a Pensioner under Act 1832, who died on the 23rd of March 1837, of Lincoln County, in the State of Tennessee, who was a Private in the Company commanded by Captain Walton of the Regiment commanded by Colonel _____ in the North Carolina Line for 13 months.

Inscribed on the Roll of Pulaski, at the rate of 43 dollars, 33 cents per annum to commence on the 23rd day of March, 1837.

Certificate of Pension issued the 25 day of February 1846, and sent to Hon. G.W. Jones, House of Representatives.
Arrears to the 4th of Sept 1845 $_____
Semi-anl allowance ending in March $_____
                                                     $_____

Recorded by D. Brown, Clerk   Revolutionary Claim
Book C   Vol 1   page 198   Act July 4, 1836
                                             Section 3.

Declaration:
In order to obtain the benefit of the Act of Congress of the 7th July 1838, entitled "An Act granting half pay and pension to certain widows".
State of Tennessee]
Bedford County   ]
On this 6th day of October A.D., 1845, personally appeared before the Worshipful in County Court of said County, Rachel Gray, a resident of Lincoln County in the State of Tennessee, aged eighty six years, who being first duly sworn according to law, doth on his oath make the following declaration in order to obtain the benefit of the provision made by the Act of Congress passed July 7, 1838, entitled "An Act granting half pay and pensions to certain widows." That she is the widow of Samuel Gray, who was a Private in the Army of the Revolution and as such was placed upon the Pension Rolls of the United States as appears from his Pension Certificate here to appended.

She further declares that she was married to the said Samuel Gray on the 19th day of August 1773 (in the year seventeen hundred and seventy three) that her said husband, the said Samuel Gray, died on the 23rd day of March 1839. That she was married to him prior to his entering the service and previous to the first day of January, seventeen hundred and ninety four. (viz)

At the time above mentioned, sworn to and subscribed on the day and year above written, in open Court before
W.B. Rhea, Chairman   Rachel (X) Gray
Peter G. McMullin
Charles H. Edmondson
Justices, holding the County Court of the said
Lincoln County in the State of Tennessee.

State of Tennessee]
Bedford County   ]
I, William Neeld, a Justice of the Peace, in and for said County of Lincoln, do hereby certify that Austin Gray, personally appeared before me this day and made oath in due form of oath, he is the son of Samuel Gray and Rachel Gray, that Samuel Gray, his father, drew a pension under the Act 7th June 1832, as a Private in the Army of the Revolution, that his father, Samuel Gray, is now dead, that he died the 23rd of March 1837, that his mother, Rachel Gray, is or

has applied to the War Department in order to draw a pension under the Act of Congress passed the 7th July 1838, granting pensions to certain widows and that in order to draw a pension under said Act, that the applicant must make the best proof of her marriage before the 1st of January 1794, and the said Austin Gray now makes oath on the Holy Evangelist of Almighty God that from the best information and only information he has ever obtained from his father and mother, Samuel Gray and Rachel Gray and from the Family Record of his father which record he says is in his father's own handwriting, that the said Austin Gray was born the 10th of February 1788. He further states that he has four sisters now living, all of which is older than himself and which record of his father, which he has this day exhibited before me show their births to be as follows:

        Mary Gray was born 19th September, 1774
        Margery Gray was born 12th December, 1776
        Elizabeth Gray was born 24th December, 1779
        Frances Gray was born 5th September, 1782

and the record also shows the said Austin Gray was born the 10th February, 1788. Sworn to and subscribed before me in Lincoln County, Tennessee this 9th day of February 1846.

Wm. Neeld, Justice of the Peace for   Austin Gray
Lincoln County, Tennessee.

State of Tennessee]
Bedford County   ]
      I, Henry Kelso, Clerk of the County Court of said County, do certify that William Neeld is a Magistrate as above and that the foregoing signature purporting to be his and genuine.
      In testimony of whereof I have here unto set my hand and affixed my Seal of Office this 10th day of February 1846.

                              Henry Kelso, Clerk

SAMUEL GRAY BIBLE RECORD

Bible is in the possession of Mrs. William Medearis Smith, Fayetteville, Tennessee. Publisher Mathew Carey, Philadelphia October 27th 1802.
Family Record:
William M. Smith was bornd in the year of our Lord July the 10, 1813
John H. Smith was bornd December the 12, 1814
Sary Smith was bornd January the 30, 1817
Austin G. Smith was bornd December the 25, 1818

Samuel Grays Book Bornd Aprile 22, 1752

Family Record:
Marriages:
Austin Gray was bornd in the year of our Lord February the 10, 1788
Poley Gray his wife was bornd April the 22 1792 and was marred November the
        30, 1815
Darkis B. Gray was born the 26 of December 1816
Margery Gray was marred October the 8, 1817
Saray Gray was marred the 8 of January 1818

Marriages:
Martain Gray was bornd January the 6, 1795
Poley his wife was bornd January the 15, 1815
Martain Gray was marred the 27 of August 1816
Elizabeth Gray was bornd June the 7, 1817
James C. Gray was bornd in the year of our Lord the December the 26 1818
Saley G. Gray was bornd March the 16, 1821

Family Record:
Mary Gray was born September 19th, 1774
Margery Gray was born December 12th, 1776
Elizabeth Gray was born December 24th 1779
Frances Gray was born September 5th 1782
Austin Gray was born February 10th 1789
Salley Gray was born March 13th 1791

Martin Gray was born January 6th 1795
<u>Dopson</u> <u>deacon</u> was born May the 10 1808

Births:
Dorkis B. Gray was bornd December 26, 1816
Elsia B. Gray was bornd Aprile 2, 1819
Fanny B. Gray was born in the year of our Lord   October the 18 1820
Thomas C. Gray was bornd August the 24, 1822
Mary An Gray was born May the May 22, 1824
Enos h Gray was bornd May the 24, 1826
N. Aklin Gray   March 20, 1828
Rachel Gray bornd febary the 20, 1831
Saley Gray was bornd June 16, 1833
Elsibeth Gray was bornd May 25, 1835

Births:
Rachel Cheshur was born September 3the 1801
Samuel Cheshur was born August 12th 1803
A Love Rey milknees Gray was born May the 21 1812
Nancy Cheser was bornd february the 15 1813
Margery Melinda Cheser was bornd April the 18, 181_
Mathew Cheser Previt was bornd August 14, 1834

Deaths:
the age of James Meek sons James C. Meek was bornd in the year of our lord
          November the 10, 1818
Rachel 24
James Blackwell was born the 6 of November 186_

Deaths:
May frost 1774
Mary Chesser Eldest daughter of Samuel and Rachel Gray, departed this Life
          March 18th, 1847 in her seventy third year.
Marge Meeks deceased on the 21 of December 1847 and was buried on the 1 of
          January 1848.
Samuel Gray died on the 23 of March 1837, aged 85, if he had lived to the 24 of
          April 1837.

          Ref: GSA Report, Washington, D.C.
          Ref: Widow's Application for Pension
          Ref: DAR 1942 Yearbook, page 102
          Ref: Samuel Gray's Bible Record
          Ref: A 1

* * * * * * * * * *

ELIJAH GREEN

Name:	Rank:	State Served:
Elijah Green	PVT	North Carolina

Born 1752 Ireland, died 1842 Bedford County, Tennessee, buried in New Hope
Church Cemetery at Fairfield, Tennessee, with a Military Marker.

No GSA Report in Washington, D.C.

Lived in Orange County, North Carolina during the Revolutionary War. Served as
Private under Captain William Williams, 7th Orange County Militia, under Colonel
Butler. Married _____ _____.
Children: Willis, born August 14, 1798, died February 22, 1858, married
          Catherine Humphreys.

Elizabeth Green, married John M. Keller, son of Jacob Keller
Sallie Green, married M.S. Byers

Ref: Susie Gentry
Ref: Nashville Monument
Ref: DAR, Tennessee Blue Book, Roster and Soldiers, Vol 1, page 737
Ref: History of the Keller Family, Vol 1 by K. Jack Keller
Ref: Cemetery Records of Bedford County, Tennessee by Marsh

* * * * * * * * * *

ALEXANDER GREER

Name: Rank: State Served:
Alexander Greer   PVT   Virginia
Born 1752 Albermarle County, Virginia, died February 1810 near Big Spring,
Bedford County, Tennessee, married Jennie Bingham (Jane Bigham). No grave
markers in the Big Spring Cemetery. He made his location near Pleasant Grove
in 1783. A first settler.
    Alexander Greer was a son of Andrew Greer and Ruth (Kincaid) Greer.
Children of Alexander and Jennie Greer:
    1. James Greer, died young
    2. Polly (Vance) Greer, born 1787, died December 8, 1854 in Arkansas
                        and married James McKisick
    3. Minerva (Hall) Greer, died 1833 of cholera, married Dr. James G.
                        Whitney
    4. Catharine (M.) Greer, died January 2, 1836, married James R. White
    5. Louisa (B.) Greer, died 1824-31, married Nathan Evans
    6. Betsey Greer, died before 1831, married Richard S. Williamson
    7. Jane B. Greer, married Joseph McKisick
    8. Joseph Greer, died before 1841
    9. (David) Alexander Greer, born December 30, 1796, died 1868
    10. Andrew Greer

Ref: Sevier's Regiment, King's Mountain
Ref: DAR Patriot Index
Ref: McCown
Ref: King's Mountain, page 230 & 995
Ref: Bedford County Deed Book CC, page 276 and 277. Dated 11 May
          1831

* * * * * * * * * *

JAMES HALEY

Name: Rank: State Served:
James Haley   PVT   Virginia
Born 1757 Lunenburg County, Virginia, died October 27, 1841 Bedford County,
Tennessee, married ca 1778 in Virginia to _____ Haynes, who was born about
1760 probably in Charlotte County, Virginia and died before 1814 probably in
Bedford County, Tennessee. James Haley has a Military Marker placed in the
Burns Cemetery, Bedford County, Tennessee.

GSA: James Haley, S.4316, Virginia
Claim No. 25336: West Tennessee, James Haley, Davidson County, in the State of
Tennessee, who was a Private in the Regiment commanded by Captain Dixon of
the Regiment commanded by Colonel Lewis in the Virginia Line for 6 months.
    Inscribed on the Roll of West Tennessee at the rate of 20 dollars, __
cents per annum, to commence on the 4th of March 1831.
    Certificate of Pension issued the 27 fay of Decr. 1833 and C.A. Harris,
present.

Arrears to the 4th of Sept $50.00
Semi-anl allowance ending 4 March $10.00
                                                $60.00

Recorded by Daniel Boyd, Clerk   Revolutionary Claim
Book E   Vol 7   page 83   Act June 7, 1832

Dead: Paid at the Treasury under the Act of April 6th 1838 from March 4th to
         October 27th 1841   Ag - Notified July 9, 1842

Declaration:
         Declaration in order to obtain the benefit of the Act of Congress passed
the 7 day of June 1832. State of Tennessee, Davidson County, on the 25 day of
October 1832, personally appeared in open court before William Williams, Jesse
Whorton and Enock P. Connel, Esquires, Justices of the Court of Pleas and
Quarter Sessions for the said County of Davidson at Nashville, now sitting, James
Haley, a resident of Davidson County, Tennessee, who being first duly sworn
according to law doth on his oath make the following declaration in order to
obtain the benefit of the Act of Congress passes June the 7 day 1832, that he
was born in the State of Virginia and raised in Lunenburg County and is now
about seventy five years of age and was born in 1757 agreeable to the record of
my father. That he entered the service of the Revolutionary War under the
following named Officers and served ...(illegible)... stated about the first day of
March the year not recollected. I enlisted as a Minute Man for twelve months
under Captain Robert Dickson, Alexander Winn, Lieutenant and Peter Jones,
Ensign and Charles Lewis, First Colonel and Haynes Morgan, 2nd Colonel. We
met at Lunenburg Court House about the first day of May and was ordered to
march to Wake County, North Carolina, against the Tories. We marched to
Kemps' Ferry on Rone Oake then crossed Fishing Creek in Halifax County, North
Carolina. We were then ordered back to Virginia by an Officer, I think John
Blarnes, then marched to Petersburg, then to Co---ham on James River, then to
Williamsburg from thence to Gwin's Island to oppose the British and Governor
Dunsmore, who had robbed the magazine and gone to the British on Gwin's Island
where we drove the British and Dunsmore from the island and caught thirty seven
head of horses and two tinders, one of those tinders had a match left in, hereby
the British then blew up the barge and killed two of our men. We also took one
woman and a little boy about ten years old. The woman said she was the wife of
Captain that commanded the Outer Ship or Guard Ship in this expedition. I did
not go to the island myself because I had not had the small pox but three of my
men went to Gwin's Island, William Parrott, Joseph Billiss and John Cunningham.
I, myself, was in sight also and staid there about one month. Dunsmore went up
the Potomac, were then marched up the Potomac to North Hampton County and
then returned home about the first day of September. I do not recollect whether
I received a discharge or not but I received my pay, thirty two dollars at
Lunenburg Court House in Virginia. And again in August 1781, I was drafted to
oppose Lord Cornwallis in Virginia and about the 18 day of August, I
rendezvoused at Lunenburg Court House under the command of Captain Roberson
and James Vaughn Lieutenant and John Holcom Colonel. We then marched to
Petersburg then to Swan Point where we were stationed a short time. Colonel
Holcom gave me a furlough to go home, then John Smithson called on me to help
him to collect beef-cattle to drive to the Army and before we got ready to start,
Cornwallis had surrendered to the American Army and I never joined the Army
again, neither did I receive any pay nor did I receive any discharge. In 1792 and
in 1806, I moved to the State of Tennessee and have lived in Davidson County
where I now live many years past. There is no person in Tennessee that I know
of by whom I can prove my service except Mr. Richard Watkins whose deposition
is here inclosed. I hereby relinguish all claims whatever to a pension or annuity
except the present and further declares that his name is not on the Pension Roll
of the Agency of any State.
Sworn to and subscribed the day and date above.   James Haley
Test. Henry Ewing, Clerk of
Davidson County Court

         We, Guy McFadden, Clergyman, residing in Davidson County, and
William H. Nance, residing in the same, do hereby certify that we are well
acquainted with James Haley, who has subscribed and sworn to the above
declaration, that we believe him to be seventy five years of age. That we have
no doubts that he was a Revolutionary Soldier as stated in his declaration and

that he is a man of truth and honesty and entitled to the same.

Sworn to and subscribed in aforesaid   Guy McFadden
October 25, 1832,   William H. Nance
Test: Henry Ewing, Clk. of
Davidson County Court.

State of Tennessee]
Davidson County   ]
          Court of Pleas and Quarter Sessions, October Term A.D., 1832, and the
said Court   hereby declare their opinion after the investigation of the matter
and after putting the interrogatories prescribed by the War Department.   That
the above named applicant was a Soldier of the Revolutionary Army and served
as he states and the COurt further certifies that it appears to them that Guy
McFadden, who has signed the preceeding Certificate, is a clergyman in the
County and State aforesaid and that William H. Nance who has also signed the
same, a Justice of the Peace for said County and residents of said County and
are respectable person whose statement are entitled to full faith and credit.
Signed in Open Court, October 25th, 1832.

                                                        E.P. Connell
                                                        J. Whorton

          James Haley, born 1757 in Lunenbury County, Virginia, died in Bedford
County, Tennessee on October 27, 1841.   Married _____ Haynes (Hanes, one of
five daughters) about 1778.   She was born about 1760, probably in Charlotte
County, Virginia and died 1814 in probably Bedford County, Tennessee.
Service: Enlisted as Minute Man from Lunenburg County, Virginia, under Captain
Robert Dickson, Lt. Alex. Winn, Ensign Peter Jones, 1st Colonel Charles Lewis,
2nd Colonel Haynes Morgan, marched to Wake County, North Carolina, against
Tories.   Drafted in 1781, under command of Colonel Roberson and James Vaughn.
Children:
          1. Edward Taylor Haley, born 1779, married Susanna (Susan) Pratt
          2. Woodson Haley, born about 1782, married Polly Neill on March 29, 1809
                              in Williamson County, Tennessee
          3. Polly (Mary) B. Haley, born about 1785, married Henry Clanton on
                              January 26, 1816 in Davidson County, Tennessee
          4. William W. Haley, born about 1790, married Wincy W. Lavender on
                              August 30, 1820 in Williamson County, Tennessee

          Ref: GSA Report, Washington, D.C.
          Ref: Texas Society DAR Roster Revolutionary Ancestors, Vol II, page
                              910

                    * * * * * * * * * *

BARZILLIA HARRISON

Name: Rank: State Served:
Barzillia Harrison   PVT   North Carolina
Born ca 1754, died 1817 in Bedford County, Tennessee, married 12th December
1775 to Ann _____, in Bedford County, Virginia.

GSA: Barzillia Harrison, R.4675, North Carolina, wife Ann.
State of Tennessee]
Bedford County   ]
          On this 12th day of March 1844, personally appeared before me, James
Foster, a Justice of the Peace for the County aforesaid, Ann Harrison, a resident
of the County, and State aforesaid, aged ninety years and thirty days, who being
first duly sworn sccording to law, doth on her oath, make the following
declaration in order to obtain the benefit of the provision made by the Act of
Congress passes July 4th 1836.   That she is the widow of Barzillia Harrison, who
was a Private in the Drafted Militia of the State of North Carolina, in the
Revolution, as a drafted Militia Man, in the month of January 1781, but the day
of the month she cannot remember, that he entered the service in the Company
command by Samuel Dyer and William Adkin Lieutenant.   His Field Officers she
is unable to specify.   She thinks he was in the army commanded by General

Gates. Her said husband continued in the service under the same Company Officers, eight months, and as well as she remembers, he served under one term of engagement, but she is certain as to the length of the term of his service. Her said husband resided in Surry County, North Carolina when he was drafted and entered the service, and was mustered into service, according to the best of her recollection, at Surry Court House. She states that her said husband was in the Battle of Camden, as she always understood from him, and as she always believed. She is unable to state the County through which her husband marched, not having been along with him in his marches. She has no documentary evidence in support of her claim to a pension. She further declares that she was married to the said Barzillia Harrison on the 12th day of December, 1775, which date she is able to state positively and accurately, she believes, from a record of her marriage in her possession, made by her said husband in his own handwriting, shortly after it took place, that her husband , the aforesaid Barzillia Harrison, died in Bedford County in the State of Tennessee, where he had removed, he died in 1817, but she cannot state the day or month of his death. Her memory not serving her and having no record of the date and she states that she has remained a widow every since the death of her said husband, as will more fully appear by reference to the proof accompanying this declaration.
Sworn to and subscribed on the day and year above written before me.
James Foster, J.P.   Ann (X) Harrison
for said County.

State of Tennessee]
Bedford County   ]
        I, James Foster, a Justice of the Peace of the County aforesaid, certify that, Ann Harrison, appeared before me, at her residence on this day and date above specified and made the foregoing declaration, being too aged and infirm to go to Court to make it. Given under my hand this 12th day of March 1844.
                                        James Foster, J.P.
                                        for said County.

State of Tennessee]
Bedford County   ]
        On this 29th day of September 1846, personally before me, James Foster, an acting Justice of the Peace in and for the County, Mrs. Ann Harrison, a resident of said County, aged ninety two years, who doth on her oath make the following declaration in order to obtain the benefit of the provision made by the Act of Congress passed July 4th 1836, and July 7th 1838 and 3rd March 1843 and 17th June 1844, that she is the widow of Barzilla Harrison, who was a Soldier from Surry County, North Carolina in the War of the Revolution and served as stated by her in a former declaration which she made in 1843 or 1844, which declaration was sent to the War Office by C. Ready. She further declares that she was married to the said Barzillia Harrison on the 12th December, seventeen hundred and seventy five in Bedford County, Virginia, that her husband, the said Barzillia Harrison died in April 1817.   That since his death, she has not intermarried but still remains his widow. She further states that the annexed family record is in the James Record which contains the correct dates of her marriage and of the births of her children and is in the hand writing of her husband, the said Barzillia Harrison. That she also here attaches a certificate of Samuel (Thomas,?) certifying to her husband having taken the Oath of Allegiance, that the Officers under whom he has served was Captain Samuel Dyer, Lt. William Atkins.
Sworn to and subscribed the dates above   Ann (X) Harrison
James Foster, (J.P.)

State of Tennessee]
Bedford County   ]
        I, James Foster, an acting Justice of the Peace in and for said County do hereby certify that I am well acquainted with Mrs. Ann Harrison, who has this day appeared and made oath to the above declaration, before me, that she is a woman of truth and veracity that full faith and credit is due and ought to be given to her statements and I further certify that she is the same Ann Harrison who was qualified some three or four years ago to a declaration in order to get a

pension and further I certify that from old age and bodily infirmity, she is not able to attend the Court in order to make this declaration in open court. This 29 September 1846.

James Foster (J.P.)

Barzillia Harrison, born ca 1754, died April 1817 in bedford County, Tennessee married 12 December 1775 in Bedford County, Virginia to Ann ____, born ca 1754, died after 1846 (aged 92).

> Ref: GSA Report, Washington, D.C.
> Ref: Widow's Application for Pension
> Ref: Tennessee DAR 1940 Yearbook, page 81

* * * * * * * * * *

WILLIAM HARRISON

Name:	Rank:	State Served:
William Harrison	---	North Carolina

Born about 1749 in North Carolina, died January 22, 1833 in Bedford County, Tennessee.

> Ref: Texas Society DAR Roster Revolutionary Ancestors,
> Vol I & II, page 972.

* * * * * * * * * *

JOSEPH HASTINGS

Name:	Rank:	State Served:
Joseph Hastings	Patriot	North Carolina

Born November 25, 1757 in North Carolina, died January 30, 1816 in Bedford County, Tennessee, married Susannah Holloway, born 1755, died August 29, 1842. Both buried with markers in the New Hope Church Cemetery, Bedford County, Tennessee.

Patriot Services, Patriot, married to Susannah Holloway, born 1755 in North Carolina and died August 29, 1842.
Children:

1. Martha, born 1779, married Thomas Sykes Cates
2. Joseph, born November 18, 1782, married Nancy Pittman
3. Henry, born 1783, married Sarah ____.
4. Robert, born February 7, 1785, married Jane Pittman
5. Stephen
6. Susannah, married Samuel Pollock

"Joseph Hastings born November 25, 1757 North Carolina, died Jan 30, 1816 in Bedford County, Tennessee, married Susannah Holloway in 1778, born 1755 in North Carolina and died August 25, 1842 in Bedford County, Tennessee."

> Ref: Tennessee "Blue Book" Roster and Soldiers, DAR, Vol I, page 809
> Ref: Cemetery Records of Bedford County, Tennessee by Marsh

* * * * * * * * * *

ABRAHAM HELTON

Name:	Rank:	State Served:
Abraham Helton	PVT	North Carolina

Born ca 1752 in Orange County, North Carolina, died after 1840 Bedford County, Tennessee.

GSA: Abraham Helton, S.4353, North Carolina.
Claim No. 13965: West Tennessee, Abraham Helton, Senr., of Bedford County, in the State of Tennessee, who was a Private in the COmpany commanded by Captain Rogers in the Regiment commanded by Colonel O'Neal in the North Carolina Line for 7 months.

Inscribed on the Roll of West Tennessee at the rate of 23 dollars, 33

94

cents per annum, commence on the 4th day of March, 1831.

Certificate of Pension issued the 18th day of July 1833 and sent to J. McKisick, Shelbyville.

Arrears to the 4th of March	$46.66
Semi-anl allowance ending 4 Sept	$11.66
	$58.32

Recorded by Daniel Boyd, Clerk	Revolutionary Claim
Book E Vol 7 page 57	Act June 7, 1832

Declaration:

Declaration in order to obtain the benefit of the Act of Congress passed the 7th June 1832.

State of Tennessee]
Bedford County   ]

On this 7th day of February in the year of our Lord, one thousand eight hundred and thirty three, personally appeared in open court before the worshipful Samuel Phillips, William McClure and John B. Armstrong, Esquires, gentlemen Justices of the Peace, appointed to hold the Court of Pleas and Quarter Sessions for said County, now sitting, Abraham Helton, Senr., a resident of said County, aged _____, said deponent states agreeable to the information he recalled from his parents, eighty years and upwards, who after being sworn according to law, doth on his oath make the following declaration in order to obtain the benefit of the Act of Congress passed the 7th June 1832. That he entered the service of the United States under the following named Officers and served as herein stated, viz, that he entered the service of the United States in the County of Orange and the State of North Carolina, he thinks in the month of September 1780, as a volunteer in a Company of Volunteers under the command of Captain William Rogers in a Regiment commanded by Colonel William O'Neal in General Butler's Brigade of North Carolina Militia and was mustered into service at Ramsour's Mill on Deep River in Chatham County in said State, and after remaining there some time, was taken sick and permitted to return home. He says he recovered his health in a short time and was ordered out again and marched to Hillsborough in said County of Orange to assist in conveying and guarding some Tory prisoners from that place to Harrisburg in Granville County, North Carolina, which he did and saw them confined in a jail at that place. He states he was then marched back into Orange County and in a few ·days was marched out again and placed under the command of Lieutenant Harmon and were marched on a scouting or spying expeditions through Randolph and Chatham Counties in said State of North Carolina, in order as he was informed, assertain the movements of the Tories, who were at that time very numerous in that section of the County, and that he remained in service until the next Spring, he thinks in April or May 1781 but from the great length of time, he is not certain which. Deponant further states that from old age and the consequent loss of memory, he is not able at this period of his life to swear to the precise length of time he was in the service of the United States but according to the best of his recollection, he served not less than seven months in actual service for which he claims a pension. And that he has no documentary evidence whatever and that he knows of no person whose testimony he can procure who can testify as to his service, except what he can prove by the testimony of Henry Moore, Senr., and Martin Shofner. And declares that his name is not on the Pension Roll of any agency in the United States to his knowledge and that he hereby relinguishes all claim to any pension or annuity, except the present.

Interrogatories by the Court

Q. 1st: Where and in what year were you born?
A.   I was born in Orange County and State of North Carolina, agreeable to what my parents informed me, but the month and year, I know nothing about.
Q. 2nd: Have you any record of your age, and if so where is it?
A.   I have no record of my age whatever.
Q. 3rd: Where were you living when called into service? Where have you lived since the Revolutionary War and where do you now live?
A.   I was a citizen of Orange County and State of North Carolina during

the time I was in service and remained a citizen until after the close of the war and until the year 1806, when I removed to Bedford County, Tennessee, where I have lived ever since and where I now live.

Q. 4th: How were you called into service, were you drafted, did you volunteer, or were you a substitute and is a substitute, for whom?

A.   I was a volunteer altogether.

Q. 5th: State the names of some of the Regular Officers who were with the troops where you served, such Continental and Militia Regiments as you can recollect, and the general circumstances of your service.

A.   I was not acquainted with any Regular Officers, nor do I recollect the names or number of any particular Regiment.

Q. 6th: Did you ever receive a discharge, and if so, what has become of it?

A.   I never did receive a discharge in writing.

Q. 7th: State the names of persons to whom you are known in your present neighborhood who can testify as to your character for veracity, and their opinion of your service as a Soldier of the Revolution.

A.   Mr. Henry Moore, Thomas Cummings, Thomas Cook, Martin Shofner, John Davis and _____ _____, but have no intimate acquaintance with any clergyman whose attendance I can at this time procure.

Sworn to in Open Court this 7th day of February 1833.

Jas. McKisick, Clk.   Abram (X) Helton

State of Tennessee   ]
Bedford County Court]

This day, Henry Moore, Senr., personally appeared in open court and made oath in dur form of law, and saith, that he was a Soldier of the Revolution and while serving as such, he became acquainted with Abraham Helton, who subscribed and was qualified to the foregoing declaration at Ramsour's Mill in the .....(unfinished statement)......

State of Tennessee]
Bedford County   ]

This day, Martin Shofner, Senr., a resident of said County, aged upwards of seventy four years, who after being sworn according to law, deposeth and saith that sometime, he thinks in the year 1780, he said deponent, was in the service of the United States, where he became acquainted with and knew Abraham Helton, Senr., at Ramsour's Mill in Chatham County in the State of North Carolina, and that said Helton was then a Soldier in the American Army, but how long, he remained in service, deponent does not know, deponent further says that he has been well acquainted with said A. Helton in Bedford County for a number of years and believes his character for veracity to be unimpeachable.

Sworn to and subscribed this 18th day of April 1833.

Jacob Coble, (J.P.)   Martin Shofner (Seal)

I, Jacob Coble, an Acting Justice of the Peace for Bedford County in the State of Tennessee, do hereby certify that Martin Shofner, Senr., who has subscribed and sworn to the following affidavit is a citizen of said County and is a man of strict honesty and integrity and that his character for veracity has never been questioned by any person to my knowledge and I believe him to be the age he states he is.

Given under my hand this 18th day of April 1833.

                                   Jacob Coble   (J.P.)

1835, aged 80, Private, North Caroline Line.

      Ref: GSA Report, Washington, D.C.
      Ref: 1835 Bedford County, Tennessee Pension List.

* * * * * * * * * *

JOSHUA HOLT

Name:	Rank:	State Served:
Joshua Holt	-----	---------------

Born November 3, 1768 in Orange County, North Carolina, died October 20, 1839 in Bedford County, Tennessee. Buried in Holt Camp Ground Cemetery.

In 1850 Census of Bedford County, Tennessee:
Eleanor Holt, age 86 years, born in North Carolina, in the house with her is Jane Eady, 13 years, born in Tennessee.

Tombstones in the Center Church Cemetery (Holt Camp Ground), Bedford County, Tennessee:

Joshua Holt, Sen.
Born in Orange Co., N.C.
Nov 3, 1768 & Died
Oct 20, 1839
Aged: 70y, 11m, 17d.

Elanor C. Holt
Apr 6, 1763
Dec 24, 1852
Aged: 89y, 8m, 18d.

Michael Holt and wife Jean Holt.   (Will of Michael Holt)
Michael's children by his first wife:
Joseph Holt, Margaret Powell, Elizabeth Smith, Sarah Hardin, Joshua Holt, Isaac Holt, Mary Thompson, Catherine Holt, Michael Holt, and William Holt.
Executors: Wife Jean, sons Isaac and Joshua.
Witnesses: J. Scott, Wm. Rainey, John Holt.

Holt, Joshua (1768-1839)
House, 14th & 15th General Assembly, 1821-25; representing Bedford County, Tennessee. Born in Orange County, North Carolina, November 3, 1768, son of Michael and Jean (Lockhart) Holt. Married in Orange County, North Carolina to Eleanor C. Family name of wife thought to be Burrow. First child born ca 1791. He erected a mill on Flat Creek, Bedford County, Tennessee in 1814, owned large acreage in Bedford County. Commissioner of Poor House in 1827. Trustee Pleasant Garden Methodist E. Church, Bedford County, 1818. Died in Bedford County October 20, 1839, buried in Holt Camp Ground Cemetery.
Ref: Mrs. Isabel Stebbins Guiloezan, family genealogist, Affton, MO.
Ref: Goodspeed History of Bedford County, Tennessee, page 863.
Ref: Abstracts of Wills, Orange County, North Carolina 1752-1850
     by Shields, Section 1, page 121.
Ref: Cemetery Records of Bedford County, Tennessee by Marsh

* * * * * * * * * *

SHADRACK HOLT

Name:	Rank:	State Served:
Shadrack Holt	PVT	North Carolina

Born 12th day of December 1753 in Culpepper County in the State of Virginia, died 15th day of April 1838, married March 1775 to Martha _____.

GSA: Shadrack Holt, R.5185, wife Martha. Service in North Carolina.
Claim No. 30763(5), West Tennessee, Shadrack Holt of Bedford County in the State of Tennessee who was a Private in the Company commanded by Captain Gwinn of the Regiment commanded by Colonel O'Neal in the North Carolina Line for 6 months.
Inscribed on the Roll of West Tennessee at the rate of 20 dollars, 00 cents per annum, to commence on the 4th day of March 1831.
Certificate of Pension issued the 19th day of July 1836 and sent to John H. Anderson, Shelbyville, Tennessee

Arrears to the 4th March 1836	$100.00
Semi-anl allowance ending 4 Sept	$ 10.00
	$110.00

Recorded by D.D. Addison, Clerk
Book B   Vol 7   page 92

Revolutionary Claim
Act June 7, 1832

Rept'd '36 (1836)
Order to _ 12 Oct 1837
Letter to J. Neil 12 Oct 1837

State of Tennessee]
Bedford County   ]
On this 5th day of November 1832, personally appeared in open court before John B. Armstrong, Jno. L. Neill and Samuel Phillips, Esqrs., Justices appointed to hold the Quorum Court of Pleas and Quarter Sessions for the County of Bedford in the State of Tennessee. The same being a Court of Record, Shadrack Holt, a resident of said County in the State aforesaid, aged about seventy nine years next December, who being first duly sworn according to law doth on his oath make the following declaration in order to obtain the benefit of the Act of Congress passed June 7, 1832.

This applicant states that about the first of June 1779, this spring, as well as he now recollects, he was drafted in the State of North Carolina where he then resided for the term of three months and was placed under the command of Captain Edward Gwin, in a Regiment commanded by William O'Neill as Colonel, and John Campbell as Major, so well as he now recollects, during the time he was drafted as aforesaid, his family was indisposed and he hired a substitute, who served in his room some short time, after the expiration of the three months tour above stated, he was again drafted for the term of twelve months, this draft or call, he is confident took place about the 1st of June, and he believes in the year 1779. Applicant's family still running and disagreeably situated and it being convenient for him so to do, he hired a man named Thomas Willis, as a substitute during this tour, who was received in his place and as deponent is informed was in the Battle of Camden, known better by the name of General Gate's Defeat, where said substitute was killed as report says. Applicant states it was some little time after he was drafted the 2nd time, before he was called into actual service, the time however he does not now recollect. He supposes it might have been 3 or 4 months. After this second draft and hiring a substitute, the time he cannot recollect, but has no doubt it was the same Fall of Fall of 1779. Applicant states his horse and gun were pressed into the service of his Country. He resisted the call, stating what he had done for his Country as above recited. He was informed his own services could not be required but those of his arms and other property could. He then told them if one went the other would. He accordingly volunteered in the service of his Country for no particular period, as he recollects, but was to serve whenever called upon. He states he did serve from that time until the close of the war, under Captain Edward Gwin and in the Regiment commanded by Colonel William O'Neal and Major John Campbell. He states according to the best of his recollection, he volunteered in the Fall of 1779 and served until sometime in the year 1782, sometime after the capture of Lord Cornwallis. He states he volunteered in Orange County, State of North Carolina, at the time aforesaid and was discharged near Wilcox's Iron Works on or near Deep River in the State of North Carolina. He further states he received a written discharge signed by Colonel O'Neill but that the same is now and has been for a long time past, lost or destroyed so that he cannot produce it. He believes in moving from North Carolina to Georgia, or from Georgia to Tennessee, it became worn out or lost, he has never since seen it. He states he was in the service about two years and from six to nine months, so well as he recollects. He was during that time engaged principally in scouts after the Tories and some British, in the Counties of Orange, Cumberland and some of the adjoining Counties. He was in a little skirmish with some of Colonel Fanning's men at the Buffalo Ford on Deep River. The Tories were beaten. He was next in a little battle on a water course called Cane Creek when he was informed Colonel Fanning commanded the Tories in person, in the battle the Tories were also beaten. Some other small skirmishes took place which he supposes unnecessary to mention as they probably have never obtain a place in history. Applicant well recollects to have seen many of the Soldiers on their return home from General Gates Defeat. Whilst he was out as Volunteer as aforesaid and recewived the news of Gate's Defeat from them. He was also within 25 miles of Guilford Court House on the day of the battle was fought between Green and Cornwallis. He distinctly recollects to have heard the reports of the cannon at that battle. The men to which he belonged were then in pursuit of Colonel Fanning, who was reported to have one thousand men, going on to the aid of Cornwallis and the subject of his Commander was as he was told to prevent their junction.

Applicant further states that he has no record of the time when or place where he was born but from the information given to him by his parents and which he believes to be true, he was born in Culpepper County in the State of Virginia in December 1753, which will make him seventy nine years old next December 1832. He further states that during his service as volunteer as aforesaid above named. He further states he knows of no person by whom he can prove the facts or any of them, except Jacob Rich and Joshua Holt, whose affidavits he has procured and are appended to this declaration as part of the same.

He hereby relinguishes every claim whatever to a pension or annuity

except the present and declares that his name is not on the Pension Roll of the agency of any State or Territory in the United States.
Sworn to in open court 5th November 1832.
Jas. McKisick, Clk.   Shadrack (S H) Holt

This day, Joshua Holt, a citizen of Bedford County, Tennessee, appeared in open court and made oath that he was acquainted with Colonel William O'Neill, Major John Campbell and Edward Gwin. The officers mentioned the foregoing declaration, he states he has seen them mustering men frequently in the County of Orange for the purpose of pursuing and taking Fanning and his men and other Tories as he was informed and has always understood. He states further that he has been acquainted with Shadrack Holt, the applicant in the foregoing declaration ever since he can recollect, being born in the same neighborhood where said <u>Shaderick</u> Holt lived. He distinctly recollecting that at different times, when the officers above named were mustering their men and at different times when they were marching as this deponent recollects and were informed. He does recollect to have seen the said applicant among the Soldiers who were commanded by the Officers above named and he does further state that he always understood that said applicant was a Revolutionary Soldier and no doubt remains on his mind that said applicant was in the service and served as he states, and that he is a man of correctness and his statements entitled to full credit.
Sworn to in open court 4 November 1832.
Jas. McKisick, Clk.   Joshua Holt

I, Humphry C. Furgerson, a Clergyman, residing in the COunty of Bedford and State of Tennessee, hereby certify that I am well acquainted with Shadrack Holt, who has subscribed and sworn to the above declaration, I do further believe him to be age he represents in his said declaration. That he is reputed and believed in the neighborhood where he resides to have been a Soldier of the Revolution and that I concure in that opinion.
Sworn to in open court 4 November 1832.
Jas. McKisick, Clk.   H.C. Ferguson

State of Tennessee]
Franklin County   ]
This day personally appeared before me, John R. Patrick, an Acting Justice of the Peace in and for said County and State, Jacob Rich, a resident of said County, aged seventy years old, who after being duly sworn deposeth and saith that he was a Lieutenant in the Army of the Revolution, and that he knows that Shadrack Holt, now of Bedford County, Tennessee, did serve against the Tories in the War of the Revolution.

                              Jacob (R) Rich

I hereby certify that the said Jacob Rich swore and subscribed to the above affidavit before me, this day and that said Rich is of good character and standing and that I believe said Rich to be a man of truth and that he is the age of seventy years. Given under my hand and seal this 28th day of January 1833.
                              John R. Patrick (Seal)
                              Justice of the Peace.

State of Tennessee
I, Edward Russell, Clerk of the Court of Pleas and Quarter Sessions for Franklin County, do hereby certify that John R. Patrick, whose name is signed to the within Certificate, is now and was of the time he signed the same, an acting Justice of the Peace in and for the County of Franklin, duly commissioned and qualified as such and that forth and credit is due and ought to be given to all his Official Acts as such.
In testimony whereof I have hereunto set my hand and affixed the Seal of said Court at Office, this 28th day of January 1833.
                              E. Russell, Clk.
                              of Franklin County Court.

An Amendment to the declaration of Shadrack Holt, made at November Term 1832 of Bedford County Court, in order to obtain the benefit of the Act of Congress passed the 7th June 1832.

State of Tennessee]
Bedford County   ]
        On this 13th day of June one thousand eight hundred and thirty three, personally appeared before me the undersigned, a Justice of the Peace in and for the said County, Shadrack Holt, Senr., who subscribed and was qualified to the declaration above alluded to, who after being duly sworn according to law, deposeth and saith that by reason of old age and the consequent loss of memory, he cannot swear positively to the precise length of his service but according to the best of his recollection, he served not less than the periods below, and in the following grades, to wit, That to the best of his recollection, he entered the service of the United States as stated in his former declaration, in the Fall of the year 1779, the 1st of October, as a volunteer in Captain Edward Gwin's Company who was under the command of Colonel William O'Neill and Major John Campbell, and was marched from Orange County, North Carolina to a Fort on Deep River called the Buffalo Ford, where he says he was in a battle or skirmish with the Tories, under the command of a Tory Colonel by the name of Fanning and that the Tories were defeated. Deponent does not recollect the month or day that this skirmish took place, but thinks it was after Christmas in the early part of the year 1780 and that he recollects very well it was in Chatham County, North Carolina, and from there he was marched to Wilcox's Iron Works on Deep River where he was kept for some time, and at that place the troops that he was with were joined by a reenforcement under the command of Colonel Paislley and Daniel Gillespie and from there he was marched to Brush Creek, he thinks in Cumberland County, North Carolina, where the troops under O'Neill, Paislley and Gillespie attacked a band of Tories and British and defeated them. He says he can not recollect the day or month at this time, that it took place, but thinks it was a short time before the Battle of Camden, and from there he was marched to Cane Creek, in the lower end of Orange County or upper end of Chatham, in said last mentioned State, where he says he was in another small skirmish against the Tories under Fanning and that the Tories gave way and fled in every direction and from there he says he was marched to the Raft Swamps in said Cumberland County where he says he was stationed for some weeks, and from that place he was marched to the Redfield Ford on Haw River where he was kept for some time but the precise length of time he does not now recollect, and from there he was marched to various other places through the Counties of Orange, Chatham, Cumberland and Randolph, to prevent the Tories from imboding and committing depredidations on the Whig families who were often left without any protection. Secondly, this applicant states that the whigs were thought to be more safe in the army or in actual service that at home and that as his services were still solicited by his Officers. He continued in service until after the surrender of Cornwallis, when he was marched to Wilcox's Iron Works, where he received a discharge in writing for more than two years. For although he cannot read writing himself, he was frequently heard persons read his discharge, which was always read to him for two years and nine months but that he is very certain to the best of his recollection he had served not less than two years in the actual service of the United States, during the Revolutionary War as a Private Soldier and volunteer for which he claims a pension.
Sworn to and subscribed the day and year aforesaid, before me
E. Hord, Justice of the Peace   Shadrack (S H) Holt (Seal)

Interrogatories by the Court

Q. 1st: Where and in what year were you born?
A.   I was born in Culpepper County in the State of Virginia on the 12th day of December 1753, agreeable to the best information I have been able to get.
Q. 2nd: Have you any record of your age and if so where is it?
A.   I have no record of my age except a letter I received from a cousin of mine, a son of my uncle Michael Holt of Orange County, North Carolina, who could write and as I have been informed, kept the age of my father's family in his Bible, and my cousin in his letter to me says he took it from the original record that I was born as above stated.
Q. 3rd: Where were you living when called into service? Where have you lived

100

A.   since the Revolutionary War and where do you now live?

A.   I was a citizen of Orange County and State of North Carolina when I was called into service and continued to be until after the close of the war when I removed to the State of Georgia, I think in the year _____ where I lived until the year _____ when I removed to Bedford County, Tennessee where I have resided ever since and where I now reside.

Q. 4th: How were you called into service? Were you a volunteer, a substitute, or were you drafted?

A.   I was a volunteer all the time I was in service.

Q. 5th: State the names of some of the Regular Officers who were with the troops where you served, such Continental and Militia Regiments as you can recollect and the general circumstances of your service.

A.   I was not acquainted with any Regular Officers with the troops where I served, nor do I now recollect any name or number to the Regiment I belonged to, except Colonel O'Neill's Regiment of Volunteers.

And I believe the foregoing declaration and the amendments thereto, are the most prominent and general history of my service that I am able at this advance stage of my life to give.

Q. 6th: Did you ever receive a discharge and if so what has become of it?

A.   I did receive a discharge in writing, signed by Colonel William O'Neill, to the best of my recollection, as it was read to me for a term of service of two years and nine months, but has been worn out or lost long since.

Q. 7th: State the names of persons to whom you are known in your present neighborhood, who can testify as to your character for veracity, and their opinion of your service as a Soldier of the Revolution.

A.   I am known to Mr. Willis Green and Wm. Culley.

Sworn to and subscribed before this 13th day of June 1833.

E. Hord, Justice of the Peace.   Shadrack (S H) Holt (Seal)

State of Tennessee]
Bedford County   ]

      This day, Willis Green and Wm. Culley, personally appeared before me the undersigned, and after being sworn agreeable to law, deposeth and say that they are well acquainted with Shadrack Holt, who subscribed and was qualified to the foregoing amended declaration and have been acquainted with him for the last fifteen years, that he is reputed and believed in the neighborhood where he now resides to have been a Soldier of the Revolution and that they concur in that opinion, that further say they believe said Shadrack Holt to be a man of strict honesty and integrity and that his character for veracity has never been questioned by any person to their knowledge, and that they believe his statements on oath to be entitled to credit in any court whatever.

Sworn to before me this 13th day of June 1833.

E. Hord, Justice of the Peace.   Willis Green
                                           William Culley

State of Tennessee]
Bedford County   ]

      I, James McKisick, Clerk of the Court of Pleas and Quarter Sessions for Bedford COunty in the State aforesaid, do hereby certify that Edmond Hord, Esq., before whom Shadrack Holt was qualified to the foregoing amendment to his original declaration, and before whom Willis Green and William Culley were qualified to the foregoing affidavit, is now and was at the time an acting Justice of the Peace in and for said County, duly commissioned and sworn and that the full faith and credit are given to all his Official Acts as such.

      In testimony whereof I have hereunto set my hand and affixed the Seal of Bedford County Court at Office this 17th day of June 1833.

                                        Jas. McKisick, Clerk

      And the said Court do hereby declare their opinion after the investigation of the matter, and after putting the interrogatories prescribed by the War Department, that the above applicant was a Soldier of the Revolution and served as he states. They further certify that H.C. Furguson who has signed the foregoing certificate is a citizen Clergyman in the Presbyterian Church, residing in Bedford County, and that Joshua Holt, who has subscribed the foregoing certificate is a respectable citizen and entitled to full credit and that the statements of the applicant and witness are entitled to full credit.

Jno. L. Neill
Samuel Phillips
John B. Armstrong

State of Tennessee]
Bedford County   ]
        I, James McKisick, Clerk of the Court of Pleas and Quarter Sessions of the County of Bedford in the State of aforesaid, do hereby certify that the foregoing contains the original proceedings of said court in the matter of the Pension Claim of Shadrack Holt, Senr., I further certify that Fergus Hall before whom said Shadrack made oath to the amendment made to his original declaration is an acting Justice of the Peace in and for said County of Bedford duly commissioned and sworn and that full faith and credit ought to be given to his Office Acts.

James McKisick, Clerk

Declaration of Martha Holt:

State of Tennessee]
Franklin County   ]
        On this 25th day of July 1840, personally appeared before James Byrom, one of the Justices of the Court of Franklin County, State of Tennessee, Martha Holt, a resident of the aforesaid County and State, aged eighty four years, and after having been duly sworn according to law, doth on her oath make the following declaration in order to obtain the benefit of the provision made by the Act of Congress passed the fourth day of July, eighteen hundred and thirty six, entitled, "An Act Supplementry to the Act for the relief of certain widows of Officers and Soldiers of the Revolution." That she is the widow of Shadrack Holt, who was a pensioner under the Act of Congress of 1832. She further declares that she was married to the said Shadrack Holt in the month of March, seventeen hundred and seventy five. That her husband, the aforesaid Shadrack Holt, died on the fifteenth day of April 1838 and that she has not been married since. She further declares that she had three children at the time of the Battle of Guilford Court House which was near her residence at the time.
Sworn to and subscribed on the day and date above written before
James Byrom, J.P   Martha (X) Holt (Seal)

State of Tennessee]
Franklin County   ]
        I, James Byrom, one of the Justices of the COurt of Franklin County, State of Tennessee, do hereby certify that Martha Holt whose name is subscribed to the above declaration, is a lady of sound mind, of good reputation and entitled to full credit and belief on her oath from my personal knowledge and that she is entirely unable from her age and bodily infirmity to appear before the Court.
Given under my hand ans seal, this 25 day of July 1840.

James Byrom (J.P.) (Seal)

State of Tennessee]
Franklin County   ]
        I, Isaac Estill, Clerk of the County Court of said County, do hereby certify that James Byrom is and was at the time of certifying the within, a Justice of the Court of Records, duly commissioned and legally qualified as such and that he is entitled to faith and credit in all his Official Acts.
        In testimony whereof I have hereunto set my hand and affixed my Seal of Office in Winchester on the 28th day of July 1840.
No. 5296   Isaac Estill, Clerk

State of Tennessee]
Franklin County   ]
        On this 25th day of August 1840, personally appeared before James Byrom, one of the Justices of the Peace in and for the aforesaid County, State of Tennessee, John Lokey, resident of the aforesaid County, personally known to

said Byrom of good repute and entitled to full credit and belief and after being duly sworn according to law, doth on his oath, testify and say that he married the second child of Mrs. Martha Holt, who is applying for a pension under the Act of Congress of 1836, making provisions for certain widows. That his wife is now according to the best of our knowledge and belief and from the declaration of her parents, sixty two years of age, that I have great grand children, the great great grandchildren of said Martha Holt, that the eldest child of my wife is now forty years of age, my wife being the second child of said Martha Holt. That there is no family record of the births of the children as far as we know, said Martha Holt being a resident of my family at this time.
Sworn to and subscribed the day and date above written before me,
James Byrom, J.P.   John (X) Lokey

State of Tennessee]
Franklin County   ]
        I, Wm. E. Taylor, Clerk of the County Court in and for the County and State above written would hereby certify that satisfactory evidence has been produced to show that Martha Holt, widow of Shadrack Holt, died on the twenty eighth day of November, eighteen hundred and forty six and that Nancy Lokey, Elizah Holt and Elizabeth Byrum(Byrom) are her only surviving children.
        I would further certify that D.D. Smith, Esq., before who the foregoing declaration and affidavits were return, is an acting Justice of the Peace in and for the County and State aforesaid, duly commissioned and sworn and the signatures purporting to be his are genuine.
        In testimony whereof I have hereunto set my hand and affixed my Seal of Office at Office in Winchester, this 7th day of July A.D. 1852.
                                                        Wm. E. Taylor, Clk.

        In order to obtain the bebefit of the Acts of Congress passed July 7th 1838, 3rd March 1843 and the 17th June 1844.
Declaration:
State of Tennessee]
Franklin County   ]
        On this 1st day of July in the year of our Lord, one thousand eight hundred and fifty two, personally appeared before the subscriber, An Acting Justice of the Peace in and for the County, Mrs. Elizabeth Byrom, aged sixty two years past, and being first duly sworn according to law doth on her oath make the following declaration, that she is the daughter and one of the heirs at law of Martha Holt, the widow of Shadrack Holt, who was a Pensioner of the United States for services in the War of the Revolution. That the date of the death of her father, she cannot tell and must refer to the proof on file and the likenesses in the department with her father. That her mother, Martha Holt, above stated , died on the twenty eighth day of November in the year eighteen hundred and forty six, leaving the following named children: Nancy Lokey, Elizah Holt and affiant Elizabeth Byrom. That her father was married to her mother, Martha Holt, prior to the first day of January in the year seventeen hundred and ninety four, for the proof of which affiant must refer to the proof on file and the proof accompanying this declaration. Affiant further declares that her father drew a pension of _____ dollars per annum.
                                                Elizabeth (X) Byrom

Sworn and subscribed before me, an Acting Justice of the Peace in and for said County and I would certify that Nancy Lokey, Elizah Holt and Elizabeth Byrom, are the only surviving heirs at law of Martha Holt, deceased, who was the widow of Shadrack Holt, who was a Pensioner of the United States. I further certify that Elizabeth Byrom who makes the above declaration is the daughter of Shadrack and Martha Holt, as she states, and that she must be of age she states that is sixty two years. I further certify that satisfactory evidence has been produced to show that Martha Holt died on the twenty eighth day of November, eighteen hundred and forty six, and that Mrs. Elizabeth Byrom is a person in whom full faith and credit may be placed.
        In testimony whereof I have hereunto set my hand, this 1st day of July A.D., 1852.   D.D. Smith, J.P. for
        Ref: GSA Report, Washington, D.C.   Franklin County, Tenn.

JOSEPH JACOBS

Name:	Rank:	State Served:
Joseph Jacobs	PVT	North Carolina

Born April 1750 in Maryland, died 9th December 1838, married 1st March 1771 to Lucy who was born about 1751.

1835, age 69, Private, North Carolina State Troops.

GSA: Joseph Jacobs, W.7875, wife Lucy.

Claim No. 26532: West Tennessee, Joseph Jacobs of Bedford County in the State of Tennessee, who was a _______ in the Company commanded by Captain Grimes of the _____ commanded by ________ in the North Carolina Line for 6 months service in Infantry. 3 months service in Cavalry.

      Inscribed on the Roll of West Tennessee at the rate of 32 dollars, 50 cents per annum, to commence on the 4th day of March 1831.

      Certificate of Pension issued the 6 day of March 1834 and sent to John Bruce, Shelbyville.

Arrears to the 4th March	$ 97.50
Semi-anl allowance ending 4 Sept	$ 16.25
	$113.75

Recorded by Daniel Boyd, Clerk	Revolutionary Claim
Book E Vol 7 page 85	Act June 7, 1832

Declaration in order to obtain the benefit of the Act of Congress passed 7th June 1832.

State of Tennessee]
Bedford County   ]

      On this 5th day of February 1834, personally appeared in open court in the Court of Pleas and Quarter Sessions of Bedford County in the State of Tennessee, before the Worshipful, Samuel Phillips, William Murphy and William Carter, Esquires, and members appointed to hold same court, now sitting, Joseph Jacobs, a residence of Bedford County in the State of Tennessee, aged eighty three years, eight months and a few days, who being first duly sworn according to law, doth on his oath, make the following declaration in order to obtain the benefit of the Act of Congress passed June 7, 1832.

      That sometime in the year 1777 or 1778, as well as he now recollects, he entered the service of the United States under the following named Officers and served as herein stated, that he first went into Captain Grimes' Company as a Miitiaman, being drafted in the North Carolina Line. Does not recollect his Colonel's name. His General was Rutherford. That he joined Captain Grimes in Rowan County in North Carolina and from there was marched through several Counties in the State of North Carolina, in persuit of the Tories till he had served three months at the end of which to me Captain Grimes gave him a written discharge but he has lost it. That during the tour aforesaid, he was acquainted with Captain Grimes, Captain Colvell and with General Rutherford, that after said Captain Grimes gave him said written discharge, he went home to Rowan County in North Carolina and continued there several months, but owing to the great lapse of time and the consequent loss of memory, he cannot now recollect with certainty how long, after which, he went into service again, into Captain Read's Company as a Militia, being drafted in the North Carolina Line, that Rutherford was his General, that he does not recollect that he had any Colonel or Major. That he joined Captain Read in Rowan County, North Carolina and from there he marched through different parts of North Carolina till the expiration of three months. At the expiration of which time Captain Read gave him a written discharge but he has lost it. That during his second tour was only acquainted with General Rutherford and Captain Read. As he was only out in a scouting party against the Tories during his second tour. That after he served the second tour, he returned home to Rowan County and continued there several months and afterwards he volunteered as a horseman and went into Captain Nighte's Company in the Militia in the North Carolina Line. Smith was his Colonel, Rutherford was his General. That he joined Captain Nighte's Company in Rowan County in North Carolina Line and from thence he marched till he arrived near Wilmington in North Carolina at which place he was in a battle with

the British and Tories in which battle the Americans were victorious, but there was but one of the Americans killed and but little execution done on this side, the battle aforesaid was called "The Battle of Wilmington" and soon after the battle aforesaid, he returned home and after his arrival at home in Rowan County, Captain Nighte gave him a written discharge but he has lost it, that his third tour was three months, that during the three months last aforesaid, he was acquainted with Captain Nighte, Colonel Smith and Captain Kenedy, Captain _____, Captain Cleveland and General Rutherford, that he served in all nine months. That he has no documentary evidence and that he knows of no person whose testimony he can procure except that of Greenberry Jacobs which he has already produced, who can testify to his service. He states there is but one clergyman in his neighborhood and he is by the name of William Keal (Keel) but from the information he has received, he has strong reasons to believe that he doesn't believe the said Keal (Keel) will not certify for any Revolutionary Soldier and not even for his own father. He hereby relinguishes every claim whatever to a pension or annuity except the present and declares that his name is not on the Pension Roll of the agency of any State or Territory in the United States. Sworn to and subscribed the day and year aforesaid.
Sworn to in open court 5th February 1834.
Jas. McKisick, Clerk   Joseph (X) Jacobs

Questions asked Joseph Jacobs

Q.1st: Where and in what year were you born?
A.   I was born in the State of Maryland but does not recollect what County, and in April 1750.
Q. 2nd: Have you a record of your age and if so where is it?
A.   I have not, it was put down in some book of my father's but I know not where it is at this time.
Q. 3rd: Where were you living when called into the service, Where have you lived since the Revolutionary War and where do you now live?
A.   When called into service, I lived in Rowan County in the State of North Carolina and after the Revolutionary War ended, he removed to Anderson County in Tennessee, then removed to Wilson County, Tennessee, then to Rutherford County, Tennessee, then he removed to Bedford County, Tennessee, where he now lives.
Q. 4th: How were you called into service? Were you drafted or did you volunteer or were you a substitute and if a substitute for whom?
A.   The first time, I was drafted, the second time I was drafted and the third time I volunteered.
Q. 5th: State the names of some of the Regular Officers who were with the troops where you served, such Continental and Militia Regiments can recollect and the general circumstances of your service.
A.   I was acquainted with General Rutherford who was a _____ Officer with Colonel Smith, Captains Grimes, Read, Nighte, Colvell, Cleveland and Kenedy, _____ all of whom are Militia Officers and the general circumstances of my service are herein stated.
Q. 6th: Did you ever receive a discharge from the service and if so by whom was it given and what has become of it?
A.   That the expiration of my first tour of service, Captain Grimes gave me a written discharge but I have lost it and at the expiration of my second tour, Captain Read gave me a written discharge but I have lost it, and st the end of my third tour Captain Nighte gave me a written discharge but I have lost it.

No. 3949: Tennessee, Lucy Jacobs, widow of Joseph Jacobs, North Carolina, who died on the 9th December 1838, of Rutherford County, in the State of Tennessee, who was a Private and Sgt. in the Company commanded by Captain Grimes of the Regiment commanded by Colonel _____ in the North Carolina Line for 9 months.

Inscribed on the Roll of Nashville, at the rate of 32 dollars, 50 cents per annum, to commence on the 10th of September 1838.

Certificate of Pension issued 29 day of April 1841 and sent to H. Yoakum, Murfreesboro, Tennessee.

105

Arrears to the 4th of March 1841 $72.39
Semi-anl allowance ending 4 Sept 1841 $16.25
                                                        $98.64

Recorded by W.W. Tyler, Clerk   Revolutionary Claim
]Book C   Vol 3   page 198   Act July 4, 1836
                                             Section the 3rd.

State of Tennessee]
Rutherford County]
     On this twenty fifth day of March 1841, personally appeared before the Judge of the Circuit Court of said County of Rutherford, in open court, Lucy Jacobs, a resident of Rutherford County and State of Tennessee, aged ninety years, who being first duly sworn according to law, doth on her oath make the following declaration, in order to obtain the benefit of the provision made by the Act of Congress passed July 4, 1836, that she is the widow of Josepj Jacobs, who was a Private of Infantry and Cavalry in the Army of the Revolution, or an evidence of which she offers his Pension Certificate dated 4th March 1834 and numbered 26532. She further declares that she was married to the said Joseph Jacobs, the identical person named in said previous certificate, on the first day of March in the year seventeen hundred and seventy one (1771). That her husband, the aforesaid Joseph Jacobs died on the nineth day of December in the year eighteen hundred and thirty eight (9 Dec 1838) and that she has remained a widow ever since that period as will more fully appear by ____ to the proof hereto annexed. She has no record of her said marriage but offers such as herewith said.
Sworn and subscribed in open court this 25th day of March 1841.
Samuel F. Hodge, Clerk   Lucy (X) Jacobs (Seal)
of Rutherford Circuit Court

State of Tennessee]
Rutherford County]
     Before me, Francis L. Manning, Justice of the Peace in and for said County of Rutherford, this day, personally appeared, Greenberry Jacobs, who after being first duly sworn, says that he is the fifth (5th) child of Joseph Jacobs and Lucy Jacobs. He was born as he has been informedly told, in July 1778. He further states that his father, the said Joseph Jacobs died the 9th day of December 1838. Lucy Jacobs, his mother is still his widow, and has not married since his death. Witness has no record of his own age.
Inscribed and sworn before me this 25 March 1841, as I do further certify that said witness is worthy of full credit, and is opinion of good character.
Francis L. Fanning (Seal)   Greenberry Jacobs
Justice of the Peace.

     Ref: GSA Record, Washington, D.C.
     Ref: Widow Application for Pension.
     Ref: A 1
     Ref: 1835 Bedford County, Tennessee Pension List.
     Ref: Tennessee DAR 1941-1942 Yearbook, page 102.

* * * * * * * * * *

NATHANIEL JOHNSTON

Name:	Rank:	State Served:
Nathaniel Johnston	PVT & Ensign	North Carolina

Born 1755/56 in Rowan County, North Carolina, died after 1834 (Pension), buried in the Old City Cemetery, Shelbyville, Tennessee, without marker.

1835, age 78, Private Infantry & Cavalry, North Carolina Militia.

GSA: Nathaniel Johnson, S.1841, North Carolina
Claim No. 6342: West Tennessee, Nathaniel Johnson of Bedford County in the State of Tennessee who was a Private and Ensign in the Company commanded by Captain Brandon of the Regiment commanded by Colonel Rutherford in the North Carolina for Militia for 14 months from ...
     Inscribed on the Roll of Tennessee at the rate of 45 dollars, 33 cents

per annum, to commence on the 4th of March, 1831.

Certificate of Pension issued the 28 day of Sept 1833 and sent to Hon. Jas. K. Polk, H.R.

Arrears to the 4th of Sept 1832	$72.49
Semi-anl allowance ending 4 March 1833	$24.16
	$96.65

Recorded by H.H. Sylvester, Clerk   Revolutionary Claim
Book D   Vol 7   page 151   Act June 7, 1832

Declaration:
State of Tennessee]
Bedford County   ]

On this 10th day of August 1832, personally appeared in open court before Samuel Phillips, John B. Armstrong and John L. Neill, Justices of the Quorum, appointed to hold the Court of Pleas and Quarter Sessions for Bedford County, State of Tennessee for the year 1832, and now sitting, Nathaniel Johnston, a resident in Bedford County and State of Tennessee, aforesaid, aged seventy six years or seventy seven years, who being first duly sworn according to law, doth on his oath make the following declaration in order to obtain the benefit of the Act of Congress passed June 7, 1832. That he entered the service of the United States under the following named Officers, and served as herein stated, viz, He was born in Rowan County, North Carolina in the year 1756 as he has been informed and believes. In which County and State he resided until the year 1823, when he removed to the County of Bedford in the State of Tennessee, where he has ever lived and now resides.

He first entered the service of the United States in an expedition against the Cherokee Indians, under Captain Brandon. The expedition as he believes by General Rutherford, whether Rutherford was at the time of this expedition, a Colonel or General, he does not recollect. He entered the service as a volunteer and served a five months tour. They traversed that part of North Carolina now called East Tennessee, particularly the County lying on the Little Tennessee also the nothern part of Georgia, through the Country lying on T(upelo) River. Burned and destroyed the Indian Towns and Settlements and skirmishes with the Indians, but no general battle or engagements, took prisoners and killed many of the Indians. This expedition commanded in the early part of June and ended about the first of November. He cannot say what year. He is confident it was before the Battle of Camden called Gates Defeat. He recollects the names of Colonel or General Rutherford, Colonel Brandon, Major Smith and knows they were in this expedition as Officers bearing the above or foregoing titles, many others, probably not recollected and many Captains. Captain Brandon commanded the COmpany to which deponent belonged. Sometime after he was discharged from the Indian Expedition, he again volunteered in the service of the United States under Captain Brandon, against an Army of Tories, who were embodied in Lincoln County, North Carolina. This expedition was commanded by Colonel Lock and Major Rutherford, we met with the Tories at a place called Ramsour's Mill in Lincoln County where he had a battle, in which the Tories were defeated. The whig party lost this battle, about 20 killed and several wounded. Among our killed were Captain Falls, Armstrong and Patton. I served in the expedition as well as I can recollect from one to two months. After the Battle of Ramsour's above mentioned, a call was made for volunteers to go in persuit of Colonel Bryan who had collected a body of Tories and was marching to join the British at an _____ Camden, South Carolina. This expedition was commanded by Generals Davidson and Locke. I volunteered and went under them in this expedition. I do not recollect the name of my Captain. I think it was Captain Brandon. We rendezvoused at Montgomery and Anson Counties to the Cheraw Hills in South Carolina _____ on in the persuit and returned home. We were in the service, I think, about two months in this trip. I then volunteered in the Light Horse Company, at the time the British came up to Charlotte from South Carolina, this was under Captain Brandon, and the call was made to raise men to check the British in their march through the upper part of North Carolina as deponant understood. This expedition lasted about two months, as well as deponant recollects, and was commanded by Colonel Davie and Major Graham the principal Officers. All the above mentioned expeditions and tours was performed and completed previous to the Battle of Camden, better known by Gates Defeat. But the precise time when they were performed, I cannot state, nor do I know of any persons by whom I can prove it. He states further that he afterwards volunteered under Captain Huggins in a tour of three months, which he served, General Rutherford was the Chief Commander, at the commencement of this term of service. The Army commanded by General Rutherford rendezvoused at Salisbury from thence we marched towards Camden and formed a junction with General Gates' Army not very far from the Cheraw Hills, and we then marched with the main Army to there the battle was fought. I was in the Battle of Camden called Gates' Defeat. He further states he knew General Gates who commanded at this battle, also General Rutherford and General Butler and General Caswell, Colonels Ledbetter, White, Majors Allcorn, White, Captain Huggins, and Wilson.

He states further, he volunteered in the service of his country, after the Battle of Gates' Defeat as aforesaid, and served one or two months as Ensign and Commander of the Company the Captain and Lieutenant both being absent. This Company or Army of Volunteers was raised at this time. Lord Cornwallis crossed the Catawba River. He was in a little skirmish on the Catawba River, at a place called Cowen's Ford, between the Wiggs (Whigs) and the British. At which place General Davidson was killed. The principal Officers who commanded this expedition were General Davidson and Davie. The length of this tour was about one month, as he believes. He further states that he did at several times after this period, enter the Army of his Country, in some of which he served a longer and in some a shorter period of time. He cannot pretend to say what would be the time he subsequently served, but supposes it would not exceed four months. He believes he served his country during the Revolutionary War in the whole a period not less than eighteen months and probably not much more, but of the precise time he cannot undertake to state. He states further that at the end of every term of service or aforesaid, he obtained a discharge for the same as he believes but he did not know they were then or even would be useful to him. He states he has no knowledge of the manner in which he has lost them but has no hesitation in saying they were now lost or mislaid in this case. He has no documentary evidence in his possession of the facts spoken of and detailed in the foregoing declaration, nor does he know of any person by whom he can prove the service aforesaid.

He does further hereby relinguish all and every claim or claims whatever to a pension or annuity except the present, and declares that his name is not on the Pension Roll of the agency of any State in the United States.
Sworn to in open Court 10th August 1832,
Jas. McKisick, Clerk   Nathaniel Johnston

Whereupon the Court consisting of the members first above mentioned, prepounded the following interrogatories to said Nathaniel Johnston in open court, this 10th day of August 1832.

Q. 1st: Where and in what year were you born?
A.   I was born in Roan (Rowan) County, State of North Carolina in the year
          1755 or 1756, as I am informed and believed.
Q. 2nd: Have you any record of your age and if so where is it?
A.   I have not.
Q. 3rd: Where were you living when called into service, Where have you lived
          since the Revolutionary War, and where do you now live?
A.   I was living in Rowan County, North Carolina when I was first called
          into the service of my country. I continued to live in said County and
          State during the Revolutionary War and even since, until the year 1823,
          at which time I moved to Bedford County in the State of Tennessee, in
which last County and State I have lived ever since, and am now living in the
          same.
Q. 4th: How were you called into service? Were you drafted? Did you
          volunteer? Or were you a substitute, and if a substitute, for whom?
A.   I was a volunteer in all the terms above mentioned. One instance not
          mentioned in my foregoing declaration, I would wish to mention, viz, We
          were all classed into classes of seven or eight persons, each of which
          classes had to furnish a man if called for, one of the class to which I

belonged was called for, I prepared to the orders to go if they would give me a certain term, this they agreed to, and whilst I was preparing to start, a young man proposed to take my place for much less, I accordingly substituted him. I have been advised I cannot claim any benefit for his service although he served. Unless this transaction might be considered as a substitute business and which is not mentioned in my previous declaration, and to which I would be entitled for pay. I have in all the cases been a volunteer. This term was for twelve months.

Q. 5th: State the names of some of the Regular Officers who were with the troops where you served, such Continental and Militia Regiments as you can recollect and the general circumstances of your service.

A. The Continental and Regular Officers which I now recollect were: General Gates and General Caswell. I think General Caswell is Regular, but not certain. The Militia Officers were: General Rutherford, Butler, Davidson and Locke and Colonel Davie. I probably could recollect names, but have not at this time any recollection of them. I have no recollection of the names or numbers of the Continental and Militia Regiments. The general circumstances have all been detailed in my declaration heretofore stated.

Q. 6th: Did you ever receive a discharge from the service? If so by whom was it given? And what has become of it?

A. I did receive discharges for every tour of service I rendered. Who gave them, I cannot now say, nor do I know what has become of them, they are lost and cannot now produce them. I recollect that it was a general practice for the Captains of our Companies to give the discharges. I believe Captain Brandon gave me several and served under him more than one tour, but I could not state the above fact on oath at this time.

Q. 7th: State the names of persons to whom you are known in your neighborhood, and who can testify as to your character for veracity, and their belief of your services as a Soldier of the Revolutionary War.

A. I know a good many persons who can state about my character in the neighborhoos of Shelbyville, Bedford County, Tennessee, where I now live, there are not many living in my immediate neighborhood who knew me in other States or had much acquaintance with me there, I know of Robert Morgan, Isaac Anderson and James Graham who have known me for many years.

Sworn to and subscribed in open court this 10th August 1832.
Jas. McKisick, Clk.   Nathaniel Johnston

We, Robert Morgan and James Graham, residing in Bedford County, Tennessee do hereby certify that we are well acquainted with Nathaniel Johnston who has subscribed and sworn to the above declaration and interrogatories, that we have been acquainted with him ever since they could recollect. They believe upwards of fifty years, that they believe him to be of the age represented in the foregoing declaration. They further state he is reputed and believed in the neighborhood where he now resides, and was reputed and believed in Rowan County, State of North Carolina where he lived when we first knew him to have been a Soldier of the Revolution. We further state, we have often heard him converse with others who were reputed Soldiers of the Revolution about events of the war, and in those conversations they appeared to agree as to many of the facts. We never heard his Revolutionary Services doubted or disputed and we concur in that opinion that he was a Soldier of the Revolution. They further state that said Nathaniel Johnston, the above applicant, has been a member of the Presbyterian Church for about forty years, for which time his ...(incomplete)...

Department of the Interior, Bureau of Pensions, Washington, D.C.

Dates enlisted	length served:	Rank:	Officers under whom served: Captains:	Colonel:	State Served:
June 1, 1776	5 mos.	Pvt	Brandon	Rutherford	N.C.
1777	2 "	"	"	Locke	
1780	2 "	"	"	Davie	

1781	3 mos.	Pvt.	Huggins
1781	1 "	Ensign	

Battles engaged in: Skirmishes during Cherokee Expedition, Ramsour's Mill and Camden, Cowens Ford of Carawba River.
Residence of Soldier at Enlistment: Rowan County, North Carolina.
Date of application for Pension: Aug 10, 1832
Residence at date of application: Bedford County, Tennessee
Age at date of application: 76 or 77 years. (Born Rowan Co., N.C. 1755/56)
Remarks: No family data

      Ref: A 1
      Ref: Susie Gentry
      Ref: Nashville Monument
      Ref: GSA Report, Washington, D.C.
      Ref: 1835, Bedford County, Tennessee Pension List

* * * * * * * * * *

THOMAS JUSTICE

Name:	Rank:	State Served:
Thomas Justice	PVT	North Carolina

Born 14 January 1765 in Halifax County, Virginia, died after 1834.

1835, age 69, Private, North Carolina State Troops.

GSA: Thomas Justice, S.1842, North Carolina.
Claim No. 7220: West Tennessee, Thomas Justice, of Bedford County in the State of West Tennessee, who was a Private in the Company commanded by Captain Nevil of the Regiment commanded by Colonel Earl in the North Carolina Line for 2 years.

    Inscribed on the Roll of West Tennessee, at the rate of 80 dollars, ___ cents per annum to commence on the 4th day of March 1831.

    Certificate of Pension issued the 16th day of March 1833 and sent to John Bruce, Shelbyville, Tennessee.

Arrears to the 4th of March 1833	$160.00
Semi-anl allowance ending 4 Sept	$ 40.00
	$200.00

Recorded by Daniel Boyd, Clerk	Revolutionary Claim
Book E Vol 7 page 85	Act June 7, 1832

Declaration:
    In order to obtain the benefit of Act of Congress passed June 7, 1832.
State of Tennessee]
Bedford County   ]

    On this 13th day of November 1832, personally appeared in open Court of Pleas and Quarter Sessions of and for the County in the State aforesaid, before Samuel Phillips, John L. Neill and John B. Armstrong, Esquires, Justices of the Peace, appointed to hold said Court, now sitting, Thomas Justice, aged sixty seven years and ten months, who being first duly sworn according to law, doth on his oath, make the following declaration in order to obtain the benefit of the Act of Congress passed 7 June 1832. That he entered the service of the United States, under the following named officers, and service as herein stated. That on the twenty first day of January 1781, he enlisted in the service of the United States and went into Captain William Nevil's Company as a volunteer in the North Carolina Line, that J---- Earl was his Colonel and he believes his General was Jonas Miller, that he joined Captain Nevil at the (Brook) Fort in Rutherford County, in North Carolina and that he served under same Captain Nevil two years against the Indians and Tories, during which time he marched through different parts of Rutherford County in North Carolina, and a fact he served all the time aforesaid Rutherford County except as following the Summer of 1781, he believes in July 11, 1781, he marched from Rutherford County, North Carolina into Spartenburg, South Carolina and continued there a _____ against the Tories, at the end of ten weeks, aforesaid, he marched back to Rutherford County in North Carolina and continued in Rutherford until the end of the two years,

110

about one year and nine days of which time he served during the Revolutionary War, having as his _____ called about the last of January or first of February 1782, but the _____ continued to be troublesome _____ several _____ after the Revolutionary War, called, that during the two years aforesaid, he was acquainted with General James Miller, Colonel John Earls, Major Arrington J. Wood, Captain Nevil, _____. That at the end of the two years aforesaid as he believes __ 21 of January 1782, he received verbally discharge by his Colonel John Earl. That he has no documentary evidence nor does he know of no person whose testimony he can procure who can testify as to his service. He thereby relinguishes every claim whatever to a pension or annuity except the present and declares that his name is not on the Pension Roll of the agency of any State or Territory in the United States.
Sworn to and subscribed this day and year aforesaid.
Jas. McKisick, Clerk   Thomas Justice

Interrogatories by the Court:

Q. 1st: Where and in what year were you born?
A.   I was born in Halifax County in the State of Virginia on the 14th day of January 1765.
Q. 2nd: Have you any record of your age and if so where is it?
A.   I have in a large Bible which formerly belonged to my father.
Q. 3rd: Where were you living when called into service, where have you lived since the Revolutionary War and where do you now live?
A.   I lived in Rutherford County, North Carolina, when called into service and lived there six years after the end of the Revolutionary War, then removed to Buncombe County, I believe 25 years, North Carolina, except I lived in Rutherford County, Tennessee during 1831, then to Bedford County.
Q. 4th: How were you called into service? Were you drafted? Did you Volunteer? Or were you a substitute and if a substitute for whom?
A.   I volunteered.
Q. 5th: State the names of some of the Regular Officers who were with the troops. State your services such Continental and Militia Regiment as you can recollect and the general circumstances of your service.
A.   General James Miller, Colonel John Earl, Major Arrington, Major Wells and Wood and Captain William Nevil, Captain Coulter and Captain McClure(?) and the general circumstances of my service are who he stated.
Q. 6th: Did you ever receive a discharge from the service and if so by whom was it given and what has become of it?
A.   I only received a verbal discharge from Colonel John Earls.
Q. 7th: State the names of persons to whom you are known in your neighborhood and who can testify as to your character for veracity and their belief of your service as a Soldier of the Revolution.
A.   Thomas Smith, Esquire, Nicholas Woodfin, Samuel Woodfin, James McClure, John Keller and Jas. M. Lynch, Clerk of the Justices.

          Ref: GSA Report, Washington, D.C.
          Ref: 1835 Bedford County, Tennessee Pension List.

* * * * * * * * * *

NELSON KELLY

Name: Rank: State Served:
Nelson Kelley   -----   North Carolina
Born _____, died by 1813.

Nelson Kelley, listed as a charter member of the New Hope Baptist Church at Fairfield, Bedford County, Tennessee, in 1809, was a Revolutionary Soldier from North Carolina. State Records of North Carolina, Vol XVII, page 1060, lists Nellson Kelley as a member of Captain William Brinkley's Company of the First Regiment of North Carolina Militia commanded by Colonel Samuel Jarvis.

          He received Revolutionary Pay Voucher No. 699 from Salisbury District in 1782 in the amount of 1200 lbs, signed by Alexander Ervin and David Vance.

Nelson Kelley was the father of Reuben Kelley. Nelson Kelley may be buried in the Keller Cemetery which was on land donated by Reuben Kelley. Nelson Kelley's name is on the 1813 New Hope Baptist Church Roll, marked "deceased". There is a possibility that Nelson Kelley could be buried at New Hope Church Cemetery.

Ref: Colonial and State Records of North Carolina, Vol XVIII, page 1060
Ref: Treasurer's and Comptrollers Papers, North Carolina

* * * * * * * * * *

EDWARD KING

Name:	Rank:	State Served:
Edward King	PVT	South Carolina

Born 1756, died after 1834.

GSA: Edward King, S.38895, South Carolina.
Claim No. 17.067: West Tennessee, Edward King of Bedford County in the State of Tennessee who was a Private in the Regiment commanded by Colonel Pinkney of the South Carolina Line, for the term of 2 years.

Inscribed on the Roll of Tennessee at the rate of 8 dollars per month to commence on the 10 of June 1819.

Certificate of Pension issued the 22 of March 1820 and sent to P.W. Humphries, Esq., Shelbyville, Bedford County, Tennessee.

Arrears to 4th of March 1820 $ 70.63
Semi-anl allowance ending 4 Sept 1820 $ 48.00
    $118.63
Revolutionary Claim
Act 18th March, 1818

September Term, May 5th 1821 per .... Esqr., ... illegible..........

Declaration:
State of Tennessee
June 10, 1819

Edward King, a resident of the State of Tennessee, Bedford County, represents that, during the American Revolution, he enlisted as a Soldier in the Continental Establishment in the First South Carolina Regiment, commanded by Colonel Pinkney and served in the Company of Captain Drayton and was regularly discharged by the commanding officer of said Regiment, in the year 1780 or 1781.

After the expiration of his term of service having served about two years, he afterwards enlisted in the year 1781, in the First Regiment of the North Carolina Line commanded by Colonel Archibald Lytle and in the company of Joseph Thomas Rhodes in the Continental Establishment and continued to serve in said Regiment until he was discharged at the close of the war. Both of his discharges, he has, has been lost by times and accident, so that he cannot now produce either of them. He was discharged in South Carolina, after the close of the war and returned to North Carolina, his place of residence and resided there for sometime and then removed to the Western Country where he has resided about twenty two years. He represents that he is about sixty one years of age and was a poor man. He is dependant on his bodily labour for his support and is so infirm from his age and delicacy of body that he cannot support himself without much difficulty and stands in need of the aid of his government and deserves a pension agreeable to the provision of the late Act of Congress on that subject. He has heretofore never received any pension from his government and release any claim he might have to a pension under any former law.
Sworn and subscribed the day and date above.
Parry W. Humphreys   Edward (X) King

Military Record

Revolutionary War:
Edward King, South Carolina (1st S.C. Regiment by Colonel C. Pinkney)

Copied from Rolls
Date of Enlistment, July 23, 1776
Discharge, 19th August 1778
Vol 9   page 172

Declaration:
District of West Tennessee   ]
Bedford Courts   ]
January Quarter Sessions, 1821]

      On this 4th day of January 1821, personally appeared in open court in the Court of Pleas and Quarter Sessions for the said County of Bedford the same being a Court of Records, Edward King, aged sixty two, resident in the County of Bedford in said District, who being first duly sworn according to law, doth on his oath declare that he served in the Revolutionary War as follows: In the year 1777, he enlisted for two years in Captain Glen Draden's Company in the First Regiment commanded by Colonel Pinkney in the South Carolina Line, on the Continental Establishment and was discharged from the service in October 1779 in Charleston, South Carolina. He again, in the year 1782, enlisted for 18 months in the company commanded by Captain Joseph Rhodes, in the First Regiment commanded by Colonel Archibald Lytle in the North Carolina Line in the Continental Establishment that he continued to serve eighteen months in said Corps, when he was discharged in South Carolina. He made an original declaration on or about the 10th of June 1819 and obtained a Pension Certificate the number of which is not recollected, he having lost or mislaid the said certificate accidentally out of his possession. And I do solomnly swear that I was a resident citizen of the United States on the 18th of March 1818, and that I have not since that time, by gift or sale or in any manner, disposed of any property or any part thereof, with intent thereby, so to deminish it as to bring myself within the provisions of the Act of Congress entitled, "An Act to provide for certain persons engaged in the Land and Naval Service of the United States, in the Revolutionary War," passed on the 18th day of March 1818, and that I have not nor has any person in trust for me, any property or securities contracts or debts, due to me, nor have I any income and _their_ then what is contained in the schedule hereto annexed by me.
Subscribed,
Schedule of Property belonging to Edward King, 4th January, 1821.

1 horse, $50.	2 pots Dutch oven & skillet, 4
9 head cattle, $50.	1 Pewter dish & 4 pewter plates, $1.75
23 do hogs, $15.	4 earthern plates .50
1 cotton wheel & cards $1.00	9 sausers, 11 cups $1.25
1 Flax wheel $1.50	1 old saddle $1.00
2 tin buckets $1.00	1 coffee pot .50
1 can of knives & forks $1.00	notes due him $300.00
6 spoons & 1 tin pan $1.00	12 fowls .75
1 pail & tuggin .75	$431.50
1 churn .50	

         E. King

     The said, Edward King, further declares on oath, that he is a farmer by occupation, but that he is now so old and infirm that he cannot pursue his business with much success as to ensure a competent support. He has a wife living with him named Sarah, aged sixty four years, also grandchild five years old named Harriet McIntosh, who ______ his can support and protection.
Sworn to and subscribed in open court, this 4th day of January 1821.
____________, Clerk   Ed. King

     Ref: GSA Report, Washington, D.C. <u>NOTE:</u> See Addendum.

* * * * * * * * * *

SAMUEL KNOX

Name:	Rank:	State Served:
Samuel Knox	PVT	South Carolina

Born ca 1753, died July 7, 1843 in Rutherford County, Tennessee, married

Catharine ________.

GSA: Samuel Knox, W.302, South Carolina, wife Catharine.
Claim No. 7499: West Tennessee, Samuel Knox of Bedford County in the State of Tennessee who was a Private in the Company commanded by Captain Brown of the Regiment commanded by ______ in the ______ Line for 22 months.

Inscribed on the Roll of West Tennessee at the rate of 73 dollars, 33 cents per annum to commence on the 4th day of March 1831.

Certificate of Pension issued the 16 day of April 1833 and sent to Jas. McKisick, Shelbyville.

Arrears to the 4th of March

	$146.66
	$ 36.66
	$183.32

Recorded by Daniel Boyd, Clerk   Revolutionary Claim
Book E   Vol 7   page 86   Act June 7, 1832

State of Tennessee] Court of Pleas and Quarter Sessions of said County.
Bedford County   ]

On this day, personally appeared in open court, now sitting, before these Justices named herein, Samuel Knox, a resident of the County of Bedford in the State of Tennessee, aged seventy nine years of age or there abouts, who being first duly sworn according to law, doth on his oath, make the following declaration in order to obtain the benefit of the Act of Congress passed June 7th, 1832.

That a short time before the attack by the British on Fort Mooler in South Carolina, he entered the service of the United States in Captain Brown's Company in Sumpter's Regiment as a substitute for his brother William Knox, then an enlisted soldier in said company. That he was in Fort Mooler during the attack made upon by the British. That soon after which he marched on an expedition against the Cherokee Indians in the same company. General Williams commanding this expedition that they penetrated Indian Country, had a fight with the Indians, near end of their tours, defeated them and burnt their towns. That on his return, he got a furlough to go home with the sick. That he soon after, accompanied by his brother William Knox, joined the Army at Charleston. That he enlisted for nine months in the same company. That when his term of service expired, he joined a Volunteer COmpany under Captain Phillip Walker and joined Sumpter's Army. That he then served six months in said Company. That after his term in this company expired, he joined another Volunteer Company in Chester County, South Carolina, commanded by Captain McClure during which term of service he was in the fight at the Rocky Mount, thinks it was on a Sunday and that on the following Sunday, he was in the action of the Hanging Rock, where his commanding officer Captain McClure was killed. That he was in the action of Black Stock when General Sumpter was wounded. And that all his engagements were honorably discharged. The great length of time however, and the consequent decay of his memory prevents him from being positively certain whether the difficult facts stated by him is in correct chronological order or not but that they are substantially true. He further states that he has no documentary testimony, that he knows of no person who can testify to his service except the evidence accompanying muster declaration.

He hereby relinguishes all and every claim to a pension or annuity except the present and declares his name is not on the Pension Roll of any agency of any State.

Sworn to and subscribed in open court 7th August 1832.
Jas. McKisick, Clk.   Sam'l (X) Knox

We, William Keel, a Clergyman of the Baptist Order, residing in Rutherford County and State of Tennessee but also a near neighbor of Samuel Knox and Theodrick F. Bradford at this time a Senator of the Legislature of the State of Tennessee also residing not far from the said Samuel Knox, do hereby certify that we are well acquainted with Samuel Knox, the applicant aforesaid. That we believe him to be about the age he purports himself to be. That he is reputed and believed in the neighborhood where he resides to have been a Soldier of the Revolution and that we fully and entirely concur in said opinion and of the correctness which we have no doubts.

Sworn to and subscribed in open court 7th August 1832.
Jas. McKisick, Clk   William Keel
                                                      Newt Bradford

No. 8.034: West Tennessee, Catharine Knox, widow of Samuel Knox, who was a
Private, Captain Brown, South Carolina, in the Revolution.
            Inscribed on the Roll at the rate of 73 dollars, 33 cents per annum, to
commence on the 4th day of March, 1843.
            Certificate of Pension issued the 7th day of December and sent to W.E.
Jones, of Tennessee. Present.
Recorded in Book A   Vol 2   page 193   Acts of March 3, 1843
                                                      and 17 June 1844

State of Tennessee]
Rutherford County]
            On this twenty eighth day of October A.D., 1843, personally appeared
before me, Lewis Howell, a Justice of the Peace in and for the County of
Rutherford aforesaid, Catharine Knox, a resident of said County aforesaid, about
eighty two years, who being first duly sworn according to law, doth on her oath,
make the following declaration, in order to obtain the provision made by the Act
of Congress passed July 7, 1838, entitled "An Act granting half pay and pension
to certain widows". That she is the widow of Samuel Knox who was a Private in
the Army of the Revolution and was a Pensioner under the Act of 7th June 1832,
and received a Certificate for seventy three dollars and thirty three cents per
annum, dated 16 April 1833, and numbered 7499. Which Certificate she has sent
to Nashville to draw a balance of pension due her, up to her husband's death.
She further declares that she was married to the said Samuel Knox, in the latter
part of the year seventeen hundred and eighty one, or the first part of the year
seventeen hundred and eighty two (1781 or 1782) that by reason of age and
infirmity, she has forgotten the day and month of the marriage. She remembers
that it was about the close of the war, and remembers of some deprevations by
the Tories being committed about the time or shortly before her marriage. She
has no record of said marriage, but remembers that she was married by her uncle
John Simpson, a Presbyterian Preacher. That her husband, the aforesaid Samuel
Knox, died in Rutherford County, Tennessee on the seventh day of July in the
year eighteen hundred and forty three (7th July 1843). That she was not married
to him prior to his leaving the service, but the marriage took place previous to
the first of January seventeen hundred and ninety four, viz, of the time
aforesaid.
Sworn to and subscribed on the day and year above written before me and I
certify that said declarant by reason of age and bodily infirmity is unable to
appear in Court of Record.
Lewis Howell (J.P.)   Catharine (X) Knox
Justice of the Peace   A Attest: F. Summers
                                                              F. Youkam

KNOX BIBLE RECORD

William Knox born the 5 of November 1788
Mary Knox born the 26 day of September 1792
Elizabeth Knox born on the 27 of November 1794

John G. Walker, October 23th, 1843

Elizabeth Knox was born the 2 day of June 1783
Catharine Knox born the 7th day of December 1784

William Knox was born the 5 of November 1788
Mary Knox was born the 26 day of September 1792
Elizabeth Knox was born the 27 of November 1794
Margaret Knox was born the 11 of June 1797
Jinnet Knox was born February the 12 in the year 1799

Samuel Knox: / 6 / S.C., 6th South Carolina Regiment
              Revolutionary War
Appears on a Book: Copied from Roll

Date of Enlistment: August 27, 1776

In 1840, Samuel Knox was with William Eoff.

Ref: GSA Report, Washington, D.C.
Ref: 1840 Bedford County, Tennessee Pensioner List.

* * * * * * * * * *

BENJAMIN LENTZ

Name: Rank: State Served:
Benjamin Lentz (Lents)   PVT   North Carolina
Born March 6, 1755 in Fairfield County, South Carolina, died July 7, 1833 in Bedford County, Tennessee, married in 1787 to Rosena (Rosena Crowell). He was son of John Lentz.

GSA: Benjamin Lentz, W.379, wife Rosena, North Carolina Line.
Claim No. 7595: Benjamin Lentz of Bedford County in the State of West Tennessee who was a Private in the Company commanded by Captain Phifer of the Regiment commanded by Colonel Alexander in the North Carolina Line for 20 months.

Inscribed on the Roll of West Tennessee at the rate of 55 dollars, 66 cents per annum to commence on the 4th day of March 1831.

Certificate of Pension issued the 3 day of May 1833 and sent to Jas. McKisick, Shelbyville.

Arrears to the 4th of March $133.33
Semi-anl allowance ending 4 Sept $ 33.33
                                                              $166.66
Recorded by Daniel Boyd, Clerk   Revolutionary Claim
Book E   Vol 7   page 87   Act June 7, 1832.

Declaration:
State of Tennessee

Declaration in order to obtain the benefit of an Act of Congress passed 7th June 1832.

On this 13th day of November in the year of our Lord, one thousand eight hundred and thirty two, personally appeared in open court before the Worshipful, John L. Neill, Samuel Phillips and Jno. B. Armstrong, Gentlemen Justices of the Court of Pleas and Quarter Sessions for the County of Bedford in the State aforesaid, now sitting, Benjamin Lentz, a resident of said County, aged seventy seven years, eight months and seven days, who being first sworn according to law, doth on his oath made the following declaration in order to obtain the benefit of An Act of Congress passed 7th June 1832. That he entered the service of the United States under the named Officers and served as herein stated, to wit, That he entered the service of the United States in the County of Mecklenburg County and State of North Carolina, sometime, he thinks, in the month of July or the first of August 1776 as a substitute for his father, John Lentz, who was drafted in said County and was placed in Captain John Phifer's Company who was attached to a Regiment under the command of Colonel Adam Alexander and he thinks a COlonel Smith and was marched to a place called Pleasant Gardens as a Colonel McDawal's in Burke County, North Carolina, where they joined General Rutherford and from that place he was marched up the Catawba waters and across the mountains to the head waters of Savahhan River in the Cherokee Nation to an Indian Town, where he says General Rutherford remained some days mailing for General Williamson from South Carolina, who came on and passed General Rutherford and he was told had an engagement with the hostile Cherokees the next day at the Valley Towns, and was marched from that to, he thinks, across French Broad River to Watauga Town and from that to another town, the name of which he does not recollect, where he says the army divided and the Company that he was attached, marched to what was then called the Overhill Town, he says he was marched back again to the main army.

Deponent states that the Americans were engaged in several small skirmishes with the Indians, but none of much magnitude, he says he was then with the main army, marched back to Mecklenburg County and was discharged, after serving a tour of five months or thereabouts, in writing by his Colonel and countersigned by his Captain, on the last day of the year, for he recollects he fired his gun with others at Captain Phifers on the same evening, New Years Eve on his way home, a practice very common in that Country, particularly with the Germans.

Deponent further states that he afterwards entered the service of the United States again as a substitute for one John Simmons in Rowan County, North Carolina, and was placed in a Company under the command of Captain James Barr, who was attached to a Regiment of nine months, were under the command of Colonel McDawal and was mustered into service at Grahams Crossroads about the first of September in the year 1778 or 79 but is not certain which and was marched from there to a little town called, at that time, Perrysburg, in the State of South Carolina on Broad River, and from that to Bacon's Bridge on Ashley River in the last mentioned State where he joined the main army under the command of General Benjamin Lincoln, and he thinks General Butler commanded the Brigade, he was attached to, and from there he was marched to Stone's River where the Americans were attacked by the British, commanded he thinks by Lord Redden, where General Lincoln lost thirty six killed and ninety and upwards wounded. He himself, said deponent, received a wound in his left leg, he thinks by a buckshot, and that General Lincoln retreated from that place about fifteen miles to an encampment he previously erected on Mansford Creek where he remained for some time and from there he says he was marched about twenty miles to a Mr. Lashings or Lassings where he says his term of nine months expired and he was discharged by General Lincoln, he recollects his discharge was a printed discharge and with red ink.

Deponent further states that he entered the service of the United States again as a substitute in Lancaster County and State of South Carolina, sometime about the first of August 1780 in the room and stead of one Thomas Glaze and was placed in Captain John Walker's Company and mustered into service called Stewart's Old Fields in Fairfield County in the last mentioned State on the 12th day of August 1780 and was marched under the command of General Samuel Lacy to Camden and from there on within 18 miles of Georgetown, where information was received that the British had left that place. He says he was then marched into North Carolina to a Mr. Clayton's Plantation on Capeferry River and joined General Rutherford with his troops, he says he was marched in a few days after to Wilmington, North Carolina, but the British had left there, he says he saw three of their vellels before they were out of sight, and was marched back to Claytons and from there to General Caulston where he was mustered out of service the 12th day of February 1781, and in about four or five days after he says he received a discharge in writing, signed by General Rutherford at Salisbury in Rowan County, North Carolina, making in all a term of service of twenty one months.

Deponent further states that he has no documentary evidence whatever and that he knows of no person whose testimony he can procure, except what he can prove by George Smith, who can testify as to his service, and that he relinguishes all and every claim whatever to a pension or annuity except the present and declares that his name is not on the Pension Roll of any agency in the United States.

Interrogatories by the Court:

Q. 1st: Where and in what year were you born?

A.   I was born in Fairfield County in the State of South Carolina on the 6th day of March in the year 1755, agreeable to my grandfather's record.

Q. 2nd: Have you any record of your age and if so where is it?

A.   I have a record of my age at my house in this County taken from my grand father's family record.

Q. 3rd: Where were you living when called into service? Where have you lived since the Revolutionary War? And where do you now live?

A.   I was a citizen of Mecklenburg County in the State of North Carolina when I first entered the service and the last time I was a citizen of Lancaster County, South Carolina and mustered into service at Stewart's Old Field in Fairfield County, South Carolina, after the close of the war, I settled in Rowan County, North Carolina where I lived until the

117

year 1815, when I removed to Bedford County, Tennessee where I have lived every since and where I now live.

Q. 4th: How were you called into service? Were you drafted? Did you volunteer or were you a substitute and if a substitute for whom?

A. I was a substitute all the time I was in service. First, for my father, second for John Simmons and the last time for Thomas Glaze.

Q. 5th: State the names of some of the Regular Officers who were with the troops where you served, such Continental and Militia Regiments as you can recollect and the general circumstances of your service.

A. I recalled General Benjamin Lincoln at the Battle of Stones, and I think Colonel Clark was a Regular Officer, the Regiment of State Troops that I was in was 19th Regiment and the 6th Brigade, I do not recollect the names or numbers of any Continental or Militia Regiment, whatever at this time, except the one I was in.

Q. 6th: Did you ever secure a discharge and if so what has become of it?

A. I received three discharges in writing, one signed by General Lincoln and wrote with red ink, and I think two of my discharges were thrown into the fire about the time I started to move to this County and one I brought with me but cannot find it among my papers and do not know what has become of it.

Q. 7th: State the names of persons to whom you are known in your present neighborhood who can testify as to your character for veracity and their opinion of your service as a Soldier of the Revolution.

A. The Rev. William Jenkins, Mr. George Smith, Michael Fisher, Esq., and Benjamin Strickler.

Sworn to in open court the day and year aforesaid.
Jas. McKisick, Clk.   Benj. Lentz

State of Tennessee]
Bedford County   ] November Term 1832

This day, George Smith, Senr., a resident of said County, personally appeared in open court and after being duly sworn according to law, deposeth and saith that he is well acquainted with Benjamin Lentz who has subscribed and sworn to the foregoing declaration, both in the State of North Carolina and in his present neighborhood in the State of Tennessee for many years and that he knew said Lentz to be and was himself a Soldier of the Revolution, he says he became acquainted with said Lentz at a Mr. Clayton's not far from Wilmington on Capeferry River, and that said Lentz was in a Company commanded by a Captain Walker. He also states that said Lentz is reputed and believed to have been a Soldier in the Revolution, in the neighborhood where he now resides, and that he believes him to be the age he states he is.
Sworn to in open court this 13th day of November 1832.
Jas. McKisick, Clk.   George Smith

We, William Jenkins, a Clergyman, residing in Bedford COunty in the State of Tennessee, and Benjamin Strickler, residing in the same, do hereby certify that we are well acquainted with Benjamin Lentz, Senr., who has subscribed and sworn to the following declaration, that we believe him to be seventy seven years, eight months and seven days of age, that he is reputed and believed in the neighborhood where he now resides to have been a Soldier of the Revolution, and that we concure in that opinion.
Sworn to and subscribed in open court this 13th day of November 1832.
Jas. McKisick, Clk.   William Jenkins
                                                       Benjamin Strickler

And the said court do hereby declare their opinion after the investigation of the matter and after putting the interrogatories prescribed by the War Department who appear to be of sufficient age to know and states and after securing the affidavit of George Smith, that the said applicant was a Soldier of the Revolution and served as he states and that William Kenkins who has signed and qualified to the foregoing certificate is a clergyman of good standing in the Lutheran Church, and a resident of the County of Bedford and State aforesaid, and that Benjamin Strickler, who also signed and was qualified to the same, is at this time a respectable merchant and citizen of this County, and a creditable person, and that his statements are entitled to full faith and credit. Done in open court this 13th November 1832.

J.L. Neill
John B. Armstrong
Samuel Phillips

I, James McKisick, Clerk of the Court of Pleas and Quarter Sessions for Bedford County in the State of Tennessee, do hereby certify that the foregoing contained the original proceeding of the said county in the matter of the application.

Line for a decision

In testimony whereof I have hereunto set my hand and Seal of Office at Office in Shelbyville, 28th December 1832.

Jas. McKisick, Clk.

Claim No. 4719: West Tennessee, Rosena Lentz, widow of Benjamin Lentz, deceased, who was a Pensioner under the Act of 1832, and who died on the 7th July 1833 of Bedford County in the State of Tennessee who was a Private in the COmpany commanded by Captain Phifer of the Regiment commanded by Colonel Alexander in the North Carolina Line for 20 months.

Inscribed on the Roll of West Tennessee at the rate of 66 dollars, 67 cents per annum, to commence on the 4th day of March 1836.

Certificate of Pension issued the 13th day of December 1839 and sent to H. Yoakum, Murfreesboro, Tennessee.

Arrears to the 4th of Sept 1839	$233.33
Semi-anl allowance ending 4 Sept 1840	$ 33.33
	$266.66

Recorded by D.D. Addison, Clerk   Claim July 7, 1838
Book _ Vol 2 page 208

Claim No. 3565: West Tennessee, Rosena Lentz, widow of Benjamin Lentz, who was a Private in the North Carolina Line.

Inscribed on the Roll at the rate of 66 dollars and 67 cents per annum, to commence on the 4th day of March 1843.

Certificate of Pension issued the 9th day of December 1843 and sent to Claimant, Shelbyville, Tennessee.

Act of March 3, 1843

Recorded in Book A Vol 1 page 220.

State of Tennessee]
Bedford County   ]

On this twenty second day of August eighteen hundred and thirty nine, personally appeared before the Circuit Court sitting for said County of Bedford, at the Court House in Shelbyville, the Hon. Samuel Anderson, Judge, presiding, Rosena Lentz, a resident of said Bedford County, aged about seventy two years, who being first duly sworn according to law, doth on her oath, make the following declaration in order to obtain the provision made by the Act of Congress passed July 7, 1838, entitled "An Act granting half pay and pension to certain widows". That she is the widow of Benjamin Lentz, who was a Soldier (perhaps a Private) of the Revolutionary War. That he has proved his services, and the proof she believes is now on file in the Pension Office at Washington City. That under that proof, he (in his life time obtained a Pension of ____ dollars per annum, perhaps per Act of June 7, 1832). That after his death, she obtained a balance of pension, dur up to the period of his death and his Pension Certificate was there deposith at the Agency for paying Pensions in Nashville, Tennessee. She has no copy of the Certificate, nor can she say exactly the amount he drew. It was sixty or seventy dollars per annum.

She further states that she was married to the said Benjamin Lentz on the __ day of ___ in the year seventeen hundred and eighty seven. That her husband the aforesaid Benjamin Lentz died on the seventh day of July, eighteen hundred and thirty three. That she was not married to him prior to his leaving the service, but the marriage took place previous to the first of January seventeen hundred and ninety four. She has no documentary or record evidence to prove her marriage, but the same took place at the time above stated.

Prescribed and sworn to in open Court at the date above written. In testimony whereof I, John L. Neill, Clerk of said Court, have hereunto set my hand and affixed my Private Seal, having no Seal of Office, this 22nd day of August, A.D., 1839.

John L. Neill, Clerk   Rosena (X) Lentz
of Bedford Circuit Court, Tennessee

State of Tennessee
        I, Samuel Anderson, one of the Judges of the State of Tennessee, presiding in and for the County of Bedford, do certify that John L. Neill, who has made the above certificate, is and was at the date of making the same, Clerk of our said Court of said County, duly elected and quarlified and that said certificates in one form of law. Given under my hand and seal this 22nd day of August 1839.

                                        S. Anderson
                                        Judge, Tennessee

Benjamin Lentz Bible Record

NOTE: This Bible is written in German and has been translated into English by Daniel L. Barringer, August 22, 1839. He was Chairman of Germanic Languages, University of North Carolina, Chapel Hill, North Carolina.

1. Catharine Lentz, daughter of Benjamin Lentz was born 11th Feb. 1788
2. Elizabeth, was born 7th March 1790
3. George, was born 2nd December 1792
4. Margaret, was born 4th September 1795
5. Annamaria was born 9th December 1797
6. Benjamin was born 2nd February 1800
7. Henry was born 26th March 1802
8. John was born 9th December 1804
9. Rosanna was born 8th December 1807
10. Valentine was born 11th November 1810
(The additions to the above consists mainly of the names of the Baptismal sponsors, to each child)
        Bible owned by Mrs. Annie Lentz Fisher.

        Ref: GSA Report, Washington, D.C.
        Ref: Widow's Application for Pension

                    * * * * * * * * * *

JACKSON LILE

Name: Rank: State Served:
Jackson Lile   PVT   North Carolina
Born December 10, 1761 in North Hampton County, North Carolina, died May 4, 1843 in Bedford County, Tennessee, married July 18th, 1793 to Elizabeth Hester who was born November 1, 1774.

1835, age 72, Private, North Carolina Line.

GSA: Jackson Lile (Lisle), W.116, wife Elizabeth, North Carolina.
Claim No. 25088: West Tennessee, Jackson Lile of Bedford County in the State of Tennessee who was a Private in the Company commanded by Captain Harring of the Regiment commanded by Colonel Butler in the North Carolina Line for 14 months.
        Inscribed on the Roll of West Tennessee at the rate of 46 dollars, 66 cents per annum, to commence on the 4th day of March 1831.
        Certificate of Pension issued the 29 day of September 1833.
Arrears to the 4th of Sept $116.65
Semi-anl allowance ending 2 March $ 23.33
                                                $139.98
Recorded by Daniel Boyd, Clerk   Revolutionary Claim
Book E   Vol 7   page 87   Act June 7, 1832

Jas. McKisick, Clk.   Dead - letter to Elizabeth Lile, May 4, 1843.

State of Tennessee]
Bedford County   ]
          On this 7th day of August eighteen hundred and thirty two, personally appeared in open court before the Quorum of the Court of Bedford County, now sitting, Jackson Lile, a resident of Bedford County in the State of Tennessee, aged seventy years and eight months, who being first duly sworn according to law, doth on his oath, make the following declaration, in order to obtain the benefit of the Act of Congress passed June 7th, 1832. That he entered the service of the United States under the following named officers and served as herein stated. That he was drafted as a Militiaman under Captain Isham Harris and exchanged to the command of Peter Bennets, both companies under the command of Colonel Butler. Lile cannot recollect the exact period but to the best of his recollection it was in June ____, to the Battle of Camden. He continued to serve under the command of Bennet until after the Battle of Camden in which Battle _____, part of a common soldier.

          After the defeat of the American Army at Camden, this applicant's term expired ___ _____ enlistment ____ the three months. He then enlisted as volunteer in a Company of Dragons, commanded by an Officer whose name the applicant cannot at this time remember, being with strangers to each other at the time of his enlistment, at the expiration of that term of service, he again colunteered under the command of Captain John Henderson, whose Lieutenant was _____ Henderson under the command of Captain Henderson, this applicant fought at the Battle of Guilford, the whole commanded by General Green.

          After this he continued his enlistment as a volunteer until near the close of the war, after the capture of Cornwallis, when he secured his discharge from a Frenchman who commanded his Regiment whose name was Matmedy, as well as this aplicant can pronounce the name.

          Applicant never held any commission and never attaching any importance to his discharge, had it lost or destroyed, a number of years ago. He knows of no person now living by whom he could procure his services nor has he any documentary evidence by which he can show the facts. He was enlisted in Granville County, North Carolina, marched to Hillsborough, thence through Salisbury into South Carolina to Camden, after that battle the troops rendezvoused at Hillsborough, when he volunteered for a second time of service.

          Applicant was born in North Hampton County, North Carolina in the year 1761, then moved to Granville County. He has the record of his age in a Bible at home, taken from a record in his father's Prayer Book. He was living in Granville County, North Carolina, when called into service and since then, has lived in the same County unti the last nine years. He now lives in Bedford County, Tennessee, applicant was drafted for the first three months at the age of eighteen, after that term of service he volunteered. He now cannot recollect the names or the Regular Officers, he recollects Colonel Washington being in it and Green and except the two Battles of Camden and Guilford, there was no inportant transaction, some small skirmishes with parties of Tories. Colonel William Barnett, William Norvell, Esq., William Allison, Esq., James Allison and John Rushing. a minister of the Gospel, are acquainted with the applicant, character for veracity and the said Jackson Lile, hereby relinguishes every claim whatever to a pension or annuity except the present and declares that his name is not on the Pension Roll of the agency of any State.
Sworn to in open court, 7th August 1832.
Jas. McKisick, Clerk   Jackson Lile

          We, John Rushing, a clergyman, residing in the County of Bedford, State of Tennessee and William Barnett, William Norvell, William Allison, residing in the same, hereby certify that we subscribed and sworn to the above, we believe him to be seventy years of age. That he is reputed and believed in the
          neighborhood where he now resides, to have been a Soldier of the Revolution and that we concure in that opinion.
Sworn to in open court, 7th of August 1832.
Jas. McKisick, Clerk   William Norvell
                                                         William Barnett
                                                         John Rushing

Jackson Lile Bible

Jackson Lile was born December 10th day A.D. 1761
Elizabeth Hester was born November 1st A.D. 1774

Jackson Lile and Elizabeth Hester was married July 18th day 1793

James Hester Lile, first child of Jackson and Elizabeth Lile was born October
       12th day A.D. 1794
Benjamin Lile was born March 17th day A.D. 1797
Sally Lile was born September 4th day A.D. 1798
William Lile was born September 25th day A.D. 1800
Rebecca Lile was born July 8th day A.D. 1803

Sally Lile was married 23 Jan 1816
James H. Lile was married 7th Nov 1816
Wm. Lile was married 29 Aug 1820
Rebeca Lile was married 29 Oct 1821
Benjamin Lile was married 5th Sept 1822
Jackson Lile was married 25 Dec 1834
Elizabeth Lile was married 2nd April 1835

Nancy Lile was born March 4th day 1810
Clary Lile was born August 29th day 1812
Elizabeth Lile was born the 9th May 1814
Jackson Lile was born March 2nd day 1816

In 1850 Census of bedford County, Tennessee: 9th District, Visit No. 87:

Elizabeth Lile	76 F	N.C.
Clary Lile	37 F	N.C.
Nancy E. Bullock	5 F	Tenn.

1835, age 72, Pvt, North Caroline Line.

> Ref: GSA Report, Washington, D.C.
> Ref: Jackson Lile Bible Record
> Ref: 1835 Bedford County, Tennessee Pension List

* * * * * * * * * *

NICHOLAS LOYD

Name:	Rank:	State Served:
Nicholas Loyd	PVT	North Carolina

Born 14th March 1753 in Bute County, North Carolina, died after 1834.

1835, age 81, Private, North Carolina Militia.

GSA: Nicholas Loyd, S.4569, North Caroline Line.
Claim No. 7675: West Tennessee, Nicholas Loyd of Bedford County in the State of Tennessee, who was a Private in the company commanded by Captain Harrison of the Regiment commanded by Colonel Moore in the North Carolina Line for 8 months from 1780.

       Inscribed on the Roll of West Tennessee at the rate of 26 dollars, 66 cents per annum, to commence on the 4th day of March 1831.

       Certificate of Pension issued 11 day of May 1833 and sent to Jas. McKisick, Shelbyville.

Arrears to the 4th of March 1833	$53.33
Semi-anl allowance ending 4 Sept 1833	$16.33
	$66.66

Recorded by William Allison, Clerk	Revolutionary Claim
Book e Vol 7 page 81	Act June 7, 1832

Declaration:
State of Tennessee

       Declaration in order to obtain the benefit of an Act of Congress passed the 7th June 1832.

       On this 10 day of November in the year of our Lord, one thousand eight hundred and thirty two, personally appeared in open court before the Worshipful Samuel Phillips, John B. Armstrong and John L. Neill, Esquires, Gentlemen

122

Justices of the Peace appointed to hold the Court of Pleas and Quarter Sessions for Bedford County in the State of Tennessee, now sitting, Nicholas Loyd, aged seventy nine years, seven months and __ days, who being first duly sworn according to law doth on his oath make the following declaration in order to obtain the benefit of an Act of Congress passed the 7th June 1832. That he entered the service of the United States under the following named Officers and served as herein states (to wit), that he entered the service of the Unites States as a Volunteer in Captain Samuel Sneed in the County of Granville and State of North Carolina about the last of September in the year 1779 or 1780 but is not certain at this time which, and was marched to Hillsborough, Orange County and State of North Carolina, where he says he received a musket cartridge box &c, and attached himself to a Company by Captain Richard Harrison, Lieutenant James Hays and Ensign Shadrack Parrish and was there mustered into service about the first of October in one of the years last aforesaid and in a short time after he was marched under the command of General Butler and Colonel William Moore, to Bell's Mill upon Deep River, he thinks in Chatham County, North Carolina, where he was stationed for sometime, and from there he was marched to the Island Ford on the Yadkin River in Rowan County, North Carolina, about seven miles from Salisbury where he was kept for about three or four weeks, and was then marched on through Salisbury towards the State of South Carolina to a place called the Three Mile Creek, where he says the Americans brought to that encampment a number of British and Tory prisoners. He recollect the British prisoners were in their Red Coat Uniforns. He also states that he assisted of that place to build a log pen to confine them in and was kept there as one of the guard for some weeks. He says he was then marched under Colonel Moore with about four hundred _____ men, and Officers to attack a set of Tories which had embodied in Leadfords Cave, on Callaways Creek, and he says the Tories surrendered themselves as prisoners to Colonel Moore without much resistance and that they marched said prisoners to General Butler's Headquarters where he remained with said troops until his term of three months service expired, when he was discharged in writing by his Captain and returned home. He further states that afterward about the first of August in the year 1781, he enlisted under Colonel Robert Burton at Williamsborough (Williamboro) in Granville County, North Carolina for six months. And was ordered to take charge of the Public Pack Horses, as an enlisted soldier, with others, he recollects Lewis Parrish as one, and John ___uit, as another soldier who was placed there at the sametime. He says he was sent from that place to Guilford Court House with expresses and to Governor Burks also, and to Colonel Joseph Taylor, but how often he went on these expeditions, he cannot now recollect. He states that afterwards, he was ordered to take charge of the public wagon and team which he did and was engaged in conveying Governor Burk's household plunder from Buckingham County in the State of Virginia back to Hillsborough (Hillsboro), North Carolina, under the command of Anderson Smith and that he remained in service of the United States as an enlisted soldier under said Colonel R. Burton for five months. He thinks he was discharged about the first of January 1782, in writing, signed by said Colonel R. Burton and returned home making in the whole a tour of service of eight months, deponent declares, although said last mentioned tour of duty was performed as above states. It was not upon Civil Contract, but as an enlisted soldier in the State Troops of North Carolina and in that way he received his discharge.

He says he has no documentary evidence whatever at this time, and that he knows of no person whose testimony he can procure who can testify as to this service, and that he hereby relinguishes all and every claim to a pension or annuity whatever except the present and declares that his name is not on the Pension Roll of any agency in the United States.

Interrogatories by the Court:

Q. 1st: Where and in what year were you born?
A.   I was born in the County of Bute County in the State of North Carolina, on the 14th of March in the year 1753, agreeable to my father's family record, was at my house in this County.
Q. 2nd: Have you any record of your age and if so where is it?
A.   I have my father's family record at my house in this County, where my

123

my age is recorded.

Q. 3rd: Where were you living when called into service? Where have you lived since the Revolutionary War and where do you now live?

A.   I lived in Granville County, State of North Carolina all the time I was in the service of the Revolution and after the close of the war I moved to South Carolina, and acted as overseer for one year for Colonel Henderson and there to the State of North Carolina again and from there to Grainger County in the State of Tennessee and from there to Bedford County, Tennessee, about 25 years ago, where I now live.

Q. 4th: How were you called into service? Were you drafted? Were you a volunteer or were you a substitute and if a substitute for whom?

A.   I was a volunteer the first tour and the last I was an enlisted soldier.

Q. 5th: State the names of some of the Regular Officers that were with the troops where you served, such Continental and Militia Regiments as you can recollect and the general circumstances of your service.

A.   I recollect to have sen General Davidson, but do not now recollect the names of any other Regular Officers whatever. I think the Regiment that I was in was the 4th but I cannot recollect the names or numbers of any other Regiment whatever at this time, and believe I have given a history of the most pertinent circumstances of my services.

Q. 6th: Did you ever secure a discharge and if so what has become of it?

A.   I did receive two discharges but what has become of them, I cannot recollect at this time.

Q. 7th: State the names of persons to whom you are known in your present neighborhood who can testify as to your character for veracity and their opinion of your service as a Soldier of the Revolution.

A.   Stephen Murphree, Esq., William Norvell, Esq., and John T. Frazer, but have not formed an acquaintance with any clergyman.

Sworn to in open Court the day and year aforesaid.

Jas. McKisick, Clk.

Nicholas (X) Loyd

State of Tennessee]
Bedford County   ] November Term 1832

On this 10th day of November in the year of our Lord, 1832, personally appeared in open court, Stephen Murphree, Esq., and William Norvell, Esq., who after being first duly sworn according to law, deposith and saith that they are now and have been for the last twenty years, well acquainted with Nicholas Loyd who has subscribed ...(incomplete) ...

1835, age 81, Private, North Carolina Militia.

Reg: GSA Report, Washington, D.C.
Ref: 1835 Bedford County, Tennessee Pension List.

* * * * * * * * * *

HUGH McCAREY (McCRORY)

Name:	Rank:	State Served:
Hugh McCarey	PVT	North Carolina

Born 1758 Ireland, died 28th March 1836 in Bedford County, Tennessee, married Jane Clark in 1786 in Mecklenburg County, North Carolina. Both are said to be buried in Old Samel Cemetery at Bell Buckle, Tennessee, without markers.

Jane (Clark) McCrory died 9 February 1838, aged 88 years.

Children:

1. Hannah, 1st born, born 1787 married John Majors in 1815
2. John, 2nd born, born 1788 married Ann Wilson
3. Mary, youngest, born 1794 married Samuel Elliott in 1814. (both Hannah and Mary were married in Bedford County.)

GSA: Hugh McCrory, S.46.254, North Carolina, wife Jane.

Claim No. 7520: West Tennessee, Hugh McCrory of Bedford County in the State of Tennessee, who was a Private in the Company commanded by Captain Raford of the Regiment commanded by Colonel Thaxton in the North Carolina Line for

15 months in Inf. and 7 months in Cav.

        Inscribed on the Roll of West Tennessee at the rate of 79 dollars, 16 cents per annum, to commence on the 4th day of March 1831.

        Certificate of Pension issued the 20 day of April 1833 and sent to Jas. McKisick, Shelbyville.

Arrears to the 4th March 1833	$158.32
Semi-anl allowance ending 4 Sept	$ 39.58
	$197.60

Recorded by Daniel Boyd, Clerk   Revolutionary Claim
Book E   Vol 7   page 88   Act June 7, 1832

Declaration:
State of Tennessee]
Bedford County   ]

        On this the 19th day of August in the year 1832, personally appeared before John B. Armstrong, John L. Neill and Samuel Phillips, Esqrs., Justices appointed to hold the Court of Pleas and Quarter Sessions for the County and State aforesaid for the year 1832. Hugh McCrory, a native and resident in the County aforesaid and State of Tennessee, aged about seventy four years, who being fully sworn according to law doth on his oath make the following declaration in order to obtain the benefit of the provision made by the Act of Congress passed the 7th June 1832.

        This deponent states that he volunteered in the service of his country in the month of May 1778 for nine months at Guilford Court House in the State of North Carolina, under Captain Raford of the North Carolina Line, 4th Regiment.

        We were marched to Moores' Creek in Caswell County, North Carolina where we remained but a short time before we received furloughs to return home, to rendezvous again at a minute warning, in the month of November of the same year, we received orders to join our companies and rendezvous with the Army at Salisbury from which place we were ordered to Charleston in the State of South Carolina. We were then marched to what was called the Ten Mile House, near the Town of Charleston, when we were ordered to Savannah in the State of Georgia, the Officers in command were Colonel Litle, Colonel Thaxton was highest in command, until said troops arrived at a little town on Savannah River, which he thinks was called Parrisburg at which place he thinks General Sumner took command. He further states that the troops remained in said Parrisburg during the winter and were as he thinks under the command of General Howe, a short time and afterwards General Lincoln who was highest in command after the departure of General Thaxton. He further states that in the spring, they were marched up the Savannah River on the South Carolina side, opposite the town of Augusta in the State of Georgia, at which place, the said troops crossed the Savannah River into the town of Augusta. At which place deponent believes never lost, said that British Army had crossed the Savannah River at or near the town of Parrisburg and were directing their course towards Charleston in the State of South Carolina. The troops were then marched down the Savannah River on the Georgia side to the mouth of Briar Creek where they recrossed into the State of South Carolina, directing their course toward Charleston. He states that on their march to Charleston, they has a small skirmish with a party of British Troops from whom they took several wagons loaded as he understood and believed with rum. This skirmish, he thinks, was on Edisto River, though he cannot say certainly that it was. He states that the American Army followed on after the British Troops, until they arrived at a place called Bacon's Brigades, where the Americans halted. He states that the American guards were attacked at this place, but does not think any person was killed. He states that he still continued with the said troops in their marches and assunder marches and the several skirmishes that preceded the battle at Stones and that he was in said engagement, which he thinks was on the 20th of June and on Sunday, he also thinks Colonel Roberts was killed in this engagement. He further states that from the vicinity of this battle ground, they were marched near a place called Fort Royal as he understood and believes to prevent the British from having Bluford Island, at which place he remained until his term of service expired, that he was then marched to Bacon's Bridage, from which place he was marched to the Ten Mile House, where he again volunteered to guard some prisoners at Salisbury in the State of North Carolina, which service he also performed. He was then legally discharged from the service of his country. His discharge was signed by Colonel Litle, dated in 1781 but he does not recollect the month or day of the month, which discharge he has lost many years past. He recollects the names of General Howe and Lincoln, as commanding at different times in this campaign. General Sumner, who he believes was a Brigadier General of the North Carolina Line. Colonels Little, Thaxton and Armstrong. Majors Armstrong and Dickson. Captains Raford, Lewis, Roads and Chapman.

Deponent further states that he again volunteered in the service of his country in the year 1780, under Captain Forbes, in a Regiment commanded by Colonel Pasely in General Davidson's Brigade. He does not recollect the name or number of this regiment, in Rowan COunty in the State of North Carolina on the Yadkin River. From there he marched to Six Mile Creek in Mecklenburg County, North Carolina, where he remained during nearly all that winter. When he was again discharged from the service of his country by Colonel Fifer to whose Regiment he had been transferred, this discharge as he believes was dated February 1781. Which discharge has also been lost. He believes he was serving this term upwards of three months, but cannot say the precise time. Deponent further states that he again volunteered in the service of his country in 1781 and as he believes in the month of March, in the Light Horse, in Captain Walker's Company and was commanded by Colonel or Major Lee. He states that he volunteered in Guilford County and was in a few days after being mustered into service taken prisoner at Colonel O'Neal's, the State of North Carolina by Tarlton Troopers. The same day, he was taken prisoner, he understood and believed that a battle was fought between Colonel Lee and a Tory Colonel by the name of Piles. This battle was fought within two miles of place where said deponent was taken prisoner. He was kept under close confinement by the British for some time. He cannot now recollect exactly how long. He was afterwards reoffered to return home or parole where he remained as he now believes about two weeks, when he broke his parole and again volunteered in the service of his country in the County of Guilford, State of North Carolina, in a Company of Light Horse, commanded by Captain Bashares and joined General Rutherford's Army on the Cape Fear River, near the Raft Swamps, from which place we marched to a place called the Governor's Bridge in the vicinity of Wilmington, where they remained until the British left the said Town of Wilmington, when they took possession in the said town. From which place we were ordered home and dismissed from the service of his country. He said deponent does not recollect whether he received any regular discharge for these two last terms of service or nor can he now say how long he was in actual service during these two latter terms, that thinks it must have been between three and four months. Deponent further states that he again volunteered in the service of his country for three months under a man who was called Major Rutherford, and who he supposed was a Quarter Master, to ride expresses and assist in the public store at Guilford Court House in the State of North Carolina, which term of service he faithfully performed and was legally discharged by said Major Rutherford. This discharge was dated as he believes in the year 1782, and has since been lost. Said deponent further states that he does not know if any person now living by whom he could prove more fully his several terms of service, than he has heretofore done by the depositions of Benjamin Starrett and Francis McAmy, whose deposition are now in the Office of the Secretary of War, or the Secretary of the Treasury, to which he wishes references made, as the said Starrett and McAmy have, since said depositions were made, removed to such distance from said deponent, that his bodily infirmities under it almost impossible for him to see them and procure new depositions to forward with this declaration.

I, Hugh McCrory, do hereby relinguish every claim whatever to a pension or annuity except the present and declares that his name is not on the Pension Roll of the agency of any State in the United States.

Interrogatories by the Court:

Q. 1st: Where and in what year were you born?
A.   In Ireland and about the year 1758 as I have been informed.

Q. 2nd: Have you any record of your age?
A.   I have no such record.
Q. 3rd: Where were you living when called into service? Where have you lived
         since the Revolutionary War? And where do you now live?
A.   In the County of Guilford in the State of North Carolina. From thence I
         removed to Mecklenburg County in the State of North Carolina. From
         there I removed to the County of Bedford and State of Tennessee where
         I lived ever since.
Q. 4th & Q. 5th: The two next interrogatories are fully answered in the body of
         the above declaration.
Q. 6th: State the names of some persons to whom you are known in your
         present neighborhood, and who can testify to your veracity and their
         belief of your service as a Soldier of the Revolution.
A.   The Rev'd Richard Cardwell, William Norvell, Esqrs., B------ Coldwell,
         Colonel Samuel Clay, Colonel Samuel Mitchell, Noble L. Majors, Esqrs.,
         Reuben Manley and Nathan Chaffin, Esqrs.
Sworn to and subscribed in open court the day and year aforesaid.
Jas. McKisick, Clk.   Hugh (X) McCrory

        We, Richard Cardwell, a Clergyman, residing in the County of Bedford
and State of Tennessee and William Norvell, residing in this County and State,
aforesaid, hereby certify that we are well acquainted with Hugh McCrory, who
has subscribed and sworn to the above declaration that we believe him to be
seventy four years of age, that he is reputed and believed in the neighborhood
where he resides to have been a Soldier of the Revolution, and we concure in
that opinion.
Sworn to and subscribed the day and year aforesaid.
Jas. McKisick, Clk.   Richard A. Cardwell
                                                 William Norvell

Declaration in order to obtain the benefit of the Act of Congress of the 7th July
1838. Entitled "An Act granting half pay and pensions to certain widows".
State of Tennessee]
                   ] December Term 1843
Bedford County   ]
        On this 20th day of December 1843, personally appeared in open court,
John McCrory and Reuben Manley, Esqrs., of the Last Will and Testament of
Hugh McCrory, deceased, before the Honorable Samuel Anderson, Esq., Judge of
the 5th Judicial Circuit of the State of aforesaid, who after being sworn
according to law, doth on their oath make the following declaration in order to
obtain the benefit of the provision made by the Act of Congress passed July 7th,
1838, entitled "An Act granting half pay and pensions to certain widows."
        This deponent further states that the aforesaid Hugh McCrory, departed
this life on the 28th day of March 1836, leaving a widow, to wit, Jane McCrory,
who has since departed this life in said Bedford County on the nineth day of
February 1838, at the advanced age of eighty eight years. They further state
that they found the Pension Papers of said Hugh McCrory, deceased, a Pension
Certificate in the words and figures following, to wit, "War Department
Revolutionary Claim", I certify that in conformity with the law of the United
States of the fifth June 1832. Hugh McCrory of the State of West Tennessee,
who was a Private in the Army of the Revolution is entitled to receive seventy
nine dollars and sixteen cents per annum, during his natural life commencing on
the 4th March 1831 and payable Semi-anl on the 4th of March and 4th of
September in every year. Given at the War Office of the United States, this
17th day of April, one thousand eight hundred and thirty three. Len Cass,
Secretary of War. Examined and countersigned, J.R. Edwards, Commissioner of
Services. Payment to be made at Nashville by the First of U.S.A. Bank, Agent
for paying Pensions in the Agency of West Tennessee. Recorded in the Pension
Office in Book E, Vol 7, page 88 by Daniel Boyd, Clerk. They further state that
there is no record of the marriage of the said Hugh McCrory to his wife Jane
McCrory now deceased, and that she has not since the death of her said husband
Hugh McCrory, intermarried with any other person whatever. They therefore
claim a pension for the lawful heirs of the said Jane McCrory, deceased, placed
in their hands for the benefit of said heirs as the Executors of said Hugh
McCrory, deceased.

Sworn to in open court 20th day of December 1843.
John L. Neill, Clerk   John McCrory
                                                             Reuben (X) Manley

        This day being 22nd day of December 1843, personally appeared in open
court before the Hon. Samuel Anderson, Judge and Noble L. Majors and James
Frizzell, residents of Bedford COunty in the State of Tennessee, who after being
duly sworn according to law, doth on their oath, depose and say that they were
present when said Hugh McCrory, mentioned in the foregoing Pension Certificate,
departed this life on the 28th day of March 1836, and that they saw him buried.
They also state upon their oaths that they were present when said Jane McCrory,
the wife of said Hugh McCrory, departed this life or shortly afterwards. They
state positively that they saw her buried and that she departed this life on the
9th day of February 1838.
Sworn to in open court 22nd of December 1843.
John L. Neill   Noble L. Majors (Seal)
                                                             James (X) Frizzell (Seal)

State of tennessee]
Bedford County   ]
        On this the 14th day of April 1852, personally appeared before me, R.S.
Thomas, an Acting Justice of the Peace in and for the County and State
aforesaid. John McCrory, aged about sixty four (64) years who being duly sworn
according to law, doth on his oath, make the following declaration in order to
obtain the benefit of the Act of Congress passed 4th July 1836.
        To wit, That he is the second child and heir at law of Hugh McCrory,
who was a Pensioner under Act of Congress passed 7th June 1832, given to him
for service rendered in the Army of the Revolution, which pension he received up
to the time of his death at eighty dollars or more. My aforesaid father and
mother were married in 1786. My sister, Hannah, age about sixty five years old
is father and mother's first child, and Mary, age about fifty eight years old is
father and mother's youngest child and that he has a record of all their ages
which he now presents, the record is in the Old Family Bible and he has always
heard it said that his father and mother were married in Mecklenburg County,
State of North Carolina. That his sister, Hannah, father and mother's first child
was married to John Majors in 1815 and my father and mother's youngest child,
Mary, was married in 1814, she was the youngest and was married first. They
were both married in bedford County, Tennessee. I must respectively ask the
Hon. Commission to cause their claim to be allowed.
Given under my hand this 14th day of April 1852.
Sworn to and subscribed before me on the day and year aforesaid.
R.S. Thomas, J.P.   John McCrory (Seal)
for Bedford County
        I do certify that the word "Mary" was erased in the declaration.
                                             R.S. Thomas (J.P.)

Affidavit of Reuben Manley

        Making the following affidavit, to wit, that he was well acquainted with
Hugh McCrory, deceased, he got acquainted with him about the year 1814 and I
have always heard it said that they were married in Mecklenburg County, North
Carolina, and that the aforesaid Jane McCrory, deceased, was the widow of Hugh
McCrory, the said Pensioner, who received his pension for service rendered in the
Army of the Revolution. I knew both of the aforesaid persons for a numerous of
years and heard them speak of their marriage frequently. The aforesaid Jane
McCrory was known as a lady of veracity and respectability amongst us and to
the best of my knowledge, I then ... (incompleted) ...

        Know all men by these present that I, John McCrory, one of the children
of Jane McCrory, deceased, the widow of Hugh McCrory, deceased, who was a
Pensioner when living, under the Act of Congress passed 7th June 1832, given to
him for services rendered in the Army of the Revolution. Do by virtue of these
present niminate, constitute and appoint S.S. Williams, my true and lawful
attorney, for us and in our names to prosecute my mother's aforesaid claim or
claims in and to any pension or pensions due under Acts of Congress passed 4th

July 1836 or any other Act of Congress heretofore passed for the services of my said father in Army of the Revolution and to administer on estate of my aforesaid mother in court or courts holding in and for the United States and do any other Act being deem proper, my aforesaid father died on March 28th 1836 and my mother died on 9th day of February 1838 and left the following persons: Hannah, John, Mary and Hugh, the latter died after his mother.

Sworn under my hand and seal on this 14th of April 1852.

In presence of   John McCrory (Seal)

R.S. Thomas, J.P.   for the heirs.

State of Tennessee]
Marshall COunty   ]

 This day being the fifth day of October in the year of our Lord, one thousand eight hundred and forty three, personally appeared before me, James V. Ewing, an acting Justice of the Peace in and for the County and State aforesaid, Benjamin Thompson, a citizen of said County of Marshall, aged seventy three years, and upwards, who after being duly sworn agreeable to law, doth on his oath depose and say that he was well acquainted with Jane Clark of Mecklenburg County in the State of North Carolina, previous to her intermarriage with Hugh McCrory, and for many years after their marriage, lived a near neighbor to them in said County of Mecklenburg, all of which took place previous to the first day of January, seventeen hundred and ninety four and that they passed as husband and wife during the whole time of his acquaintance with them.

Sworn to and subscribed before me the day and year above written.

James V. Ewing (Seal)   Benjamin (X) Thompson

J.P. for Marshall County.

Hugh McCrory, born in Antrim, Ireland, 1758, in America April 1775, married 1786 to Jane Clark in Mecklenburg County, North Carolina. Jane (Clark) McCrory, born in Mecklenburg County, North Carolina died 9th February 1838, aged 88 years.

Hugh McCrory died 28th March 1836, both Hugh and Jane died in Bedford County, Tennessee and buried in Old Salem Cemetery, no markers.

Children:

Hannah, born in North Carolina, married John Majors, 1815, in Bedford County, Tennessee.

John, born in North Carolina, married Ann Wilson, both are buried in Old Salem Cemetery, Bedford County.

Mary, youngest, married 1814 in Bedford County, Tennessee to Samuel Elliott.

Hugh, another child.

 Ref: GSA Report, Washington, D.C.
 Ref: 1835 Bedford COunty, Tennessee Pension List.
 Ref: Duck River Valley Pioneers by Jacobs. 1968, page 92.

* * * * * * * * * *

JAMES McCUISTON

Name:	Rank:	State Served:
James McCuistion	Patriot	North Carolina

Born May 18, 1758 in Rowan County, North Carolina, died March 27, 1826 in Bedford County, Tennessee, married September 11, 1792 to Jean Nicholson in Guilford County, North Carolina. Jean was born January 1767 in Maryland and died November 18, 184_ in Ray COunty, Missouri. Moved to Tennessee in 1806.

Children:

1. Thomas, born December 12, 1792, married February 21, 1816, died March 7, 1880.

2. Ann, born November 22, 1794, married Schooler or Schuler, lived and died in Tennessee.

3. Margery, born October 11, 1796, married Dr. Bell, lived and died in Huntington, Tennessee.

4. James, born September 20, 1798, died November 5, 1798.

5. Anthony, born October 20, 1800, married twice, died June 7, 1881.

6. Jane Elizabeth, born March 9, 1802, married Samuel Ingram, died in Tennessee.
7. James, born September 15, 1805, married March 1825, died September 1869.
8. Benjamin Franklin, born January 20, 1808, married 1830, died January 30,
    1901.

Another record of James McCuistion's children:
1. Thomas, born December 12, 1792, married Nancy Jordan.
2. Ann, born 1794, married _____ Schuler.
3. Margery, born 1796, married Dr. Bell.
4. Jane, born 1798.
5. Anthony, born October 25, 1800, married Nancy Winsett.
6. James, born 1802, died infancy.
7. James, born September 15, 1805.
8. Benjamin F., born January 20, 1808.

Ref: Texas Society DAR Roster Revolutionary Ancestore, Vol III.

* * * * * * * * * *

WILLIAM McGUIRE

Name: Rank: State Served:
William McGuire   Lieutenant   Virginia
Born March 12, 1748 in Virginia, died 1834 in Bedford COunty, Tennessee,
married February 23, 1778 to Mary Shirley in Virginia who was born February 17,
1762 in Virginia and died 1845 in Bedford County, Tennessee. Both are buried in
the Horse Mountain Cemetery with a Military marker.

Military Marker:
Lieut. Wm. McGuire   &   Mary Shirley McGuire
1 Art Regt   born Feb 17, 1762
Cont'l Troops   died   1845
born Mar 12, 1748
died   1834
married   1777

GSA: Military Record. Continental Troops Va.
    William McGuire, Lieutenant
     List: not dated
    of Officers who are
      prisoners of war   Rank, Lieutenant
         No. 10   Remarks: Officer of Artillery
No. of Record 62   J.C. Handley

List: List of Redundant Officers belonging to the 1st Regiment of Artillery
        Not dated   Rank: Lieut.   No. 5
Remarks: Officer who is prisoner of War.

Pay Master General's Return   Jany 10, 1786
Pay due in 1782 $100.
Pay due 1783   133.30
Pay received in 1782   100.
Pay received in 1783   133.30
Remarks: Deranged Jan 1, 1783 but Prisoner till May 1783

Book of Accounts
William McGuire, Lt. Arty.
        To cash for pay for Feb, Mar & April 1783 $100.
        To cash for pay for subsistance July 1783   8.
Vol. 139   page 23

List of Officers and Soldiers of the Virginia Line on Continental Establishment
Not dated: Regiment, Artillery
Number of acres: 200
Warrent, when issued, 25th Augt. 1789

William McGuire was an Ensign, 3rd Virginia Regiment, 1780, and Lieutenant in 1st Regiment, Artillery, Continental Army of Virginia. Was Captured (with wife and son) and held a prisoner of war in Canada until October 1782. He resided in Virginia.

Children:

1. Michael, born about 1779, died in Canada
2. Thomas, born August 1, 1781 in Canada, married Ann Lee (went to Texas)
3. Polly, born December 4, 1783
4. Kate, born 1789, married Peter Lee
5. William, born November 15, 1794, married Mary (Fabra) Ditto
6. Cornelius "Neely", born October 5, 1798, married (1) Jane _____, (2) Jane _____ (went to Texas)
7. John (Dr.), born June 29, 1801, married Mary "Polly" Yell
8. Elizabeth "Bettie", born July 22, 1803, married Henry Holt

      Ref: GSA Report, Washington, D.C.
      Ref: Bedford County, Tennessee Cemetery Records by Marsh
      Ref: Texas Society DAR Roster Revolutionary Ancestors, Vol III, pages 1394 & 1924
      Ref: DAR Tennessee Blue Book Roster & Soldiers, Vol 1, page 1184

* * * * * * * * * *

DANIEL McKISICK

Name:	Rank:	State Served:
Daniel McKisick	Captain	North Carolina

Born 1755 Scotland, died November 19, 1818 in Bedford County, Tennessee, married 1776 to Jane Wilson in Lincoln County, North Carolina, who was born 1759 in Rowan County, North Carolina and died July 4, 1842 in Benton County, Arkansas.

GSA: Daniel McKisick, W.26251, wife Jane, Service in North Carolina. His name appears on a list of applicants for invalid pension returned by the District Court for the District of North Carolina, submitted to the House of Representatives by its Secretary of War on March 2, 1795 and printed in the American State Papers Class 9, page 168.

Rank: Captain
Regt.: Troop of Horse Militia
Disability: Wounded by a musket ball in his left arm
When and where disabled: June 20, 1780, near Ramsour's Mill
Residence: Lincoln County
Remarks: Militia
Evidence incomplete: 1st: No evidence when he left the service
              2nd: The examining Physician do not state the degree in which he is disabled from obtaining a livelihood by labor

Declaration:
State of Arkansas]
Benton County   ]

      On this 14th day of August, one thousand eight hundred and thirty nine, personally appeared before the subscriber, an Acting Justice of the Peace in and for the County of Benton and State of Arkansas, Jane McKisick, aged eighty years, who being first sworn according to law, doth on her oath make the following declaration in order to obtain the benefit of the provision made by an Act of Congress passed July the fourth 1836.

      That she is the widow of Captain Daniel McKisick, who served in the War of the Revolution, that her husband the said Daniel McKisick, commanded a Company of Volunteers or Militia in the COunty of Lincoln in the State of North Carolina, and the 20th day of June in the year 1780, her said husband was in an engagement with the enemy at Ramsour's Mill in said County, received a gunshot wound in his left arm and cause further, of which, he was never able to perform manual labour during the remainder in his life. The ball having entered near the

elbow, and lacerated the line up to near the shoulder where it came out, in consequence of receiving, which wound, he was placed on the list of Invalid Pensioners, as well be more fully understood and explained by a Certificate to the evidence on file in the Pension Office as she believes, in the City of Washington. She cannot at this remote period recollect who commanded the Whigs at the Battle of Ramsour's Mill where her said husband Captain Daniel McKisick, received the wound as above described, but she is inclined to believe that the command devolved on Captain Bells (Wells) who was fell in the action, at the time of the battle, above referred to, said husband, Daniel McKisick, lived about eight or ten miles from said Ramsour's Mills, during the day on the morning of which the battle was fought. She informed that an engagement had taken place with the enemy, and that her husband, the said Captain Daniel McKisick was wounded, she immediately proceeded to the battle ground and found her husband with others, wounded in the action at Rineharts House on a large farm which lay south and near to Ramsour's Mills. On the evening of the same day on which the engagement took place, General Rutledge came up with the Brigade but not in time to take part in the action. The detachment of the enemy consisted principally of Tories and was commanded by a Colonel Moore, as she was then and many times afterwards informed. She cannot at this remote period state exactly the date of her marriage with her husband, the said Captain Daniel McKisick, deceased, but to the best of her recollection, it was in the year 1776 or 1777, she distinctly recollects that her second child was at the breast at the date of said Battle of said Ramsour's Mill, when her said husband was wounded. She was married in the County of Lincoln in the State of North Carolina. The marriage ceremony was performed by a Presbyterian Clergyman by the name of Lyle, who is dead as she believes. She has no documentary evidence of the marriage or the date through papers that point to the accompanying evidence as best she can at this time procure. .Her dead husband, the said Captain Daniel McKisick, drew a pension for many years before and up to the time of his death, she thinks he was placed on the list of Invalid Pension for the State of Tennessee, after moving to that State. His Pension Certificate and any he had, has been lost or mislaid and cannot now be found. The only documentary evidence she has of his being an Invalid Pensioner is the the Power of Attorney with the oath annexed together with his signatures, she knows to be in the handwriting of her dead husband Daniel McKisick. She with her husband and such of her children as were then married, left the State of North Carolina, Lincoln County, in the month of October 1807 and settled in Bedford County, Tennessee, where he resided until the time of his death which was on the 17th of November 1818. She resided at the same place where her husband died until the month of May 1836 when she set out for the State of Arkansas, where she arrived in the month of June in the same year and has since lived in the County of Benton in said State, that she has remained a widow ever since the death of her husband, as will most fully appear by reference to the proof hereto annexed. Sworn to and subscribed on the day and year above written.
David Mitchell, J.P.   Jane McKisick

District of Columbia, Claim No. 4022
        Jane McKisick, widow of Daniel McKisick, who died in the month of November 1818 of ______ in the District of Columbia, who was a Captain of Dragons in the ______ commanded by Captain ______ of the ______ commanded by ______ in the ______ Line for ______.
        Inscribed on the Roll of the District of Columbia at the rate of 31 dollars, 66 cents per annum, to commence on the 4th day of March 1831.
        Increased from $175.
        Certificate of Pension issued the 8th day of May 1845 and sent to H.H. Sylvester, Present.

Recorded by D. Brown, Clk.   Revolutionary Claim
Book C   Vol A   page 222   Act July 4, 1836
                                                   Section the 3.

Reps see letter
Transferred Ark. M 1845 to D.C.

State of Tennessee]
Bedford County   ]

On this 11th day of October 1839, personally appeared before the subscriber, an acting Justice of the Peace, in and for the County, aforesaid, Mary Patton, the widow and relict of John Patton, deceased, aged seventy six years on the 16th day of September last, who being first duly sworn according to law deposith and says that she is the sister of the said, Jane McKisick, the applicant and widow of Daniel McKisick, deceased, and was living with her sister, Jane, a part of her time during the Revolutionary War, and was living in the family at the time the engagement took place between a detachment of the American Army and the enemy at Ramsour's Mill in the County of Lincoln in the State of North Carolina. She was then young but very distinctly recollects the circumstance of the said Daniel McKisick, deceased, being wounded at said Ramsour's Mill, that on the same day on which the battle was fought, the said Jane McKisick, the applicant went on to the place where the engagement was fought, and she, this deponent, went to her father's house four or five miles distance from where said Daniel McKisick then resided, that about three or four days to the best of her recollection, after going to her father's, the said Daniel McKisick with others who were wounded in the engagement were brought there. She cannot at this remote period state the year in which she said, Jane McKisick, the present applicant was married to the said Daniel, deceased. She was present at the time of the marriage, being as above states, a younger sister of the said Jane, the applicant. She distinctly recollects that the said Jane had two children at the time the said Daniel McKisick was wounded, the youngest of which was at the breast, and was left in her care at the time, at the time the said Jane was absent with her wounded husband, the said Daniel McKisick, deceased. That the said Jane removed from the COunty in the Spring of 1836 and which time she has not seen her, that up to that time she remained a widow since the death of her husband, Daniel McKisick, that she is credibly informed and believes the fact so to be, that she is alive and still is a widow being in Benton County, Arkansas. Sworn to before me this day and date above enters.

John Barrett (Seal)   Mary Patton

I, John Barrett, a Justice of the Peace in and for the said County of Bedford in the State of Tennessee, do hereby certify that I am well acquainted with the above named, Mary Patton, who has sworn to and subscribed the foregoing deposition, and that her proof is entitled to full credit. Given under my hand this 11th day of October 1839.

John Barrett, J.P. in and
for for Bedford County,
Tennessee.

"A"
Referred to:

Know all men by these present, that I, Daniel McKisick, of the County of Bedford, in the State of Tennessee, for divers consideration and good causes me hereunto, have made, ordained, constituted and appointed by these presents do make, ordain, constitute, and appoint "William Baylor, Esquire" of the City of Raleigh, in the State of North Carolina, my true and lawful attorney for me, in my name and to my use, to ask, demand and receive of and from Sherwood Haywood, Esquire, Commissioner of the Loan Office in and for North Carolina, the sum of two hundred and forty dollars, money of the United States, the same being my Pension due and owning to me as an Invalid Pensioner for two years commencing September 1808. I, by these present, giving and granting to my said attorney, my sole and full power and authority to obtain the same for me and to _____ and on the receipt thereof to make and _____ the same for me and in my name, ratifying, allowing and confirming whatsoever my said attorney shall lawfully do, in and about the execution of the promises by virture of these present. In witness whereof, I have hereinto set my hand and seal the 10 day of September in the year of our Lord, one thousand eight hundred and ten.

Dan'l McKisick (Seal)

State of Tennessee]
Bedford County   ]

This day, Daniel McKisick, personally appeared before us, Joseph Steele and Ho'l Dawdy, two of the Justices assigned to keep the Peace in the County of Bedford, of the State aforesaid, presence duly acknowledged the foregoing Power of Attorney, in witness whereof, we have hereunto set our hands and seals the (Date missing).

> Joseph Steele
> Ho'l Dawdy
> (Howel Dawdy)

Daniel McKisick lived in Lincoln County, North Carolina. Captain in North Carolina Dragons Militia. Wounded at Battle of Ramsour's Mill, June 20, 1780. Also in expedition against the Cherokees, married 1776 in Lincoln County, North Carolina, to Jane Wilson, born 1759 and died 1844 in Benton County, Arkansas. Daniel McKisick was born 1755, and died November 19, 1818 in Bedford County, Tennessee. He had a grave marker but the cemetery has been long destroyed. The cemetery was on the Old Coggins Farm, south of Shelbyville, Tennessee.

Jane (Wilson) McKisick, wife of Daniel McKisick, was the child of James Wilson and Margaret Wilson. Jane was a sister to Mary Wilson who married John Patton.

Children of Daniel and Jane (Wilson) McKisick:

1. Margaret, born May 11, 1777, died 1865 in Avoyelles Parish, Louisiana, married 1792 to John Dickson who was born March 8, 1772, died October 2, 1827.
2. Mary, born 1780 Lincoln County, North Carolina, died June 2, 1853 in Arkansas, married 1802 to Ezekiel Dickson who was born February 1, 1782, died May 14, 1858 in Arkansas. (Came to Tennessee in 1803)
3. James, born February 24, 1783, died January 12, 1848 in Arkansas, married Mary Vance Greer who was born 1787, died December 8, 1854 in Arkansas. (Went to Arkansas in 1835)
4. John, born 1784, died 1846.
5. David, born December 11, 1786, died November 9, 1863, married October 27, 1814 to Margaret Robinson who was born December 11, 1796, died July 23, 1873. Margaret was a daughter of John Robinson. (Went to Benton County, Arkansas in 1835)
6. Daniel, born 1789, married Margaret Henderson.
7. Joseph, born 1791, died before CSA in Arkansas, married Jane Greer, a sister to Mary.
8. Wilson Harmon, born May 10, 1794, died March 28, 1852, married April 9, 1829 to Theodocia Greer who was born April 9, 1810, died December 23, 1835.
9. Elizabeth Louise, born 1797.

State of Arkansas]
Benton County   ]

On this 17th day of August 1839, personally appeared before the subscriber, an acting Justice of the Peace in and for the County of Benton, John Robinson of said County, aged __ years, who being first duly sworn according to law, deposeth and says that he was a Soldier of the Revolutionary War, he lived in Mecklenburg County in the State of North Carolina and belonging to General Rutherford's Brigade. That in the month of June in the year 1780, according to the best of his recollection, the General marched with the troops under his command from Charlotte in said County to Ramsour's Mill in Lincoln County in said State, that on the morning of the same day which General Rutherford arrived with his Brigade at said Mills, a battle had been fought between a portion of the Militia and Volunteers of the State of North Carolina and a detachment by a Colonel Moore, on their march from Charlotte to Ramsour's Mills, General Rutherford's men took some prisoners among who was and who represented himself to be a brother of the said Moore who commanded the enemies at Ramsour's Mills ... (incompleted) ...

State of Arkansas]
Benton County   ]
        On this 14th day of August 1839, personally appeared before the
subscriber, an acting Justice of the Peace in and for the County aforesaid,
Ezekiel Dickson, aged fifty six years, who being first sworn duly and according to
law, deposeth and says that he was intimately acquainted with Captain Daniel
McKisick and with all his family. He knew him well while he lived in Lincoln
County in the State of North Carolina and also after he moved to the County of
Bedford in the State of Tennessee, in the course of many years he had many
conversations with him and often business with him. He knows that he was
disabled in the left arm and has heard him speak of the cincumstances of his arm
being disabled by a gunshot wound that he received in an action with the enemy
during the War of the Revolution at Ramsour's Mills. He is also well acquainted
with the applicant, Jane McKisick and knows her to be the widow of the said
Daniel McKisick and having been intimate in the family from his boyhood up to
the present time. That the said Daniel McKisick died in the County of Bedford
in the State of Tennessee in the Fall of 1818. The precise day of his death he
could not state from recollection but on examining the family record, he finds
that it then states that he died on the 19th of November in the said year. He
has no knowledge of the marriage between the said applicant, Jane and the said
Daniel McKisick, and as that much have taken place before deponent was born,
they having two children older than deponent, he now knows they lived together
as man and wife up to the time of the death of the said Daniel McKisick and as
deponent was often at their house and has frequently slept under the same roof.
The said Jane McKisick has remained a widow since the death of her husband,
Daniel McKisick. Deponent further states ...(not complete) ...

        Ref: GSA Report, Washington, D.C.
        Ref: Widow's Application for Pension.
        Ref: Dickson-McEwen and Allied Families by Austin W. Smith, 1945.
        Ref: Tennessee DAR Blue Book Roster & Soldiers, Vol 1, page 1190
        Ref: Heitman: Officers of the American Revolutionary War
        Ref: Tennessee DAR Yearbook 1933-34, page 67

* * * * * * * * * * *

GEORGE McLAIN

Name:	Rank:	State Served:
George McLain	PVT	North Carolina

Born October 14, 1760 in Lincoln County, North Carolina, died November 30,
1834 in Bond County, Illinois, married 25th July 1789 in Mecklenburg County,
North Carolina to Rebecca. George and Rebecca McLain had eight children.
One son, Josiah Thomas McLain, who was 46 years old in 1844 and living in Bond
County, Illinois.

1835, George McLain, age 74 years, Private in North Carolina Militia in Bedford
        County, Tennessee.

GSA: George McLain, W.21793, wife Rebecca.
Claim No. 7591: West Tennessee, George McLain of Bedford County in the State
of West Tennessee, who was a Private in the Company commanded by Captain
Martin of the Regiment commanded by Colonel Barber in the North Carolina Line
for 22 months.
        Inscribed on the Roll of West Tennessee at the rate of 75 dollars, 33
cents per annum, to commence on the 4th day of March 1831.
        Certificate of Pension issued the 3 day of May 1833 and sent to James
McKisick, Shelbyville.

Arrears to the 4th of Marsh	$146.66
Semi-anl allowance ending 4 Sept	$ 36.66
	$183.32
Recorded by Daniel Boyd, Clerk	Revolutionary Claim
Book E Vol 7 page 88	Act June 7, 1832

Declaration:
State of Tennessee]
Bedford County   ]

On mthe seventh day of November, personally appeared in open court before us, John B. Armstrong, Samuel Phillips and John L. Neill, Justices of the Court of Pleas and Quarter Sessions for said County, now sitting, George McLain, a resident of the County and State of Tennessee, aged about seventy two years, who being first duly sworn according to law doth on his oath make the following declaration in order to obtain the benefit of the Act of Congress passed June the 7th, 1832.

That he entered the service of the United States under the following named Officers and served as herein stated.

That he was born October the 14th in the year 1760 in Lincoln County, North Carolina, that he had no written record of his age and only think from what he had always understood from his parents, that when first called into service, he lived in said County of Lincoln, where he continued to reside until the year 1798 when he removed to the County of Mecklenburg, North Carolina and lived there until the Autumn of 1816 when he removed to the County of Bedford aforesaid where he has ever since resided and now resides. That in the month of July 1780, he volunteered in the County of Lincoln for three months under Captain Samuel Martin, with John Barber as his Colonel, James Patterson was Lieutenant and John Walker was Ensign under Samuel Martin that he marched to Camden, South Carolina and from there to Ninety-Six to observe the Tories and that they continued to scout the engagement, that at the end of the three months, he returned home and in the next April, colunteered for another tour of three months under Captain John Mattocks, whose Lieutenant was named Aaron McKinzie and whose Ensign was named John Hall, that their Colonel was named William Graham of said County of Lincoln. That a part of said term, they were scouting the County of Lincoln for Tories, and the balance, they were in the County of York, South Carolina and ranging between that and Broad River, all with the subject of keeping down the Tories. That at the end of the tour, he again returned home, that in the next Fall, he again volunteered for three months under Samuel Martin, with John Berry his Lieutenant and James Glenn the Ensign and John Barber the Colonel. That during this tour, they marched in the direction of King's Mountain to join Campbell against Ferguson. That on the evening before the Battle of King's Mountain, they were about encamping a short distance from the mountain, when they were scouted by Tories of Ferguson's Dragons, and scattered and when they heard the firing on the next day, he and five others made towards where it was and joined Campbell just after the Battle had closed. That he was left with four others of his Company to guard the Tory Prisoners and take care of Campbell's wounded, that there were about twenty left for that duty. That the COlonel of his Company went on with the other troops and that he joined them no more during that tour. That immediately upon the close of the last mentioned term, he volunteered for another term of three months under the same last mentioned Officers and marched into South Carolina and joined Sumpter at Clem's Branch and remained there during the remainder of the tour, that during that term, Sumpter kept his headquarters at Clem's Branch, that immediately after the expiration of that last mentioned term, he again volunteered for another term of three months under Captain John Walker of Lincoln County, with William Rankin his Lieutenant and John Hoyle his Ensign and John Barber his Colonel. That they marched into South Carolina and again joined Sumpter at Clem's Branch near where Fishing Creek empties into the Catawba River. That he was out on a foraging party when the British surprised Sumpter in his encampment at Clem's Branch and defeated him, that he was returning to camp from the foraging expedition when he met Sumpter at Colonel Bratton's. On the day after the defeat and Sumpter took him and five others with him to pilot him across the country towards Virginia. Thay they crossed the Catawba at Tuckalgee Ford and crossed the Yadkin at Long's Ferry where he left Sumpter and returned home and joined Captain Frank ______ and spent the balance of the term reconnoitering about Charlotte which was then occupied by Cornwallis. That he returned home and remained there. He does not recollect how long when he again volunteered for another term of three months under

Captain John Walker, William Graham was the Colonel, but he was not with them during the tour, that Major Joseph Dixon had the principal command of them. That when they heard that Cornwallis was _____ Virginia, they followed him until he crossed the South Fork of Catawba River. That between the South Fork and the main river, at a creek called Dutchman's Creek, they killed 4 Tories. That when Cornwallis came to the main river, it was up and he lay there two days and nights. That on the night before Cornwallis crossed the river, this affiant with about forty others under Major Joseph Dixon lay about half a mile behind the British and on the opposite side from where Davidson was killed. That Dixon sent him to South Carolina with an express to Colonel Barber to join him in pursuing Cornwallis. That he took the express to Barber and that Barber was marching to join Dixon when they learned at the South Fork of Catawba, that Cornwallis had not halted in Salisbury but marched across the Yadkin to Guilford and they pursued no further, then he returned home and then remained until the next August when he again volunteered for three months under Captain Robert White, the Lieutenant was named Phillips and the Ensign Mathew Armstrong, the Colonel was Robert Smith, who was over an officer in the Regular Army. That they marched to a place called Little River and there joined General Rutherford and remained with him only two days, when they left him and marched down the country through the Scotch Settlement towards Wilmington. That they met with a company of Tories at a place called the Raft Swamp and entirely routed them in and killed about twenty of them. That they marched down to the Buck Horse near Wilmington and met with another company of Tories and took about twenty of them prisoners and killed about a dozen. That whilst in the neighborhood of Wilmington, their term expired and Smith wanted them to stay a month longer. That Captain White refused to stay, and marched home with all the men except eighteen of whom applicant was one, when they elected Lieutenant Null their Captain and remained another month, that a party of British had occupied the Brick House and they attempted to dislodge them, but that they were compelled to retreat with two men wounded. That during the balance of the month, they ranged the country between Wilmington and Georgetown, South Carolina, when they returned home and were verbally discharged by their Colonel. That he never acted with any of the Continental Regiments except under Sumpter. That he belonged to the Mounted Infantry in all of his tours and was principally employed in scouting parties to overcome the Tories and to hang upon the rear of the enemy, that he has no documentary evidence by which he can prove his claim, as he never received any but verbal discharges, but he can prove by William Maxwell of Rutherford County in this State, that affiant was in the skirmishes of the Raft Swamp and the Brick House and also that he was under Captain Frank _____ when the British were stationed in Charlotte as stated above. That he knows of no person now living by whom he can prove of his services in the Revolutionary War. He relinguishes every claim whatever to a pension or annuity except the present and declares that his name is not on the Pension Roll of any agency of any State.
Sworn to and subscribed in open court this 7th day of November, 1832.
Jas. McKisick, Clk.   George McLain

Claim No. 4384: Illinois, Rebecca McLain, widow of George McLain, who served in the Revolutionary War as a Private. Incd from $30.

Inscribed on the Roll at the rate of 73 dollars, 33 cents per annum, to commence on the 4th day of March 1848.

Certificate of Pension issued the 1st day of August 1850 and sent to M.G. Dale, Coms., Greenville, Bond County, Illinois.
Recorded on Roll of Pensioners under Act Feb 2, 1848, page 347, Vol 3.

State of Illinois]
Bond County   ]
On this fourth day of March in the year of our Lord, one thousand eight hundred and forty four, personally appeared in open court before the Judges of the County Commissioners Court of Bond County in the State aforesaid, a Court of Record of said County now holding the March Term A.D. 1844, of said Court, Robert Keyes, being presiding Judge of said Court, Rebecca McLain, a resident of Bond County aforesaid, aged seventy four years on the 18th September last, who being first duly sworn according to law, doth on her oath, make the

following declaration in order to obtain the benefit of the provision made by the Act of Congresspassed July 7, 1838, entitled "An Act granting half-pay and pensions to certain widows."

That she is the widow of George McLain, who was late of Bedford County, State of Tennessee, deceased, who was late a Private in the Army of the Revolution, and who for services rendered during the said war, was placed on the Pension Roll of the United States, at the rate of seventy three dollars, thirty three cents per annum. That she, this deponent, in the year one thousand eight hundred and thirty five surrendered the Certificate of Pension granted by the War Department to her husband, in order to draw the arrears of pension due up to the day of his death, which she did draw, to which said Certificate and such other documentary evidence as may have been furnished by her husband in his life time and which remain on file in the respectfully refers, the Department.

She further declares that she was married to the said George McLain on the twenty fifth day of July, one thousand seven hundred and eighty nine. That her husband, the aforesaid George McLain, died on the thirtieth day of November, one thousand eight hundred and thirty four. That she was not married to him prior to his leaving the service, but the marriage took place previous to the first of January, seventeen hundred and ninety four, viz, at the time above stated, that she was elgally married in Mecklenburg County, North Carolina, that the marriage ceremony was performed by _____ ' Tygert, Esq., then an acting Justice of the Peace of said Mecklenburg County, that she knows of no record existing of said marriage, that she has diligently searched and employed council to search in said Mecklenburg County and elsewhere for a long time past but can obtain no record proof of the same.
Sworn to in open court March 4, 1844, before me, I,
Robert Keyes, Presiding Judge   Rebecca (X) McLain

At the same time before said court, now open in the Judicially sitting, personally came, Elias W. Alexander of said County of Bond, State of Illinois, aged sixty four years, who being duly sworn deposes and says, that in the summer of the year, one thousand seven hundred and eighty nine, Rebecca McLain, here in Court and who had signed the foregoing affidavit, and George McLain came to my father's house in Mecklenburg County, North Carolina, as man and wife. I was not at the marriage but understood, and it was the understanding of all present, that they had just been married and were making the wedding tour.

I lived in the neighborhood with him in North Carolina from that time till about the year 1816, when they moved to Tennessee, I moved at the same time to Tennessee and remained in their neighborhood till the year eighteen hundred and twenty nine.

They were persons entitled to full credit, having good reputation for truth and veracity.
Witness my hand said 4th day of March A.D. 1844.

Robert Keyes
Presiding Judge
NOTE: An affidavit was made by Josiah T. McLain, part of which was not completed ... "still remains the widow of said George McLain".
Sworn to and subscribed before me and credibility of witness certified to by me, in open court, March 4, 1844.
Robert Keyes   Josiah T. McLain
Presiding Judge

State of Illinois]
Bond County   ]
I, James Bradford, Clerk of the County Commissioners Court, a Court of Record in and for said County, certify that Robert Keyes, whose name appears to the foregoing affidavits, was at the time of the date thereof the Presiding Judge of said Court, duly elected and sworn and that full faith and credit are due to his acts as such. I further certify that the said four signatures purporting to be his are his genuine signatures.

In testimony whereof I have hereunto set my hand and affixed the seal of said Court at Greenville, said County, this 4th day of March A.D. 1844.
J. Bradford, Clerk

State of Illinois]
Bond County   ]
    I, Robert Keyes, the Presiding Judge of the County Commissioners
Court, a Court of Record in and for the said County, do certify that James
Bradford, whose name appears to the foregoing certificate, was at the time of
making the foregoing certificate, and still Clerk of said Court duly commissioned.
I further certify that the said Rebecca McLain, Elias W. Alexander, Josiah N.
Alexander and I, Thomas McLain, are respectable persons, residents of said
County of Bond and State of Illinois.

Robert Keyes
Presiding Judge

Ref: GSA Report, Washington, D.C.
Ref: Widow's Application for Pension.
Ref: 1835 Bedford County, Tennessee Pension List.

* * * * * * * * * *

FRANCIS McKAIMY

Name:	Rank:	State Served:
Francis McKaimy	PVT	North Carolina

Born 15th August 1758 in Orange County, North Carolina, died after 1834 (78
years old in 1834 Pension List)

1835, aged 76, Private, North Carolina Militia.

GSA: Francis McKaimy, S.1853, Served in North Carolina.
Claim No. 6346: West Tennessee, Francis McKaimy of Bedford County in the
State of Tennessee, who was a Private in the Company commanded by Captain
Brasher of the Regiment commanded by Colonel Paisley in the North Carolina
Militia from 1780 for 7 months, 24 days.
    Inscribed on the Roll of Tennessee at the rate of 26 dollars, __ cents
per annum, to commence on the 4th day of March, 1831.
    Certificate of Pension issued the 28 day of February 1833 and sent to
Hon. Jas. K. Polk, H.R., Jas. McKisick, C. Bedford Co., Tennessee.

Arrears to the 4th of September 1832	$39.00
Semi-anl allowance ending 4 March 1833	$13.00
	$52.00

| Recorded by Henry H. Sylvester, Clerk | Revolutionary Claim |
| Book D   Vol 9   page 154 | Act June 7, 1832. |

State of Tennessee
Declaration in order to obtain the benefit of the Act of COngress passed 7th
June 1832.
    On this 13th day of November in the year of our Lord, one thousand
eight hundred and thirty two, personally appeared in open court before the
Worshipful Samuel Phillips, John B. Armstrong and John L. Neill, Esquires,
Gentlemen Justices of the Peace appointed to hold the Court of Pleas and
Quarter Sessions for the County of Bedford in the State aforesaid, now sitting,
Francis McKaimy, aged seventy four years and some months, who after being
duly sworn according to law, in open Court, doth on his oath make the following
declaration in order to obtain the benefit of the Act of Congress passed June the
7th 1832.
    That he entered the service of the United States under the following
named Officers and served as herein states, to wit, That he entered the service
of the United States as a drafted soldier in the County of Guilford and State of
North Carolina on the first of January in the year 1780 and was placed in a
Company commanded by Captain Brasher and rendezvous at Guilford Court House
when he says he was taken from the ranks of said Company by order of Colonel
John Paisley, the Commanding Colonel, and ordered to take charge of Public
Wagons and Team as a driver of the same and said wagon was used in conveying
public arms, powder and lead from Halifax Court House in Virginia to Salisbury in
the State of North Carolina, and to Guilford in the last mentioned State and to
various other places until his term of three months expired when he says he was

dismissed by Major Rutherford and returned home.

Deponent further states that he was drafted again in the same County (Guilford) between the 15th and 20th January 1781 and was placed in Captain Barnett's Company and was again taken from the ranks by order of the Commanding Officers to take charge of another Public Wagon as a driver, in company with about twenty two others, and went to Newbourn in the State of North Carolina for salt for General Green's Army. He states that before they returned about fifteen miles below Hillsborough he received information that the British were then in Hillsborough and he says they were conveyed from there under the command of Colonel Gillespie across Roanoak River at Taylor's Ferry into the State of Virginia where he says they remained until after the Battle of Guilford, when they returned home and was discharged after delivering up the wagons to the Public Officers for a tour of three months service although he says he was very little more than two months in actual service. Deponent further states that while he was on this last mentioned tour of duty, his brother James McKaimy was killed by the Tories and some of Tarlton's men. And that he then volunteered immediately under Captain Brasher's Company under the command of Colonel Paisley and was marched to Deep River in Randolph County in the State of North Carolina in persuit of a man by the name of Fanning, a Tory Colonel, and from there he says he was marched into Chatham County where the Army under Colonel Paisley and Colonel O'Neal joined their Armys together and encamped at Ramsey's Mill on Deep River for some time, and while the troops remained there he says he was in an engagement or skirmish with the Tories in which three Tories were killed and one American, and from there he was marched to some old barracks in Chatham County and remained there some time. He says he was then dismissed til further orders, after serving six weeks and 42 days, he states that after that he was called on again by the same Captain and Colonel and joined them at Guilford Court House, in about ten days after he was dismissed in Chatham, and was marched in search of Tory Captain by the name of Piles. He was called Doctor Piles who it was said collected a band of Tories near the County Line between Chatham and Cumberland Counties and after serving on this expedition four weeks, he was dismissed again until further orders. He further says that he was called on again by the same Captain and Colonel and was marched in search of another Tory Captain by the name of Fields but before the American Troops reached the place where Fields and his men were they had all fled off and he says he was marched back home and then dismissed, he thinks he served two weeks on this expedition, making in the whole a term of actual service of eight months and that he has no documentary evidence whatever and that he knows of no person, except what he can prove by Matthew Cunningham affidavit which accompanies this his declaration, whose testimony he can procure who can testify as to his service, and also that he hereby relinguishes all and every claim to a pension or annuity except the present and declares that his name is not on the Pension Roll of any agency in the United States.

Interrogatories by the Court:

Q. 1st: Where and in what year were you born?

A. I was born 15th of August 1758 in Orange County and State of North Carolina agreeable to the information secured from my parents.

Q. 2nd: Where were you living when called into service? Where have you lived since the Revolutionary War? And where do you now live?

A. I have lived in Guilford County, North Carolina all the time I was in service and after the close of the Revolution until the year 1811 when removed to Bedford County, Tennessee, where I have lived ever since and where I now live.

Q. 3rd: Have you any record of your age and if so where is it?

A. I have not, but from the information of my parents, I am the age stated in the foregoing declaration.

Q. 4th: How were you called into service? Were you drafted? Did you volunteer? Or were you a substitute and if a substitute for whom?

A. I was drafted in Guilford County, North Carolina, the two first tours I served and then I was a volunteer until I was finally dismissed.

Q. 5th: Did you ever receive a discharge and if so what has become of it?

A. I never received a discharge in writing but verbally dismissed for all my

140

services.

Q. 6th: State the names of some of the Regular Officers that were with the troops where you served. Such Continental and Militia Regiments as you can recollect and the general circumstances of your service.

A. I knew Major Rutherford at Guilford and Major John Campbell but do not recollect the names or numbers of any Regiment either Continental or Militia, and my declaration this day subscribed and sworn to, contains a history of my services in the Revolution as near as my memory at this advanced age will permit.

Q. 7th: State the names of persons to whom you are known in your present neighborhood who can testify as to your character for veracity and their opinion of your services as a Soldier of the Revolution.

A. Colonel James McKisick and William Norvell, Esq.

Sworn to anc subscribed in open court the day and year aforesaid.

Jas. McKisick, Clk.   Francis McKaimy

State of Tennessee]
Bedford County   ] November Term, 1832

On this 13th day of November in the year of our Lord 1832, personally appeared in open court, Colonel James McKisick and William Norvell, Esqrs., who being duly sworn according to law, doth on their oaths depose and say, that Francis McKaimy, who has subscribed and sworn to the foregoing declaration is reputed and believed in the neighborhood where he resides to have been a Soldier of the Revolution and that they concure in that opinion, and that they believe his statements upon oath are entitled to credit in a Court of Justice, and also that they believe him to be the age he state he is.

Sworn to in open court the day and year aforesaid.

Jas. McKisick, Clerk   Jas. McKisick
                                                  Wm. Norvell

And the said court do hereby declare their opinion of the matter after the investigation, and after putting the interrogatories prescribed by the War Department. That the said Francis McKaimy, who has subscribed and sworn to the foregoing declaration, was a Soldier of the Revolutionary War and served as he states, and that James McKisick who has subscribed and sworn to the foregoing affidavit is at this time and has been for many years Clerk of the Court of Pleas and Quarter Sessions for this County, and that William Norvell, Esq., who has also signed the same, is a Deputy Sheriff in said County and has formerly been the High Sheriff of the same. That they are credible persons and full faith and credit are due their statements upon oath or otherwise.

Given under our hands this 13th day of November 1832.

                                                  Jno. L. Neill
                                                  Samuel Phillips
                                                  John B. Armstrong

I, James McKisick, Clerk of the Court of Pleas and Quarter Sessions for Bedford County in the State of Tennessee, do hereby certify that the foregoing contains the original proceedings of the said Court in the matter of the application of Francis McKaimy for a pension, and that Jordan C. Holt, Esq., before whom the accompanying affidavit was sworn to is now and was at the time of signing the same an acting Justice of the Peace in and for Bedford County, duly commissioned and qualified as such.

In testimony whereof I have hereunto set my hand and Seal of Office in Shelbyville, the twentieth day of December 1832.

                                                  James McKisick, Clk.

          Ref: GSA Report, Washington, D.C.
          Ref: 1835 Bedford County, Tennessee Pension List.

                    * * * * * * * * * *

DAVID McROBERTS

Name: Rank: State Served:
David McRoberts   -----   --------------

Born ca 1747, died after 1832

84 years old in 1832 Pension List.

Ref: A 1

* * * * * * * * * *

ROBERT MAJORS

Name: Rank: State Served:
Robert Majors   PVT   North Carolina

Born March 14, 1761 in Dorchester County, Maryland, died April 29, 1847 in Bedford County, Tennessee, married Huldah Ladd on July 26, 1781, probably Surry County, North Carolina. Both are buried in Old Salem Cemetery, Bell Buckle, Tennessee, with markers.

<table>
<tr><td>

Sacred to the Memory of
Robert Majors
who was born 14th March
1761 and departed this life
life April 29th 1847
Aged : 86 years, 1 month
& 15 days. "Was a Soldier
in the Revolutionary Army,
was a member of the Methodist
Church 62 years, died as he lived
a Christian."

</td><td>

Sacred to the Memory of
Huldah Majors
Consort of Robert Majors
who was born Oct 1st 1764
and departed this life the
24th of Jan 1845.

</td></tr>
</table>

GSA: Robert Majors, S.2002, wife Huldah, Service of North Carolina.
Declaration:

Declaration in order to obtain the benefit of the Act of Congress passed 7th June 1832.

On this 15th day of August in the year one thousand eight hundred and thirty two, personally appeared in open court before the Worshipful John B. Armstrong, Samuel Phillips and John L. Neill, Esquires, Gentlemen Justices of the Peace, appointed to hold the Court of Pleas and Quarter Sessions for Bedford County in the State of Tennessee, Robert Majors, a resident of said County, aged seventy one years, five months and one day, who being first duly sworn according to law doth on his oath make the following declaration in order to obtain the benefit of the Act of Congress passed 7th June 1832. That he entered the service of the United States under the following named officers and served as herein stated, to wit, That he entered the service of the United States, as a drafted soldier in the County of Surry and State of North Carolina, in the year 1778 as he believes. He states that one John Davis was one of the proper number to be called out, but was absent at that time and he states that he was ordered to rendezvous at Richmond, the County Town, on a particular day, by the proper Officers. He further states that his brother John Majors, substituted in the place of some person whose name he has forgotten, to go with him. He also states that when he and his brother appeared according to orders, the aforesaid John Davis appeared and filled his own place according to his number. He states he was then released but in order to accompany his brother who had manifested so much brotherly affection for him, he states he substituted also in the place of one John Carmichael and was placed under the command of Captain James Shepherd, and the Major's name was Richard Good. He states he was marched from Surry County to Salisbury in Rowan County, North Carolina. He states, at that place, he was taken sick and was hauled in a wagon to a place called the Hanging Rock in the State of South Carolina. He states that after he recovered, he traveled on to headquarters, Powellsburg on the Savannah River. He states that he was marched from that place to what he thinks was called the Two Sisters, and drom that, on up to what was called the Black Swamps on Savannah River. He states the troops were under the command of General Rutherford and Colonel Lock and Major Good. He states that soon after he joined the main army, after his sickness, he understood that a part of General Rutherford's Army and the British had a small skirmish on Briar Creek on the Georgia side of the Savannah River. He states that they remained there until the 10th April 1779, when he states he was discharged in writing. He thinks his discharge was signed by General Rutherford, but not being able to read writing, he is not certain. He states he served five months on this expedition. He states that during the balance of the year 1779 and the year 1780, he was frequently engaged in reconnoitering through the country on the Yadkin River in search of bands of Tories. He states he joined Captain John Halbert and a Major Smith, both citizens of Surry County, North Carolina. He further states that afterwards in the year 1781, he volunteered in Captain Minor Smith's Company of Light Infantry, and marched down the Yadkin River, passing the town of Crosscreek, and thence on down to Drounding Creek, a distance of about one hundred and fifty or two hundred miles. He states that at or near that place, he saw a Company of Dragons belonging to the American Army, under the command of Major Graham and Captain Charles Polk. He states that during this tour of duty, the company he belonged to, was fired on by the Tories, and one of the Americans Killed, and the next morning our troops killed one of the Tories. He states he was then marched near to General Rutherford's headquarters, where he states they were discharged or dismissed and sent home with their Captain. He states he served nine weeks on this last tour.

He relinguishes all claims whatever to any pension or annuity except the present and declares that his name is not on the Pension Roll of any agency in the United States. He further says that he had no documentary evidence at this time and that he knows of no person whose testimony he can procure.

Interrogatories by the Court:

Q. 1st: Where and in what year were you born?

A.   I was born in Dawset (Dorchester) County in the State of Maryland in the year 1761, the 14th March, as I have been informed by my parents.

Q. 2nd: Have you any record of your age and if so where is it?

A.   I have a record of my age at my dwelling house in this County in my book called Wesley's Sermons, taken from the record in my father's Bible.

Q. 3rd: Where were you living when called into service? Where have you lived since the Revolutionary War? And where do you now live?

A.   I lived in the County of Surry in the State of North Carolina, where I was first called into service, and in the same County when I was last called into service, and I remained in the same County until the year 1806 when I moved to Bedford County in the State of Tennessee, where I have lived ever since and where I now live.

Q. 4th: How were you called into service? Were you a volunteer? Were you drafted? Or were you a substitute and if a substitute, for whom?

A.   I was first drafted and released, and then I substituted in order to go with my brother, for to fill the place of one John Carmichael and in my tour against the Tories, I always volunteered and in my last tour under Captain _____.

Q. 5th: State the names of some of the Regular Officers who were with you, or the troops where you served, such Continental and Militia Regiments as you can recollect and the general circumstances of your service.

A.   I recollect Lieutenant Joel Lewis of the Regular Troops, who commanded the 9 months men. I have seen some Regiments of Militia but do not recollect their number, I saw some Regular Troops on Savannah River, but do not know any thing about their numbers or the names of their Officers, and I only know such Officers and Regiments as I have given in my declaration.

Q. 6th: Did you ever secure a discharge? And if so, what has become of it?

A.   I received one discharge from General Rutherford, I think, but what has become of it, I do not know.

Q. 7th: State the names of persons to whom you are known in your present neighborhood who can testify as to your character for veracity and their belief of your service as a Soldier of the Revolution.

A.   The Rev. R.W. Cardwell, William Norvell, Esquire, Matt Martin, Esq., and John Tilman.

The foregoing sworn to in open court this 15th day of August 1832.

Jas. McKisick, Clk.   Robert (X) Majors

143

Children of Robert and Huldah Majors:
1. John, born January 1, 1783 (John Consentine, 1785)
2. Constantine, born January 1, 1783
3. Henry D., born June 20, 1783 (conflict information)
4. Mary Ladd, born September 9, 1784
5. Forsh M., born March 1, 1786
6. John P., born June 18, 1790
7. Noble (Able) L., born June 18, 1790, married May 8, 1820 in Bedford County,
       Tennessee, to Mary Bouldin.
8. Amy D., born June 24, 1793
9. Sarah W., born March 1, 1796, married Dr. Billy Smith
10. Theodosia H., born October 17, 1798, married Richard C. Clardy
11. Robert Howell, born July 3, 1801, married (1) Sarah Campbell Fugitt, (2) Lucy
       F. Rucker Smith
12. Alexander Wilson, born July 3, 1803
13. Joseph Ladd, born May 26, 1806

> Ref: GSA Report, Washington, D.C.
> Ref: Texas Society DAR Roster Revolutionary Ancestors, Vol III, pg
>   1423
> Ref: 1835 Bedford County Tennessee Pension List

* * * * * * * * * * * *

JOHN F. MARION

Name:	Rank:	State Served:
John F. Marion	PVT	North Carolina

Born 14 October 1760 in Lancaster County, Pennsylvania, died after 1834 (Pension List).

GSA: John F. Marion, S.2747, North Carolina
Claim No. 25--: West Tennessee, John F. Marion, Bedford County in the State of Tennessee, who was a Private in the Company commanded by Captain Alexander of the Regiment commanded by Colonel Polk in the North Carolina Line for 10 months. Prof Cavalry & 10 months prof Infantry.

Inscribed on the Roll of West Tennessee at the rate of 75 dollars, ___ cents per annum, to commence on the 4th day of March 1831.

Certificate of Pension issued the 18 day of December 1833 and sent to J.K. Polk, H.R.

Arrears to the 4th of Sept	$187.5-
Semi-anl allowance ending 4 March	$ 37.5-
	$225.0-

Recorded by Daniel Boyd, Clerk   Revolutionary Claim
Book E   Vol 7   page 93   Act June 7, 1832

State of Tennessee
Declaration in order to obtain the benefit of the Act of Congress passed 7th June 1832.
State of Tennessee   ]
Bedford County Court]

On this 7th day of November in the year of our Lord, one thousand eight hundred and thirty two, personally appeared in open court before the Worshipful, Samuel Phillips, John L. Neil and John B. Armstrong, Esquires, Gentlemen Justices of the Peace, appointed to hold the Court of Pleas and Quarter Sessions of the County aforesaid, John F. Marion, a resident of Bedford County in the State of Tennessee, aged seventy two years and thirteen days. Who being sworn according to law doth on his oath make the following declaration, in order to obtain the benefit of the Act of Congress passed 7th June 1832. That he enlisted in the Army of the United States in the year 1779 and served as herein after stated under the following named Officers, to wit, that he enlisted in the late Troops of North Carolina sometime in the month of June 1779, under Captain William Alexander in the town of Charlotte in the County of Mecklenburg and State of North Carolina and was marched with his Captain under the command of

Colonel Charles Polk to Ingram's Old Fields on the Congaree River where he says they joined General Sumpter of South Carolina and after remaining there about two months they were _____ to the Eutaw Springs. He states he was in an engagement at that place between the British and Americans and was wounded through the right leg and his horse was killed under him. He says that General Greene commanded the American Army as Commander in Chief on that day. He says he then wmarched back to Ingram's Old Field and was sent to Doctor Paulton at Strawberry Ferry on Ashley River where he remained until he was cured of his wound. He says that after serving in said State Troops the term of ten months, he then enlisted under Colonel Wade Hampton during the war in his Regiment of Light Horse and was placed in Captain James Simmons' Company belonging to said Regiment of United States Troops. He states he was marched from that place to a place called Monks Corner in South Carolina where he was stationed until within a few days of Christmas Day, and he says that on Christmas Day, the British sent away their troops from Charles Town, Soutn Carolina and the Americans under General Greene marched into the town and remained there until the next Fall, when he says he was furloughed agreeable to an Act or Resolution of Congress as he was told, and was never called into service upon said enlistment afterwards, he thinks _____ _____ on this last mentioned tour about eight months, making in a whole, a term of service twenty eight months for which he claims a pension and that he has no documentary evidence whatever, and that he knows of no person whose testimony he can procure who can testify as to his service. He hereby relinquishes all and every claim to a pension or annuity whatever except the present, and declares that his name is not on the Pension Roll of any agency in the United States.

Interrogatories by the Court:

Q. 1st: Where and in what year were you born?
A.   I was born in Lancaster County and State of Pennsylvania on the 14th of October in the year 1760, agreeable to my father's family record.
Q. 2nd: Have you any record of your age and if so where is it?
A.   I have a record of my age at Mr. James Wilson's in this County where I make my home.
Q. 3rd: Where were you living when called into service?
A.   I was a resident of Mecklenburg County in the State of North Carolina when I first entered the service of the United States, and the last term, I entered the service, it was on the bank of the Congaree River in South Carolina but I do not know what County.
Q. 4th: Where have you lived since the Revolutionary War and where do you now live?
A.   I went to the Moravian Town in the State of North Carolina shortly after the close of the Revolutionary War, where I enlisted in Captain Hadley's Company in a Regiment of Troops that was raised by virtue of
a   an Act of General Assembly of the State of North Carolina for the protection of the white settlers in the country. Then called "Cumberland" and was marched under Major Thomas Evans to what is now called Davidson County in the State of Tennessee, where I remained in that service for two years, and from there I moved to Williamson County, in the same State, and from there to what is now Bedford County, where I have lived ever since and where I now live.
Q. 5th: How were you called into service? Were you drafted? Were you a volunteer? Were you a substitute and if a substitute for whom or did you enlist?
A.   I was an enlisted soldier in the State of South Carolina the whole time I was in the Revolutionary Army.
Q. 6th: State the names of some of the Regular Officers who served with the troops where you served, such Continental and Militia Regiment as you can recollect and the general circumstances of your service.
A.   I knew Colonel Stewart, General Greene and General _____ Wayne, Captain Joshua Hadley, Colonel W. _____, Major Conjars, Captains James and Thomas _____ Lee and Captain James, also Colonel Wade Hampton, I know Colonel Washington's Dragons and some other Regiments of Regulars that do not recollect the names or numbers of

145

any of the Regiments at this time, and I believe my declaration contains as near a general history of my service as I am able at this time to give.

Q. 7th: Did you ever receive a discharge and if so what has become of it?

A. I never did receive a discharge but was furloughed by Act of Resolution of Congress.

Q. 8th: State the names of persons to whom you are known in your present neighborhood who can testify as to your character for veracity and their opinion of your service as a Soldier of the Revolutionary War.

A. Captain John Wortham, James Brittain, Esquire, Colonel Robert Cannon, and Mr. James Wilson.

Sworn to and subscribed the day and year aforesaid.
Jas. McKisick, Clk.   John F. Marion (Seal)

Declarant further makes oath that there is no Minister or Regular Preacher living in his neighborhood whose testimony he can procure who knows anything of his service or character as a Revolutionary Soldier or otherwise that he knows.

Sworn to in open court 1st February 1833.
Jas. McKisick, Clerk   John F. Marion

Ref: GSA Report, Washington, D.C.
Ref: 1834 Pension List

* * * * * * * * * *

BARCLAY MARTIN

Name:	Rank:	State Served:
Barclay Martin	Colonel	North Carolina

Born June 13, 1756 in Charlotte County, Virginia, died November 16, 1815 in Bedford County, Tennessee, married Rachel Clay. No children. Both Barclay and Rachel (Clay) Martin are buried in the Martin Family Graveyard, near Fairfield, Bedford County, Tennessee. Rachel (Clay) Martin has a grave marker but no inscription. Colonel Barclay Martin's grave marker reads:

"Sacred to the Memory of Col. Barclay Martin, a native
of Virginia, Born June 13, 1756. He emigrated to South
Carolina during her Colonial dependency, and at an early
period, was identified with its cause of the Revolution
and served his Country with zeal and fidelity of a
Patriotic Soldier and a meritorious Officer. A Deacon
of the Baptist Church. His life was an example of Piety
and unselfishness. Died on the 16th of November 1815, in
the full hope of the blest, inheritance of the just. His
Memory will ever be sacred."

Colonel Barclay Martin, son of Abram and Elizabeth (Marshall) Martin, brother of Matthew Martin, married Rachel Clay, cousin to Henry Clay of Kentucky, had no children. Revolutionary War, Captain and Colonel under George Washington.

Colonel Barclay Martin, after settlement in Bedford County, died childless and now lies buried alongside of his wife, Rachel Martin.

Ref: SR (1909-1910 year DAR Report ot Smithsonion)
Ref: See Matt Martin's sketch
Ref: Cemetery Records of Bedford County, Tennessee by Marsh
Ref: Sketches of Prominent Tennesseans by Hon. William S. Speer,
Nashville, 1888

* * * * * * * * * *

GEORGE MARTIN

Name:	Rank:	State Served:
George Martin	-----	---------------

Born ca 1742, died after 1836

GSA: George Martin, R. 6946, Tennessee Residence
     George Martin, Tennessee, Rejected. See Letter, 13 December 1836.
                                        Hon. C. Johnson

Letter:
          Letter 20th December 1836, sent to Hon. C. Johnson
          "Did not serve six months in a regular organized Corps during the
          Revolutionary War."

                                        Act, 1832

          The Commissioners of Pension would much oblige me by inclosing the
Pension papers of George Martin that they present them to Congress.
                                        E. Johnson

          In Lincoln County, Tennessee, Minute Book said he was living in Bedford
County, Tennessee by 1811, with brother Richard Martin. Also, surveying Lincoln
County, Tennessee area in 1784.

          George and Richard Martin and Amos Balch's Grant No. 16. 3,234 acres
from State of North Carolina. Paid 10 lbs per 100 acres. Situation: Middle
District. On south side of Duck River, on both sides of Sugar Creek, beginning
on west side of a creek, borders James Bradshaw, Charles M. Commons and Amos
Balch. 10th July 1788.

          Ref: GSA Report, Washington, D.C.
          Ref: 1811 Minute Book of Lincoln County, Tennessee
          Ref: Bedford County, Tennessee Deed Book a, page 26.

                         * * * * * * * * * *

JOSIAH MARTIN

Name: Rank: State Served:
Josiah Martin   Lieutenant   North Carolina
Born February 1757 Cumberland County, Pennsylvania, died September 17, 1835
in Rutherford County, Tennessee, married May 28, 1783 Mecklenburg County,
North Carolina to Mary McClary who was born September 15, 1765 in
Mecklenburg County, North Carolina, died 1852 in Rutherford County, Tennessee.

1835, age 77, Private, North Carolina Line. (Bedford County, Tennessee Pension
List.

          Josiah Martin's home was in the shadow of King's Mountain. In Battle
of Ramsour's Mill. In Captain Barber's Company, Colonel McDowell's Regiment.
He married Mary McClary, daughter of Robert and Abigail McCleary of
Mecklenburg County, North Carolina. She survived him and drew a pension. He
married May 28, 1783 in her father's house.
Children:
1. Abigail, born March 28, 1784, married 1803 to William Dinwiddie Baird
2. William, born December 8, 1786, married (1) 1814 to Isabella Martin, (2) Mrs.
          Caroline E. Griffin
3. Hannah, born October 20, 1790, married March 17, 1812 to Aaron J. Wilson
4. Robert, born November 10, 1793, married Mary Aston Baker
5. Clarrissa, born August 15, 1796, married Edwin Hunter
6. Marilla, born September 29, 1799, married November 4, 1823 to William Davis
Baker
7. Mary, born November 16, 1806, married September 28, 1825 to David Davis
8. Matilda, born February 15, 1808, married 1825 to Jas. McC. Killough

Another list of children has:
1. Abigail, born 1790
2. Robert, born 1793
3. Clarissa born 1796
4. Marilla, born 1799
5. Polly McDowell, born 1806
6. Matilda, born 1808

Ref: 1835 Bedford County, Tennessee Pension List
Ref: Tennessee DAR Blue Book, Vol I, page 1074
Ref: A 1

* * * * * * * * * *

MATT MARTIN

Name: Rank: State Served:
Matt Martin   PVT   Georgia, North Carolina &
                                                  Virginia.

Born December 26, 1763 in Charlotte County, Virginia, died October 16, 1846 in
Bedford County, Tennessee, married Sally Clay on March 8, 1787 in Edgefield,
South Carolina (Charlotte County, Virginia), born November 16, 1765 in
Cumberland County, Virginia, died January 2, 1842 in Bedford County, Tennessee.
Both Matt and Sally (Clay) Martin are buried in the Martin Family Graveyard
near Fairfield, Bedford County, Tennessee. Both have markers:

Sacred to the Memory of
Capt. Matt Martin, born 26
of December 1763. At an early
age of 16 years, he became a
Soldier in the defense of his
Country during her struggle
under Gen. Greene, in the
Battle of Gilford and under
Clark and Sumpter in many
other battles. He continued
to discharge the duries of a
Patriotic Soldier until the
close of the war. He was a
humane Master, a kind neighbor
and unwavering friend. Tender
and affectionate. Father and
devoted Husband. Died 16th of
October 1846, in the esteem of
all who knew him. Kind to his
children, a friend made evidence
in his last days the consoling
reflections that their loss was
his infinate gain.

Mrs. Sally Martin, wife
of Capt. Matt Martin,
Born Nov. 16, 1765.
Member of the Baptist
for near a half Century
Died Jan 2, 1842.

"Revolutionary Soldier"
1763-1846
Placed by Belle Meade
Chapter DAR.
(DAR Marker now gone in
1968)

GSA: Matt Martin, S.2726, Service in Georgia, North Carolina and Virginia.
Claim No. 7593: West Tennessee, Matt Martin of Bedford County in the State of
West Tennessee, who was a Private in the Company commanded by Captain
Martin of the Regiment commanded by Colonel Clark in the Virginia Line for 14
months and 26 days.
    South Carolina, Georgia and Virginia Line Records corrected.
    Inscribed on the Roll of West Tennessee, January 26, '_4, at the rate of
49 dollars, 33 cents per annum, to commence on the 4th day of March 1831.
    Certificate of Pension issued 3 day of May 1833 and sent to applicant,
Shelbyville, Tennessee.

Arrears to the 4th of March $ 98.66
Semi-anl allowance ending 4 Sept $ 24.66
                                                 $123.32

Recorded by Daniel Boyd, Clerk   Revolutionary Claim
Boom E   Vol 7   page 88   Act June 7, 1832.

                    Died Oct 16, 1846
                    Agency Book.

Declaration:
State of Tennessee]
Bedford County   ] Court of Pleas & Quarter Sessions, Feb Term 1833

    On this seventh day of February, eighteen hundred and thirty three,
personally appeared in open court before Samuel Phillips, James Brittain and

William McClure, now sitting, Matt Martin, a resident of said County of Bedford, State of Tennessee, aged sixty nine years, December last, who being first duly sworn according to law, doth on his oath make the following declaration in order to obtain the benefit of the Act of Congress passed June the 7th, 1832.

That he entered the service of the United States and in the following named Officers and served as herein stated. He thinks it was in the month of February 1780, he entered the service as a substitute for George Martin, without compensation, he being a brother, at a camp on Cupboard Creek, near Augusta in the State of Georgia with Militia Company commanded by Barclay Martin, a Lieutenant, does not recollect the name of the Captain, in the Regiment commanded by Colonel Leroy Hammond of the Militia of South Carolina, General Andrew Williamson commanded, who sometime afterwards turned Tory and joined the British at Charleston. We continued for sometime at that camp and afterwards marched into Augusta, when a short time after the surrender of Charleston, we were dismissed. He cannot recollect certainly that he served three months in that tour, but believes he did. There was a small number of Continental Troops stationed at Augusta at that time, but does not remember who commanded them. The object of stationing the troops there was to watch the motions of the British and Tories in that Country as he believes. At the time of entering the service he was sixteen years old, his place of residence was at Martin Town in Ninety-Six District, South Carolina.

After the surrender of Charleston, he again entered the service of the United States (with three brothers who had been at the Seige of Augusta under the command of Colonel Elijah Clark) in Rutherford County, State of North Carolina in the Volunteer Frontier Corps of Mounted Men commanded by Captain Frederick Stallions, James Stallions First Lieutenant and Edmond Martin Second Lieutenant, in the Regiment commanded by Colonel Elijah Clark and Colonel Chandler. The Regiment was composed principally of refugees from Georgia and South Carolina, who had refused to take the benefit of British protection. He thinks he entered this service about the last of September or early in the month of October 1780. We were engaged sometime in scouring the country on the British Lines and then joined General Sumpter on the waters of Broad River, then marched under Sumpter to Sh----- Ferry on Broad River. Then marched under Sumpter where we expected to attack a party of British, when we got there, they were on the north side of the river and no engagement took place. Then took down the river to Summers Mill, then struck off and made up the country thirteen miles and encamped. On the next morning, Colonel Chandler was detached with fifty men, declarent among the number to return and destroy said Mills which was effected by cutting the running gear, left there and marched all day and night to catch up with Sumpter, which we did the next day at Blackstock on Tyger River where we were attacked at our camp by the British under Tarlton. A sevier engagement ensued and the enemy were beaten off of the ground. General Sumpter was wounded and we marched away that night to Warford's Ironworks and went into North Carolina to recruit, he forgets the name of the place. They remained there a few days. Then marched into South Carolina and beat about the place to place endeavoring to suppress the Tories and to strengthen the cause of the Whigs, on the borders of Ninety-Six when this declarent was in a severe engagement. The Tories and British on Long Cane Creek, now in Abbeville District in which we were defeated having twenty men killed and wounded out of a setachment of one hundred and four, Colonel Elijah Clark was among the wounded. We retreated and made for North Carolina, when we dispersed being withour provisions and almost naked. We were permitted to go to our friends. Declarent with his brothers went to Halifax County, Virginia, where some of his friends and relatives lived, to obtain clothing and subsistance, in that service to the best of his recollection, he served three onths. He got no discharge. None was necessary.

This declarant next in the County of Halifax, be believes in the month of February 1781, volunteered 2nd in the Company commanded by Captain Bird Walls in the Virginia Regiment commanded by Colonel Nathaniel Cocke in the Brigade commanded by General Stephens, entered the service on the north side of Dan River, near Irvin's Ferry. We were detached down the river to destroy books and other crafts to prevent the British from crossing as low down as one Peyton

Stephen's, while engaged in that service General Greene recrossed Dan River going to the south and we rejoined him at Wiley's. We then continued with him, marched and countermarched through the country and thence to Guilford Court House but before we reached there, were joined by a reinforcement of Virginia Troops under General Lawson, and North Carolina Militia under General Butler according to his recollection. Declarant was in the Battle of Guilford in which General Stephens was wounded. I saw General Greene, Colonels Washington, Lee and Greene in that campaign. After the battle, we rendezvoused at Troublesome Iron Works about ten miles from the field of battle. The army lay there a few days and was marched in pursuit of Cornwallis to Ramsey's Mills on Deep River, where the enemy crossed first before we arrived. The Virginia Militia was then dismissed. The declarant served in this tour two months according to the best of his recollection. He then returned to Halifax County and took the place of one Charles Edwards, his brother-in-law, as a substitute without pay, in the Company of Virginia Militia commanded by Captain Richard Jones. We conducted, under guard, a small party of British prisoners from Pittsylvania County, to Winchester in Virginia, were then marched back and discharged by the Captain in Halifax County. He believes he was engaged in that service twenty days. The precise time, he cannot tell and cannot recollect with certainty the time leaving the service. He well remembers it was about the time the Legislature of Virginia fled from Charlottesville.

Declarant then returned to Ninety-Six in South Carolina and in the year of 1781, he believes in September, he again volunteered a substitute for one Joseph DePugh with Company commanded by Captain Thomas Key in the Regiment commanded by Colonel Leroy Hammonds. The Lieutenant Colonel was named John Lane. We joined General Andrew Pickens and were engaged in scouting the swamps of Edisto, when it was understood a large party of Tories were secreted. Upon our approach, they dispersed, we marched to the Ridge House in Ninety-Six and declarant was discharged at that place having served twenty days in this tour as a Mounted Gunmen. Shortly afterwards, he again joined General Pickens as a Mounted Volunteer in the Company commanded by Lieutenant Henry Ware in the Regiment commanded by Major Tutt. We marched against the Cherokee Indians, at a town called Chota, surprised the Indians, killed thirty and took as many prisoners, distroyed their town and returned with the prisoners to Major Tutts' in Ninety-Six District where declarant was discharged having served to the best of his recollection in that tour, one month.

Again in 1782, he entered the service in Ninety-Six, South Carolina as a Militia Man for three months, he does not remember the name of his Captain, his Lieutenant was Barclay Martin and Robert Briant in the Regiment, South Carolina Militia commanded by Colonel Leroy Hammond. We marched to Greene's headquarters near Bacon's Bridge before Charleston, then staid until the time expired, when we were discharged, having served three months, to the best of his rememberance.

In the Fall of 1782, declarant joined an expedition against the Cherokee Indians, under General Pickens, his Company was commanded by Captain Drury Pace, on the frontier of Georgia (does not recollect the name of the place) was joined by a re-enforcement of Georgians, commanded by Colonel Elijah Clark, we marched to Down's Town on the Chattahoochee, Beamers Town on the Hightower River, thence down the same to the Long Swamp, thence to Vann's Settlement and to the Pine Log where a council was held with the Indians. The Indians could not be brought to battle, fleeing at our approach. Declarant was detached under Captain Robert Maxwell in an expedition to collect and recover some property which the Tories had taken. We passed by Coosawhatchie Town and up the Coosa River and recovered seven negroes, then returned and met with General Pickens at the mouth of Long Swamp, then marched home and this declarant was dismissed, was in this tour not less than six weeks. Declarant states that his memory has greatly failed him and it is out of his power to state with certainty the times of entering, having the service on the several tours of duty performed by him, but according to the best of his recollection, he served the several tours herein stated, in all, amounting to fifteen months for which he claims a pension. He was born in the COunty of Charlotte, State of Virginia on the 26th day of December 1763, according to the information of his family and as appears from his Father's Register in an Old Bible, now in his possession. He lived since the

Revolutionary War at Martin Town in South Carolina now Edgefield District until 1806 when he removed to Bourbon County, State of Kentucky, from whence he removed in September 1808 to Bedford County, Tennessee where he has resided ever since and where he now resides. He does not recollect of ever receiving a discharge, his impression is that none was given to the Militia or Volunteers with whom he served. He has no written documentary evidence of his service within his power that he can refer to or know of, unless the South Carolina or Virginia Rolls will show, nor does he know of any person whose testimony he can procure who can testify as to his claim.

He is known in his present neighborhood by the Rev'd George Newton, Andrew Erwin, Jr., and William Norvell, who can testify as to his character for veracity and their belief of the services as a Soldier of the Revolution. He hereby relinguishes every claim to whatever a pension or an annuity except the present, and that his name is not on any agency roll of any State.
Sworn to and subscribed the day and year aforesaid.
Jas. McKisick   Matt Martin

State of Tennessee]
Bedford County   ]
We, George Newton, a Clergyman, residing in the County of Bedford and who lived many years in the vincinity of Matt Martin and Andrew Erwin, Jr., and William Norvell, who resides in the immediate neighborhood of the applicant and in the County of Bedford, hereby certify that we are well acquainted with Captain Matt Martin who has subscribed and sworn to the above declaration.

Matt Martin, was the youngest of eight brothers who served in the Revolution, was a Private in a Company of Infantry commanded by his brother George. His eldest brother, William, was Captain of Artillery at Augusta, where he was killed. Barclay, John, Edmond, James and Marshall were all officers and survived the war. He was born in Virginia and was a Pensioner when he died in Bedford County, Tennessee.

Sally Clay Martin carried important despatches by night in 1781 to General Nathaniel Greene. These documents were taken by her sisters, armed as Soldiers, from British Couriers enroute to the beleagered Fort, Ninety-Six.

Martin Family:
John Martin of King and Queen and Caroline County, Virginia, born 1685 married Martha Burwell (of Virginia and daughter of Lewis Burwell of Gloucester County), born 1703 and died May 27, 1738.
Mary, born 1703, married ______ Clark
John, born 1705
Susan, born 1710
Thomas, born 1714
Abram*, born 1716
Eliza, born 1721, married ______ Douglass

*Captain Abram Martin, born February 7, 1716 in Edgefield District, South Carolina, died 1780 (youngest son of John and Martha Burwell Martin). Married October 2, 1744 to Elizabeth Marshall Smith, born March 1, 1726, died 1797 (She was widow of John Smith and daughter of Captain John and Elizabeth Markum Marshall).
1. Captain William, born September 26, 1745 and killed at Battle of Augusta, Georgia, married Grace Waring.
2. Letty, born September 25, 1747, married (1) Edmond Wade, (2) Charles Edward, a Soldier of the Revolution.
3. Lt. James, born October 14, 1749, married 1775 to Obedience Bugg. He was a Soldier of the Revolution.
4. John, born November 19, 1751 in South Carolina, died August 7, 1813, married (1) Elizabeth Terry of Virginia, 1756-1800.
5. Capt. George, born June 4, 1754, died 1804, a Soldier of the Revolution, married Alice Freeman.
6. Col. Barclay, born June 13, 1756, Soldier of the Revolution, married Rachel Clay, daughter of Henry and Rachel (Purvell) Clay of Charlotte County, Virginia. No children.

7. Lt. Edmund, born January 10, 1759, married Katherine Tutt. He was a Soldier
        of the Revolution.
8. Marshall, born February 10, 1761, a Soldier of the Revolution, married May 9,
        1784 to Mary Isham Key.
9. Matt, born December 26, 1763 in Virginia, a Soldier of the Revolution, died
        October 16, 1846 in Bedford County, Tennessee.

Children of Matt and Sally (Clay) Martin:
1. Mary "Polly" Clay, born January 17, 1788, married John Marshall.
2. Rachel (Rochee) Powell, born January (May) 16, 1789, married John Tillman.
3. Rebecca, born July 11, 1791, married Thomas Bedford Mosley.
4. Lucy Green, born August 5, 1793, married Theoderic Bradford.
5. Letitia "Letty", born April 6, 1795, died young.
6. Henrietta Bedinger, born May 10, 1797, died young.
7. Sallie Clay, born November 17, 1798, married Col. John L. Neill.
8. Abram, born November 22, 1800, married Betty Lane.
9. Barclay, born December 17, 1802, married (1) _____ Suggs, (2) Maria Ruth
        Williams, (3) _____.
10. Elizabeth "Betty" Marshall, born December 13, 1804, married Edward Archer
        Mosley.
11. Henry Clay, born November 26, 1806, married.Amanda Davenport.
12. Molley (Mattie) Bedford, born December 2, 1808, married Samuel R. Rucker.
13. Matt (General), born June 18, 1812, married (1) Sara Quincy Williams, (2)
        Elizabeth B. Martin.

Deed:
        A. Jackson to Matt Martin   640 acres
15 June 1809. A. Jackson of Davidson County to Matt Martin of Bedford County,
Tennessee, for $1000 for 640 acres in Bedford County, in the 2nd District, 6th
Range and 6th Section and on the Middle Fork of Duck River. Beginning on the
north west bank of said Middle Fork at 2 beech trees, marked NP & P. & E.,
borders 5000 acres of John Gray Blount, No. of Grant 217, another tract 5000
No. 220, crosses Puncheon Camp Creek and crosses a creek and a fork of the
Middle Fork of Duck River in all 422 ...
Witnesses: William P. Anderson, John Drake, John Coffey and John A.S.
Anderson.

Deed:
        Same as above for 640 acres.   15 May 1809
2 District, 6th Range and 4th Section.
Situated on Middle Fork of Duck River, borders John Donalson's 640 acres and
borders two Blounts (above).

        Ref: GSA Report, Washington, D.C.
        Ref: Cemetery Records of Bedford County, Tennessee by Marsh
        Ref: Texas Society DAR Roster Revolutionary Ancestore, Vol III, pg
            1445.
        Ref: Bedford County, Tennessee Deed Book A, page 328 & 330
        Ref: 1835 Bedford County, Tennessee Pension List.
        Ref: DAR Lineage, Vol 60, page 14.
        Ref: Tennessee and King's Mountain Papers by Draper, Madison, Wisc.

            * * * * * * * * * *

RICHARD MARTIN

Name: Rank: State Served:
Richard Martin   -----   ---------------
Born ca 1752, died after 1811.

Richard Martin was living in Bedford County, Tennessee in 1811, and he also was
surveying in Lincoln County, Tennessee area in 1784. Brother to George Martin
(see George Martin).

State of Tennessee]
Bedford County   ]

George and Richard Martin and Amos Balch's Grant No. 16, 3,234 acres from State of North Carolina. Paid 10 lbs per 100 acres. Situated: Middle District. On south side of Duck River, on both sides of Sugar Creek, beginning on west side of a creek, borders James Bratshaw (James Bradshaw), Charles M. Commons and Amos Balch. Dated 10th July 1788.

Ref: Lincoln County, Tennessee Minute Book.
Ref: Bedford County, Tennessee Deed Book A, page 26.

* * * * * * * * * *

DANIEL MEADORS

Name:	Rank:	State Served:
Daniel Meadors	PVT	North Carolina

Born November 14th, 1762 in Granville County, North Carolina, died after 1834.

GSA: Daniel Meadors, S.1699, North Carolina.
Claim No. 22195: West Tennessee, Daniel Meadors of Bedford County in the State of Tennessee was a Private (Cav & Inf) in a company commanded by Captain Sneed of the Regiment commanded by Colonel Taylor in the North Carolina Mil. Line for 6 months and 8 days for 1778.

Inscribed on the Roll of West Tennessee at the rate of 23 dollars, 38 cents per annum, to commence on the 4th day of March 1831.

Certificate of Pension issued the 17th day of October 1833, and sent to John Bruce, Shelbyville.

Arrears to the 4th of Sept 1833 $58.45
Semi-anl allowance ending 4 March 1834 $11.69
                                                   $70.14

Recorded by William S. Allison, Clerk   Revolutionary Claim
Book E   Vol 7   page 93   Act June 7, 1832.

1835, age 70, Private in Inf & Cav, North Carolina Militia.

Declaration:
State of tennessee]
Bedford County   ]

On this 15 day of August 1832, personally appeared in the open Court of Pleas and Quarter Sessions before Samuel Phillips, John B. Armstrong and John L. Neill, members to hold Court, Daniel Meadors, aged sixty nine years and nine months, and on this who being duly sworn according to law, doth on his oath, saith he, the following declaration in order to obtain the benefit of the Act of Congress passed the 7th June 1832.

That he entered the service of the United States in August 1778 with Captain Sneed's Company of Horsemen, North Carolina Line in a Regiment of Horsemen commanded by Colonel Phillip Taylor and as he believes the Brigade in which he served was commanded by General Butler, that he served as a Horseman three months the first time he went into service. That during the term of service aforesaid, he went from Granville County in the State of North Carolina to Salisbury in the State last aforesaid, from there he marched to a little town called Pinetree in the State of South Carolina. Afterwards, the name of said little town was changed to some other name which he does not now recollect and from thence he marched to a little town called Charleston in the State of aforesaid. At which place he remained only one day and then he marched to a little stream called Rocky River in the State of North Carolina, from thence he marched to the town of Hillsborough in the State of North Carolina, where he was discharged. That during the term of service aforesaid, he was acquainted with General Butler, Colonel Phillip Taylor, Major McClure and Hunt and Captain Farraw, Captain James Saxton, Captain John G--ation, Captain John Henderson. At the expiration of the three months aforesaid Company ___ Phillip Taylor gave him a written discharge but he has lost or mislaid, said Discharge and has discharge and has searched for it, but cannot find it, and he does not know where it is at this time. That he has no documentary evidence and that he knows of no person whose testimony he can procure who can testify as to his service during the three months aforesaid.

He states that afterwards, sometime in the year 1779, he does not know in what month, he again volunteered and went into service as a Horseman in Captain John G-----'s Company of Horsemen, who went out with his company as a scouting party to persue the British and Tories. That he served about seventeen days under Captain John G-----. At the expiration of which time said G----- left same company and went to Hillsborough in the State of North Carolina and after G----- he himself from said company. The Lieutenant's said Company 's name, he does not recollect the name. The does not recollect who took command of said company. That he served three months in the company last aforesaid. That during the three months last aforesaid, he marched through different parts of Granville, Orange and Wake Counties, all in the State of North Carolina. That during the three months last aforesaid, he was acquainted with Captain G----- at the expiration of the three months last aforesaid, Captain John G----- who had returned back to his company again, gave him a written discharge but he has lost it and does not know where it is at this time. That he has no documentary evidence and that he knows of no person whose testimony he can procure who can testify as to his second term service.

That some time in the year 1779, he volunteered as a Horseman in Captain John Henderson's Company. That he volunteered under said Henderson was then all sign to serve three months but at the expiration of eight days, Captain John Henderson verbally discharged him, there being no necessity for him to serve any longer at that time. That during the eight days aforesaid he was acquainted with Captain John Henderson, that during the eight days last aforesaid, he marched from Granville County in the State of North Carolina to the town of Halifax in the State of last aforesaid, and the town of Halifax, he was discharged. That he has no documentary evidence nor he knows of no person whose evidence he can procure who can testify as to any of his services whatever. That he served in all six months and eight days. He hereby relinguishes every claim whatever to a pension or annuity except the present and declares that his name is not on the Pension Roll of the agency of any State or Territory in the United States.

Sworn to and subscribed on this 16 day of August in the year 1832.

Jas. McKisick, Clerk   Daniel (X) Meadors

Questions to be ask:

Q. 1st: Where and in what year were you born?

A.   I was born in Granville County in the State of North Carolina, the 14 day of November 1762.

Q. 2nd: Have you any record of your age?

A.   I have not. It was put down in my father's Bible and said Bible was either destroyed or worn out. I know not where it is.

Q. 3rd: Where were you living when called into service? Where have you lived since the Revolutionary War and where do you now live?

A.   I was living in Granville County in the State of North Carolina at time I went into service and resided there till about fifteen years ago, I removed from there to Sumner County, State of Tennessee, remained there one year then I removed to Warren County in the aforesaid State, remained there several years, he does not recollect how long, he removed to Bedford County in State of Tennessee where he has lived every since.

Q. 4th: How were you called into service? Were you drafted? Did you volunteer? Or were you a substitute and if a substitute for whom?

A.   I volunteered all three times.

Q. 5th: State the names of some of the Regular Officers who were with the troops where you served, such Continental and Militia Regiments as you recollect and the general circumstances of your service.

A.   I was acquainted with General Butler, Colonel Phillip Taylor, Major William Hunt, Captain Farrow, Captain James Lanxton, Captain John G---- and Captain John Henderson and Captain Samuel Snead and the general circumstances of my service are above stated.

Q. 6th: Did you receive a discharge from the service and if so by whom was it given? And what has become of it?

A.   Colonel Phillip Taylor gave me a written discharge at the expiration of my first term of service but I do not know where it is at, the expiration of my second term of service, Captain John G---- gave him a written discharge which is lost and at the expiration of the third term of service, Captain Henderson gave him a verbal discharge.

Q. 7th: State the names of persons to whom you are known in your present neighborhood and who can testify as to your character for veracity and their belief of your services as a Soldier of the Revolution.

A. Samuel Haggard, John A. _____, The Reverand William G. Wood, and James Haggard.

Sworn to in open court 16th August 1832.

Jas. McKisick, Clerk   Daniel (X) Meadors

We, Richard Cunningham, residing in the County of Bedford, in the State of Tennessee and James Haggard, Junr., residing in the same, hereby certify and sworn to the above declaration that we believe him to be sixty nine years and nine months ... incomplete ...

Ref: GSA Report, Washington, D.C.
Ref: 1835 Bedford County, Tennessee Pension List.

* * * * * * * * * *

JAMES MILLER

Name: Rank: State Served:
James Miller   ------   ---------------

Born 1754, died March 16, 1840, aged 86 years, married Elizabeth who was born 1760 and died March 13, 1830, aged 70 years. Both are buried in the Green Cemetery, Bedford County, Tennessee.

Tombstones:

    "Revolutionary Soldier"   Elizabeth Miller
       James Miller   departed this life
    departed this life   Mar 13, 1830
    Mar 16, 1840   Aged 70 years
    aged 86 yrs.   "Gone but not
    "I have fought a goof fight   forgotten."
    and have gone home."

No GSA Report in Washington, D.C.

Ref: Cemetery Records of Bedford COunty, Tennessee by Marsh

* * * * * * * * * *

PETER MILLER

Name: Rank: State Served:
Peter Miller   -----   ---------------

Died after 1834 and before 1840, married Dolly.

Both are buried in the Miller Cemetery, no markers, on Fay Creek, 3rd District, Bedford County, Tennessee, near Wiley Miller.

Ref: Cemetery Records of Bedford County, Tennessee by Marsh
Ref: Susie Gentry
Ref: Nashville Monument

* * * * * * * * * *

HENRY MOORE

Name: Rank: State Served:
Henry Moore   PVT   North Carolina

Born 11th day of May 1760 Chester County, Pennsylvania, died 1833/34 in Bedford County, Tennessee, married in North Carolina to Catherine Robinson who died before 1830. Catherine Moore was a daughter of Michael Robinson. Children of Henry Moore are: Henry, Samuel, Michael, David R., Martha Delk, Mary, Margaret, and Elizabeth.

GSA: Henry Moore, S.2851, North Carolina

Claim No. 7413: West Tennessee, Henry Moore of Bedford County in the State of West Tennessee who was a Private in the company commanded by Captain Sanders of the Regiment commanded by Colonel Brannen in the North Carolina Line for 10 months, Private of Cavalry and 6 months Private of Infantry.

Inscribed on the Roll of West Tennessee at the rate of 51 dollars, 66 cents per annum to commence on the 4th day of March 1831.

Certificate of Pension issued the 9 day of April 1833 and sent to Samuel Henderson, Shelbyville.

Arrears to the 4th of March	$103.32
Semi-anl allowance ending 4 Sept	$ 25.83
	$129.15

Recorded by Daniel Boyd, Clerk   Revolutionary Claim

Book E   Vol 7   page 88   Act June 7, 1832

NOTE: First part of this declaration is missing....

. . . Major whose name he does not recollect but he was called by the troops DeBeren and Major Henderson. They marched through Chatham and back through Orange into Guilford and were round the lines at the Battle of Guilford but had not arrived in time to see General Green or to be placed under his command. It was supposed by the soldiers to be Colonel Malmady's intention to capture the enemies baggage but was misled or deceived by the pilot. We marched back to Chatham and attacked the British Pickett at Ramsey's (Ramsour's) Mills on Deep River and followed the British Army to Wilmington from Wilmington we marched to Duplin County and from there to Dobbs County on New River where I was discharged, having been in service the last tour five or six months, making the whole time I was in actual service of the United States during the Revolutionary War was sixteen or seventeen months.

This declarent cannot at this distance of time recollect the days or were months he volunteered his service the four different tours he served nor the days or months he received his discharge at the end of the different periods, he has lost all his discharges not believing they would ever be of any service to him. He can only state generally he volunteered first in the Fall of 1779, say in October or November, the 2nd tour of three months, he thinks, probably in February or March 1780, his 3rd tour of five months, he supposes, was in July or August 1780, and his last tour of five months or six months, he supposes, must have been in January or February 1781.

This declarent states he was born on the 11th day of May 1760 in Chester County, Pennsylvania as he has been informed by his parents, and according to a register of his birth which he has at home in his Bible given to him by his father. His father removed into Orange County, North Carolina in the year 1766, in which County this declarent lived at the commencement of the Revolutionary War. After the close of the war he resided in said County of Orange, North Carolina until the year 1798 when he removed to Davidson County, Tennessee where he lived one year. He then removed to Warren County, Kentucky where he lived seven years. He then removed to Maury County, Tennessee where he lived six years. He then removed to Bedford County where he has resided ever since. He has no documentary or other evidence of his service in his power except the affidavits accompanying this declaration.

This declarent further states that in addition to the officers already mentioned in the foregoing declaration that he became acquainted in his first tour with a Major Nickens and General Caswell. In the 2nd tour he became acquainted with Major Griffis. In the 3rd tour he became acquainted with Captain Bledsoe, Captain Colo--- and Captain Douglass and in the 4th tour he became acquainted with Captain Taylor and Captain Byass, tho he thinks all these officers as well as those mentioned in his declaration were of the Militia with the exception of Colonel Mabane and the French Colonel Malmady and the French Major _____.

He further states he is known in the neighborhood where he resides by John Robinson, James Rhea, John Philips, Absolem Hays, Samuel Balch and a great many others and in fact all his acquaintances all of whom he believes would testify to his character for veracity and their belief of his services as a Soldier of the Revolution. There is no clergyman residing in his immediate neighborhood he believes sufficiently acquainted with him to testify as to his belief of his Revolutionary services.

He hereby relinguishes every claim whatever to a pension of annuity except the present and declares that his name is not on the Pension Roll of the agency of any State whatever.

Sworn to and subscribed this 6th of November 1832.

Jas. McKisick, Clk   Henry Moore

I, John Robinson, aged between sixty two and sixty three, residing in the County of Bedford, State of Tennessee hereby certify and make oath that I was raised in Orange County, North Carolina in the same neighborhood where Henry Moore who has subscribed and sworn to the above declaration resided. I was acquainted with the said Henry Moore from my earliest recollection and saw him frequently before he entered the service of the United States and altho I was never in service myself, being too young, I have a distinct recollection of the different times the said Henry Moore was absent from the neighborhood and was said to be in the service of the United States as a Soldier in the Revolutionary War. I have been and conversed with many persons who was with Henry Moore in service and have heard such persons speak of serving with said Henry Moore and in conversing with him relate various incidents which occurred during their service together. He further states that he resides at this time within 7 or 8 miles of said Henry Moore and are at this time and have been since my earliest recollection well acquainted with him. I believe him to be 72 years of age and he is reputed and believed in the neighborhood where he resides to have been a Soldier of the Revolution and I concur in that opinion.

Subscribed and sworn to this 6th day of November 1832.

Jas. McKisick, Clk   John Robinson

I, Abraham Hilton (Helton), aged about eighty years of age, residing in the County of Bedford, State of Tennessee, hereby certify that I am well acquainted with Henry Moore who has subscribed and sworn to the foregoing declaration. I believe him to be 72 years of age, that he is reputed and believed in the neighborhood where he resides to have been a Soldier of the Revolution. He further states that he knew and was acquainted with said Henry Moore while he was in service of the United States as a Soldier of the United States. He served in the same regiment with this deponent one tour of service if no more. He has a distinct recollection of seeing said Henry Moore in service shortly before the skirmish with the Tories at Lenly's Mills. He recollects he was sick and was left with some of the troops at Ramsey's (Ramsour's) Mills on Deep River and I recollect said Henry Moore marched with the detachment to Linly's Mills when he understood they had a skirmish with the Tories at the latter place and he always understood from said Moore and others said Moore was in that engagement and he was not only concur in the opinion that said Henry Moore was a Soldier of the Revolution in the service of the United States but he has a knowledge personally of that fact.

Subscribed and sworn to this 6th November 1832.

Jas. McKisick, Clk.   Abraham (X) Helton

And the said Court do hereby declare their opinion after the investigation of the matter and after putting the interrogatories perscribed by the War Department that the above named applicant was a Revolutionary Soldier and served as he states. And the Court further certifies that it appears to them that John Robinson and Abraham Helton who have subscribed and sworn to the proceeding certificates are residents of Bedford County and are incredible persons and that their statement is entitled to credit.

                                    Jo. L. Neill
                                    Samuel Phillips
                                    John B. Armstrong

I, James McKisick, Clerk of the Court of Pleas and Quarter Sessions of Bedford County do hereby certify that the foregoing contains the original proceedings of the said Court in the matter of this application of Henry Moore for a pension.

In testimony whereof I have hereunto set my hand and Seal of Office this 7th day of November 1832.   Jas. McKisick, Clk.

Brief in the case of Henry Moore of Bedford County in the State of Tennessee
(Act 7th June 1832)
Henry Moore, age 72, entered service in Orange County, North Carolina

In 1777 3 months,   Private   Col. Brannen, Capt. Sanders] NC Mil
In 1780 3 months   Private   Col. Mabane, Capt. Farland]
In 1780 5 months   Cavalry   Col. O'Neal, Capt. Christman - NC
In 1781 5 or 6 months Cavalry   Col. Malmady, Capt. M----

Henry Moore died 1833/24 in bedford County, Tennessee, married in North Carolina to a daughter (Catherine) of Michael Robinson. She died before 1830. Known children: Henry, Samuel, Michael, David R., Martha Delk, Mary, Margaret, and Elizabeth.. Served in the Revolution with neighbor Abraham Helton.

Ref: Abraham Helton deposition, S.4353
Ref: GSA Report, Washington, D.C.
Ref: Bedford County Deed Book EE, page 16 & 17
Ref: Will of Michael Robinson of Orange County, North Carolina
Ref: 1835 Bedford County, Tennessee Pension List

Additional information on Henry Moore:

Letter from Thomas N. McClain to James K. Polk:
Mr. James K. Polk   Richmond, Bedford County, Decm 8th 1831.
I have inclosed you a petition for a postoffice at my store twelve miles south west of Shelbyville in the neighborhood of Henry Moore, James Ray, Esqr., Col. Blackwell, Capt. Medearis, and Thos. Suduth[1] between Rock and Sinking Creek four & one half miles south of the Lawrenceburg Route on the road leading from the Fishingford to Fayetteville. Please forward the petition[2].
Thos N. McClain

Addressed to Washington.
1: Moore and Medearis were Revolutionary War Veterans, and Blackwell was probably Shrewsbury Blackwell, who was a Colonel in the Militia. Ray and Susuth have not been identified.
2: The petition was successful. A post office was established at Richmond, and McClain served as its postmaster.
Ref: Correspondence of James K. Polk, Vol 1, page 424.

Henry Moore was in the 1830 Census of Bedford County, Tennessee, age 90-100 years, living in the Richmond area.

* * * * * * * * * *

JOHN MOORE, SR.

Name: Rank   State Served:
John Moore, Sr.   PVT   North Carolina
Born September 5, 1761 in Louisa County, Virginia, died January 6, 1842 in Bedford County, Tennessee, married Eleanor Marbrey in Rowan County, North Carolina in Fall of 1787. Both are buried in Mt. Moriah Cemetery with marked graves, Bedford County, Tennessee.

Tombstones:

John Moore   Eleanor G., Consort of
1760 - Jan 6, 1842   John Moore
Aged: 82 yrs.   1760 - Dec 9, 1851
                        Aged: 91 yrs.

GSA: John Moore, W.40, Eleanor, wife.
Claim No. 8102: Nashville, Tennessee, Eleanor Moore, widow of John Moore, who was a Pensioner under the Act of 1832 and who died on the 6th January 1842 of Bedford County, in the State of Tennessee, who was a Private in the Company Regiment commanded by Colonel _____ in the North Carolina Line for 8 months.
Inscribed on the Roll of Nashville at the rate of 26 dollars, 66 cents per annum, to commence on the 4th day of March 1836.
Certificate of Pension issued the 14 day of February 1844 and sent to

Hon. G.W. Jones, H.R.

Total Amount $133.30

Recorded by F.L. Swann, Clerk
Book D   Vol 1   page 351

Act July 7, 1838

John Moore, D.40, Nashville, Tennessee, widow of John Moore who was a Private in the North Carolina Line.

Inscribed on the Roll at the rate of 26 dollars, 66 cents per annum, to commence the 4th day of March 1843.

Certificate of Pension issued the 21 day of Feby 1844 and sent to Hon. G.W. Jones, H. of Reps.

Recorded in
Book A   Vol 1   page 220

Act of March 3, 1843

Declaration:

Declaration in order to obtain the benefit of Act of Congress passed the 7th June 1832.

State of Tennessee]
Bedford County   ]

On this 13th day of August in the year of our Lord, one thousand eight hundred and thirty two, personally appeared in open court before the Worshipful John B. Armstrong, John L. Neill and Samuel Phillips, Esquires, Gentlemen Justices of the Peace, appointed to hold the Court of Pleas and Quarter Sessions for the County of Bedford in the State of Tennessee, John Moore, Senr., a resident of the County and State aforesaid, aged seventy years, eleven months and ten days, who being first duly sworn according to law doth on his oath make the following declaration in order to obtain the benefit of the Act of Congress passed the 7th June 1832, that he entered the service under the following named officers and served as herein stated, to wit, That he volunteered in the County of Rowan and State of North Carolina, he thinks in the year 1778 or 1779, under a Captain Robert Gillespie, he states, he was marched from that to Moore County, North Carolina. He states the Company he belonged to was frequently _____ _____ _____ but had ne engagement with the Tories. He states he was then marched down on Pee Dee in South Carolina, near to where General Marion (or he was informed) had lately been with his army, and it was said the Tories had all fled or had become quiet. He further states that he was then marched home to the Garrison at Salisbury and discharged. He states that he only remained at home six or seven days before his mother informed him that she had heard a report in circulation that the Tories had threatened to take his life and advised him to go and join the Americans again which he states he did and joined Captain Peter Hedrick's Company of Mounted Men at Salisbury in the State of North Carolina in a few days after I received the above information from my mother, he states he was marched from that place pretty nearly the same route as when the Captain Gillespie, called the Crossroads, killed one Tory and chased the balance into a swamp. He states that he was marched from said place to another where the Captain was informed the Tories had embodied and returned home again, and was discharged, served a tour of duty two months or thereabouts, he states that he had not been home more than three or four days before General Morgan came to his father's, in person being an old acquaintance of his father where he states he joined General Morgan and was attached to Captain Washington's Company of General Morgan's Riflemen, he states he was marched out with General Morgan and belonged to the Regiment at the Battle of Cowpens. He states he was attached to the guard who guarded prisoners from the Cowpens to that place the Americans sunk the flat boat by leading _____ _____ _____ _____ _____ _____ through his Battalion _____ _____ _____ and weighting her down with rocks. He states that the British who were in persuit of them made their appearance on the bank of the river in a short time, he states, it was on this night and bright moon light and at the place Morgan formed his men for action and gave his men to understand that from the two discharges from their rifles, he, General Morgan, would necessarily have to retreat and requested that who could go on further, to meet him again that night about three miles below there at Ramsour's Ferry and those who could not go further, to make their way home the best way could. He states that his father only lived

about one mile and a half from this place and came to meet him the same evening and on finding that the British was coming, he saw the said John Moore the present applicant's house. He also states that the engagement anticipated by General Morgan did take place and that Morgan retreated. He states that he made his way to his father's but had not been at his father's more than two hours before he was made prisoner by the Tories. On the same night, the leading Tories were, his father's near neighbors, by the name of John Smith and 'Bama Beavers, both Captains of Tory Companies. He states they marched next morning, about day, to Cornwallis and delivered him up to him, he says Cornwallis asked him how long he had been in the Rebel Service, to which he says he answered that, that he had not been in the Rebel Service, that father and mother were Quakers (which was the fact) and that he understood the Quakers were not compelled to bear arms. He states that Cornwallis told him he could return home but to be sure never to take up arms against his King, which promise he says he made but on the next day, he went to Salisbury and joined Captain Gillespie and continued with him until 'Wallis was defeated. He was arresting Tories and imprisoning them and guarding the jail and a _____ he had in Salisbury. He states that he thinks in the two last mentioned tours of duty, he served six months. He states he does not recollect of being acquainted with Regular Officers of any Regiment belonging to the American Army nor does he recollect the number of any Regiment of Militia,'if he did, at that time he has since forgotten it. He states that he thinks the whole time he served was at least eight months. He further states that he has no documentary evidence whatever at this time and that he knows of no person whose testimony he can procure, who can testify as to his service. And that his name is not on the Pension Roll of any agency in the United States. And he hereby relinguishes all claim to a pension except the present.
Sworn to and subscribed the day and year aforesaid.

____________, Clerk   John Moore, Senr.

Interrogatories by the Court:

Q. 1st: Where and in what State were you born?

A.   I was born in Louisa County in the State of Virginia on the 5th day of September 1761, agreeable to my father's record.

Q. 2nd: Have you any record of your age, if so where is it?

A.   I have a record of my age at my house in this County, taken from my father's Bible and written in my own Bible.

Q. 3rd: Where were you living when you were called into service? Where have you lived since the Revolutionary War and where do you now live?

A.   I lived in Rowan County, in the State of North Carolina when I entered the service of the United States and I remained in the same County until I moved to the County of Bedford in the State of Tennessee in the year 1810, where I have lived ever since and where I now live.

Q. 4th: How were you called into service? Were you a volunteer? Were you drafted, or were you a substitute and is a substitute for whom?

A.   I was a volunteer the whole time of my service, first with Captain Robert Gillespie, second, with Captain Peter Hedrick, the third, with Captain Washington under General Morgan and the fourth time, and last time, with Captain Gillespie.

Q. 5th: State the names of some of the Regular Officers who were with you, or the troops where you served, such Continental and Militia Regiment as you can recollect and the general circumstances of your service.

A.   I did not become acquainted with any of the Regular Officers while in service, nor do I recollect the names of any Officers of any Regiment nor the number of them, except those set forth in my declaration.

Q. 6th: Did you ever receive a discharge from the service? And if so, where is it or what has become of it?

A.   I never did receive a written discharge.

Q. 7th: State the names of persons to whom you are known in your present neighborhood who can testify as to character for veracity, their belief of your service as a Soldier in the Revolution.

A.   The Rev. John Brooks, Thomas McGuire, David Norvell, Jacob Martin, Thomas Holland and William Ditto and others.

Sworn to in open Court 15th August 1832.
Jas. McKisick, Clk.   John (X) Moore

        We, John Brooks, a Clergyman, residing in Bedford County, Tennessee
and William Ditto, a resident of the same County and State, do hereby certify
that we are well acquainted with John Moore, Senr., who has sworn to and
subscribed the foregoing declaration in order to obtain the benefit of the Act of
Congress passed the 7th June 1832, that we believe him to be seventy years,
eleven months and ten days, that he is reputed and believed in the neighborhood
where he resides to have been a Soldier of the Revolution and that we concur in
that opinion.
Sworn to and subscribed the 15th day of August 1832 in open Court.
Jas. McKisick, Clk   Jno. Brooks
                                                    Wm. (X) Ditto

        And the said Court do hereby declare their opinion after the
investigation presented by the War Department, that the above named applicant
was a Revolutionary Soldier and served as he states. And the Court further
certifies that it appears to them that John Brooks who has signed the foregoing
certificate is a Clergyman of good standing in the Methodist Church and that
William Ditto who has signed the preceeding certificate as a resident of the
County aforesaid, and is a creditable person and that his statement is entitled to
credit.
                                          J.L. Neill
                                          Samuel Phillips
                                          John B. Armstrong

State of Tennessee   ]
Bedford Circuit Court] December Term, 1843
        This day being the 18th day of December in the year of our Lord, one
thousand eight hundred and forty three, personally appeared, Elenor Moore, a
resident of said County of Bedford, aged eighty years and upwards, in open court
before the Honorable Samuel Anderson, Esquire, Judge of the 5th Judicial Circuit
of the State of Tennessee, who after beinh duly sworn according to law, doth on
her oath make the following declaration in order to obtain the benefit of the
provision made by the Act of Congress passed July 7th, 1838, entitled "An Act
granting half pay and pensions to certain widows." That she is the widow of John
Moore, now deceased. She further states that her husband John Moore drew a
pension from the United States as a Private Soldier of the Revolution of
twenty-six dollars and some cents, that when she drew the arrearages of pension
due her, at her husband's death, his Pension Certificate was filed with the Agent
for paying Pensions in Nashville, Tennessee, as she is informed and believes. She
further declares that she was married to her said husband, John Moore, in the
County of Rowan and State of North Carolina, sometime in the Fall of the year
seventeen hundred and eighty seven. She further states that she knows of no
record by which her marriage can be established, and that she was not married to
her said husband, John Moore, until after he left the service of the United
States, but that it took place as above stated sometime in the Fall of 1787. She
further declares that she has not since the death of her said husband, John
Moore, intermarried with any other person whatsoever.
Sworn to and subscribed in open court this 8th day of December 1843.
John L. Neill, Clerk   Elenor (X) Moore (Seal)

State of Tennessee
        I, John L. Neill, Clerk of the Circuit Court of Bedford County, being a
Court of Record, having common law issued term, do certify that Elenor Moore
whose name is inscribed to the foregoing declaration, appeared in the Circuit
Court of Bedford County, at the Courthouse in the town of Shelbyville, on the
8th day of December 1843 and was duly sworn in open court to the facts stated
in said declaration. I do further certify that Locke Marberry and Redding George
also appeared in open court on said 8th day of December 1843 and was duly
qualified to the facts stated in the within affidavits by them respectively
subscribed and that on the 9th day of December 1843, Robert Moffatt appeared
in said open court and was duly sworn to the facts stated in the affidavit by him
subscribed. I do further certify that Samuel Anderson whose name appears to the

above Certificate is one of the Judges of the Circuit Court of the State of Tennessee assigned by law to hold the Circuit Court in the Fifth Judicial Circuit of the State of Tennessee, said Courts being Courts of Common Law Jurisdiction (the County of Bedford, composing a part of the Juducial Circuit). I do further certify that the foregoing signatures of Samuel Anderson are genuine. In testimony whereof I have hereunto set my hand and affixed my private seal there being no Seal of said Court, done at my office in Shelbyville on this 9th day of December 1843.

John L. Neill, Clerk

This day being the 8th day of December 1843, personally appeared in open court before the Honorable Samuel Anderson, Judge, and Redding George, a resident of Bedford County in the State of Tennessee, who after being duly sworn according to law, doth on his oath, depose and say that he was present and assisted in placing the identical, Jno. Moore, in his coffin, mentioned in the foregoing declaration made by his widow, Elenor Moore, that he departed this life on the sixth day of January 1842 in bedford County and State of Tennessee, and that he is a near neighbor of said Elenor Moore, that she is a woman of undoubted veracity.
Sworn in open court, 8th of December 1843.
John L. Neill, Clerk   Redding George (Seal)

This day being the 9th day of December 1843, personally appeared in open court before the Honorable Samuel Anderson, Esq., Judge of the 5th Judicial Circuit Court of the State of Tennessee, who after being duly sworn according to law, doth on his oath, state that he is well acquainted with Mrs. Elenor Moore, the applicant in the foregoing declaration, he states that he wrote Powers of Attorney for John Moore in his lifetime for pensions to draw his pension from the agency in Nashville and is satisfied the amount of pension per annum was twenty six dollars and he thinks sixty six cents. He further states that he the said John Moore, now deceased, is the identical John Moore mentioned in the foregoing declaration of said Elenor Moore. He further states that she is a woman of good character and for honesty and truth is unimpeachable.
Sworn to in open court 9th of December 1843.
John L. Neill, Clerk   Robert Moffett (Seal)

I, Samuel Anderson, one of the Circuit Judges in and for the State of Tennessee, now presiding in Bedford County, do certify that L. Marberry, Redding George and Robert Moffatt, whose signatures are to the foregoing affidavits, are persons of creditability as it appears to me from information I have obtained from their acquaintances with them. I am personally acquainted with Robert Moffatt whose signature is to be the last affidavit and certify he is a man of good character and creditability of my own knowledge of his private and general character.
Given under my hand this 9th day of December 1843.

S. Anderson, Judge Cit.

Children of John and Elenor Moore:
1. John, born September 30, 1795, died July 11, 1868 and buried in Mt. Moriah Cemetery, Bedford County, Tennessee, married Nancy Yell who was born July 13, 1803, died March 27, 1883 and are buried in Mt. Moriah Cemetery.
2. Tabitha Williams, born 15 August 1800, married Morgan Smith.
3. Green, married _____ Cooper.
4. D.C.
5. Sally, born ca 1797, married Isaac West.
6. Frances, born ca 1795, married Abraham Shriver.

In 1850 Census of Bedford County, Tennessee, 4th District, Visit No. 163:
Eleanor Moore was in the house of Abraham Shriver and wife Frances (who was a daughter of John and Eleanor Moore). Frances, born 1795 in North Carolina.

Ref: GSA Report, Washington, D.C.
Ref: Widow's Application for Pension.
Ref: Cemetery Records of Bedford County, Tennessee by Marsh.
Ref: DAR Tennessee 1941 Yearbook, page 102

Ref: Tennessee Pension Roll, page 47
Ref: 1850 Census of Bedford County, Tennessee, visit No. 163.
Ref: Texas Society DAR Roster Revolutionary Ancestors, Vol III, pg 1528.

* * * * * * * * * *

RANDOLPH MOORE

Name:	Rank:	State Served:
Randolph Moore	PVT	North Carolina

Born January 10, 1758 in Edgecomb County, North Carolina, died July 7, 1833 Bedford County, Tennessee, married June 12, 1783 in Johnson County, North Carolina to Elizabeth Stanstill.

GSA: Randolph Moore, North Carolina, wife Elizabeth, W.52.
Claim No. 6345: West Tennessee, Randolph Moore of Bedford County in the State of North Carolina, who was a Private in the Company commanded by Captain Thomas of the Regiment commanded by Colonel Caswell in the North Carolina Militia for 12 months and 4 days.

Inscribed on the Roll of Tennessee at the rate of 40 dollars, 44 cents per annum to commence on the 4th day of March 1831.

Certificate of Pension issued the 28th day of February 1833 and sent to Jas. McKisick, Clk.

Arrears to the 4th of Sept 1832	$60.66
Semi-anl allowance ending 4 March 1833	$20.22
	$80.88

Recorded by Henry H. Sylvester, Clerk   Revolutionary Claim
Book D   Vol 7   page 154   Act June 7, 1832.

Claim No. 6088: Tennessee, Elizabeth Moore, widow of Randolph Moore, deceased, who was a Pensioner under the Act of 1832, and who died on the 7 July 1833 of Bedford County, Tennessee in the State of Tennessee, who was a Private in the Company commanded by Captain Thomas of the Regiment commanded by Colonel Caswell in the North Carolina Line for 1 year and 4 days.

Inscribed on the Roll of Nashville at the rate of 40 dollars, 44 cents per annum to commence on the 4th day of March 1836.

Certificate of Pension issued the 9th day of March 1841, and sent to Hon. H.M. Watterson, Member of Congress.

$202.22
Recorded by D.M. Curdy, Clk   Act July 7, 1838
Book A   Vol 2   page 208

State of Tennessee   ]
Bedford County Court]   November Term, 1840

The declaration of Elizabeth Moore in order to obtain the benefit of the Act of Congress passes 4th July 1836.

On this second day of November in the year of our Lord, one thousand eight hundred and forty, before the Worshipful, Jacob Greer, William Burnett and Price C. Steele, Gentlemen Justices of the Peace in and for the County and State aforesaid, personally appeared in open court, Elizabeth Moore, a citizen of Bedford County aforesaid who after being duly sworn agreeable to law, deposeth and saith that she was born in Babbs County and State of North Carolina on the 9th day of July 1766, agreeable to the record of her parents, that her father and mother removed to Johnson County in North Carolina, where she intermarried with Randolph of said County on the 12th day of June 1783. Sometime after they removed to wake County and from there to Bedford County in the State of Tennessee, where she now resides. She further states that sometime in the year 1832, her said husband applied and obtained a pension from the government of the United States for the sum of forty dollars and some cents. She cannot recollect which sum it was at present, which pension she states her said husband drew the 4th March 1831 until the 4th of March 1833. She further states that she drew the balance of pension on her said husband, by a Power of Attorney to Thomas Davis. She states her husband, Randolph Moore departed this life on the 7th of July 1833 in said County of Bedford.

Sworn to in open court the day above written.
Test: Robert Hurst, Clerk of   Elizabeth Moore (Seal)
Bedford County Court.

State of Tennessee]
Bedford County   ]
   This day Isham O'Neal, a citizen of Marshall County in the State of aforesaid, personally appeared in open court and after being duly sworn according to law, deposeth and saith that he was intimately acquainted with Randolph Moore and his wife Elizabeth, formerly of Johnson County and State of North Carolina, and that they were always considered as man and wife while residents of said Johnson County and he further states that he was acquainted with said Randolph and Elizabeth Moore since they moved to Bedford County, Tennessee and have always been reputed as man and wife until the death of the said Randolph Moore.
Test: Robt. Hurst, Clerk of   Isom O'Neal
Bedford County Court

State of Tennessee]
Bedford County   ]
   I, Robert Hurst, Clerk of the County Court of said Bedford County do hereby certify that the foregoing contains the original proceedings of the said court in the matter of the application of Elizabeth Moore for a pension.
   In testimony whereof I have hereunto set my hand and Seal of Office this fifth day of November A.D. one thousand eight hundred and forty.
           Robert Hurst, Clerk

   I, H.M. Watterson, Member of Congress from the nineth Congressional District of the State of Tennessee, certify that I have been acquainted with Isom O'Neal, of the County of Marshall and State aforesaid, for about six years and that he sustains a fair and good character, none I presume will or can question his veracity. His age is near sixty years. Given under my hand and Seal, this 5th day of November 1840.

        H.M. Watterson (Seal)

State of Tennessee]
Marshall County   ]
   This day personally appeared before me, J.T. Harris, an Acting Justice of the Peace for said County at the dwelling house of Isham O'Neal in said County, Mrs. Milley Campbell, a resident of the said County of Marshall, aged eighty two years, formerly of Johnson County and State of North Carolina, being so aged and infirm as to be unable to attend a Court of Record, after being duly sworn according to law deposeth and saith that she was well acquainted with Randolph Moore and Elizabeth Stansell in Johnson County, North Carolina, previous to the marriage of the said Randolph Moore and Elizabeth Stansell which she believes took place sometime in the year, one thousand seven hundred and eighty and that she knew ans saw them pass as husband and wife for some years previous to the first of January, one thousand seven hundred and ninety four.
Sworn to and subscribed before me this the 30th day of January 1841.
John T. Harris (Seal)   Milley (X) Campbell (Seal)
Justice of the Peace for
Marshall County.

   I do certify that the lady whose signature appears to the above is entitled to full credit for truth and veracity and that she stands fair in security. This the 30th day of January 1841.

        J.T. Harris (Seal)
        Justice of the Peace for
        said County.

State of Tennessee]
Marshall County   ]
   I, Martin W. Oakley, Clerk of the COunty Court of said Marshall County, certify that John T. Harris, whose signature appears to the foregoing affidavit and certificate is and was an Acting Justice of the Peace for said County at the time he signed the same, he having been duly commissioned and as

such.

       In testimony where of, I have hereunto set my hand and affixed my Seal of Office at Office in Lewisburg, this 6th day of February A.D. 1841.

Martin W. Oakley, Clerk
of said Court.

State of tennessee]
Marshall County   ]

       I, Benjamin Williams, chariman and residing Magistrate of the County Court of said Marshall County, do certify that Martin W. Oakley, who made the above certificate is and was at the time of making the same, the Clerk of our said County Court duly elected and qualified, and that the certificate is a duly form of law, sealed with our County Seal and the signature genuine.
Given under my hand and seal this 6th day of February A.D. 1841.
Hon. H.M. Watterson, M.C.   B. Williams (Seal)

1835, age 76 years, Private in North Carolina Militia.

Randolph Moore, served as Private under Captain Needham Bryant. Colonel Richard Caswell, North Carolina Regiment, under Captain Philip Thomas, Colonel Brown, North Carolina Regiment, under Captain Joseph Sessions. Colonel Linton and Richard Dobbs, North Carolina Regiment. At Battle of Moore's Creek. Pension from bedford County, Tennessee, aged 76 years in 1832, Pension List. 1834 P.L.W. , File W.52. Married June 12, 1783 in Johnson County, North Carolina to Elizabeth Stansill, born July 9, 1766 and died 1843.
Children:
1. Elizabeth, born 1794
2. Stansill, born 1796
3. Nathan, born 1798
4. John, born 1800
5. James, born 1802
6. Thomas, born 1804, married 1833 to Nancy Carr Allen*
7. Silpha, born 1806 (Zilpha)
8. Celia, born 1807, married _____ Dyer
9. Rebecca, born 1809
10. Piety, born 1811.

* Notes from a sketch of John Randolph Moore, originally from Bedford County, Tennessee, born 1834, gives his parents as Thomas and Nancy (Allen) Moore, natives of Wake County, North Carolina, and Warren County, Tennessee, respectively, the father born 1804 and was son of Randolph Moore, a native of Virginia, Soldier of the Revolutionary War. The latter came to Bedford County, Tennessee in 1830. His children were: Elizabeth, Stansil, Nathan, John, James, Thomas, Zilphia, Rebecca, Celia and Piety. Piety died in Lincoln County, Tennessee. The paternal grandmother of John Randolph Moore was Elizabeth Stansil, died in bedford County, Tennessee, 1843. His father, Thomas Moore was reared in bedford County, married Miss Allen while in Tennessee, both were born 1812(?). Her father, John Allen was a native of Mecklenburg County, North Carolina and his wife Miss Nancy Carr (Karr) born in the same County, daughter of Joseph Carr (Karr), a native of Ireland and a Revolutionary War Soldier.

      Ref: GSA Report, Washington, D.C.
      Ref: Widow's Application for Pension
      Ref: 1835 Bedford County, Tennessee Pension List
      Ref: Pension File No. W.52
      Ref: Tennessee DAR 1941 Yearbook, page 103
      Ref: "Dropped Stitches", Column, Commercial Appear, Memphis, Tennessee.
      Ref: Tennessee DAR Blue Book Roster and Soldiers, Vol 1, page 1125

Name: Rank: State Served:
John Morrison   PVT   North Carolina

Born March 28, 1763 in Pennsylvania, died December 7, 1846 in Bedford County, Tennessee, married April 5, 1791 to Jane Bradshaw who had six children and died January 5, 1803. Married second July 31, 1804 to Dolly Rogers and had about thirteen children and died in 1854.

1835, age 69 years, Private in the North Carolina Line.

GSA: John Morrison, S.2867, North Carolina. Born in Pennsylvania.
Claim No. 1919(7 or 3): West Tennessee, John Morrison of Bedford County in the State of Tennessee, who was a Private in the Company commanded by Captain Barnes of the Regiment commanded by Colonel Davidson on the North Carolina Line for 7 months and 25 days.

Inscribed on the Roll of West Tennessee at the rate of 26 dollars, 11 cents per annum, to commence on the 4th day of March 1831.

Certificate of Pension issued the 14th day of April 1833 and sent to John Bruce, Pensioner, Shelbyville.

Arrears to the 4th of March $52.22
Semi-anl allowance ending 4 Sept $13.05
                                                    $65.27

Recorded by Daniel Boyd, Clerk   Revolutionary Claim
Book E   Vol 7   page 89   Act June 7, 1832

Declaration:
State of Tennessee]
Bedford County   ]

This 14 day of August 1832, appeared John Morrison, in open Court of Pleas and Quarter Sessions of Bedford County in the State aforesaid, before Samuel Phillips, John B. Armstrong and John L. Neill, Esquires, members appointed to hold such Court, about sixty nine years of age, make the above declaration to obtain the benefit of an Act of Congress of 1832, and being first duly sworn according to law deposeth and says as follows: That in the year 1780, he volunteered and went into service, into Captain Peter Barnes' Company of Militia, Second Regiment in the North Carolina Line, commanded by Colonel Locke in General Rutherford's Brigade. That he and the said Company in which he served were called Minute Men and were directed to march at any time on the approach of the enemy that occasionally he got permission from his Captain to go home and return back again for about five months, to wit, from sometime in the year 1780, October, that at the time he volunteered, he resided in Mecklenburg County in the State of North Carolina. That during the term of service aforesaid, he was in the Battle of the Waxhaws with the Tories, at which battle, thirteen of the Tories were killed and the Tories defeated. That Major Davis commanded the said battle, there being no officers higher than a Major with the Whigs at that time, that said battle was fought in September 1780. That during the term of service aforesaid he was acquainted with General Davidson and General Rutherford and Colonel Locke, Colonel Evin and with Major White and Major Davis, Major Harris, Captain Peter Barnes, Captain Riley, with John _____ and Hue Paterson, who acted as adjutant in the regiment in which he served. At the expiration of the term of service aforesaid Major White gave him a written discharge stating in said discharge that deponent had been in actual service one hundred days after his return home, he gave said discharge to his father for safe keeping but his father had since departed this life and he does not know where said discharge is at, at this time. That he has no documentary evidence by which he can prove his term of service, but John Roberson, Esquire, saw him in service during the term of service aforesaid, he is the only person he now knows of that whom he can prove his term or service, and he lives in the western part of this State about one hundred miles from this place and deponent does not know in what County he lives and consequently, it would be very inconvenient for deponent to produce his affidavit. And in October 1780, shortly after he was discharged as aforesaid deponent again volunteered and went into service as a waggoner, under John Huggins as Wagon-master and went into the Second Regiment of Militia in the North Carolina Line, commanded by General

Davidson, General Rutherford who formerly commanded said Regiment having been taken a prisoner in General Gates' Defeat, that he served as a waggoner about three and one half months during which time he saw all the Officers with whom he was acquainted during his first term of service except General Rutherford and Major Davie(s). That during the term of service aforesaid, he marched through different parts of Mecklenburg County in the State of North Carolina and at the expiration of the last term of service, he believes he received no discharge but his father acquired as he believes a written discharge for him, but he does not know where it is at this time, having never seen it in his life. That he has no documentary evidence by whom he can prove the last term of service but during the last term of service aforesaid, he saw one Samuel Bowman but he now lives at this time in an adjoining County, about forty miles from this place, and he is very old and infirm and deponent does not know whether he recollects of ever seeing deponent in the service aforesaid deponent knows of no person by whom he can prove the term of service last aforesaid except John Roberson, Esquire, who lives in the western part of this State as aforesaid , except Samuel Bowman recollects of seeing him in the service during his second term of service, and in August 1781, deponent volunteers as waggoner into the Second Regiment of North Carolina Militia in the North Carolina Line, commanded by General Davidson and served three weeks during which term of service, he saw very few Officers as he was then fauling for the benefit of the hospital, at the expiration of the last term of service, a discharge, as he believes, was given to his father but he does not know where it is at this time, as he never saw it in his life. That at the different times, he volunteered his services, he resided in Mecklenburg County in the State of North Carolina and he hereby relinguishes all and every claim whatever to a pension or annuity except the present and declares that his name is not on the Pension Roll of the agency of any State or Territory in the United States. That he served in all seven months and twenty five days.
Sworn to and subscribed the day and year aforesaid.
Sworn to in open Court 14th August 1832.
Jas. McKisick, Clerk   John Morrison

Questions to be asked John Morrison:

Q. 1st: Where and in what year were you born?
A.   In the State of Pennsylvania but does not know in what County on 28 March 1763.
Q. 2nd: Have you any record of your age and if so, where is it?
A.   I have it at home, it was written in my father's Family Bible and I translated it from his Family Bible into my own Bible, which I now have.
Q. 3th: Where were you living when called into service? Where have you lived since the Revolutionary War and where do you now live?
A.   I was living in Mecklenburg County in the State of North Carolina when called into service and I have lived in the County and State aforesaid till about fifteen years ago, at which time I removed to Bedford County in the State of Tennessee, where I have resided ever since.
Q. 4th: How were you called into service? Were you drafted? Did you volunteer? Or were you a substitute and if a substitute for whom?
A.   I volunteered all three times.
Q. 5th: State the names of some of the Regular Officers who were with the troops where you served such Continental and Militia Regiment as you can recollect and the general circumstances of your service.
A.   I saw Colonel Washington during my second term. Major White gave me my first discharge and I do not know who gave my father my other two discharges of service. Was not acquainted with him and I was acquainted with General Rutherford, General Davidson, Colonel Locke, Colonel Ewin, Major Davie, Major White, Captain Peter Barnes, Captain Riley, John Allison and Hue Paterson who acting as Adjutants.
Q. 6th: Did you ever receive a discharge from the service and if so by whom was it given and what has become of it?
A.   I received a discharge at the expiration of my first term of service but I do not know where it is and my father as I believe received one discharge at the expiration of my two terms of service but I do not

167

know where they are at this time.

Q. 7th: State the names of the persons to whom you are known in your present neighborhood and who can testify as to your character or veracity and their belief in your service as a Soldier in the Revolution.

A.   The Reverand John Rushing and Colonel William Burnet and as to the general circumstances of my services, they are above stated.

Sworn to and subscribed on the day and year aforesaid.

Sworn to in open Court 14th August 1832.

Jas. McKisick, Clerk   John Morrison

Shelbyville, Tennessee	John Morrison, Bedford County
E.	No. 6666
John Bruce	from 1780 first return
7 months, 25 days $20.11	10.16 Barnes - Davidson 11 Mar 1833, N.C.Pen.

John Morrison's known children:

1. Cynthis, married Joel B. Alexander, remained in Mecklenburg County, North Carolina.
2. Elias Denson, born 1800 Mecklenburg County, North Carolina, married Jennie (Jane) Kimmons in 1820 in Hickman County, Tennessee. Elias D. lost 5 of 7 sons during the Civil War.
3. Siah Watson, married Sarah Rodgers and went to Coles County, Illinois in 1836
4. Whitfield W., went to Illinois.
5. Zenas C., married first ____, settled in Graves County, Kentucky in 1848 or 1849, married 2nd in 1841 in Williamson COunty, Tennessee to Elizabeth Maxwell.
6. James, went to Arkansas.
7. McKemie Wilson, last known living in Bedford County, Tennessee at the homeplace in 1850.
8. Tirza
9. Rev. Silas Hall, died in Alabama.
10. Rev. Levi Rogers, died in Missouri.
11. Rev. George M., died in Texas.
12. William, born 1840 when his mother died.
13. James
14. John
15. Elizabeth
16. Robert

     Ref: 1835 Bedford County, Tennessee Pension List

     Ref: GSA Report, Washington, D.C.

     Ref: Times Gazette, May 10, 1959 by Mrs. Katholene M. Privett, Alton, Illinois.

     Ref: Tennessee Blue Book DAR Roster and Soldiers, Vol 1, page 1138.

* * * * * * * * * *

JAMES MOSELY

Name:	Rank:	State Served:
James Mosely	SGT	Virginia

Born 1760 in Virginia, died 25th September 1836 in Marshall County, Tennessee, married Martha _____ 27th March 1821.

GSA: James Mosely, W.25721, Wife Martha, B.L.Wt. 31297-160-55

Claim No. 18.779: West Tennessee, James Mosely of Bedford County in the State of Tennessee, who was a Sergeant in the Regiment commanded by Colonel Matthews of the Virginia Line, for the term of 4 years from 1775.

Inscribed on the Roll of West Tennessee at the rate of 8 dollars per annum, to commence on the 9th of July 1822.

Certificate of Pension issued the 25th of October 1823 and sent to S.R. Rucker, Esqr., Murfreesboro, Tennessee.

Arrears to 4th of Sept 1822	$14.99
Semi-anl allowance ending 4 March 1823	$48.00
1 month	$62.99

Revolutionary Claim
Act 18th March 1818
Act 1 May 1820

Declaration:
District of West Tennessee

On this 9th day of July 1822, personally appeared in open court, the Court of Pleas and Quarter Sessions for the County of Bedford in said State, the same being a Court of Records, James Mozley, resident in said County of Bedford, aged sixty two years, who being first duly sworn according to law doth on his oath make the following declaration in order to obtain the provision made by the Act of Congress of the 18th of March 1818 and the 1st of May 1820. That he the said James Mozely, enlisted for the term of twelve months in the 1775 in the COmpany commanded by Captain William Fountain in the Regiment commanded by Colonel Parker in the Line of the State of Virginia. That he continued to serve in said "Corps" until his time expired when he was discharged at the city of Williamsborough, Virginia. During this service, he was in the Battle of Gwinns Island when Governor Dunsmore commanded the enemy. Afterwards in the year 1776, he enlisted for three years in the company commanded by Captain Samuel T. Cabel in the 9th Regiment commanded by Colonel George Matthews in the Virginia Line on the Continental Establishment. He continued to serve in said Corps for about 18 or 20 months when he was transferred to Captain Lambert's Company in Colonel Morgan's Rifle Regiment, he served sometime in said company when he was transferred to Henderson's Company in the same Regiment, in which Corps, he served the remainder of the three years for which he had enlisted, when he was discharged at Trenton in New Jersey. He was in the Battle of Brandywine, Germantown, Monmouth, Camden, Blufords Defeat, and Little York, and he has no evidence now in his power of his said services excepting his oath, his discharge having been destroyed accidentally by fire near twenty five years since.

And in the persuance of the Act of the 1st of May 1820, I do solemnly swear that I was a resident citizen of the United States on the 18th day of March 1818 and that I have not since that time by gift, sale or in any manner disposed of my property so to dimish it as to bring myself within the provisions of an Act of Congress entitled "An Act to provide for certain persons engaged in the Land and Naval Service of the United States during the Revolutionary War, passed on the 18th day of March 1818." And that I have no property nor has any person in trust for me any property or securities, contracts or debts due me, nor have I any income other than what is contained in the schedule hereto annexed and by me subscribed.

Schedule of the property of James Mozely:

2 feather beds & furniture	$30.00	2 Pails	$ 1.00
2 bed steads	3.00	1 washing tub	.50
2 pots	5.00	1 Piggin tub	.25
1 Oven	1.50	2 Spinning wheels	3.00
4 pewter Plates	1.00	1 H___ Saw	1.50
2 Earthen Plates	.50	1 Drawing Knif	.75
½ doz Knives & Forks	2.00	1 Club Axe	$ 1.50
1 tin Bucket	1.00		$52.50
		1 Cow	9.00
		1 Yearling	2.00
			$63.50

James Mozely

His occupation is that of farming and owning to his age and increase of debility of constitution, he does not think that by his personal industry and exertions, he can procure a necessary and competent support for himself and family. He has a wife named Martha aged 38 years, three daughters living with them:
Mary aged 12 years
Maria ten years
Jane six years old
He has three boys:

William 8 years old
Dixon 4 years old
Daniel Seaborn aged weeks
Their children ought to be educated in such manner as to make them useful and respectable citizens. The Defenders and the Mothers of the Defenders of the Rights and Independence of the Republic.

The means of accomplishing this laudable object is not in the power of the declarent, who was toiling in the service of his Country, which others were recumulating property for themselves and their children.

Sworn to and declared on this 9th day of July 1822, in open Court.

Jas. McKisick   James Mozely

Claim No. 3573: Tennessee, Nashville, Martha Mosely, widow of James Mosely, Virginia, who served in the Revolutionary War, as a Sergeant.

Inscribed on the Roll at the rate of 96 dollars, 00 cents per annum, to commence on the 3rd February 1853.

Certificate of Pension issued 3rd day of February 1854 and sent to Ezra Halstead, South Harpeth, Davidson County, Tennessee.

Recorded on Roll of Pensioners under Act February 3, 1853, page 187, Vol. A.

186.771: Act March 3, July 10, 1855: Martha Mosely, widow of James Mosely, Sergeant, Revolutionary War. Feb.

William James, Charlotte, Dixon County, Tennessee

State of Tennessee]
County of Dickson]

On this second day of April A.D. 1853, personally appeared before me, an acting Justice of the Peace in and for the County and State aforesaid, Mrs. Martha Mosely, a resident of Dickson COunty in the State of Tennessee, aged sixty eight years, who being duly sworn according to law doth on her oath make the following declaration in order to obtain the benefit of the provision made by the Act of Congress passed 3rd February 1853. That she is the widow of James Mosely, who was a Pensioner on the Pension Roll at the agency at Nashville, Tennessee, and drew at the rate of ninety six dollars per annum. She declares that she was married to the said James Mosely, to the best of her recollection, on the 27th of March A.D. 1821, and that her husband, the aforesaid, James Mosely died in Marshall County, Tennessee on the 25th September 1836. That she was married to him at the time above stated. That she knows of no public record containing the date of her marriage, and has no family record containing who was present when she was married to hereto annexed. She further swears that she was a widow at the passage of the Act, and is still a widow and that she has never before made application for a pension.

Sworn to and subscribed on the day and year above written before me,

William Denagan, J.P.   Martha Mosely

Bounty Land Claim:

James Mosely of Virginia, Sergeant in Infantry, on Book of Revolutionary War. Received by George Pickett.

Day when: June 21, 1783
Sum: 77lbs, 19. 4
Vol. 176, page 203

Ref: GSA Record, Washington, D.C.
Ref: Widow's Application for Pension
Ref: Bounty Land Claim

* * * * * * * * * *

JOSEPH MULLINS

Name:	Rank:	State Served:
Joseph Mullins	PVT	Virginia

Born March 2, 1739 in Prince Edward County, Virginia, died after 1834 Bedford County, Tennessee, married to Mary ______.

GSA: Joseph Mullins, S.4248, wife Mary.
Claim No. 7676: West Tennessee, Joseph Mullins of Bedford County in the State of Tennessee who was a Private in the Company commanded by Captain Bates of the Regiment commanded by Colonel Rogers in the Virginia Militia for 6½ months from 1780(1).

        Joseph Mullins Record O.K.   March 29 '04

        Inscribed on the Roll of West Tennessee at the rate of 21 dollars, 66 cents per annum to commence on the 4th day of March 1831.

        Certificate of Pension issued the 11 day of May 1833 and sent to James McKisick, Shelbyville.

Arrears to the 4th of March 1833 $43.33
Semi-anl allowance ending Sept 4, 1833 $10.83
                                                  $54.16

Recorded by William Allison, Clerk   Revolutionary Claim
Book E   Vol 7   page 88

State of Tennessee
Declaration:
        Declaration in order to obtain the benefit of the Act of Congress passed June the 7th 1832.

        On this 9th day of November in the year of our Lord, one thousand eight hundred and thirty two, personally appeared in open court before the Worshipful John B. Armstrong, Samuel Phillips and John L. Neill, being Gentlemen Justices of the Peace, appointed to hold the Court of Pleas and Quarter Sessions of Bedford County, now sitting, Joseph Mullins, a resident of the County and State aforesaid, aged ninety three years, eight months and six days, who being first duly sworn according to law, doth on his oath make the following declaration in order to obtain the benefit of the Act of Congress passed 7th June 1832. That he entered the service of the United States under the following named Officers and served as herein stated, to wit, That he entered the service of the United States as a drafted soldier in Halifax County in the State of Virginia, sometime about the first week in January 1781 and was placed in a Company under the command of Captain Hezekiah Powell and was marched to Portsmouth where he was mustered into service and placed in a Regiment commanded by Colonel Gaskins under the command of General Mucklenburg and was marched from Portsmouth to a Colonel Babbs in the State of Virginia but he does not recollect the name of the County where the American Troops remained for sometime. When they were attacked by the British Army when a general engagement took place, and the Americans under General Mucklenburg proved victorious, he says he was then marched back to Portsmouth and at that place his Captain was sick and died, where he remained until his term of three months service expired when he was discharged by his Lieutenant in writing. (Which discharge accompanies this declaration). Deponent further states that afterwards, about the first week in July 1781, he was drafted again the same County (Halifax) as a Militiman and was placed in Captain Flemming Bates' Company under the command of Colonel John Rogers and a Major Boyce and was marched to Little York where he was mustered into the command of general George Washington where he says he continued until after the Seige of York, that he was in the engagement when Wallace was taken and remained at Little York until something like two weeks after his term of three months service expired. With a view to perform another tour of duty in the character of a volunteer with his Captain who had agreed to go against a party of hostile Indians. He was told Creek Indians, but he is not certain, but was taken sick and ordered to be discharged which was accordingly done by his Cpatain on the 19th day of October 1781. Making in the whole a term of service in all of writings and have accompanied this his declaration. He hereby relinguishes every claim whatever to a pension or annuity except the present and declares that his name is not on the Pension Roll of any agency in the United States.

Interrogatories by the Court:

Q. 1st: Where and what year were you born?
A.   I was born in Prince Edward County in the State of Virginia on the 2nd day of March in the year 1739 as he was informed by his parents to the

171

best of his present recollection.

Q. 2nd: Have you any record of your age and if so where is it?
A. I have no record of my age whatever.
Q. 3rd: Have you any discharges, and if so where is it?
A. I have two discharges, here let them accompany my declaration.
Q. 4th: Where were you living when called into service? Where have you lived since the Revolutionary War, and where do you now live?
A. I was a citizen of Halifax County in the State of Virginia when I entered the service of the United States, and remained so until many years after the close of the Revolutionary War when I moved to Henry County in said State and from that I removed to Pittsylvania County in said State and from there to Grainger County in the State of Tennessee and from there to Jefferson County and from there I moved to Bedford County in the last mentioned State where I now live.
Q. 5th: How were you called into service? Were you drafted? Were you a volunteer or were you a substitute and if a substitute for whom?
A. I was a Drafted Soldier the whole time I was in service.
Q. 6th: State the names of some of the Regular Officers who were with the troops where you served, such Continental and Militia Regiments as you can recollect and the general circumstances of your service.
A. I recollect Mucklenburg at the Portsmouth expedition and General Washington at the Seige of York but do not recollect the names of any other Officers in the Regular Army. I do not recollect the numbers or names of any Regiments of Militia or Continental whatever and I believe I have given a history of the general circumstances of my service as near as I can at this period of my age in the foregoing declaration.
Q. 7th: State the names of persons to whom you are known in your present neighborhood who can testify as to your character for veracity and their opinion of your service as a Soldier of the Revolution.
A. The Rev. William Martin, John Webb and Samuel Cox.

Sworn to and subscribed the day and year aforesaid.
Jas. McKisick, Clk.   Joseph (X) Mullins

We, William Martin, a Clergyman residing in bedford County and State of Tennessee, and John Webb and Samuel Cox of the County of Lincoln and the State aforesaid, hereby certify that we are well acquainted with Joseph Mullins, who has subscribed and sworn to the foregoing declaration, that we believe him to be ninety three years, eight months and six days of age. That he is reputed and believed to have been a Soldier of the Revolution and that we concur in that opinion.

Sworn to in open Court the day and year aforesaid.
Jas. McKisick, Clk.   William Martin
                                                             John Webb
                                                             Samuel Cox

And the said Court do hereby declare their opinion after the investigation of the matter, and after putting the interrogatories prescribed by the War Department that the above named applicant was a Revolutionary Soldier, and served as he states, and the Court further certifies that John Webb and Samuel Cox, who have signed the preceding certificate. And that the Rev. William Martin who has also signed the same is a Clergyman of good standing in the Baptist Church in Bedford County, Tennessee, and a citizen of the same.

                                                             John L. Neill
                                                             Samuel Phillips
                                                             John B. Armstrong

I, James McKisick, Clerk of the Dourt of Pleas and Quarter Sessions for Bedford County in the State of Tennessee, do hereby certify that the foregoing contains the original proceedings of the same Court, in the matter of the application of Joseph Mullins for a pension.

In testimony whereof, I have hereto set my hand and Seal of Office at Shelbyville, the twenty seventh day of December eighteen hundred and thirty two.

                                                             James McKisick, Clk.

Ref: GSA Report, Washington, D.C.
Ref: A 1
Ref: 1835 Bedford County, Tennessee Pension List

* * * * * * * * * *

JAMES MURRAY, SR.

Name:	Rank:	State Served:
James Murray, Sr.	-----	Virginia/North Carolina

Born July 7th, 1754 in Caroline County, Virginia, died September 17, 1840 Bedford County, Tennessee. He is buried in Holt Camp Ground Cemetery, grave marked with a tombstone.

Tombstone:
Sacred to the Memory of James Murray,
was a Soldier of the Revolution.
Born in Caroline County, Va.,
7th July 1754, emigrated to Franklin
County, North Carolina, departed this life
17th Sept. 1840.
Aged: 86 years and 10 days.

No GSA in Washington, D.C.

Ref: Cemetery Records of Bedford County, Tennessee by Marsh
Ref: Susie Gentry, Nashville Monument

* * * * * * * * * *

JAMES NORSWORTHY

Name:	Rank:	State Served:
James Norsworthy	SGT	North Carolina

Born 1756, died after 1823, married Barbara, born ca 1756.

GSA: James Norsworthy, S.38.961, wife Barbara, North Carolina Service.
Claim No. 15.953: West Tennessee, James Norsworthy of Bedford County in the State of Tennessee, who was a Sergeant in the Regiment commanded by Colonel Hogan of the North Carolina Line, for the term of two years.

Inscribed on the Roll of West Tennessee at the rate of 8 dollars per month to commence on the 6 April 1819.

Certificate of Pension issued the 25 of November 1819 and sent to Alfred M. Harris, Pulaski, Tennessee.

Arrears to the 4th of Sept 1819	$39.73
Semi-anl allowance ending 4th March 1820	$48.00
	$87.73

Notification sent May 4th 1821 to   Revolutionary Claim
S.R. Rucker, Esq., Murfreesborough   Act 18th March 1818
West Tennessee.

State of Tennessee, ss
On this 11th day of October 1819, before me, the subscriber, one of the Judges of the Circuit Court, for the said State, personally appeared James Norsworthy, aged sixty four years, resident in Bedford County in the said State, who being by me first duly sworn according to law, doth on his oath make the following declaration, in order to obtain the provision made by the late Act of Congress, entitled "An Act to provide for certain persons engaged in the Land and Naval Service of the United States in the Revolutionary War", that he, the said James Norsworthy, enlisted for the term of three years on the __ day of January in the year 1777, in the Bute, now Warren County, in the State of North Carolina in the Company commanded by Captain Samuel Ealey of the Regiment commanded by Colonel James Hogan in the line of the State of North Carolina on the Continental Establishment, that he continued to serve in the said corps, or in the service of the United States until the expiration of his said term of service, when he was discharged from service in South Carolina. And that he

was in the Battles of Brandywine, Germantown, and at Gates' Defeat, and several unconsiderable skirmishes that he served frequently in Captain John Mecacon's Company, served as orderly sergeant, and that he is in reduced circumstances, and stands in need of the assistance of his Country for support. And that he has no other evidence now in his power of his said services, except his Captain's Certificate. Sworn to and declared before me, the day and year aforesaid.

Alfred M. Harris, Judge of the   James Norsworthy (Seal)
Judicial Circuit of that State
of Tennessee.

I, Alfred M. Harris, Judge, &C, as aforesaid, do certify that it appears to my satisfaction that the said James Norsworthy did serve in the Revolutionary War, as stated in the preceding declaration, against the common enemy, for the term of nine months at one time, on the COntinental Establishment, and I now transmit the precedings and testimony taken and had before, to the Secretary for the Department of War, pursuant to the directions of the forementioned Act of Congress. I am also satisfied that he needs the assistance of his Country for support.

Given under my hand and Seal, this 11th October, 1819.

                (Seal)   Alfred M. Harris, Judge of
                                      the 6th Judicial Circuit of
                                        the State of Tennessee.

District of West Tennessee]
Bedford County, 1821   ]
January Quarter Session   ]

On this 4th day of January 1821, personally appeared in open Court in the Court of Pleas and Quarter Sessions for the said County of Bedford, the same being a Court of Records, James Norsworthy, aged sixty five years, resident in said County of Bedford, after being first duly sworn according to law, doth on his oath declare that he served in the Revolutionary War as follows: That in the year 1777, he entered the service under the expectation of being appointed Ensign for three years, and serve as a First Sergeant in Captain John Meeken's Company in the 7th Regiment commanded by Colonel James Hogan in the North Carolina Line on the Continental Establishment, that he served eighteen months in that Corps, when he was recommended and got the appointment of Adjutant and acted as such in the First Regiment, commanded by Colonel Richard Caswell of the North Carolina Line on the Continental Establishment and was discharged a few days after Cornwallis' Surrender at Little York, near Halifax in North Carolina. He made an original declaration on the 6th day of April 1819. Has received a pension, the number of his Pension Certificate is 15.953.

And I do solemnly swear that I was a resident of the United States on the 18th day of March 1818 and that I have not since that time, by gift, sale or in any manner disposed of any property or any part thereof, with intent thereby so to diminish it or to bring myself within the provisions of an Act of Congress, entitled "An Act to provide for certain persons engaged in the Land and Naval Services of the United States, in the Revolutionary War, passed on the 18th day of March 1818. And that I have not nor has any person in trust for me, any property or securities contracts or debts due to me nor have I any income other than what is contained in the schedule hereto annexed and by me subscribed.

Schedule of real and personal property belonging to James Norsworthy:

106 Acres of land	$500.
5 head horses & colts	150.
8 head of Cattle	40.
8 head of sheep	12.
50 head of hogs	45.
Amt.	$777.

                                         James Norsworthy

The said James Norsworthy further declares on oath, that he is by occupation, a farmer, and that by reason of the many infirmities insident to age, he cannot pursue his business so as to insure a necessary support for himself and wife. His wife living with him being sixty five years old, feeble and decrepid, her name is Barbara. He has also an orphan girl living with him, named Lucy

Pate, 17 years old, but also is no relation by blood or marriage. Has no other persons living with him who contribute to his support.
Sworn to and declared on in open Court this 4th day of January 1821.
Jas. McKisick   James Norsworthy

James Norsworthy received land Grant of 320 acres for his Service in North Carolina, Warrent No. 144, entered 21st day of August 1807, land lying in Bedford County, Tennessee on the waters of Sugar Creek. He gave by Deed of Gift to his son, Thomas Norsworthy 164 acres, dated April 6th, 1819. Also, to son Neal Norsworthy by Deed of Gift 106 acres, dated 1820. His two sons sold their land in 1831 and 1832. James Norsworthy was in Perry County, Tennessee January 14, 1823, when he gave Power of Attorney to his son Thomas to transact all his business.

Ref: GSA Report, Washington, D.C.
Ref: Bedford County, Tennessee Deed Book L, page 118-119.
Ref: Bedford County, Tennessee Deed Book Q, page 35.

* * * * * * * * * *

DAVID OSTEEN

Name: Rank: State Served:
David Osteen   PVT   North Carolina
Born 11 April 1761 in Carteret County, North Carolina, died before 2 June 1845 in Bedford County, Tennessee. He is buried in Cedar Grove Cemetery with a grave marker.

1840 Pension List of Bedford COunty, Tennessee, he was 79 years old.

GSA: David Osteen, S.4637
Claim No. 7985: West Tennessee (Alabama) of Morgan County in the State of Alabama, who was a Private in the Company commanded by Captain West of the Regiment commanded by _____ in the North Carolina Line Militia for seven months. $23.33
Inscribed on the Roll of Alabama at the rate of 23 dollars, 33 cents per annum, to commence on the 4th day of March 1831.
Certificate of Pension issued the 2nd day of May 1833 and sent to M.M. McKenzie, Morgan County, Alabama.
Arrears to the 4th of March 1833 $46.66
Semi-anl allowance ending 4 Sept 1833 $11.66
                                                        $58.32

Recorded by Wm. R. Labner, Clerk   Revolutionary Claim
Book E   Vol 8   page 49   Act June 7, 1832

Sent to West Tennessee from 4 Sept 1837. 7 March 1839 notifies, sends to Amos Morrill, Shelbyville, Tennessee.
Paid at the Treasury under the Act of the 6th April 1838 from 4 Sept 1837 to 4th Sept 1838. Notified 15 June 1839.

Declaration:
Declaration in order to obtain the benefit of the Act of Congress of the 7th June 1832.
State of Alabama]
Morgan County   ]
On this 28th day of January 1833, personally appeared in open court, before Charles M. Peters, Judge of the Orphans Court of Morgan County aforesaid, now sitting, David Osteen, a resident of the County of Morgan aforesaid, aged seventy two years of age on the 11th day of April next, who being first duly sworn according to law, doth on his oath, make the following declaration in order to obtain the benefit of an Act of Congress passes June 7, 1832. That he entered the service of the United States under the following named Officers and served as herein stated, to wit, He entered the service under the following named Officers, to wit, General Ash and Captain William Dennis and Lieutenant Eli West, Ensign Belshasen Fuller and he entered the service early in the Fall of the year seventy eight and the tour was six months, he got home

the last of April 1779 and he was under another engagement of one month, he entered in April 1780 under Eli West as Captain and served one month. He states that he resided in Carteret County, State of North Carolina when he entered the service in both tours and that he was drafted the first tour but was a volunteer the second. He states that during the first engagement on tour of duty, he joined Colonel Lincoln in South Carolina and marches to Augusta in Georgia and marched from there down the river to Briar Branch, where we had an engagement with the British when the Americans were defeated. They then retreated back into South Carolina and were discharged in April 1779 as above mentioned. He was discharged from service in Wilmington, North Carolina, was Major Blount who gave a discharge which he has lost and in the second tour of duty, he was in an engagement with the British at Bluford and he received no discharge when the British left the place, we were dismissed.

He was born in Carteret County, North Carolina in the year seventeen hundred and sixty one. He has in his possession a record of his age. He was living in Carteret County, North Carolina when he entered the service. He removed after he married and had a family to the adjoining County of Anson where he lived twelve years and from there he moved to the State of Tennessee, Davidson County, and lived there seven or eight years and then moved to Maury County in the same State and from there to Wayne County in the same State and from there to Limestone County, State of Alabama and from there to Morgan County, Alabama, where he has resided and has resided for nine years past.

He was drafted when he was first called into service and volunteered the second tour.

He states that he does not recollect any Continental Officers except General Lincoln, he has in his possession parts of his declaration stated the general circumstances of his services. He has stated in his declaration in the first part the circumstances of his discharge and by whom given and the type of it. He states that he is known to Cooley Whitney and Samuel Winton and John Maxwell, in his neighborhood, who can testify as to his character for veracity and their belief of his service as a Soldier of the Revolution.

He hereby relinguishes every claim whatever to a pension or annuity except the present and declares that his name is not on the Pension Roll of the agency of any State.
Sworn to and subscribed the day and year aforesaid.
M.M. McKenzie, Clk.   David Osteen

We, Cooley Whitney, Samuel Winton and John Maxwell, all of whom reside in the County of Morgan, State of Alabama, hereby testify that we are well acquainted with David Osteen, who has subscribed and sworn to the above declaration that we believe him to be seventy two years old the 11th of April 1833. That he is reputed and believed in the neighborhood where he resides to have been a Soldier of the Revolution and we concur in that opinion.
Sworn to and subscribed the day   Cooley Whitney
and year aforesaid   John Maxwell
M.M. McKenzie, Clerk   Samuel W. Martin

State of Tennessee]
Bedford County   ]
On this day the 22 December 1838, before me the subscriber, an acting Justice of the peace in and for the County aforesaid, personally appeared, David Osteen, who on his oath declares that he is the same person, who formerly belonged to the Company commanded by Captain William Dennis in the Battalion commanded by Major Blount of the Line of the State of Georgia in the service of the United States. That his name was placed on the Pension Roll of the State of Alabama from whence he has lately removed, that he now resides in the State of Tennessee, in the County of Bedford, where he intends to remain and wishes his pension to be there payable in future. The reason for his removal is, that he may live with his relations, upon whom he is mainly dependent for his subsistance.
Sworn to and subscribed before me this day and year aforesaid.
Test: W. Perry (J.P.)   David (X) Osteen

Known children of David Osteen:
1. George Osteen, in Wayne County, Tennessee in 1840.
2. Samuel Osteen, born 1790 Carteret County, North Carolina, in Bedford County, Tennessee in 1840.
3. Hillary Osteen, born 1798 Onslow County, North Carolina, married Sarah ____, was in Maury County, Tennessee in 1840 and in Bedford County, Tennessee in 1850.
4. Edward Osteen, born September 1, 1801 Onslow County, North Carolina, married (1) Elizabeth Stem, (2) Mrs. Nancy Elizabeth (Wilson) Houston. In Bedford County, Tennessee by 1818.

      Ref: GSA Report, Washington, D.C.
      Ref: Cemetery Records of Bedford County, Tennessee by Marsh
      Ref: DAR No. 649077, Texas

* * * * * * * * * *

JAMES ORR

Name:	Rank:	State Served:
James Orr	PVT	North Carolina

Born ca 1734, died after 1834 (in 1834 Pension List of Bedford COunty, Tennessee, married Sara Catherine Snell.

GSA: Military Record.

James Orr, Polk's Company, North Carolina Militia.
      Appears on an account of the province of North Carolina with Captain Charles Polk's Company of Militia Foot Soldiers. Account dated July 1776. Days: 25. Swain, copyist.
      Appears on an account of the North Carolina with Captain Charles Polk's Company of Militia Foot Soldiers. Account Dated: (no date). Days: 25. Swain, copiest.
      James Orr, Private, appears on an account of the State of North Carolina with Captain Charles Polk's Company to Cross Creeks.

Account dated Halifax, January 15, 1779. Days: 26. Clark, copiest.

      Ref: GSA Military Report.

* * * * * * * * * *

JAMES PATTON

Name:	Rank:	State Served:
James Patton	-----	North Carolina

Born February 20, 1764 in Buncombe County, North Carolina, died August 9, 1827 in Bedford County, Tennessee, married August 3, 1784 in Buncombe County, North Carolina to Sarah Cunningham who was born December 12, 1765 in Buncombe County, North Carolina and died August 13, 1825 in Bedford County, Tennessee. Both are buried in the Couch Cemetery in Bedford County, Tennessee with markers.

Tombstones:

James Patton	Sarah Patton
died Aug 9, 1827	died Aug 13, 1825
Age: 63 years	Age: 60 years
left 12 childrens.	leaving her husband and 12 children.

No GSA Report.

James Patton born Buncomb County, North Carolina. Lived in Burke County, North Carolina during War. Served as Soldier in the 11th North Carolina Cavalry Regiment. Married August 3, 1784 in Buncombe County, North Carolina to Sarah Cunningham who was born December 12, 1765 in Buncombe County, North Carolina and died August 13, 1825 in Bedford County, Tennessee.

Children:
1. Margaret, born October 5, 1785, married William Hannah

2. Rhoda, born March 12, 1787, married Thomas Couch
3. Jane, born March 14, 1789, married Joseph Erwin (Irwine)
4. Sarah, born March 28, 1791, married Joseph Haynes
5. Thomas, born March 11, 1793, died in infancy
6. Elizabeth, born November 30, 1794, married Robert Haynes
7. Katherine, born July 10, 1796, died March 10, 1886, married November 4, 1813
    to Joseph Couch.
8. Magdaline, born December 16, 1797, married Robert Waite
9. James Erwin, born April 5, 1799, married (1) Mary Cowser, and (2) Mrs. Mary
    Snead
10. Abigail, born December 11, 1800, married Jacob Anderson
11. Mary, born April 10, 1802, married Enoch Haynes
12. Nancy Ann, born August 8, 1803, married Rev. Silas Hall Morrison*
13. Humphrey, born July 21, 1805, died in infancy
14. Keziah, born February 24, 1809, married Hanceford M. Davidson

* See sketch on John Morrison, page 166.

James Patton, State of North Carolina. Morgan District. No. 4842. This Certificate that the board of Auditors have allowed James Patton, two pounds, four shillings for Military Service, 1st day of October 1784, William Erwin C.B., A.M. Erwin, Ben Elledge. Militia Service. Soldier in North Carolina, 11th Cavalry.

> Ref: Certificate No. 4842 for Military Service from State of North
>   Carolina, 11th Cavalry.
> Ref: Roster and Soldiers, Tennessee Society DAR, Vol 2.

* * * * * * * * * *

JOHN PATTON

Name: Rank: State Served:
John Patton   PVT   South Carolina

Born February 14, 1755 in Augusta County, Virginia, died February 28, 1838, married January 19, 1785 in Lincoln County, North Carolina to Mary Wilson who was born September 16, 1764, died March 1845. She was sister to Daniel McKisick (see page 131).

John Patton was son of Captain Thomas Patton (1726-1808) and Margaret Erwin. He was also grandson of Matthew Patton and Jane Alexander. John Patton had three brothers and one sister: Matthew, Janes (see page 177), Joseph Ervin, and Margaret Patton.

GSA: John Patton, W.162, wife Mary.

Claim No. 6347: West Tennessee John Patton of Bedford County, in the State of Tennessee, who was a Private in the Company commanded by Captain Duff in the Regiment commanded by _____ in the South Carolina Militia for 7 months and 2 days, from 1779.

> Inscribed on the Roll of Tennessee at the rate of 23 dollars, 55 cents per annum, to commence on the 4th day of March 1831.

> Certificate of Pension issued the 28 day of February 1833, and sent to Hon. J.K. Polk, H.R.

Arrears to the 4th of Sept 1832 $35.32
Semi-anl Allowance ending 4 March 1833 $11.77
                                                   $47.09

Recorded by Henry H. Sylvester, Clerk   Revolutionary Claim
Book D   Vol 7   page 157   Act June 7, 1832

Reverse side of claim:
Notes: See letter to Hon. J.K. Polk 18 Apr 1834
            do   7 Aug 1834
        Order to pay 12 Oct 1837
        Letter to J.L. Neil, 12 Oct 1837
        Letter 23 Apr '39, H. Jackson

Declaration:
        Declaration in order to obtain the benefit of the Act of Congress passed June 7th, 1832.
State of Tennessee]
Bedford County   ]
        On this 10th day of August, personally appeared in open Court before Samuel Phillips, John B. Armstrong, John L. Neill, Justices of the Court of Pleas and Quarter Sessions of the County of bedford in State of Tennessee aforesaid, John Patton, a resident of said County, aged seventy six years, who being first duly sworn according to law, doth on his oath make the following declaration in order to obtain the benefit of the Act of Congress passed 7th June 1832.

        That he entered the service of the United States under the following named Officers and served as herein stated, as a Revolutionary Soldier about the year 1778 or 1779 as well as he now recollects, he was drafted in York District in the State of South Carolina and enrolled in a Company of Light Horse commanded by Captain Duff and went on an expedition called the Stone Campaign against a detachment of Tories who were collected on Kittle Creek on the west side of Broad River in the State of South Carolina, said Tories were attacked and defeated by the main body of the detachment, but that this declarent nor the Company to which he belonged, were not in the action, being ordered on other duty which prevented them from participation in the engagement.   After returning from the above mentioned expedition, he was drafted in another expedition which was ordered out against a band of hostile Cherokee Indians who were committing depredations on the frontiers of the State of Georgia.   He was then enrolled in Captain Andrew Loves Company.   The detachment or regiment which went on this tour of duty was commanded by Colonel Neil of South Carolina after returning home and being discharged from the Campaign against the Indians, he with fifteen or twenty others from the said District of York, South Carolina, determined to enter the service again and traveled up to the State of North Carolina and on the Battle Ground at Ramsour's Mills, which was in Lincoln County.   Joined General Sumpter's Brigade as a volunteer under the command of Captain Thompson and remained a volunteer in Sumpter's Brigade so long as the British and Tory hostilities existed in that section of the country, with the exception of a tour of duty he performed in what was called the Seige of Ninety-Six, in which expedition he was under the commande of Colonel Henderson, at this place General Green commanded in person.

        After joining Sumpter's Brigade at Ramsour's Mills, he went with said Brigade into South Carolina and at a place called Brattons Farm, attacked and defeated a detachment of British and Tories under the command of Colonel Turnbull, in this engagement, they killed and wounded a consider number of Turnbull's men and took nearly thirty prisoners.   After disposing of the dead, wounded and prisoners, they continued their march after Turnbull, who had fortified his Regiment at Rocky Mount on the Catawba River.   At this place, we again attacked Turnbull but were unable to dislodge him, he being advantageously posted, we were then marched to Graves Ford on the Catawba River, about seven miles above Camden, South Carolina to prevent a party of the British from crossing to join the main Army at Camden.   We were encamped at this place at the time General Gates was defeated.   We were then marched up the river to a place called Graves Farm at the mouth of Fishing Creek at which place we were attacked by Tarlton's Cavalry and badly defeated, having lost about three hundred men, after General Sumpter's Brigade was again enlisted and organized for service.   We were ordered to march down the country and attack a Fort occupied by the British on the Congree River called for sometime but without much effort and General Sumpter discovering that Watson had more than doubled the number of men under his command at that place, ordered a retreat which we effected in good order, the British seeming not to incline to pursue us.   We then returned to headquarters in Mecklenburg County, North Carolina, when the troops were concentrating to attack Ferguson at King's Mountain.   This declarent set out with a part of General Sumpter's men with the expectation of being engaged in that action but was taken sick on the line of march and became unable to travel.   This declarent further represents that he has no documentary evidence to

assist his recollections. He having received no discharge from General Sumpter
or any other person, and half a century now lapsed since the time of his service
he presumes many things have escaped his recollection which might be necessary
stated in his declaration. He is not certain that he recollects all the skirmishes
he may have been engaged in, many of the Officers together with their names
with whom he was then familier, he has entirely forgotten. He is unable to state
precisely at this remote period, the length of time, he was engaged in the service
of the United States as a Revolutionary Soldier, according to the best of his
recollection, it was upwards of two years. So much over that time he cannot
now say. He hereby relinguishes every claim whatever to a pension or annuity,
except the present, and declares that his name is not on the Pension Roll of the
agency of any State.
Sworn to and subscribed the day and year aforesaid in open Court.
Jas. McKisick, Clk.   John Patton

Interrogatories by the Court:

Q. 1st: Where and in what year were you born?
A.   I was born in Augusta County, in the State of Virginia.
Q. 2nd: Have you any record of your age and if so where is it?
A.   My age is recorded in a book which I now have at home, and according
          that record I was born on the 14th of February 1755.
Q. 3rd: Where were you living when called into service? Where have you lived
          since the Revolutionary War, and where do you now live?
A.   I was living in York District in the State of South Carolina, near Hill's
          Iron Works when I entered the service, after the Revolutionary War was
          over, I married in Lincoln County in the State of North Carolina in
          which County I settled and lived until the Fall of 1805, at which time I
          moved to this State (Tennessee). I lived three years in Wilson County in
          this State. In the year 1808, I moved to this County (Bedford) in which
          I now live and have lived since the year 1808.
Q. 4th: How were you called into service? Were you drafted? Did you
          volunteer or were you a substitute and if a substitute for whom?
A.   In the two first campaigns which I served, I was drafted, as before
          stated in the declaration, all my other services were preformed as a
          volunteer. I performed no duty as a substitute.
Q. 5th: State the names of the Regular Officers who were with the troops which
          you served such Continental and Militia Regiments as you can recollect.
A.   At the time General Sumpter was defeated, there were 300 Regulars
          attached to his Brigade and under his command to which Regular
          Officers they belonged. I am not certain, perhaps to General Roundous'
          Brigade, if he was a Continental Officer, and my recollection is that he
          was. General Sumpter never encamped with General Rutherford's Line,
          was ment at General Gates Defeat where General Rutherford was made
          a prisoner by the British. We were guarding Grasses' Ford on the
          Catawba River and could very distinctly hear the artillery during the
          action. The general circumstances in relation to my service and dated
          as correctly as I can recollect them in my declaration with the
          exception of an attack made upon a British Fort in Grandy, South
          Carolina, at which place the British had armed five or six hundred
          negroes belonging to the South Carolina Planters. We beseiged this plan
          and could have taken it from the British Officers and negroes in the
          Fort, had not Colonel Watson, a British Officer arrived with a strong
          reinforcement at a very lucky moment for them and an unfortunate time
          for us.
'Q. 6th: Did you ever receive a discharge from the service and if so by whom
          was it given and what has become of it?
A.   I never did receive a discharge from General Sumpter or any other
          persons for my Revolutionary services. When I joined his Brigade at
          Ramsour's Mills as a volunteer, my engagement was during the War.
Q. 7th: State the names of persons to whom you are known in your present
          neighborhood and who can testify as to your character for veracity and
          their belief of your service as a Revolutionary Soldier.
A.   I have been well acquainted with James McKisick, the Clerk of the

180

Court, from his childhood also with Ezekiel Dickson, both of these men have known me from their childhood to the present day. I am acquainted with the people generally in the neighborhood where I believe I am acquainted with the members of the Court, with the Sheriff of this County and many other persons in Bedford County, having lived in the County for upwards of twenty years last past.

John Patton

Personally appeared in open Court, Robert Cowden, a citizen of this said County of Bedford who makes the following statement an oath in relation to the ...incompleted ...

Claim No. 7342: Tennessee, Mary Patton, widow of John Patton, of Captain Duff of South Carolina, who was a Private in the South Carolina Line. Inscribed on the Roll at the rate of 23 dollars, 55 cents per annum, to commence on the 4th day of March 1843.

Certificate of Pension issued the 13th day of October, 1845 and sent to John Bruce, Murfreesborough, Tennessee.

Act of March 3, 1843 &
17 June, 1844

Recorded in Book A   Vol 2   page 196

State of Tennessee]
Bedford County   ]   To wit:

On this third day of December in the year of our Lord, eighteen hundred and thirty eight, personally appeared before the Hon. the Circuit Court of Tennessee holding for the said County of Bedford aforesaid at the Courthouse in the town of Shelbyville, Mary Patton, a resident of the County of Bedford aforesaid, aged seventy four years, who being first duly sworn according to law, doth on his oath make the following declaration in order to obtain the benefit of the provision made by the Act of COngress, July 7th, 1828, entitled "An Act granting half pay and pensions to certain widows," that she is the widow of John Patton, a Private in the Revolution, that his services in the War are fully set forth in the testimony by him, in his lifetime, sent to the Pension Office to obtain a pension for said services, which said pension, he obtained, as will be seen by the accompanying Certificate, Marked "A". The accompanying Record of the marriage of this declarent with her husband the said John Patton, was made by him in his own hand writing, about fifty eight years since. She further declares that she was married to the said John Patton on the nineteenth day of January, in the year seventeen hundred and eighty five. That her husband the aforesaid John Patton died on the twenty eighth day of February in the year, eighteen hundred and thirty eight. That she was not married to him prior to his leaving the service, but the marriage took place previous to the first day of January, seventeen hundred and ninety four, vis, at the time above stated.
Sworn and subscribed to in open Court the date above stated.
Hon. Samuel Anderson, Presiding   Mary Patton

In testimony whereof, I, John L. Neil, Clerk of the Circuit Court for the County of Bedford, aforesaid, have hereunto set my hand and affixed my private seal, having no Seal of Office. This third day of December A.D. 1838.

John L. Neil, Clerk of
Bedford Circuit Court,
Tennessee

State of Tennessee]
Bedford County   ]
I, Samuel Anderson, Judge and Presiding at the Circuit Court of Tennessee, holding for the County of Bedford aforesaid, do hereby certify that John L. Neil, who has made the above Certificate is and was at the time of making the same, Clerk of our said Court for Bedford County, duly elected and qualified, and that said Certificate is in due form of law. Given under my hand and seal, this 4 December 1838.

S. Anderson (Seal)
Judge of 5 Judicial Circuit
of Tennessee.

State of Tennessee]
Rutherford County]

Before me, William Galbreath, a Justice of the Peace in and for the County of Bedford aforesaid, this day, personally appeared, John Patton, Jr., aged forty six years, and after being first duly sworn, deposeth and saith that the annexed Family Record is a leaf from an Old Book belonged to the Family. That the said Record has been in said book from his earliest recollection. John Patton, his father, died on the 28th day of February, eighteen hundred and thirty eight. The deponent has always understood that his father and mother were married by the publication _____, his mother, Mary Patton, has remained a widow ever since the death of her said husband up to this day. Deponent's mother is a sister of Captain James Patton, who died some twenty years since in Rutherford County, Tennessee.

Subscribed and sworn to   John Patton
before me this fourth day of
Decr. 1838 and I do hereby
certify that John Patton, the above deponent, is a person of good character and worthy of credit.
W. Galbreath, Justice of the Peace.

John Patton's Family Record:

John Patton was born January 14, 1755 in Augusta County, Virginia
John Patton married January 19, 1785 in Lincoln County, North Carolina to Mary
       Wilson, born September 16, 1764
John Patton died February 28, 1838 Bedford County, Tennessee

Children of John and Mary Wilson Patton:
Jean Davis, born October 9, 1785
James, born September 19, 1787
Margret, born April 10, 1790
John, Jr., born October 10, 1792
David, born March 15, 1795
Joseph Wilson, born October 10, 1797
Betsy Barry, born November 20, 1799
Polly McKisick, born April 7, 1802
Martha W., born March 2, 1806

Captain James Wilson, brother of Mary Wilson Patton, died about 1818 in Rutherford County, Tennessee.

John Patton's Bible Record:

John Patton was born February 14th in the year 1755, and his wife
Mary Wilson, born September 16th in the year 1764, and we were mar<u>red</u> January
       11th day in the year 1785

Jean Davis Patton was born October 9th - 1785
James Patton was born September 19th - 1787
Margret Patton was born Aprile 10th - 1790
John Patton, Jnr., was born Wednesday 10th of October - 1792
David Patton was born Tuesday 10th March - 1795
Joseph Wilson Patton was born October 10th - 1797
Betsy Barry Patton was born November 20th - 1799
Polly McKisick Patton was born Wednesday 7th Aprile - 1802 - 10:06 night
Martha W. Patton was born Sunday 2d day of March - 1806 - at 5 o'clock

Editor's Note:
There is a conflict on the parents of Mary Wilson, wife of John Patton. One sourse states she was daughter of David Wilson of Sumner County, Tennessee, who owned 2000 acres at Caney Spring in Marshall County, Tennessee. Another sourse states she was daughter of James and Margaret Wilson of Lincoln County, North Carolina. She is said to have been sister of Jane McKisick, wife of Daniel McKisick and James Wilson of Rutherford County, Tennessee.

John Patton joined the New Providence Presbyterian Church on Sugar Creek, Bedford County, Tennessee on August 20, 1827, according to the Session

Minutes and an entry in the said minutes dated March 1, 1838, states "John Patton, Senr. Died".

In 1836, only one John Patton was living in Bedford County and he was living in the 21st District near the Old McKisick place and the New Providence Presbyterian Church.

Also see Daniel McKisick, page 131.

> Reg: GSA Report, Washington, D.C.
> Ref: Widow's application for Pension
> Ref: John Patton's Family Record
> Ref: John Patton's Bible Record
> Ref: Minutes of the New Providence Presbyterian Church.
> Ref: 1836 Tax List of Bedford County, Tennessee
> Ref: 1835 Bedford County, Tennessee Pension List.

WILLIAM PEARSON

Name: Rank: State Served:

William Pearson   PVT   Pennsylvania

Born April 10, 1761 in Chester County, Pennsylvania, died October 13, 1844 in Bedford County (now Moore County), Tennessee, married in 1782 to Sarah Jones, born 1762 and died 25 July 1845. Divorced in Union County, South Carolina in 1812. William Pearson is buried in the Pearson-Bobo Family Cemetery, now Moore County, Tennessee. Grave marked. Sarah Pearson is buried beside her daughter in the Cowan-Eakin Family Graveyard, in the city of Shelbyville, Tennessee. Her tombstone is in very bad condition.

Tombstones:

In Memory of	Sarah Pearson
William Pearson	Died 25th July 1845
who was born the 10th	Aged: 85 years, 2 months
day of April 1761 and	& 3 days.
died the 10 day of October	(Marker in bad condition)
1844. Aged: 83 years,	
6 months and 10 days.	

Children of William and Sarah Jones Jacks (widow of Edmond Jacks (Jacques)):
1. Elizabeth, married John Dillard, did not come to Tennessee
2. Thomas, married Ailsey Garrett
3. William, did not come to Tennessee
4. Samuel, did not come to Tennessee
5. Sally, married Elijah Bobo
6. Charles
7. Kindred, married Sidney Watson
8. Lucretia, married John Eakin
9. a son

In 1842, when Sarah Jones Jacks Pearson, was in her 84th year, while she was living in the home of her daughter Lucretia Eakin in Shelbyville, Tennessee, she wrote that she married a Jacks and had three (3) sons by him, then she married a Pearson and by him had six (6) sons and three (3) daughters. She stated that her grandfather came from Wales and settled in Virginia, her father, Samuel Jones, moved to Rowan County, North Carolina and was living there when he died.

The parents of William Pearson:
Enoch Pearson born March 25, 1718, died ___ __, 1780, married about 1751 to Tabitha Jacocks, born about 1730, died February 14, 1811.
Children:
Mary, married Josiah Prather
Thomas, married Martha ______
William, married Mrs. Sarah Jones Jacks
Margaret, married Robert Burns
Sarah, married Charlie Jones
Rachel, married George Roberts

Tabitha, married Stacy Cooper
Isaac, married Elizabeth Murphy
Enoch.

William Pearson, born 1760 Chester County, Pennsylvania, died October 19, 1844 in Bedford County (now Moore), Tennessee, married 1782 to Sarah Jones, born 1768, died 1810 Union County, South Carolina. NOTE: This date is incorrect, she died in Bedford County, Shelbyville on 25th July 1845 according to her grave marker.
Service: Private, Chester County, Pennsylvania

Enoch Pearson Bible

Dated: 1789
Owner: Elsie Caldwell
Copy furnished by Mr. Klyne Jack Keller, Madison, Tennessee.

Enoch Pearson, The son of Enoch Pearson and Margaret his wife, was born in Buckingham Township, Buck County, Pennsylvania on Sunday the 25th of May 1718.

Tabitha Jacocks, The daughter of Jonathan Jacocks and Mary his wife was born in Monmoth County in East New Jersey, on Saturday the 7th of December 1734 and married in Virginia to Enoch Pearson, above mentioned in September 1751.

Mary Pearson, the daughter of Enoch Pearson and Tabitha his wife, was born on Monday the 4th of February 1753 near one o'click in the afternoon.

Thomas Pearson, the son of Enoch Pearson and Tabitha his wife, was born on Monday the 8th of October 1754 near eight o'clock in the morning.

Margaret Pearson, the daughter of Enoch Pearson and Tabitha his wife, was born on Sunday the 17th of October 1756 near noon.

Sarah Pearson, the daughter of Enoch Pearson and Tabitha his wife, was born on Monday the 15th of January 1759 near Ten o'clock at night.

William Pearson, the son of Enoch Pearson and Tabitha his wife, was born on Wednesday the first of April 1761 about three o'clock in the afternoon.

Rachel Pearson, the daughter of Enoch Pearson and Tabitha his wife, was born on Wednesday the 3rd of August 1763, between two and three o'clock in the morning.

Tabitha Pearson, the daughter of Enoch Pearson and Tabitha his wife, was born on Saturday the 28th of September 1765 near ten o'clock at night.

Elizabeth Pearson, the daughter of Enoch Pearson and Tabitha his wife, was born the 29th day of November 1767 on Sunday between 4 and 5 o'clock in the afternoon.

Hannah Pearson, the daughter of Enoch Pearson and Tabitha his wife, was born on Saturday the 28th of January 1770 and deceased the 12th day after.

Isaac Pearson, the son of Enoch Pearson and Tabitha his wife, was born on Saturday the 29th of June before the sun set, 1771.

Enoch Pearson, the son of Enoch Pearson and Tabitha his wife was born the first day of October 1775 on Sunday morning an hour before day.

Isaac Pearson, son of Enoch Pearson was borne the 29th day of June in the year 1771, was married to Elizabeth Murphy on the 9th day of February 1792, who was borne on the 10th day of May 1769.

Thomas Pearson, son of Isaac Pearson and Elizabeth his wife, was borne the 27th day of December 1792.

William Pearson, son of the above, was borne the 12th day of September 1794.

Polly Pearson, daughter of the above, was borne December 3rd, 1796.

Rachel Pearson, daughter of Isaac Pearson and Elizabeth his wife, was borne Septr. 29, 1798.

Jefoe and Jeremiah Pearson, sons of the above, borne at one birth on the 3rd day of December 1800.

Bird Pearson, son of the above, was borne March 26th, 1803.

President Pearson, son of the above, was borne the 20th of Aprile in the year, 1805.

Elizabeth Pearson, daughter of the above, was borne the 1st day of June in the year, 1807.

Isaac Newton Pearson was borne on the 5th day of June, 1809.
A daughter was still borne on the 5th day of August, 1810.
Independence L. Pearson was borne on Tuesday the 27th day of May, 1813.

Independence Liberty Pearson and Margaret Sproall were married Nov. 17th, 1835.
Independence L. Pearson died in Columbia, California, Sept 11, 1852.

> Ref: Cemetery Records of Moore County, Tennessee by Marsh
> Ref: Cemetery Records of Bedford County, Tennessee by Marsh
> Ref: DAR National No. 221678
> Ref: Will of Enoch Pearson.   Ninety-Six District, South Carolina,
> April 20, 1775. Will Book 1776-1794, page 159.
> Ref: Will of Tabitha Townsend. District of Union, South Carolina, April
> 14, 1803. Will Book A, page 252.

* * * * * * * * * *

BAXTER RAGSDALE

Name: Rank: State Served:
Baxter Ragsdale   PVT   Virginia
Born 1758, died after 1834.

1834 Pension List of Bedford County, Tennessee.

1835 Bedford County, Tennessee Pension List, age 74 years.

1836, living in Bedford County, north of Bell Buckle, Tennessee near the
Rutherford County Line.

* * * * * * * * * *

JOHN RAINEY

Name: Rank: State Served:
John Rainey   PVT   South Carolina
Born 20 May, 1750 in Caroline County, Virginia, died prior to 3rd May 1842 in
Bedford County, Tennessee. Possibly buried at Mt. Hermon Cemetery or Pleasant
Gardens Cemetery in an unmarked grave.

GSA: John Rainey, S.4035, South Carolina.
Claim No. 13.872: West Tennessee, John Rainey of Bedford County, in the State
of Tennessee, who was a Private in the Company commanded by Captain _____
for the Regiment commanded by Colonel Thomas in the South Carolina Line for 2
years.

Inscribed on the Roll of West Tennessee at the rate of 80 dollars, __
cents per annum, to commence on the 4th day of March, 1831.

Certificate of Pension issued the 3 day of July 1833 and sent to Hon.
J.K. Polk, Columbia.

Arrears to the 4th of March 1833 $160.00
Semi-anl allowance ending 4 Sept $ 40.00
                                                   $200.00

Recorded by William Allison, Clerk   Revolutionary Claim
Book E   Vol 7   page 95   Act June 7, 1832

Paid at the Treasury under the Act of April 6th, 1838 from Sept 4th 1840 to
March 4th, 1844.
Agt notified 3rd May 1842.

Declaration in order to obtain the benefit of the Act of Congress passed June
7th, 1832.
State of Tennessee]
Bedford County   ]
On this sixteenth day of August, appeared in open Court before Samuel
Phillips, John B. Armstrong and John L. Neill, Justices of the Court of Pleas and
Quarter Sessions of the County of Bedford in the State of Tennessee aforesaid,

John Rainey, a resident of said County, aged eighty two years, two months and seven days, who being first duly sworn according to law, doth on his oath make the following declaration in order to obtain the benefit of the Act of Congress passes 7th June 1832.

That he entered the service of the United States under the following named Officers and served as herein stated. He does not know owning to the failing of his memory what time he entered the service but that it was during the time the American Army lay at Slim Oak, a place between Charleston and Savannah in South Carolina.

That in Laurens County, South Carolina, he was commissioned by one Colonel Thomas to hold a garrison at the place where Colonel Hight was killed, which was in the Cherokee Nation, just over the South Carolina line, and then remained himself with about sixty men, he had under his command nine months during which time they kept possession of the garrison, and after the nine months service, he had his company returned home. There was but one little engagement, which was about half a mile from the garrison in which engagement there was no white men killed and but one Indian.

This applicant further states that shortly after he returned home from his service in the garrison, he raised a Company of Volunteers, say about twenty and went in pursuit of the Tories, who were then going through the country and trailed them about fifty miles when he got information that Colonel Clark and General Pickens were before him and nearer the Tories than he was. He then, on that information, thought proper to return back home, and immediately himself and Colonel Rowebuck and Major Smith turns out and raised more volunteers to keep down the Tories in that part of the country and guard the frountiers, and whilst he was scouting about down below Camden, he was taken prisoner by the British and one Colonel Ferguson was the Commander of the British at the time he was taken by them, and whilst on their way with him from. Camden to King's Mountain about eighteen miles from Camden, between sunset and daylight down, he made his escape from the British, he then without delay, made back home being about forty miles distant, to hear, if he could, anything of Rowebuck, Smith or General Green. But his wife could give no account of them (and all in that neighborhood with a very few exception, were Tories). So he had no chance to make further inquiries but he immediately went on to a place in South Carolina then called Ninety-Six and near Camden, and stayed there some two or three days, being a Whig neighborhood generally speaking but could not still hear anything of the above mentioned men. He then returned home again and by this time, his wife had got information in what direction Morgan's Army was. He then immediately without staying one single night at home, went in pursuit of Morgan's Army to join him which I done. When I found Rowebuck and Smith and their Companies and mu own Company. Morgan's Army then lay about eighty miles from his house, and the morning after I joined them, the battle was fought between Morgan and Tailor (Taylor) and in which battle, Taylor and his Army was defeated and Taylor himself wounded. We pursued them on to where ColonelWallis' Army was laying and in the pursuit together with what we took on the field of battle. We captured some hundred of the British and we kept on to Halifax Court House in the State of Virginia and then we lay about six weeks. But before we got to said Court House, General Morgan gave up his command and understood went home, and General Greene took command of the whole. He further states that they marched from Halifax Court House to Hillsborough, North Carolina, and directly after they got there, they very nearly had some small engagements and some are killed, and when the army got up to High Rock, North Carolina, General Greene commissioned him to recruit men to join General Pickens at Ramsour's Mills, and he is accordingly recruited some when he thinks about thirty. He was in hearing of artillery when the Battle of Guilford was fought and the second day after the Battle of Guilford, him and his men were on march to join General Pickens, when to his great estonishment, he met his wife and all his children with her, five in number, drove out of their native State by the Tories nearly exhausted by fatigue and might add with hunger and this situation, he gave up his command to one Major Stone and they went on and he conveyed his wife off a distant of about thirty miles and procured a house for them and from thence home to South Carolina and was not in the service afterwards.

        This declarent further represents that he has documentary evidence to assist his recollection, he having received no discharge from General Greene or any other person, and half a century having now lapsed since the time of his service, he presumes many things have escaped his recollection which might be necessarily stated in his declaration. He is not certain that he recollects all the skirmishes he may have been engaged in. Many of the Officers together with their names with whom he was then familiar, he has entirely forgotten. He is unable to state precisely at the remote period the length of time, he was engaged in the service of the United States as a Revolutionary Soldier, according to the best of his recollection, it was upwards of three years how much over that time he cannot say. He hereby relinguishes every claim whatever to a pension or annuity, except the present and declares that his name is not on the Pension Roll of any agency of any State.
Sworn to in open Court 16th August 1832.
Jas. McKisick, Clk.   John (X) Rainey

        We, Malchesadic Brame, a Clergyman, residing in the County of Bedford and William Hazlett residing in said County, hereby certify that we are well acquainted with John Rainey, who has subscribed and sworn to the above declaration, that we believe him to be eighty two years of age, that he is reputed and believed in the neighborhood where he resides to have been a Soldier of the Revolution and we concur in that opinion. Sworn to and subscribed the day and year aforesaid in open Court.
Jas. McKisick, Clk.   Melch. Brame
                                                       Wm. Hazlett

Interrogatories by the Court:

Q. 1st: Where and in what year were you born?
A.   I was born in Caroline County, Virginia on the 20th day of May 1850.
Q. 2nd: Have you any record of your age and if so where is it?
A.   My age is registered in a Family Bible belonging to my father in Virginia and I have not seen it since the close of the war.
Q. 3rd: Where were you living when called into service? Where have you lived since the Revolutionary War and where do you now live?
A.   I was living in South Carolina, Laurens County when I entered the service, after the war was over I lived in the same County and State, and I removed from there to Bedford County, State of Tennessee in the year 1808, where I now live and have lived since the year 1808.
Q. 4th: How were you called into service? Were you drafted? Did you volunteer or were you a substitute and if a substitute for whom?
A.   In the first place, I was commissioned as a Captain to build the garrison as stated in the declaration, and when I enteres the service the second time, I volunteered and I was never a substitute.
Q. 5th: State the names of the Regular Officers who were with the troops where you served, such Continental and Militia Regiments, as you can recollect and the general circumstances of your service.
A.   Colonel Thomas (his christian name I do not recollect) was the man that commissioned me to built the garrison, spoken of in this declaration and he was the Colonel of Laurens County. General Morgan, his christian name I also forgot, I do not know the names of any of the Field Officers under him. I was then under General Greene, his given name I also forgot, and I knew Major Lawson who was under General Greene. The general circumstances in relation to my service are related as correctly as I can now recollect them in my declaration.
Q. 6th: Did you ever receive a discharge from the service and if so, by whom was it given and what has become of it?
A.   I never received a discharge from anyone.
Q. 7th: State the names of persons to whom you are known in your present neighborhood and who can testify as to your character for veracity and their belief of your services as a Revolutionary Soldier.
A.   I have been acquainted with Solomon Campbell, Thomas Dean, and William Hazlett, the latter two are Justices of the County of Bedford and many other persons in Bedford County, having lived in said County

187

upwards of twenty two years past.
Sworn to in open Court 16th August 1832.
Jas. McKisick, Clk.   John (X) Rainey

Personally appeared in open Court, Solomon Campbell, a citizen of the said County of Bedford, who makes the following statement on oath in relation to the services rendered by John Rainey, the before mentioned applicant. That he was not personally acquainted with said John Rainey as he now relates in this copy, but does believe from having repeated conversations together about the Revolutionary War and said Rainey speaking of certain events happening during the campaign in North Carolina, that he was certainly in the Revolutionary War and a true Whig and that the opinion of the neighborhood and served as he states and the Court further certifies that it appears to them that Melchesadic Brame who has signed the preceeding certificate, a Clergyman, resident in the said County of Bedford and that William Hazlett and Solomon Campbell who have respectively signed the foregoing certificate, are creditable persons and that their respected statements are entitled to credit.

                                    Jno. L. Neill
                                    Samuel Phillips
                                    John B. Armstrong

I, James McKisick, Clerk of the Court of Pleas and Quarter Sessions of the County of Bedford in the State of aforesaid, do hereby testify that the foregoing contains the original proceedings of said Court in the matter of the applicant of John Rainey for a pension. In testimony whereof, I have hereunto set my hand and Seal of Office of Shelbyville, the 16th day of August 1832.
                                    Jas. McKisick, Clk.

1835, age 84 years, Private in South Carolina Militia.

John Rainey had a daughter Nancy, born November 11, 1784, died October 17, 1871, married Henry Hart. Nancy is buried in the Hart-Gossage Cemetery, near Oak, Polk County, Illinois. Her tombstone reads: "Nancy, wife of Henry Hart and daughter of Capt. John Rainey of the Revolution, born Nov 11, 1784, died Oct 17, 1871. Aged 86 yrs, 11 mos & 6 days. Member of the Baptist Church for 70 years."

John Rainey lived in the extreme southern part of Bedford County; north west of New Hermon, in the area of Possum Trot Road.

In the 1820's and 1830's , other Raineys living near John Rainey were: Peter, John W., A.R., and Henry K. Rainey.
        John Rainey was living on Rainey Branch on waters of Flat Creek in 1814.

        Ref: GSA Report, Washington, D.C.
        Ref: DAR No. 655757
        Ref: Tennessee Land Grants by Marsh

* * * * * * * * * *

ANTHONY REAGOR

Name:	Rank:	State Served:
Anthony Reagor	-----	---------------

Born 1760, died 1824 in Bedford County, Tennessee, September 7th. He married Margaret Shook Brock December 11, 1789. Both are buried in the Shook Cemetery, Flat Creek, Bedford County, Tennessee with marked graves:
        A. R.   M. R.
        1760-1824   1766-1838

No GSA Report in Washington, D.C.

Anthony Reagor, born 1760, died September 7, 1824, was one of the earliest settlers "on the waters of Big Flat Creek" in Bedford County, Tennessee. He married Margaret Shook Brock, born 1766, died September 18, 1838, a widowed daughter of William Shook, on December 11, 1789. He was a Tax Payer in 1812.

Children:
1. William, born August 10, 1790 in Knox County, Tennessee
2. John, born January 3, 1792 in Knox County, Tennessee
3. Mary Magdalene, born December 9, 1793, died November 22, 1856, married
    David Floyd, born June 19, 1786, died December 18, 1856, married 1811,
    had 9 children. Both are buried in the Shook Cemetery, Bedford County,
    Tennessee
4. Jacob, born October 10, 1795, died young
5. Anthony Wayne, born June 18, 1797, died June 8, 1846, married Rhoda Boone
    on December 10, 1820, buried in Boone Cemetery, Bedford County,
    Tennessee. Tombstone: Rhoda Boone Reagor, born November 17, 1803,
    died April 23, 1846.

    Ref: Cemetery Records of Bedford County, Tennessee by Marsh
    Ref: DAR Lineage Book

NOTE: Anthony Reagor was the first Reagor, and wife a Shook, came to
    Tennessee from North Carolina, and were of German descent.

* * * * * * * * * *

DAVID REAVIS

Name: Rank: State Served:
David Reavis   -----   ---------------
Born 1758, died 1852 Bedford County, Tennessee, near Richmond. Buried in the
Reavis Graveyard in an unmarked grave.

David Reavis was son of Jesse who died in Surry County, North Carolina and
served in the Revolution under General Francis Marion, in a Volunteer Unit.
        David was twice married, raised 13 sons and 4 daughters to maturity. In
1817, he moved to Brancheville, in Bedford County, Tennessee, near Richmond
and it was here he died in 1852. Six of his sons moved with him, three younger
sons were born in Tennessee. Sons who came to Tennessee were: Solomon,
Simeon, John, Johnson, Isaac Newton and Hardy. David's last wife was Patience.

His service record is from descendents and a Reavis History, published in 1972.
No proof of this service has been found by descendents applying for membership
in the Sons of the American Revolution through David, but was found for his
father Jesse. This in no way means that David did not serve, in fact due to his
age and the fact that his father served, it is likely that David did also.

    Ref: Reavis History, published in North Carolina in 1972
    Ref: Mr. Grady W. Reavis, deceased, late of Marshall County, Tennessee

* * * * * * * * * *

JOHN REED

Name: Rank: State Served:
John Reed   PVT   North Carolina
Born 1764 in Randolph County, North Carolina, died 17th November 1839 in
Bedford County, Tennessee, married about 1794 (or before) to Sarah, born 1767,
died 1845 in Bedford County, Tennessee. No marked graves.

GSA: John Reed, R.8674, wife Sarah
Claim No. 3833: West Tennessee, John Reed of Bedford County in the State of
Tennessee, who was a Private in the Company commanded by Captain Knight of
the Regiment commanded by Colonel Belford in the North Carolina Line for 2
years.
        Inscribed on the Roll of West Tennessee at the rate of 80 dollars, __
cents per annum to commence on the 4th day of March 1831.
        Certificate of Pension issued the 3rd day of January 1833 and sent to
Hon. J.K. Polk, House of Reps.
Arrears to the 4th of Sept 1832 $120.00
Semi-anl allowance ending 4 March 1833 $ 40.00
                                                       $160.00

Paid at the Treasury was the Act of 6 April 1838
        from 4 Sept to 17 Nov 1839
        Agt. notified 27 Nov 1841

State of Tennessee]
Bedford County   ]

On this 16th day of June 1832, personally appeared in open Court before John L. Neill, Samuel Phillips and John B. Armstrong, Esqrs., Justices, appointed to hold the Court of Pleas and Quarter Sessions for Bedford County in the State aforesaid, now sitting, John Reed, a resident of said County and State, about sixty eight years of age who being first duly sworn according to law doth on his oath make the following declaration in order to obtain the benefit of the Act of Congress passed the 7th June 1832.

He states that he was born in Randolph County, North Carolina, on the waters of Deep River, but the year and month, he does not recollect. He states that he has no record of his age and to the best of his recollection, never had any and all the information he ever had in regard to his age, he received from his father.

He was living in Randolph County, North Carolina, when he first entered the service of the United States in the Revolutionary War. He first volunteered in the service between the age of sixteen and seventeen, for a term of three months under Captain John Knight, who raised a Company of Volunteers at that time in Randolph County. Knight's Company served as Minute Men and were generally engaged during this term of service in scouting about in Randolph County after the Tories. Endeavoring to put a stop to their plundering and ravages. Knight's Company was frequently along with Captain. Edward Williams', which was also a Volunteer Company performing like service with Knight. This applicant states that during this term of service, his Company had several skirmishes with the Tories, one of which was at Drowning Creek. At the expiration of this three months tour of service, he again volunteered for three months more under Captain Knight. At the expiration of this term of service, under him immediately after the close of each of these three months terms of service until he had served eighteen months from the time he first volunteered. During all these terms of service comprising eighteen months, he states that Knight's Company was principally engaged in scouting, ranging and subduing the Tories in Randolph and occassionally in Guilford County, North Carolina, and had a good many little engagements or skirmishes with them, but none of any importance. He further states that during all these three months terms of service, Colonel Belford was the Colonel in Command of Captain Knight and Captain Williams' Companies and probably others, but of this he is not certain, but just about the close of this applicants last term of three months service which completed the eighteen months above mentioned.

Colonel Belford was killed by the Tories.

This applicant states that at the expiration of the last mentioned three months of service, he again volunteered under the same Captain Knight and served under him six months before he was discharged. During this term of service, Knight's Company was still engaged in ranging and subduing the Tories in the County of Randolph and occassionally in Guilford. Part of this term, this applicant was among others, employed in guarding two Courts which sat at the Crossroads in Randolph County, against the Tories who were numerous and troublesome. At the expiration of this term of service this applicant was discharged and never served any more. He states that after the death of Colonel Belford and during this last six months term Colonel Dougan was his Colonel in Command. He further states that at the expiration of each and every term of his service, he received a written discharge from his Captain. These discharges were by him returned to the Board of War. This applicant states that he knows of no person now living by whom he can prove his services, except the one whose affidavit is hereto annexed, nor has he any documentary evidence of his services. He states that to the best of his recollection he was two years or upwards in the service of the United States during the Revolutionary War. He also states that it was about six months after the Battle of Yorktown and surrender of Lord Cornwallis, that he was finally discharged from the service. He further states that at the close of the war, he continued to reside in Randolph County, North Carolina for about twelve years. He then removed to Washington County, Virginia, from thence he removed to Blount County, Tennessee, from thence to Franklin County and from thence to Rutherford County and lastly from thence to Bedford County, Tennessee, where he has lived ten years or more and still continues to reside.

This applicant states that he is well acquainted with David Tucker, Adam Dunlap, David Phillips, John Williams and many other respectable citizens of his neighborhood who will testify as to his veracity and their belief of his services as a Soldier of the Revolution.

This applicant further states that he was acquainted with no other Officers of the Army during the Revolutionary War than those whose names are mentioned in this declaration.

This applicant hereby relinguishes every claim whatever to a pension or annuity and declares that his name is not on the Pension Roll of the agency of any State.

Sworn to and subscribed the day and year aforesaid.

Jas. McKisick, Clk.   John (X) Reed

Declaration:

State of Tennessee]

Bedford County   ]

In order to obtain the benefit of the Act of Congress of the 4th of July 1836 and of the Act of Congress passed the 7th of July 1838, entitled, "Acts granting half pay and pensions to certain widows."

On this 20th day of September 1845, personally appeared before me, one of the Acting Justices of the Peace in and for the County of Bedford and State aforesaid and one of the members of the County Court of Bedford County and in the State aforesaid, Sarah Reed, a resident of the COunty and State aforesaid, aged seventy eight years, who being first duly sworn according to law, doth on his oath to obtain the benefit of the provision made by the Act of Congress passed July the 4, 1836 and by the provosion made by the Act of Congress passed July the 7, 1838, entitled "Acts granting half pay and pensions to certain widows."

That she is the widow of John Reed who was a Soldier of the Revolutionary War, that in the year 1780 or 1781, her husband the said John Reed in Randolph County in the State of North Carolina, went into the service of the United States as a volunteer and Private Soldier and went into Captain Knight's Company in a Foot Company. That Belford was his Colonel, she does not recollect his General's name. That soon after he went into service, he marched from Randolph County in North Carolina to what was then called the Sandhills near Cross Creek. That after he arrived in the Sandhills, he was there stationed with the Army a few weeks. At the expiration of which time he was in a battle with the Tories in the Sandhills near a station in which battle the Whigs were victorious and after said battle was fought, he marched through different parts of North Carolina and continued in service till his first tour ended. That his first tour was five months. At the expiration of which time, she does not know whether he ever received any written discharge from his proper Officer or not. That a few days after his first tour ended, he again went out into the service of the United States as a Light Horseman and Private Soldier. That when he went into service the second time, he was a volunteer. That Knight was his Captain, the second time when he went into service Belford was his Colonel. She does not recollect his General's name. That he joined Captain Knight's Company in Randolph County in North Carolina. The second time he went into service and they amrched from Randolpj County through different parts of North Carolina in service against the British and Tories, till his service tour expired. That his second tour was six months. That he served in all, eleven months. At the expiration of said second tour, he was discharged but whether he received any written discharge or not, she does not at this time recollect. That when the said John Reed went into service the first and second time he resided in Randolph County in the State of North Carolina. That several years previous to the death of the said John Reed, he applied for and obtained a pension of eight dollars per annum from the Government of the United States, which he continued to draw to the time of his death. That the said John Reed died on the 17 day of November 1839. She states that she does not at this time recollect the time when the marriage with the said John Reed took place with certainty, as the record of her marriage with him was sent on to the War Department several years ago (perhaps in 1840) for the purpose of getting a pension but she is advised and believes it was previous to the first of January 1794. She further declares that she was not married to the said John Reed, her said husband, prior to his leaving the service but she believes the marriage took place previous to the first of January 1794. She states that she never has married any other person whatever since the death of the said John Reed. She states that the said John Reed departed this life in Bedford County in the State of Tennessee in which last mentioned County and State she resides at this time. She is advised and believes that the said John Reed's Pension Certificate has been sent to the pension Office at Washington City and is there filed. That she has no further documentary evidence in support of her claim, except that which has already been adverted to in this declaration. She stated the said record of her marriage was written by the said David Bowlen the next day after said marriage took place and that the same was returned and kept by her in her possession till she delivered the same to a Lawyer in morder to get a pension for her several years ago which time she advised and believes it was sent on to the Pension Office at Washington City, she prays for a pension.

And David Bowlen is dead and there is no person that she knows of in the country by whom she can prove his handwriting.

Sarah (X) Reed

State of Tennessee   ]
County of Henderson]

On this twenty seventh day of March A.D. one thousand eight hundred and fifty four, personally appeared before me, an acting Justice of the Peace within and for the County and State aforesaid, William Reed, a resident of Henderson County in the State of Tennessee, aged 59 years, a resident of Henderson County, in the State of Tennessee, who being first duly sworn according to law, doth on his oath, make the following declaration in order to obtain the benefit of the provision made by the Act of Congress passed July 7th, 1838, entitled "An Act granting half pay and pensions to certain widows," that his mother, Sarah, is the widow of John Reed, who was a Soldier of the Revolutionary War and drew a pension for his service at the agency at Nashville, at the rate of eight dollars per annum. He further declares that she was married to his father, the said John Reed, on the __ day of ___ in the year seventeen hundred and __. That she was not married to him prior to his leaving the service, but the marriage took place previous to the first of January, seventeen hundred and ninety four.
Sworn to and subscribed before Med and 2 years at (alone) written.
Eli Teague (J.P.)   William (X) Reed
for Henderson County.

It is hereby certified that satisfactory proof has been exhibited before the Court of the Tenth Judicial Circuit, for the County of Henderson, in the State of Tennessee, by the affidavits of William Horton and William Adcock, residents of Henderson County, in the State of Tennessee, who are persons entitled to credit, that John Reed, a Revolutionary Soldier, died in the County of Bedford, State of Tennessee, leaving a widow, Sally (Sarah), who died in the County and State aforesaid in the year A.D. one thousand eight hundred and forty five, and that William Reed, Jesse Reed, Elizabeth Price, and Polly Dunlap are the only surviving children of the said John Reed, who was a Revolutionary Soldier.

In testimony whereof I have set my hand and private Seal of Office, having no Seal of Office, this twenty eighth day of March in the year A.D. one thousand eight hundred and fifty four.

K.B. Jones, Clerk
Circuit Court,
Henderson County,
Tennessee

John Reed, the Soldier was allowed pension on his application executed June 16, 1832, at which time he was aged about sixty eight years and a resident of Bedford County, Tennessee. He died in that County November 17, 1839.

John Reed married July 31, 1783, place not stated, Sarah (sometimes called Sally) Bolen, daughter of David Bolen who died about 1805. The date and place of Sarah's birth and names of her parents are not known. In 1840, she was aged seventy five years and a resident of Bedford County, Tennessee. She died there in 1845.

Sarah Reed, widow of John Reed, was survived by children names as follows: Mary or Polly who in 1840 was aged fifty six years and the wife of _____ Dunlap, his given name not shown; William Reed who in 1854 was aged fifty nine years and living in Henderson County, Tennessee; Jesse Reed; Elizabeth who in 1854 was the wife of _____ Price, his given name not stated.

Reference was made to one child, namely, Samuel or Lamb Reed, whose name was not on the list of children who survived their mother, Sarah Reed. His age and other details concerning him were not given.

In 1840, one Thomas C. Price made affidavit in Bedford County, Tennessee; his relationship to Soldier's daughter, Elizabeth Price, not stated.

In 1832, one Adam Dunlap was a resident of Bedford County, Tennessee, his relationship to Soldier's daughter, Mary or Polly Dunlap, not designated.

Ref; GSA Report, Washington, D.C.
Ref: A.D. Hiller, Executive Assistant of the Administrator, GSA, Washington, D.C.
Ref: Roster of Revolutionary Soldiers and Patriots in Alabama by Julich

* * * * * * * * * *

EZEKIEL REYNOLDS

Name: Rank: State Served:
Ezekiel Reynolds   PVT   North Carolina
Born March 3, 1760 in Hartford (Hertford) County, North Carolina, died after 1840 in Bedford County, Tennessee.
1835, age 74 years, Private, North Carolina Line.
1840, in the house of Michael Reynolds in Bedford County, Tennessee.

GSA: Ezekiel Reynolds, S.2013, North Carolina
Claim No. 7522: West Tennessee, Ezekiel Reynolds of Bedford County in the State of West Tennessee who was a Private in the Company commanded by Captain Dyer of the Regiment commanded by Colonel Wright in the North Carolina Line for 10 months.

Inscribed on the Roll of West Tennessee at the rate of 53 dollars, 33 cents per annum, to commence on the 4th day of March 1831.

Certificate of Pension issued the 20 day of April 1833 and sent to Jas. McKisick, Shelbyville.

Arrears to the 4th of March 1833 $106.66
Semi-anl allowance ending 4 Sept $ 26.66
                                                    ‾‾‾‾‾‾‾
                                                    $133.32

Recorded by Daniel Boyd, Clerk   Revolutionary Claim
Book E   Vol 7   page 94   Act June 7, 1832

Declaration in order to obtain the benefit of the Act of Congress passed 7th June 1832.

On this 17th day of August in the year of our Lord, 1832. Personally appeared in open Court before the Worshipful, Samuel Phillips, John B. Armstrong and John L. Neill, Gentlemen Justices appointed to hold the Court of Pleas and Quarter Sessions for the County of Bedford in the State of Tennessee, now sitting,, Ezekiel Reynolds, a resident of the County and State aforesaid, aged seventy two years, five months and 14 days, who being first duly sworn according to law, doth on his oath make the following declaration in order to obtain the benefit of the Act of Congress passed June the 7th 1832. That he entered the service of the United States and served as herein stated, to wit, That he enteres the service of the United States as a drafted soldier in the County of Surry and State of North Carolina sometime in the Spring of the year 1776. He thinks in

April and was attached to Captain Samuel Dyer's Company and his Colonel was William Adkins, and was marched from Surry Court House to the town of Salisbury in the State of North Carolina and from that to Camden in Soutn Carolina where he states he remained for sometime during which time, he was frequently on scouting parties in search of Tories, until his term of three months service expired. When he was discharged in writing, signed by Samuel Dyer, his Captain and he then returned home. He states that shortly after he returned home, the Tories were embedding in various places through the County where he lived. Deponent states that he then volunteered for two months under Captain ____ Francis who commanded a Company of Mounted Men, he thinks it was in September in the year 1776 and was marched after joining him to a place near the Shallow Ford on the Yadkin River and on the next morning had an engagement with a band of Tories under the command of our Colonel Hezekiah Wright, where he states the Americans only about seventy six in numbers (Privates) besides the Officers, defeated about three hundred and fifty Tories, who it was thought were on their way to King's Mountain to join Ferguson. He states they got their information from a mulatto man by the name of John Morgan who they suckered up and whipped until he informed Captain Francis where the Tories were and where they would cross the Yadkin River. He states he was marched from that to King's Mountain and was in the engagement at that place. He recollects Colonel Cleveland, Colonel William Shephard and Major Joseph Winton and Major Sutton, and he says he was under Captain James Shephard on that day and from that place he was marched the 3rd day after the battle as one of the guard with the British prisoners to Moravian Town, in what is now called Stokes in North Carolina. And that there the prisoners secured by another guard and marched as he was told into Virginia. He says he was marched back there up the County and was engaged in several skirmishes in the Counties of Surry, Wilkes and Rowan until his term of service expired and was then discharged at the town of Richmond, the County Seat of Surry County. He further states that afterwards, he volunteered in a Company of Mounted Men commanded by Captain James Freeman, the Lieutenant's name was William Adkins and that the aforesaid Company was employed for sometime in annoying the British. First, the night after they crossed the Yadkin River on their march to Hillsborough, we fired on their picket guard and after that at or near Haw River, we fired on them again. He says the Company he was in followed on till the British entered Hillsborough, and at that place on the night previous to the British leaving Hillsborough, the American Volunteers and Militia kept a pretty constant firing of rifles and muskets at the British the whole night. He says their Company was ordered then to march against a supposed band of Tories in Chatham County, North Carolina, but could not find them. They were then marched from that place to another until after the Battle of Guilford, when they marched into Orange County where they took two prisoners from a cave, 5 or 6 miles below Hillsborough, one by the name Solomon McKehan, a deserter from the Maryland Line of Regulars as he understood. The other was the name of William Crabtree, a Tory, and delivered them over to General Greene near Salisbury and then returned home and was dismissed after serving about two months, and after that he thinks sometime after the Battle of Guilford in 1781. He was called on as one of the nine months men and was attached to Captain Thompson Glenn's Company and was marched to Salisbury and remained there for sometime until after the surrender of Cornwallis, and was marched from Salisbury to a little town called Pinetree in the State of South Carolina and remained there for sometime but how long he does not recollect, and was then marched back to Salisbury, North Carolina and after remaining there for sometime was marched to Richmond, Surry County, North Carolina and received a discharge for nine months service.

The Colonel Commandant was Robert Lanier and the Major's name was Joel Lewis. Making is all, a term of service of one year and eight months. He relinguishes all and every claim whatever to a pension or annuity, except the present. And declares that his name is not on the Pension Roll of any agency in the United States. That he has no documentary evidence at this time, and that he knows of no person whose testimony he can procure who can testify to his service.

Interrogatories by the Court:

Q. 1st: When and in what year were you born?

A. I was born in Hartford (Hertford) County in the State of North Carolina, on the Meherren River, on the 3rd day of March in the year of our Lord 1760.

Q. 2nd: Have you any record of your age and if so where is it?

A. I have a record of my age at my dwelling house in this County.

Q. 3rd: Where were you living when called into service? Where have you lived since the Revolutionary War and where do you now live?

A. I lived in the County of Surry and State of North Carolina when I was called into service of the United States, and remained until the close of the Revolution, in the same County, and remained there after the war until the year 1795 when I removed to Washington County, Virginia and in 1809 I removed to Wilson County in the State of Tennessee and from that I removed to the County of Bedford in 1811 and where I have lived ever since and where I now live.

Q. 4th: How were you called into service? Were you drafted? Were you a volunteer? Or were you a substitute and if a substitute for whom?

A. I was drafted the first and last tour of duty and the three other tours, I was a volunteer.

Q. 5th: State the names of some of the Officers of the Regular Army who were with you, or troops where you served, such Continental and Militia Regiments as you can recollect and the general circumstances of your service.

A. I recollect Colonel John Armstrong, General Pickens, Colonel Robert Lanier, Colonel Cleveland of the Regular Army and Colonel Joseph Williams and Colonel William Shephard of the Militia. I also recollect Colonel Washington and Colonel Lee. I saw a great many Regiments of Regulars and Militia but their names or numbers if I ever heard them, I have forgotten. I also saw a Major Butler, who it was said, was a Regular Officer. And I believe I have given as near as I can the general circumstances of my service in the foregoing declaration.

Q. 6th: Did you ever receive a discharge and if so where is it?

A. I did receive 4 discharges but what has become of it, I cannot tell.

Q. 7th: State the names of some persons to whom you are known in your present neighborhood who can testify as to your character for veracity and their belief of your services as a Soldier of the Revolution.

A. The Rev. M. Brame, a Clergyman, residing in the COunty about seven or eight miles from me, Colonel K.L. Anderson, James Shaw, Richard Long, and Abraham Mayfield.

Sworn to in open Court the 17th day of August 1832.
Jas. McKisick, Clk.   Ezekiel (X) Reynolds

We, Melchezedick Brame, a Clergyman, residing in Bedford County and State of Tennessee, and Kenneth L. Anderson of the same County and State, do hereby certify that we are well acquainted with ezekiel Reynolds who has subscribed and sworn to the foregoing declaration in order to obtain the benefit of an Act of Congress passed 7th June 1832. That we believe him to be seventy two years, five months and fourteen days old, that he is reputed and we believe in the neighborhood, where he resides to have been a Soldier of the Revolution. And that we concur in that opinion.

Sworn to in open Court   Melchezedick Brame
17th August 1832.   K.L. Anderson

Ezekiel Reynolds died while living .on the tract of land later sold by Ezekiel Reynolds, Jr., son of Michael who was a son of old Ezekiel Reynolds. Ezekiel Reynolds was likely buried in the John Darnell-Batten Cemetery near Haskins Chapel, Bedford County, Tennessee. No grave marker.

Another known child of Ezekiel Reynolds was Emily (Milly) who married Michael Cleek of West Bedford County, Tennessee.

Ref: GSA Report, Washington, D.C.
Ref: Bedford County, Tennessee Deed Book
Ref: O'Neal Family Records

JOSEPH ROGERS

Name: Rank: State Served:
Joseph Rogers   PVT   South Carolina
Born September 17, 1750 in Amelia County, Virginia, died after 1834

GSA: Joseph Rogers, S.1928, South Carolina
Claim No. 7037: Tennessee, Joseph Rogers of Bedford County in the State of Tennessee, who was a Private in the Company commanded by Captain Mobley of the Regiment commanded by Colonel Winn in the South Carolina Militia for 6 months, 14 days from 1780.

Inscribed on the Roll of Tennessee at the rate of 24 dollars, 88 cents per annum, to commence on the 4th day of March 1831.

Certificate of Pension issued 23rd day of February 1833 and sent to Hon. J.K. Polk, Hos. Reps.

Arrears 4th of March 1833 $49.76
Semi-anl allowance ending 4 Sept 1833 $12.44
                                                      $62.20

Recorded by W.L. Williams, Clerk   Revolutionary Claim
Book   Vol   page   Act June 7, 1832.

Order to pay 23 Oct 1837
Letter to E.H. Brandon, Same

Declaration:
State of Tennessee]
Bedford County   ]

Declaration in order to obtain the benefit of the Act of Congress passed 7th June 1832.

On this twenty first day of January in the year of our Lord, one thousand eight hundred and thirty three, personally appeared before me, Adam Miller, an acting Justice of the Peace in and for the County of Bedford in the State aforesaid, Joseph Rogers, a resident of said County, aged eighty two years, four months and four days, who after being sworn according to law, doth on his oath make the following declaration in order to obtain the benefit of the Act of Congress passed the 7th June 1832. That he entered the service of the United States under the following named Officers and served as herein stated, to wit, That he entered the service of the United States as a drafted soldier, in the County of Fairfield in the State of South Carolina, about the first of April in the year 1780, and was placed in a Company commanded by Captain Eleazer Mobley in a Regiment under the command of Colonel John Winn, who was under the command of General Richard Winn. He states that he was mustered into service at Shirey's Ferry on Broad River in said County of Fairfield, and State of South Carolina, and was marched from there to Saluda River to a particular Ferry on the same, the name of which he has forgotten. Where he was kept for sometime, and from there he was marched to a small village, then called the Three Sisters, not a great distance from the Savannah River, where he says he was stationed for seven or eight weeks and from there he was marched down on the Wateree River and from there up on Saluda River again to Weavers Ferry where he states he was discharged or dismissed the first week in August 1780, after serving a tour of four months. He further states that afterwards in the month of November in the year 1780, he entered the service of the United States again as a drafted soldier in the said County of Fairfield, and was placed under his former Captain (Mobley) and was mustered into service at Lister's Ford on Broad River under the same Colonel and General, as before mentioned, and was marched to a place called Wynnsborough (Winnsboro) where he was stationed for some time, and from there he was marched on down the Warteree, in search of Tories. They being very numerous at that time throughout the State of South Carolina and from there he was marched up the Warteree River to an encampment about eight miles from Camden, where he says he was kept about three or four weeks, and was dismissed sometime in the month of February 1781. After serving two months and two weeks, he further states he served in the whole a term of service of not less than six months and two weeks for which claima a pension. But that he has no documentary evidence and that he knows of no person whose testimony he can procure who can testify as to his service and declares that his name is not on the Pension Roll of any agency in the United States.

Interrogatories by the Court:

Q. 1st: Where and in what year were you born?

A. I was born in Amealy (Amelia) County in the State of Virginia on the 17th day of September 1750.

Q. 2nd: Have you any record of your age and if so where is it?

A. I have no record of my age at this time, but has seen it often where it was recorded in my father's Dictionary, in the State of South Carolina, but where it is now I cannot tell.

Q. 3rd: Where were you living when called into service? Where have you lived since the Revolutionary War and where do you now live?

A. I was a citizen of Fairfield County in the State of South Carolina when I entered the service of the United States and continued there until after the close of the war, and I think I removed to the County of Fayette and State of Kentucky in the year 1792 or 93, where I lived nearly three years, when I removed to the State of Georgia and I think I lived there fourteen years, I then removed to Rutherford County in the State of Tennessee where I lived about eight years, and from there I removed to Bedford County, Tennessee, where I have lived ever since and where I now live.

Q. 4th: How were you called into service? Were you drafted? Did you volunteer, or were you a substitute and if a substitute for whom?

A. I was a drafted Soldier all the time I was in the service of the United States.

Q. 5th: State the names of some of the Regular Officers who were with the troops where you served, such Continental and Militia Regiments as you can recollect and the general circumstances of your service.

A. I do not recollect any Regular Officers with the troops where I served, our Officers were Militia altogether and I believe I have given as general a history of my service in the foregoing declaration as I am able to do at this advanced age of my life.

Q. 6th: Did you ever receive a discharge, and if so what has become of it?

A. I never did receive a discharge to my knowledge but was dismissed by the Commanding Officers.

Q. 7th: State the names of persons to whom you are known in your present neighborhood who can testify as to your character for veracity and their belief of your service as a Soldier of the Revolution.

A. The Rev. R.W. Morris, Matthew Russell, Allen Perry, Esqr., and Martin Adams.

Subscribed and sworn to before me, the day and year aforesaid.

Attest: A. Miller (J.P.)   Joseph (X) Rogers (Seal)
Justice of the Peace for
Bedford County.

Joseph Rogers is very old and blind and very poor. He has no family except himself and wife who is also very old and helpless, and one son who is subject to fits and almost an idiot. Letter dated 25th January 1833.

Rogers served in the South Carolina Militia during the Revolution and was placed on the Pension List within a month of the date of this letter.

Ref: GSA Report, Washington, D.C.
Ref: Correspondance of James K. Polk, Vol II, page 47.

* * * * * * * * * *

JOHN SACK

Name:	Rank:	State Served:
John Sack	PVT	Georgia & Virginia

Born about 1754, died after 1834.

Tradition is that John Sack is buried in the Old Enon Church Cemetery, near the north-west corner of Bedford County, near the Rutherford County line. No grave marker.

GSA: John Sack, S.39, 062.
Claim No. 19.502: West Tennessee, John Sack, of Rutherford County in the State of Tennessee, commanded by Captain Bard of the Regiment commanded by Colonel Elbert in the Georgia Line, for the term of two years, from the Fall of 1776 to the Fall of 1778.

Inscribed on the Roll of West Tennessee at the rate of 8 dollars per month, to commence on the 28th of March 1825.

Certificate of Pension issued the 5th of September 1825 and sent to S.R. Rucker, Murfreesboro, Tennessee.

Arrears to 4th of Sept 1825	$42.09
Semi-anl allowance ending 4 March 1826	$48.00
	$90.09

Recorded   Revolutionary Claim
Book F   Vol 9   page __   Acts March 18, 1818
                                                and May 1, 1820

Duplicate Certificate issued 8th April 1841 and sent to Pension Agent, Nashville, Tennessee.
Triplicate Certificate issued 3 April 1844 and sent to Joel M. Smith, Esq., Pension Agent, Nashville, Tennessee.

District of West Tennessee]

On this 23rd day of January in the year of our Lord 1823, personally appeared in open Court, the Court of Pleas and Quarter Sessions for the County of Rutherford, State of Tennessee, the same being a Court of Record, John Sack, aged sixty nine years and resident in said County of Rutherford, who being first duly sworn according to law, doth on his oath make the following declaration, in order to obtain the provision made by the Acts of Congress of the 18th of March 1818 and of the 1st of May 1820. That the said John Sack enlisted for the term of three years, in the Fall of the year 1776 in the State of Virginia, in the Company commanded by Captain Bard in the Regiment commanded by Colonel Elbert in the line of the State of Georgia on the Continental Establishment, that he continued to serve in said Corps until Savannah was cpatured, when and where he was taken prisoner of war and put on board the British prisonship Betsy, then by consent of the Captain of said prisonship was allowed to go on board of a British Privateer to help her to weigh anchor, most of her crew having deserted, which vessel took him to Sandy Hook, when he was pressed on board the British sloop of War Hunter. Then put on board the Vulture, British sloop of war, then sailed up the North River, then was put on board the Rainbow Man of War, about the time of General Arnold's defection, from which vessel he deserted at the eastern end of Long Island, went to the City of New York then apprehended as a British deserter and compelled to return on board the ship from which he deserted or to enlist as a Soldier in the 84th Regiment of the British Army, which last alternative he preferred and embraced. He then embarked with the British Army and landed at Suffolk in Virginia, when on the second night, he deserted and joined the Army of his own country then commanded by General Eaton who gave him permission to go to North Carolina in November 1781. That he was in a battle at Frederica Island. He was in the Battles of Amelia Island and Midway Meeting House and at the Capture of Savannah and that he has no other evidence now in his power of his said services, excepting his own oath and the affidavit of Thomas Williams. He made a former declaration on the 23rd of August 1820.

In pursuance of the Act of the 1st of May 1820, I do solemnly swear that I was a resident citizen of the United States on the 18th day of March 1818, and that I have not since that time by gift, sale or in any manner disposed of my property or any part thereof with intent thereby, so to diminish it as to bring myself within the provisions of an Act of Congress entitled An Act to provide for certain persons engaged in the Land and Naval services of the United States in the Revolutionary War, passed on the 18th day of March 1818, and that I have not nor has any person in trust for me, any property or securities, contracts or debts due to me, nor have I any income other than what is contained in the schedule hereto annexed and by me subscribed, having sold his negro man mentioned in a former declaration for two hundred and fifty dollars, all of which he has expended for his necessary support excepting one hundred and fifty dollars, which he has not yet received.

Schedule of John Sack's property. One debt due him of $150.

John   S   Sack

His occupation is that of a silk weaver and for want of employment in that branch of business as also his age and infirmities of mind and body, he cannot pursue his business so as to make a necessary maintinanceand he has no wife or children living.

Sworn to in open Court 22nd January 1825.   John   S   Sack
B. Coleman, Clk.
(Blackman Coleman)

Ref: GSA Report, Washington, D.C.

* * * * * * * * *

JOHN SARK

Name: Rank: State Served:
John Sark   PVT(?)   ---------------

No information as to birth or death.   He is buried in the Hoover Cemetery in the 10th District of Bedford County, Tennessee. No grave marker.

Reg: Susie Gentry
Ref: Nashville Monument

* * * * * * * * *

SAMUEL SARRETT

Name: Rank: State Served:
Samuel Sarrett   PVT   North Carolina

Born 1754, died April 1, 1821 in Bedford County, Tennessee, married 24th May 1792 on the line of Person and Caswell Counties of North Carolina to Nancy _____.

GSA: Samuel Sarrett, W.5981, wife Nancy.

Claim No. 15.320: West Tennessee, Samuel Sarrett of Bedford County, in the State of Tennessee who was a Private in the Regiment commanded by Colonel Lamb and Shepard of the North Caroline Line, for the term of three years.

Subscribed on the Roll of West Tennessee at the rate of 8 dollars per month, to commence the 7th of September 1819.

Certificate of Pension issued the 20th of October 1819 and sent to John McNairy, Esq., Nashville, Tennessee.

Arrears to 4th of September 1819 $ 90.93
Semi-anl allowance ending 4 March 1820 $ 48.00
                                                   $138.93
11 mo 11/30   Revolutionary Claim
                                                   Act 18th March, 1818

Bible Record

Joseph Sarrett, son of Samuel Sarrett and Nancy Sarrett was born June the 3rd, 1793
James Sarrett, November 15th, 1794
Samuel G. Sarrett was born April 1st, 1796
Hiram M. Sarrett born Sept the 2nd, 1800

District of West Tennessee

Samuel Sarrett, aged sixty four, a citizen of Bedford County in the State of Tennessee, came before me and claimed to be placed on the Pension List of the United States in consequence of his services as a Soldier in the Revolutionary War and after being duly sworn, deposeth and oath, that he enlisted in Fall of 1777 as a Soldier in the Continental service under the command of Captain William Lytle in the 6th North Carolina Continental Regiment commanded by Colonel Gideon Lamb, Brigade commanded by General Francis Nash, that he enlisted as aforesaid for three years and faithfully served the said term, was taken prisoner before his term closed and continued a prisoner until the end of the war and so that he never received a discharge but then returned home.

That he is a very poor man, not worth one hundred dollars, circumstances so reduced as to stand so ___ need of and from Government. That he is very infirm and unable to labor for his livelihood, having a wife and two children very small to support. That he never had any pension from the United States or any State.

Sworn to and subscribed before me this 7th day of   Samuel Sarrett
September, 1818
John McNairy, District Judge

William Sarrett of Davidson County in said State, a nephew of the applicant, made the oath, that he is well acquainted with him, that he he a very poor man, secondly worth fifty dollars, that he is very infirm and unable to labor.

Sworn to and subscribed before me   Wilson Sarrett
this 7th day of September 1818
John McNairy, District Judge

Major Howel Tatum of Davidson County in said State made oath that the applicant has given a most minute and particular account of the Army and its movements, more so than any with whom he has enumerated so that he has no doubt but that his statements in the foregoing affidavit are true.

Sworn to and subscribed before me   H. Tatum, Capt.
on the dates above.   Wm. N. Knox, Agt.
John McNairy, District Judge

Claim No. 5.996: Georgia, Nancy Sarrett, widow of Samuel Sarrett, North Carolina, who served in the Revolutionary War, as a Private.

Inscribed on the Roll at the rate of 80 dollars, ___ cents per annum, to commence on the 4th day of March, 1848.

Certificate of Pension issued the 6th day of October 1852, and sent to Smith A. Jones, Nashville, Tennessee.

Recorded on Roll of Pensioners under Act February 2, 1848 Page 214, Vol 3.

Declaration under Acts July 7, 1838, March 3rd, 1843, June 17, 1844 and February 2nd, 1848:
State of Georgia]
Habersham County]

On this 8th day of March 1852, personally appeared before me a Justice of the Peace in and for the County and State, Nancy Sarrett, a resident of Habersham County, State of Georgia, aged eighty one years, who being duly sworn according to law, doth on her oath make the following declaration in order to obtain the benefit of the provisions made by the Acts of Congress passed, July 7th, 1838, March 3rd, 1843, June 17th 1844 and February 2nd, 1848.

That she is the widow of Samuel Sarrett, who was a Pensioner of the United States under Act of March 18, 1818 on the Roll of the Nashville, Tennessee Agency, at the rate of ninety six dollars ($96.00) per annum, that he lived in Bedford County, State of Tennessee in which County and State he died on or about the first day of April in the year eighteen hundred and twenty one (1821).

She further declares that she was married to the said Samuel Sarrett on the 24th day of May in the year seventeen hundred and ninety two (1792), on the line of Person and Caswell Counties in the State of North Carolina by one John Womack, a Justice of the Peace, that she was not married to him prior to his leaving the service, but the marriage took place previous to the first day of January seventeen hundred and ninety four (1794) viz, at the time above stated.

That she has not again intermarried but remains the widow of the said Samuel Sarrett, that her name before her marriage was Nancy Johnston, and that she has in her possession no other record or documentary evidence in support of her claim ot in proof of her marriage than that hereto annexed, and which is the genuine original Family Record, kept by her husband during his life time.

Sworn to and subscribed before me   Nancy (X) Sarrett (Seal)
this 8th day of March 1852
William C. King (J.P.)
Witness: H.M. Harper

I hereby certify that I am personally acquainted with Nancy Sarrett, the above named declarent, that she is a woman of veracity and that by reason of old age and bodily infirmity, she is unable to attend Court in order to make her declaration. Witness my hand this 8 day of March 1852.

William C. King (J.P.)

Know all men by these present, that I, Nancy Sarrett, of Habersham County, State of Georgia, do hereby constitute and appoint Smith & Jones of Nashville, Tennessee, my true and lawful attorney for me and in my name be present and prosecute my claims against the United States for Revolutionary Pension, as widow of Samuel Sarrett.

Ref: GSA Report, Washington, D.C.
Ref: Widow's Application for Pension

* * * * * * * * * *

CHRISTOPHER SHAW

Name:	Rank:	State Served:
Christopher Shaw	Captain	South Carolina

Born October 25, 1763 in Edgefield District, South Carolina, died February 22, 1832 at Fairfield, Bedford County, Tennessee, married in 1808 in Edgefield, South Carolina to Mary Butler who was born 1779 and died 1861 at Fairfield, Bedford County, Tennessee. They are both buried in the New Hope Baptist Church Cemetery at Fairfield, with marked graves.

Tombstones:

"Capt. Christopher Shaw who was born in Guinette County, South Carolina, Oct 25, 1765. Removed to Bedford County, Tenn., in 1808. Died 22nd Feb 1832. At an early age Capt Shaw engaged in the struggle of the Revolution on the side of Liberty and continued through life to be an upright honest citizen, faithful in the discharge of his duties, setting an example to all around of industrious perseverances and frugality. He was for many years a member of the Baptist Church at New Hope and finally died in the truimph of faith in his blessed Redeemer".

Mary, wife of
Christopher Shaw
Born 1779
Died 1861

Christopher Columbus Shaw, born in Edgefield District, South Carolina on October 25, 1765, died in Bedford County, Tennessee on February 23, 1831. Married Mary Butler in Edgefield, South Carolina in 1808. She was born 1779 and died 1861 (Bedford County, Tennessee).
Service: Soldier, Edgefield District, South Carolina.
Children:
1. Thomas Lewis
2. David William, married Elizabeth Cunningham
3.]
4.] Christopher George Washington Brooks , married (1) Sophia Armstrong, (2) Martha Keyser
5. Robert Charles
6. Cotesworth Pinckney, born April 17, 1817, married Sarah Ann Morris

David W.J.B. Shaw, son of C. & Mary Shaw, died January 3, 1826, aged 16 years, 5 months and 18 days. This memorial erected by his father, C. Shaw.
Buried beside his father and mother in the New Hope Church Cemetery.

James Butler, born about 1745 in South Carolina, died May 16, 1811 in Edgefield, South Carolina, married Winnifrey Brooks in 1766 in South Carolina. She was born on September 7, 1748 and died in Edgefield, South Carolina in 1831.
Service: Private, South Carolina Militia.

Children of James Butler and Winnifrey Brooks Butler:
1. Rebecca, married David Shaw, 2nd Hugh Ballentine
2. Martha B. (Patsy), born 1775, married Edward Moseley
3. Mary (Polly), born 1779, married Christopher Shaw
4. John, born 1781, married Elizabeth Cleckley
5. Anthony, born about 1811, married Polly Purcell
6. Thomas, married (1) Alethia Roby Barns, (2) Letea Bussey Bond
7. Robert, married Matilda Cooper
8. Ann, married Henry Waldrum

> Ref: Cemetery Records of Bedford County, Tennessee by Marsh
> Ref: Texas Society DAR Roster Revolutionary Ancestors, Vol IV, pg 1907, also Vol I, pg 343

* * * * * * * * * *

MARTIN SHOFNER

Name: Rank: State Served:
Martin Shofner   -----   North Carolina

Born December 3, 1758 in Orange County, North Carolina, died September 30, 1838 in Bedford County, Tennessee, married July 7, 1780 in Duplin County, North Carolina to Catherine Cook who was born May 27, 1762 and died June 14, 1823. Both are buried in the Shofner Lutheran Church Graveyard, Bedford County, Tennessee.

Tombstones:

In Memory of
Martin Shofner
was born December the
3 day 1758. Departed this
life September the 30 day
1838.

In Memory of
Catherine Shofner
was born May 27 day
1762. Joined in wedlock
to Martin Shofner July 7
day 1780. Was the mother
of ten children, deceased
June 14 day 1823.

Revolutionary Soldier
Martin Shofner
1758-1838
Placed by
Shelby Chapter DAR

Martin and Catherine Shofner were buried in the Old Shofner Cemetery on a hill behind the Shofner Lutheran Church but were later removed to the Shofner Luthersn Church Graveyard.

FOR THE RECORD: On the 21st day of June 1812, Clement Cannon sold Martin Shofner 217 acres out of his 914 acre Tennessee Grant No. 281, that had been granted and registered to him on May 3rd, 1810. This 217 acre purchase included Shofner's residence as well as the first church and burying ground, located on the hill and the present Shofner Lutheran Church and Cemetery.

> Ref: Bedford County, Tennessee Deed Book B, page 273-274.

NOTE: While historians and some qualified researching descendants have at this date been unable to document Martin Shofner's service record. It is generally accepted that he contributed to the American cause in the struggle for independence.

When Martin and Catherine Shofner were moved from the original burying ground to the present Shofner Lutheran Church Graveyard another marker was erected and read"

MARTIN SHOFNER
1758-1838
"Son of Michael, an immigrant from Frankfurt on Main, Germany
in 1760, migrated by covered wagon, horseback and afoot from
North Carolina in 1808 with his family and settled this tract
of land on Thompson's Creek. This land was granted to him by

the Continental Congress for Military Service rendered his
Country during the Revolutionary War, as a Cavalryman in a
N.C. Regiment, under Gen. Green. Near this place in a log
cabin, the first Lutheran Church in middle Tenn. was founded
in 1808, and in 1871, the present, The Shofner Lutheran Church
building was erected on land donated by his son, Austin Martin
Shofner, Pioneer Settler of Bedford Co., Patriarch of Lutheran-
ism and his wife Catherine Cook Shofner lie buried under these
stones."
(This Memorial, a gift from W.O. Jenkins of Puebla, Mexico and
designed by G. Edwin Shofner, descendants of Martin Shofner - 1961)

Children of Martin and Catherine Cook Shofner:
1. Margaret, married Philip Burrow
2. Turley (Tessy), married Adam Euless
3. John, married (1) Amelia Shofner, (2) Miss Beams (Beavers)
4. Christian, married Elizabeth Jennings (Susan Ferguson)
5. Eva, married William Holt (2nd _____ Muse)
6. Frederick (Fred), married _____ Cable
7. Austin, born August 12, 1801, died October 18, 1852, married Katherine _____,
       born April 21, 1798, died October 10, 1875
8. Dorothea, married Adam Euless
9. Polly, married (1) _____ Brown, (2) _____ Thomas
10. Elizabeth, died young

One sourse says that Austin (No. 7) married Rebecca Cook

> Ref: Cemetery Records of Bedford County, Tennessee by Marsh
> Ref: Bedford County, Tennessee Deed Book B, page 273-274
> Ref: Tennessee DAR 1941-1942 Yearbook, page 101, 102
> Ref: Texas Society DAR Roster Revolutionary Ancestors, Vol IV, pg
>   1926

* * * * * * * * * *

THOMAS ALDRICH SIKES

Name:	Rank:	State Served:
Thomas Aldrich Sikes	PVT	Virginia

Born about 1760, died 5th September 1835, married 13th October 1783 to Sarah.

GSA: Thomas A. Sikes, W.991, wife Sarah, Virginia
Claim No. 19.097: West Tennessee, Thomas A. Sikes of Rutherford County in the
State of Tennessee, who was a Private in the Company commanded by Captain
Winston of the Regiment commanded by Colonel Lewis in the Virginia Line, for
the term of 3 years from 1775.

Inscribed on the Roll of West Tennessee at the rate of 8 dollars per
month, to commence on the 25th of August 1823.

Certificate of Pension issued the 18th of October 1823, and sent to S.R.
Rucker, Esqr., Murfreesboro, Tennessee.

Arrears to 4th of Sept 1823	$ 2.86
Semi-anl allowance ending 4 March 1824	$48.00
	$50.86

Revolutionary Claim
Acts March 18, 1818
and May 1, 1820

District of West Tennessee:
On this 19th day of May 1820, before me, the subscriber, one of the
Judges of the Courts of the United States for the District of East and West
Tennessee, personally appeared, Thomas A. Sikes, aged sixty years, a resident of
the County of Rutherford in said District, who by me, first duly sworn according
to law, doth on his oath make the following declaration, in order to obtain the
provision made by the late Act of Congress entitled, "An Act to provide for
certain persons engaged in the Land and Naval service of the United States in
the Revolutionary War." That he the said Thomas A. Sikes enlisted for the term

of three years on the 9th day of January 1776, in the State of Virginia in the Company commanded by Captain Jno. Winston in the 14th Regiment commanded by Colonel Abraham Dewy in the Line of the State of Virginia on the Continental Establishment. That he continued to serve in the Land Corps, or in the service of the United States the full term of three years, when he was discharged from service that he was in the Battle of Pauless Hook. That he is in reduced circumstances and stands in need of the assistance of his Country for support and that he has no evidence now in his power of his said services.

I went to and declared before me   Thomas A. Sikes
the day and year aforesaid.
John Wrainy

District of West Tennessee
Rutherford
December Quarter Sessions 1820

      On this 26th day of December in the year of our Lord, 1820, personally appeared in open Court, the Court of Pleas and Quarter Sessions, held for the County of Rutherford aforesaid, being a Court aforesaid, Thomas A. Sikes, of the said County, aged sixty years, who being first duly sworn according to law, doth on his oath make the following declaration, in order to obtain the provisions made by the Act of Congress of the 18th of March 1818 and of the 1st of May 1820. That he the said Thomas A. Sikes, enlisted for the term of three years on the 9th day of January 1776 in the State of Virginia, in the Company commanded by Captain John Winston in the 14th Regiment commanded by Colonel Charles, was in the Line of the State of Virginia on the Continental Establishment, that he continued to serve in the said Corps the full sum of three years, when he was discharged from the said service.

      That he was in the Battle of Pauless Hook and that he has no other evidence, now in his power of his said services, excepting his own oath, his discharge being out of his power.

      And in pursuance of the Act of the 1st of May 1820, I do solemnly swear that I was a resident citizen of the United States on the 18th day of March, one thousand eight hundred and eighteen, and that I have not since that time by gift, sale or any manner, disposed of any property, or any part thereof, with intent hereby so to diminish it as to being myself within the provision of an Act of Congress entitled, "An Act to provide for certain persons engaged in the Land and Naval services of the United States in the Revolutionary War," passed on the 18th day of March 1818, and that I have not, nor has any person intrust for me, any property or securities, contracts, contracts or debts due to me. Nor have I any income other than what is contained in the schedule hereto annexed and by me subscribed.

      Schedule of real and personal property belonging to Thomas A. Sikes:

Item	Value	Item	Value
1 Sorrel Mare	$60.	Table furniture & Table	$ 3.00
1 Dun mare & sorrel colt	55.	8 chairs	4.00
2 cows & 1 yr old calf	20.	Kitchen furniture	8.00
2 sows, 5 shoats	9.00	farming tool	10.00
pork	18.00	1 shot gun	6.00
2 beds, bedsteads &		1 small chest &	
furniture	40.00	1 old chest	2.50
1 flat iron	.50	1 candle stick & snuffers	.377
1 Bell	.30	1 handsaw & 2 chisels	2.50
Old Books	1.50	2 pr. cards	1.50
1 Loom & 2 spinning wheels	7.00	2 slaighs	1.25
2 Saddles	15.00	Debts owning by the said	
Amt. of debts owing to		Thomas A. Sikes	2.00
Thomas A. Sikes	75.00	Amounting to	$286.40
2 irons wedges, shoes		Value of property	67.72
makers tools	2.00		
1 pr. chain traces & hames	1.50		
1 log chain	2.00		
1 trap hook	.50		

                      Thomas A. Sikes

The occupation of the said Thomas A. Sikes is that of a farmer, but on account of his age and bodily infirmities, he is unable to pursue his business so as to obtain a necessary maintance. He has living with him, a wife, Sarah Sikes, aged sixty years, also two daughters, one of whom is named Rebeccah Sikes, aged twenty six years, the other named Mary, aged 24 years and 2 small children, issues of Mary Sikes, one of whom is a boy named Carril, 3 years and the other a girl, named Sarena, aged one year, all of which said persons on account of age and to amount of education, can hardly contribute to their own support and much less to the support of their infirm father, Thomas A. Sikes.

Claim No. 1705: Nashville, Tennessee, Sarah Sikes, widow of Thomas A. Sikes who served in the Revolutionary War, as a Private, Virginia Line.

Inscribed on the Roll at the rate of 80 dollars, __ cents per annum, to commence on the 4th day of March, 1848.

Certificate of Pension issued the 1st day of September 1848 and sent to Smith and Kendlock, Nashville, Tennessee.

Recorded on Roll of Pensioners under ______, February 2, 1848
Page 306,   Vol 3.

State of Tennessee]
Bedford County   ]

On this twenty second day of December in the year of our Lord, eighteen hundred and thirty eight, personally appeared before me, Price C. Steele, one of the Quorum of Justices of the County of Bedford aforesaid, Sarah Sikes, a resident of the County of Bedford and State of Tennessee, aged seventy seven years, who being first duly sworn according to law, doth on her oath make the following declaration in order to obtain the benefit of the provision made by the Act of Congress passed July 7th 1838, entitled, "An Act granting half pay and pensions to certain widows." That she is the widow of Thomas A. Sikes (Sykes), a Private in the Revolutionary War. That proof of his services had been made heretofore to the War Department in order to obtain a pension under the Act of Congress passed June 7th, 1832, which pension he obtained for ninety six dollars per annum, payable at Nashville, Tennessee. The original Pension Certificate was by declarent, sent to Nashville to obtain a balance of pension due her husband at his death. She further declares that she was married to the said Thomas A. Sikes on the thirteenth day of October in the year seventeen hundred and eighty three, of which marriage, she has no documentary evidence whatever, nor does she know of any living witness by whom she can prove the fact. That her husband, the aforesaid Thomas A. Sikes, died on the fifth day of September eighteen hundred and thirty five. That she was not married to him prior to his leaving the service, but the marriage took place previous to the first of January seventeen hundred and ninety four, viz, at the time above stated.
Sworn and subscribed to before me the   Sarah (X) Sikes
date above written and I do certify
that the above declarent, by reason of
her age and bodily infirmity is unable
to appear in Court.
P.C. Steele (Seal)
One of the Justices of
Bedford County Court.

State of Tennessee]
Bedford County   ]

I, William D. Orr, Clerk of the County Court in and for the County of Bedford aforesaid, do hereby certify that Price C. Steele who was attested the above declaration is, and was, at the time of attesting the same, one of the Quorum of Justices of our said County Court, duly elected and qualified and that the signature above, purporting to be his, is genuine.

In testimony whereof, I have hereunto set my hand and affixed my Seal of Office, this twenty second day of December A.D. 1838.

William D. Orr, Clerk
of Bedford County Court.

Bible Record of Thomas A. Sikes:

Elisabeth An Sikes was born September the 5, 1785
Jese Sikes was born October the 13, 1787
Susanna Sikes was born April the 10, 1789
Rebecker Sikes was born September the 16, 1791
Jonas Sikes was born July the 3, 1793
Nancy Sikes was born July the 3, 1795
John and Mary Sikes was born August the 25, 1797
Robert Sikes was born October the 16, 1799
Anna Johns West was born July the 25, 1809
Nancy Lowe was born December the 14, 1796
William Lowe was born October the 1, 1798
        End of Bible Record.

Thomas Sikes
Dates of Enlistments or appointments: 1775
Length of Service: 3 years
Rank: Private
Captain: John Winston
Colonel: Charles Lewis
State: Virginia

Battles engaged in: Pauless Hook
Residence of Soldier at enlistment: Virginia
Date of Application for Pension: Dec 26, 1820 - His claim was allowed.
Residence at date of application: Rutherford County, Tennessee.
Age at date of application: 60 years - Died in Bedford County, Tennessee
                                           September 5, 1835.
Remarks: M. in Lunenburg Co., Va., Oct 13, 1783, Sarah _____. She was allowed
        pension by an affidavit and executed Dec. 22, 1838 while resident of
        Bedford County, Tennessee, 77 years. She died June 2, 1849.
Children: See Bible Record, above.

Military Record of Thomas A. Sikes, Soldier

Appears in a Book (of Certificates at the Auditors Office, of Soldiers & Officers
of the Virginia Line) under the following heading:
        "A List of Soldiers of the Virginia Line on Continental Establishment
who have received Certificates for the balance of their full pay agreeable to an
Act of Assembly passed November Session 1781."

Revolutionary War

by whom received: Col. Thompson
Date when   : July 27, 1786   Sum of 53 lbs - 13-
        Vol 176, page 407

        Thomas Sykes, Private, Captain John Winston's Company of the 14th
Virginia Regiment, commanded by Colonel William Davies, appears on Company
Muster Roll.
1: of the organization named for the month of Jan 1779.
    Roll dated: Camp Middlebrook, Feb 5, 17__
    Term of enlistment: 3 years
2: Month of Jan, 1779   Company Muster Roll
    Pay per month, 6 2/3 dollars
    Amount: 2 lbs Va. Cur.
3: Month of Feb, 1779   Company Muster Roll
    Dated: Camp Middlebrook, Mar 6, 1779
    Term: 3 years
4: Company Muster Roll of Feb, 1779
    Pay per month: 6 2/3 dollars
    Amount: of pay 2 lbs Va. Currency
5: Company Muster Roll, Mar 1779
    Roll Dated: Camp Middlebrook, April 5, 1779
    Term of enlistment: 3 years

206

6: Company Pay Roll, Mar 1779
   Pay per month: 6 2/3 dollars
   Amount of pay: 2 lbs Va. Currency
7: Company Muster Roll, April 1779
   Roll Dated: Camp Middlebrook, May 1779
   Term of enlistment: 3 years
8: Company Pay Roll, Apr 1779
   Pay per Month, 6 2/3 dollars
   Amount of pay 2 lbs Va. Currency
9: Company Muster Roll, May 1779
   Roll Dated: Camp Smith Clove, June 12, 1779
   Term: 3 years
10: Company Pay Roll, May 1779
   Pay per month: 6 2/3 dollars
   Amt. of pay: 2 lbs
11: Company Muster Roll, June 1779
   Roll Dated: Smith's Clove, July 1, 1779
   Enlisted: Dec 1, 1776
12: Company Pay Roll, June 1779
   Pay per Months: 6 2/3 dollars
   Amt. of pay: 6 2/3 dollars
13: Company Muster Roll, July 1779
   Roll Dated: Rammopan, Aug 3, 1779
   Enlisted: Dec 1, 1776
   Term of enlistment: 3 years
14: Company Pay Roll, July 1779
   Pay per month: 6 2/3 dollars
   Whole Amt. in dollars: 6 2/3
15: Company Muster Roll, Aug 1779
   Roll Dated: Smith's Clove, Sept 6, 1779
   Enlisted: Dec 1, 1776
   Term of enlistment: 3 years
   Remarks: On Fatigue
16: Company Pay Roll, Aug 1779
   Pay per month: 6 2/3 dollars
   Subsistence: 10 dollars
   Amt. of pay: 11 1/3 dollars
17: Company Muster Roll, Sept 1779
   Roll Dated: Ramapaugh, Oct 2, 1779
   Enlisted: Dec 1, 1776
   Term: 3
18: Company Pay Roll, Sept 1779
   Pay per month: 6 2/3 dollars
   Subsistence: 10 dollars
   Amt. of pay: 16 2/3 dollars
19: Company Muster Roll, Oct 1779
   Roll Dated: Nov 8, 17__
   Enlisted: Dec 1, 1776
   Term: 3 years
20: Company Pay Roll, Oct 1779
   Pay per month: 6 2/3 dollars
   Subsistence per month: 10 dollars
   Amt. of Pay: 16 2/3 dollars

NOTE: This list continues through the number 63.

Ref: GSA Report, Washington, D.C.
Ref: Tennessee DAR Roster & Soldiers, Vol I, page 1429

* * * * * * * * * *

Name:	Rank:	State Served:
James Slaton	PVT	Virginia

Born 1759 in Louisa County, Virginia, died April 19, 1833 in Bedford County, Tennessee, married April 23, 1782 in Pittsylvania County, Virginia to Martha Pigg who was born 1765 and died October 31, 1849 in Howard County, Missouri.

GSA: James Slaton, W.9655, wife Martha, Virginia.
Claim No. 1822: West Tennessee, James Slaton of Bedford County in the State of Tennessee, who was a Private in the Company commanded by Captain Harrison of the Regiment commanded by Colonel Davis in the Virginia Line for 13 months from 1780.

Inscribed on the Roll of West Tennessee at the rate of 43 dollars, 33 cents per annum, to commence on the 4th day of March, 1831.

Certificate of Pension issued the 12th day of November 1832 and sent to Jas. McKisick, Shelbyville, Tennessee.

Arrears to 4th of Sept 1832	$64.99
Semi-anl allowance ending 4 March 1833	$21.67
	$86.66

Recorded by Nathan Rice, Clerk   Revolutionary Claim
Book D   Vol 7   Page 160   Act June 7, 1832.

State of Tennessee]
Bedford County   ]

On this 14th day of August in the year 1832, personally appeared before John B. Armstrong, John L. Neill and Samuel Phillips, Esqrs., Justices appointed to hold the Court of Pleas and Quarter Sessions for the County and State aforesaid for the year 1832. James Slaton, a citizen of and resident in the County aforesaid and State of Tennessee, aged about seventy three years, who being first duly sworn according to law, doth on his oath make the following declaration in order to obtain the benefit of the provision made by the Act of Congress passed June 7th, 1832.

Deponent states he volunteered in the service of his Country in the year ____ under Captain Bibb of the Virginia Militia and served one month as guard about Williamsburg and York Town. At the time he entered the service of his Country, he was living in Goochland County, State of Virginia, and entered the service at Goochland Court House and was marched to Williamsburg at which place we acted as a guard for a short time and were marched to York Town where we remained a short time, returned to Williamsburg from which place we were marched back to Goochland County and discharged.

There were no Field Officers in command in this service, as there was but one Company and deponent supposes the Captain said, his orders from Governor Partick Henry while in Williamsburg as the deponent was a guard at the house of Governor several times while at said Town and while at York Town, he supposes the Captain Sec'd, his orders from General Mason who lived in or at York Town while said Company were on duty at that place. Deponent does not recollect the names of the officers in said company except Captain Bibb and Obediah Smith, who he believes was Ensign in saod Company. He states that he does not know of any person now living by whom he could prove the above service. He further states that he again entered the service of his Country in the year 1780 in the Virginia Line at Chesterfield Barracks in the State of Virginia as a substitute to clear a class of fifteen or sixteen men from a draft of eighteen months service, six months of which term expired before he was mustered into actual service at said barracks. He was mustered into service in Captain Harrison's Company who says gave him a certificate that his term of service would expire in twelve months by which certificate he was at the expiration of said term of twelve months discharge from the service of his Country. He further states that there was no General Officer in command at said Barracks at the time he entered the service, Colonel Davis, he believes, was highest in command at that time. Deponent further states that a party were ordered from said barricks to march as he understood to Suffolk against a part of the British called The Queens Rangers, and that he was with the said party in Captain Harrison's Company and that they marched through Petersburg in

Virginia, that they passed Cabin Point and encamped at Mackey's Mill where they remained a short time. At which place he believes they were under General Mulenburg. From that place, a detachment of men were sent on towards Suffolk, and that he was with said detachment and in Captain Harrison's Company on arriving near Suffolk, in the evening, we encamped with special orders to make as little noise as possible, which induced said deponent to believe that the enemy were supposed to be in the neighborhood, and that during the night several guns were fired in the neighborhood, which produced some alarm in camps. And that in the morning a file of men, under the command of a Sargeant, as he believes, found several of our own guns and accessments setting against a tree, and an examination in Camp. It was ascertained that five of our own men (viz) two brothers by the name of Private Prater, Hughs and Snider and the names of the others not recollected who he believes the officers in command, thought had deserted to the enemy and given them items of our approach, which circumstance said deponent believes caused them to retract back to Mackey's Mills, from which place they marched back to Chesterfield Barracks, where they remained during the winter. He further states that on the return of said detachment to said barracks, he thinks, General Steuben had arrived there before and detachment and as he believes was highest in command during the winter.

He, the said Slaton, further states that he was with General Steuben when he retreated from Chesterfield Barracks at James River towards the mountains, crossing James River as he believes at Carter's Ferry. he states that he was at that time in Captain Laneley's Company. The troops retreated up James River to the forks where they crossed one prong of said river into a little town called, as he believes, Pointy Fork, and that retreat was continued up the South Fork of said river, some distance and that they returned into said town in the forks of James River. That they crossed the South Fork of James River at or very shortly after we crossed the river. We discovered the British troops entering the town, we had just left. The British fired one field piece at our army and killed a mare from under an officer, who he believes was a Captain. Our troops were marched on the opposite side of a hill from which place men were dispatched to sink the boats in order to prevent the British from crossing in pursuit, on which party, he the said Slaton, went and assisted in sinking the boats. From which place the American Troops situated through several counties in Virginia and crossed Staunton River, a ferry called as he believes, Cole's Ferry, where they encamped for sometime. He further states that the troops recrossed Staunton River and _____ their retreat march, some distance of about _____ as said deponent believes General Steuben left said troops and did not as he believes rejoin the said troops. He further states that they were under the command of Colonel Gaskins. After the departure of general Steuben, until we met General Wayne and his Army, who assumed command over the troops to which said deponent was attached. The junction of these troops was as said deponent believes affixed in the upper end of Hanover County, near the residence of a noted character in them days, Colonel Dandridge. He said deponent further states that after marching through the country for sometime that he was near Captain Kirpatrick's markes at the time as he was that by one of our own soldiers, by the name of Grant, as he believes and acted a guard around the person of Grant at the time he was conveyed to the gallows to be hung for said offenceand that he saw him hung. Said Slaton further states that he continued with the army under the command of general Wayne until General Wayne marched a part of his command to Jamestown where he was informed and believes a battle was fought between General Wayne's troops and the troops or a part of the troops under the command of Lord Cornwallis, at which time deponent was left under the command of Colonel Gaskins, left near Gales Ferry on the Chickamahorning River, where they remained but a few days. The day of the Battle of Jamestown, the troops with which said deponent was left, were ordered to Jamestown to co-operate in the battle but was too late in their movements and met the American Troops on their retreat from said battleground and that the two detachments retreated together some distance. He further states that he continued under the command of General Wayne until he marched his troops nearer the British Army again, at which time he was separated from him and did not fall under his immediate any more but was marched by Colonel Gaskins to Parnunkey River near the town of Newcastle and which place he states he was legally discharged, agreeable to the Certificate he had received from Captain Harrison on entering the service of his country. This was in the year 1781 and his discharge was signed by Captain Lovely and to the best of his recollection he signed his name William Lewis Lovely. His discharge was also signed by Colonel Gaskins, who he thinks signed his name Lewis Gaskins. His discharge was dated in 1781, but he cannot recollect the month or day of the month but is confident that it was between the Battle at Jamestown and the time that Lord Cornwallis surrendered to the American Army. The great length of time that has lapsed since the above service was performed, I cannot now recollect the name or number of the Regiment to which I belonged. Colonel Gaskins was the Colonel in command and he believes Major Polson belonged to said Regiment, he does not recollect the names of any other Regular Officers but those that have been named in the foregoing statement. He also states that his discharge and Certificate were placed in the hands of a man whose name he believes was Jenkins, who resided in the County of Pittsylvania and State of Virginia, who represented that, he was going to the town of Richmond in said State, to whom deponent confided said papers for the purpose of drawing his wages for the above term of service and on the return of said Jenkins, he said he could not draw anything and that he had lost said papers, since which time deponent has not seen said papers nor does he know that they had ever been found, nor has he ever drawn any compensation for the said term of service. The said Slaton further states that at the time of entering the service of his country that he was measured and a particular description taken of him, which he supposed has been preserved. He does not know of any person now living by whom he could prove the above term of service. Except John Sladgen of Henderson County and State of Kentucky, whose affidavit is herewith forwarded. The said deponent further states that owing to the great lapse of time, the frailty of memory and bodily infirmities may cause some of the circumstances detailed in the foregoing statement to be named out of their proper order, as he has kept no record to assist in the proper arrangement of so many circumstances and he wishes here to state that he does not recollect whether Captain Kirkpatrick was shot before the Battle at Jamestown or not, although in giving a detail of the circumstances above, he believes it was, but is not certain and there may have been some other inaccuracies of a simular time.

  I, James Slaton, do hereby relinguish every claim whatever to a pension or annuity except the present and declare that my name is not on the Pension Roll of any agency of any State in the United States.

Sworn to and subscribed the day and year aforesaid

Jas. McKisick, Clerk   James Slaton

Interrogatories by the Court:

Q. 1st: Where and in what year were you born?

A.   I have been informed that I was born in the County of Louisa, in the State of Virginia and from the best information I have, was born about the year 1759.

Q. 2nd: Have you any record of your age and if so where is it?

A.   I have no such record.

Q. 3rd: Where were you living when called into the service of your country? Where have you lived since the Revolutionary War and where do you now live?

A.   In the County of Goochland in the State of Virginia, several years in Madison, Lincoln, and Garrett Counties in the State of Kentucky, from thence removed to the COunty of Bedford in the State of Tennessee, thence to the State of Missouri in the Caounty of Cape Girardeau, from which place I returned to the County of Bedford in the State of Tennessee where I now live.

Q. 4th: State the names of persons to whom you are known in your present neighborhood and who can testify as to your character for veracity and their belief of your services as a Soldier of the Revolution.

A.   Capt. Matt Martin, John Scott, Esqe., Col. Jonathan Webster, Edmond Hord, Esqr., John Tillman, Major James Walker, Mead Haile, Major Shaw and Col. Samuel Mitchell.

210

We, Samuel Mitchell and T.L.D.W. (Thomas Lewis) Shaw, residing in the County of Bedford hereby certify that we are well acquainted with James Slaton, who has subscribed and sworn to the above declaration, that we believe him to be seventy three years of age, that he is reputed and believed in the neighborhood where he resides to have been a Soldier of the Revolution and that we concur in that opinion.

Sworn to in open court 14th August 1832.　　　　　　Samuel Mitchell
Jas. McKisick, Clk.　　　　　　　　　　　　　　　　T.L.D.W. Shaw

Claim No. 5.997: Missouri, Martha Slaton, deceased, widow of James Slaton, who served in the Revolutionary War as a Private.

Inscribed on the Roll at the rate of 43 dollars, 33 cents per annum, to commence on the 4th day of March, 1848, ending 31 October 1849.

Certificate of Pension issued the 11th day of October 1852 and sent to J.J. Coombs, P

Recorded on Roll of Pensioners Act February 2, 1848, page 365, Vol 3.

Declaration of Mrs. Martha Slaton, in order to obtain the benefit of the third section of the Act of Congress of the 4th July, 1836.

State of Missouri]
County of Howard]

On this 5th day of July A.D. 1847, personally appeared before the County Court within and for the County aforesaid, Mrs. Martha Slaton, a resident of the County of Howard and State of Missouri, aged eighty two years, who being first duly sworn according to law, doth on her oath make the following declaration in order to obtain the benefit of the provision made by the Act of Congress passed July 4th, 1836.

That she is the widow of James Slaton, who was a Private in Captain Lovely's Company in the Revolutionary War, (the names of the Field and Company Officers except Captain not recollected) that said James Slaton resided in Goochland County, Virginia, at the time he entered the service, but the time at which he entered, or was discharged, the country through which he marched, the battle of which he was engaged, are not now recollected, that he was drafted, that she has no documentary evidence in support of her claim, other than the records in the Pension office at Washington, which will show that said James Slaton in his life time drew a pension.

That at the time of his death, he resided in Bedford County, Tennessee. She further declares that she was married to James Slaton on the 23rd day of April (1782) seventeen hundred and eighty two, that her husband, the aforesaid, James Slaton died on the 19th day of April 1833 and that she has remained a widow ever since that period as will more fully appear by reference to the proof hereto annexed.

Sworn to and subscribed before the undersigned Clerk, aforesaid Court in open Court this 5th day of July A.D. 1847.

Andrew J. Hemons, Clerk　　　　　　　　　　Martha (X) Slaton

State of Missouri]
County of Howard]

On this 14th day of July, eighteen hundred and fifty two, personally appeared before me, William T. Mallory, an Acting Justice of the Peace within and for the County of Howard and in the State of Missouri, Prior M. Jackson, a resident of the County and State aforesaid, who first being sworn according to law, states upon oath that he is the administrator of the estate of Martha Slaton, deceased, who was the widow of James Slaton, deceased, late of Bedford County in the State of Tennessee and formerly a Soldier in the Army of the Revolution and a Pensioner of the United States at the rate of forty three dollars and thirty three cents per annum. As well appear from his original Certificate of Pension, herewith presented. That the said James Slaton resided in Bedford County, Tennessee and made application for pension and that the attached Certificate was issued in his favor at the War Office of the United States on the 12th day of November, one thousand eight hundred and thirty two, but that the said James Slaton died on the 19th day of April, eighteen hundred and thirty three without receiving any money to his knowledge. And that after said James Slaton deceased, his widow the aforesaid Martha Slaton removed to Howard County in the State of Missouri where she remained until her decease which took place on the thirty first day of October, eighteen hundred and forty nine. That the said Martha Slaton made application for pension also but never received anything for the services of her said husband.

That the said James Slaton and Martha Slaton were married either in Pittsylvania or Goochland County in the State of Virginia on the 23rd day of April, seventeen hundred and eighty two as well appear by a certificate copy of the original Family Record kept by the said James Slaton and Martha Slaton, his wife, in their lifetime. That the said Martha Slaton remained the widow of the said James Slaton, deceased, until her death and that she, Martha Slaton, died on the day and date above mentioned, leaving the following named persons, her children and her only surviving children by the said James Slaton, deceased, viz, Susan Jackson formerly Slaton, aged sisty nine (69) years; Mary Golston formerly Slaton, aged sisty seven (67) years; Elizabeth Adams formerly Slaton, aged sixty three (63) years; Sarah Short formerly Slaton, aged fifty nine (59) years; and Rachel Baker formerly Slaton, aged fifty seven (57) years.

That he makes this declaration on behalf of the afiresaid heirs of Martha Slaton, deceased, and to the testimony on file and to the Records, he refers for evidence in support of his application.

Prior M. Jackson

Subscribed and sworn to before me the day and year above written.
14th day of July, 1852   Wm. T. Mallory, J.P.

Ref: GSA Report, Washington, D.C.
Ref: Widow's application for pension.

* * * * * * * * * *

GEORGE SMITH, SR.

Name: Rank: State Served:
George Smith, Sr.   PVT   North Carolina
Born December 24, 1763 in Rowan County, North Carolina, died August 19, 1842 in Sevier County, Arkansas, married October 25, 1786 in Rowan County, North Carolina to Phoebe _____. Phoebe Smith's grave is not marked but is said to be buried in the Crowell Chapel Cemetery, Halls Mill, Bedford County, Tennessee.

GSA: George Smith, Senr., S.31969, West Tennessee, Phoebe, wife.
Claim No. 1603: George Smith, Senr., West Tennessee, No. 1603 transferred to Arkansas.

George Smith, Senr., of Bedford County in the State of West Tennessee who was a Private in the Company commanded by Captain Heddrich of the Regiment commanded by Colonel Phifer in the North Carolina Line for 7 months.

Inscribed on the Roll of West Tennessee at the rate of 23 dollars, 33 cents per annum, to commence on the 4th day of March 1831.

Certificate of Pension issued the 3rd of May 1833 and sent to James McKisick, Shelbyville.

Arrears to the 4th of March $46.66
Semi-anl allowance ending 4 Sept $11.66
                                           $58.32

Recorded by Daniel Boyd, Clerk   Revolutionary Claim
Boom E   Vol 7   Page 96   Act June 7, 1832.

Pension and Pay Agent, June 5, 1837
Letter to Hon. J.K. Polk, 12 June 1837
Paid at the Treasury under the Act of the 6 April 1838 from 4 March 1837, to 4 Sept 1837. Agt. notified 28 July 1838.
Cer. to Pen. Agent and letter to Hon. E. Cross - 6 July 1842.
To Arkansas from 4 Sept 1838 - 19 Aug 1842, notification to Hon. E. Cross, H.R.

House of Reps.
July 4th 1842

Sirs,

I enclose you a application by George Smith and requesting the payment of his pension in Arkansas instead of Tennessee from whence he has removed with his children to the former State. I have no knowledge of sd. Smith but know personally the officers and witnesses whose names appear upon his papers. They are highly resepctable and I hope it will be in your power to make the change he desires.

Very Respectfully,
Col. J.L. Edwards   Your obv. serv't
Court of Pensions   Edw. Cross

Declaration in order to obtain the benefit of the Act of Congress passed June the 7th 1832.
State of Tennessee]
Bedford County   ]

 On this 7th day of February in the year of our Lord one thousand eight hundred and thirty three, personally appeared in open Court before the Worshipful Samuel Phillips, John B. Armstrong and William McClure, Esquires, Gentlemen Justices of the Peace appointed to hold the Court of Pleas and Quarter Sessions for Bedford County in the State of Tennessee, now sitting, George Smith, Senr., a resident of said County, aged seventy nine years, one month and fourteen days, who after being sworn according to law, doth on his oath make the following declaration in order to obtain the benefit of the Act of Congress passed the 7th June 1832. That he entered the service of the United States under the following named Officers and served as herein stated (to wit) that he entered the service of the United States as a drafted Soldier in Rowan County and State of North Carolina in the month of August 1779 and was placed under the command of Captain Peter Heddrick and his Lieutenant's name was Caleb Kimble and was marched on horseback down on Peedee River about sixty miles to Mosses' Ferry where he states he was in an engagement against the Tories under the command of a Tory Captain by the name of Kimbro, and that the Tories were nearly all killed and taken prisoners, he says he was then marched back to Rowan County and from there he was marched down into Randolph County, North Carolina about forty miles from Rowan Court House, against a supposed band of Tories said to be collecting on the waters of Deep River, where the Americans captured a few Tory prisoners and wounded one Tory, who attempted to escape by the name of Hambleton and was marched back to Rowan again and then marched in search of Tories, west of the Yadkin in said County of Rowan and from there up into neighborhood of Salem, now Stokes County, North Carolina where it was supposed the Tories were embodying in order to subdue the Whigs in that part of the Country. And from there he was marched back to Rowan about the first of November 1779. Where he says he was dismissed after serving three months. Deponent further states that afterwards, he entered the service again as a volunteer in the month of February, he thinks in the year 1781. He recollects it was about the time Cornwallis passed through Salisbury with his Army, and was marched as one of the guard in conveying the prisoners taken at Tarlton's Defeat, into the State of Virginia, he says he was under the command of Mirick Davis as Captain on this tour and that he served not less than one month. Deponent further states that he volunteered and entered the service again in said Rowan County the first of September in the year 1781, and attached himself to a Company commanded by Captain Frederick Smith who was under the command of COlonel Caleb Phifer in General Rutherford's Brigade, and he says his Major's name was arthur Harris. Deponent states he was mustered into service at one John Kimbro's on Little River and was marched through Montgomery and Randolph Counties to the Gum Swamp, and Raft Swamps in search of Tories, who were very numerous there at that time and from there to Wilmington on Cape Fear River, where he was stationed when the news of the surrender of Cornwallis was received by the Americans. He says that Colonel Phifer being elected a representative of the Legislature of North Carolina, had left the American Army and returned home to attend to that business, and from Wilmington, he says he was marched back to Rowan and discharged in writing by Major Harris, sometime about the first of December 1781, for a term of three months service, making in all a term of service of not less than seven months for which he claims a pension. Deponent states that he has no documentary evidence whatever and that he knows of no person whose testimony he can procure who can testify as to his service, except what he can prove by Benjamin Lentz. That he hereby relinguishes all claims to a pension except the present and declares that his name is not on the Pension Roll of agency in the United States.

Interrogatories by the Court:

Q. 1st: Where and in what year were you born?
A.   I was born in Rowan County in the State of North Carolina the 24th of December in the year 1763.
Q. 2nd: Have you any record of your age, and if so where is it?
A.   I have no record of my age at this time.
Q. 3rd: Where were you living when called into service? Where have you lived since the Revolutionary War, and where do you now live?
A.   I was a resident of Rowan County in the State of North Carolina during the war, and for many years there after and from there I removed to Bedford County, Tennessee, where I have resided for many years and where I now live.
Q. 4th: How were you called into service? Were you drafted? Did you volunteer or were you a substitute, and if a substitute for whom?
A.   I was drafted my first tour, the second and the last, I was a volunteer.
Q. 5th: State the names of some of the Regular Officers who were with the troops where you served such Continental and Militia Regiments as you can recollect and the general circumstances of your service.
A.   I was not acquainted with any Regular Officers, my Officers were all Militia. Nor did I become acquainted with the names or numbers of any Regiments either Continental or Militia and my declaration contains the most pertinent circumstances of my service in the War of the Revolution that I am able to give.
Q. 6th: Did you ever receive a discharge and if so what has become of it?
A.   I did receive two discharges but what has become of them I cannot tell.
Q. 7th: State the names of persons to whom you are known in your present neighborhood who can testify as to your service and their belief of your character for veracity and service as a Soldier of the Revolution.
A.   The Rev. George Newton, Michael Fisher, Esq., and James Brittain, Esq.
Sworn to in open court the day and year aforesaid.
Jas. McKisick, Clk.   George Smith

State of Tennessee

We, George Newton, a Clergyman, residing in Bedford County in the State aforesaid, and James Brittain residing in the same, do hereby certify that we are well acquainted with George Smith, who has subscribed and sworn to the above declaration, that we believe him to be sixty nine years, one month and fourteen days old, that he is reputed and believed in the neighborhood where he resides to have been a Soldier of the Revolution, and that we concur in that opinion, and we further certify that said applicant is a man of good moral character and of undoubted veracity.
Sworn to and subscribed this 7th day of February 1833.
Jas. McKisick, Clk.   Geo. Newton, V.D.M.
                                                       James Brittain

State of Tennessee]
Bedford County   ]

On this 7th day of February 1833, personally appeared in open Court, Benjamin Lentz, who after being sworn according to law doth on his oath deposeth and say that he is seventy seven years, eleven months and 12 days old, agreeable to his father's Family Bible, that he was a Soldier in the War of the Revolution and while serving . . . imcomplete . . .

Grant to George Smith, 640 acres No. 155
To whom these present shall come greetings.

Know ye that in consideration of Military Service performed by SAMUEL BROWN, to the State of North Carolina, Warrent No. 85, dated the 21st day of December 1803 and entered on the 10th day of August 1807 by No. 80. There is granted by the said State of Tennessee unto George Smith, assignee of the said EMANUEL BROWN, a certain tract or parcel of land containing six hundred and forty acres, lying in Rutherford County in the second District, Sixth Range, Fractional Section No. 1. On the waters of Elk River. Bordering James White.

214

Surveyed the 10th day of September 1807. In witness whereof John Sevier, Governor of the State of Tennessee hath hereunto set his hand on a caused the Great Seal of the State to be affixed at Knoxville on the twentieth day of April in the year of our Lord one thousand eight hundred and eight.

by the Governor
John Sevier

Known children of George Smith, Senr.:
1. George Washington, born ca 1794, died 1865, married Mary "Polly" Turrentine, daughter of James and Ellen (Neely) Turrentine. Polly born 1802 in Orange County, North Carolina, died 1886 in Sevier County, Arkansas.
2. Margaret, born January 27, 1801 North Carolina, married Archelaus Turrentine who was born 1796 in Orange County, North Carolina, died 1885 in Arkansas.

> Ref: GSA Report, Washington, D.C.
> Ref: Turrentine Records.
> Ref: Texas Society DAR Roster Revolutionary Ancestors, Vol IV, pg 1957.
> Ref: Bedford County, Tennessee Grant Book, page 88, Register's Office Shelbyville, Tennessee
> Ref: See Benjamin Lentz's Application for Pension, page 116

* * * * * * * * * *

WILLIAM SMITH

Name:	Rank:	State Served:
William Smith	-----	---------------

Born _____, died _____.

No GSA Report in Washington, D.C.

William Smith, Revolutionary Soldier, Veteran, had a son James Smith.

> Ref: Correspondence of James K. Polk, Vol II, page 30.

* * * * * * * * * *

SAMUEL SPEARS

Name:	Rank:	State Served:
Samuel Spears	PVT	Virginia

Born 1760 in Albermarle County, Virginia, died after 1834 (1834 P.L.W.)

GSA: Samuel Spears, S.1.779, Virginia
Claim No. 13591: West Tennessee, Samuel Spears of Bedford County in the State of West Tennessee, who was a Private in the Company commanded by Captain Harris of the Regiment commanded by Colonel Richardson in the Virginia Line for 6½ months.

Inscribed on the Roll of West Tennessee at the rate of 21 dollars, 66 cents per annum, to commence on the 4th day of March 1831.

Certificate of Pension issued the 21 day of March 1833 and sent to said applicant, Shelbyville (Chapel Hill)

Arrears to the 4th of March	$43.32
Semi-anl allowance ending 4 Sept	$10.80
	$54.12

Recorded by Daniel Boyd, Clerk	Revolutionary Claim
Book E Vol 7 Page 96	Act June t, 1832

Declaration:
State of Tennessee]
Bedford County   ]

On this 12th day of November 1832, personally appeared in the open Court of Pleas and Quarter Sessions of the County and State aforesaid before James Brittain, Samuel Phillips and John B. Armstrong, Justices of the Peace and members of the Court, aforesaid, Samuel Spears, a resident of the County and

State aforesaid, aged seventy two years, who first being sworn according to law, doth on his oath make the following declaration in order to obtain the benefit of the Act of Congress passed 7th June 1832.

That he entered the service of the United States under the following named Officers and Soldiers as follows: in the State of Virginia, Albermarle County, he entered the United States Army as a drafted man under Captain Benjamin Harris and was stationed at Albermarle Barracks called to guard prisoners called Burgoyne's prisoners, from that tour, he was discharged the thinks in about one month, he then entered the service as a substitute for a certain James Moore of that County for a three months tour under Captain John Toliver, James Barret Lieutenant. We marched to Richmond where he thinks the Company was attached to the First Regiment of Virginia commanded by Colonel Richardson, under General Nelson. From there this applicant states the troops marched down James River where they were re-formed and continued to march to different points at length they marched near to Williamsburg to a place called the Old Magazine where he was discharged for his three months tour. After this applicant entered the service again for himself as a drafted man, under Captain Martin and was marched first to guard the Ford on the North Fork of James River, in order to guard Charlottesville should the British come to that Ford but applicant says the British crossed at another Ford and he was in the town when Charlottesville was taken and the Legislature driven. After which the troops were immediately sent in pursuit of them and applicant was with the troops in the pursuit down to Little Fork and helped build breast works, at that place, his first Captain being promoted to the command of Major and a certain ____ commanded as Captain. Applicant recollects that he belonged to a Regiment commanded by Colonel Linsey, a Colonel, from his own County at Little York, he got his discharge for his three months tour and after he got home he heard Wallis was taken so that he thinks his discharge could not have been more than seven or eight days previous to Cornwallis' Surrender. Applicant has no documentary evidence to refresh his memory and knows of no living testimony that he could procure to testify of his actual service. He hereby relinquishes every claim whatever to a pension or annuity except the present and declares that his name is not on any Pension Roll of the agency of any State or Territory of the United States.

Sworn to and subscribed in open Court on this ...

Jas. McKisick, Clk.   Samuel (X) Spears

We, James Y. Green, a Clergyman residing in Bedford County, Tennessee and James Patterson, Esqr., residing in the same, do hereby testify that we are well acquainted with Samuel Spears, who has made and sworn to the above declaration that we believe him to be seventy two years of age, that he is reputed and believed in the neighborhood where he resides to have been a Soldier of the Revolution and that we are of that opinion.

Sworn to and subscribed the day and year aforesaid.

James McKisick, Clk.   James Y. Green
12th day of Nov. 1832   James Patterson

Interrogatories by the Court:

Q. 1st: Where and in what year were you born?

A.   In Albermarle County, State of Virginia, in the year 1760.

Q. 2nd: Do you have a record of your age?

A.   I have, from my father's Family Record.

Q. 3rd: Where were you living when called into service and where have you lived since the Revolutionary War? Where do you now live?

A.   In Albermarle COunty, State of Virginia, I was called into service. I have lived in the State of North Carolina since but am now living in Tennessee, Bedford County.

Q. 4th: How were you called into service? Were you drafted? Did you volunteer or were you a substitute, and if so for whom?

A.   I was drafted, volunteered and substituted for James Moore.

Q. 5th: State the names of some of the Regular Officers who were with the troops where you served such Continental and Militia Regiments, as you can recollect and the general circumstances of your service.

A.   I recollect of no Officers nor Regiments were there, I have set forth in my declaration.

Q. 6th: Did you ever receive a discharge and if so from whom and what has become of it?

A.   I recollect of receiving no written discharge.

Q. 7th: State the names of some of the persons in your present neighborhood who are acquainted with your character and who can testify to your veracity as a man of truth, etc.

A.   James Patterson, Esq., James Y. Green, Jos. Resson, Esq., and Hugh L. McClelan.

In 1835, Samuel Spear, aged 74, Private in Virginia Line.

> Ref: GSA Report, Washington, D.C.
> Ref: 1835 Bedford County, Tennessee Pension List.

* * * * * * * * * *

JOSIAH J. STAFFORD

Name: Rank: State Served:
Josiah Stafford   PVT   North Carolina

Born 1757, died 16th May 1835 Bedford County, Tennessee, married Patsy _____.

GSA: West Tennessee, Josiah Stafford, wife Patsy, North Carolina Line.

Claim No. 151751: West Tennessee, Josiah Stafford, of Smith County in the State of Tennessee who was a Private in the Regiment commanded by COlonel A. Shepherd of the North Caroline Line for the term of two years.

Inscribed on the Roll of West Tennessee at the rate of 8 dollars per month, to commence on the 11 of May 1818.

Certificate of Pension issued the 10 of November 1819 and sent to John McNairy, Judge, Nashville, West Tennessee.

Arrears to 4th of Sept 1819 $126.48

Semi-anl allowance ending 4 March
        15 mos   21/31 &]
                          ] 1820
        4/ 30   ] $ 48.00
                                                              $174.48
                                                              Revolutionary Claim
                                                              Act 18th March 1818

Verification sent May 5, 1837
to Graham Foster, Esq., _____, Tennessee

District of West Tennessee

On this 11th day of May 1818, Josiah Stafford of the County of Smith in the State of Tennessee, came before me and claimed to be places on the Pension List of the United States in consequence of his service in the Revolutionary War, and after being duly sworn deposeth and saith that he entered the service of the United States in the _____ service and served one year and in the command of Captain John Garland. After the end of that service that he entered as a soldier in Captain Abraham Sheppard's Company for three years. The said Company belonged to the 10th North Carolina Regiment which was afterwards dismissed and put into the 1st and 2nd North Carolina Regiment that he served the said three years and was taken prisoner at Charles Town and never got a discharge. He further states that Captain Sheppard left the service and that he served the three years under the command of Captain John Ingles. Further states that he is very poor and stands much in need of the aid of Government, that he is stricken with the palsey for 14 years and that for the four last years he is entirely unable to labor or get about. That he never has had a pension or aid either from the United States or any of the State Governments.

Sworn to and subscribed before me   Josiah (X) Stafford
on the date shown.
John McNairy, District Judge

                                                  Nashville Bank
                                                  Pension Office
                                                  5 Sept 1820
Sir,
        It appears that two pension applications have issued for Josiah Stafford,
one commencing on the 11th May 1818, another on the 13th Feb 1820, as I have
my reasons to believe they are both for the same person and as Judge McNairy
as well as myself are of the opinion that he is entitled to the one bearing date of
the first application. I herewith inclose you one of them for further information.
Mr. Stafford's first application was made while he resided in Smith County in the
State, papers made out before John McNairy, Esq., and the last application, the
papers were made out before Judge Harris. The reason Mr. Stafford assigns for
making the two applications was the delay of time in hearing from the first one
during which time he removed from Smith County to Giles County, same State
where the last application was made from. I am sinc respectfully yrs.
                                                  Stephen Cantrell
                                                  Pension Agent

State of Tennessee]
Davidson County   ]
        Howel Tatum made the oath that he was an officer in the 1st North
Carolina Regiment in the Revolutionary War. That he knew the Commanders and
most of the Officers of the different Regiments of that line, that he particularly
knew Colonel Abraham Shepherd who commanded the _____ Regiment and his son
Abraham, a Captain of the said Regiment. He also knows that the said Regiment
joined the main Army and the North Carolina Brigade at the Valley Forge in the
Spring of the year 1778 and that the Regiment was reduced under a new
arrangement of the Army about the 2nd of June in that year and the now
commissioned Officers and Soldiers transferred to the 1st and 2nd Regiment of
the State made equally. He knows nothing of Josiah Stafford who states himself
to know served under Captain John Ingle but knew Captain Jno. Ingles well and
has no boubts that Stafford had stated his services correctly as this deponent has
conversed with the said Stafford but a few days past and received such a
statement of his different marches with the army when this deponent was in
Company and related so minutely facts which took place and could not have
known to a man not in the Army so as to relate so well in connection. He states
the facts in connection that took place on the North River and _____ them on as
far as Wilmington in North Carolina and from thence to Charlestown in South
Carolina. At which place he states himself to have been cpatures. As this
deponent was on the whole of that tour and has heard Stafford relate it so
minutely and correctly, he has no doubt but Stafford actually did serve the period
mentioned in his application and is fully convinced that he did serve from the
Spring of the year 1778 until he was captures the 12th of May 1780, and further
this deponent saith no.
Sworn to and subscribed before me   H. Tatum
John McNairy

Josiah Stafford was a Revolutionary Soldier and was paid his pension until his
death which occured about four years ago states the Nashville Agency,
Tennessee.
        Mr. Stafford was entitled of Pension Money previous to his having drawn
any. Will you afford me all the information on the subject in your pawer? When
did he first receive pension money? How much did he receive prior to his death?
And what are the regulations to be followed when a pension is entitled to
unclaimed pension money.
        Your earliest reply to me at Springfield will oblige me very much.
October 23, 1840   Your ob't Servt.
                                                   W.L.D. Ewing

Josiah Stafford, West Tennessee Roll, Act. March 18, 1818
        Be pleased to say to what time he was last oaid.
                                                   Pension Office
                                                   Nov 5, 1840
Died 16th May 1835. Rec'd 3rd 1835 to date of death.   L.H. Hill

State of Tennessee
On the 10th day of February 1820, before me the subscriber, one of the Circuit Judges of the State of Tennessee for the 6th Judicial Circuit, personally appeared Josiah Stafford, aged 63 years, residing in the County of Giles in the Circuit aforesaid, who being by me first duly sworn according to law doth on his oath make the following declaration in order to obtain the provision made by the Act of Congress entitled "An Act to provide for certain persons engaged in the Land and Naval Service of the United States in the Revolutionary War." That he the said Josiah Stafford enlisted the term of three years sometime in the month of July (the day of the month not recollected) in the year 1777 to the best of his recollection, in what was at that time called Dobbs County, in the State of North Carolina, in the Company commanded by Captain A. Shepherd of the Regiment commanded by Col. A. Shepherd (Colonel and Captain reputed father and son, 10th Regiment) in the line of the State of North Carolina or the Continental Establishment. That shortly after his enlistment he was marched to the Valley Forge where he was transferred to a Company commanded by Captain John Ingles, in a Regiment commanded by Colonel Harvey. That he continued to serve in said Corps or in the service of the United States until he was taken prisoner by the British at the Seige of Charleston in South Carolina from where he made his escape in the month of July 1780 (his term of service having expired and returned home). That he never had any discharge in writing, but his conduct was approved by his officers and payment for his service rendered. That he was in the Battle of Monmouth, at the Seige of Charleston, and in several inconsiderable skirmishes. And that he is in reduced circumstances and stands in need of assistance of his country for support and that he has no other evidence now in his power (except the aforesaid affidavit of Sarah Gatlin) by which he could prove his said services.
Sworn to and subscribed before me   Josiah (S) Stafford (Seal)
the day and year aforesaid
Alfred M. Harris, Judge of the
6th Judicial Circuit of the
State of Tennessee

State of Tennessee
On this 14th day of February 1820, before me the subscriber, one of the Circuit Judges of the State of Tennessee for the 6th Judicial Circuit, personally appeared Sarah Gatlin, aged seventy one years, who being by me first duly sworn according to law, upon her oath, says that she has been intimately acquainted with the above named Josiah Stafford from his infanct, being his sister. That during the Revolutionary War, said Josiah Stafford lived with this affiant and her then husband (William illegible) who is now dead. And whilst living there enlisted himself as Regular Soldier for the period of three years. He then left the dwelling of the affiant (leaving his horse), and as she then understood and yet believes, marched with the American Troops to the north where he was gone a long time, where he returned with an army and travelled to the south, and was taken, as the affiant understood and believes, prisoner by the British at Charleston. This affiant knows that said Josiah Stafford (who is not present) was after his aforesaid enlistments as much as least as three years absent except the time of his return from the north where he only remained a part of one day, and always understood and believed that he was in the service of his country.
                              Sarah (X) Gatlin (Seal)
Subscribed and sworn to before me the day and year aforesaid
Alfred M. Harris, Judge

I, Alfred M. Harris, Judge &c aforesaid, do certify that it appears to my satisfaction that the said Josiah Stafford did serve in the Revolutionary War as stated in the preceding declaration, against the common enemy for the term of nine months, all one time on the Continental Establishment, and I now transmit the ______ and testimony taken and had before me to the Secretary for the Department of War, pursuiant to the directions of the afore mentioned Acts of Congress.

I am also satisfied that he needs the assistance of his country for support. In testimony whereof I have hereunto set my hand and seal. this 14th February 1820.

                              (Seal)   Alfred M. Harris, Judge
                                              of the 6th Judicial Circuit
                                              Court of the State of
                                              Tennessee.

State of Tennessee]
Giles County   ]
        On this 27th day of November 1820, personally appeared in open Court, Josiah Stafford, aged 63 years, who being first duly sworn according to law, doth on his oath, make the following declaration in order to obtain the provision made by the Acts of Congress of the 18th March 1818 and 1st of May 1820, that the said Josiah Stafford enlisted for the term of three years, the day of the month and year not recollected, in the State of North Carolina in the Company commanded by Captain Abraham Shepperd, Jr., in the Regiment commanded by Colonel Abraham Shepperd, Senr., in the line of the State of North Carolina on the Continental Establishment, that he continued in said Corps until removed into the Company commanded by John Ingles in the Regiment commanded by Colonel _____ and continued to serve in said Corps until taken prisoner at Charlestown from whence he made his escape and returned home. The term of his enlistment having expired consequently he was never able to get a discharge. That he was in the Battles of Charlestown, Moores' Creek and Monmouth and that he has no other evidence now in his power of his said services except the testimony of Sarah Gatland (Gatlin) who says that she is well acquainted with the applicant Josiah Stafford that she knows of his entering in the Revolutionary War but in what year and month she does not recollect, that he continued in service for the space of three years or at least he was given that length of time. Sarah Gatland (Gatlin).

                                    Josiah (S) Stafford
        And in pursuance of the Act of the 1st of May 1820, I do solemnly swear that I was a resident citizen of the United States on the 18th day of March 1818 and that I have not since that time by gift, sale or in any manner disposed of my property or any part thereof with intent thereby sb to diminish it as to bring myself within the provisions of an Act of Congress entitled "An Act to provide for certain persons engaged in the Land and Naval service of the United States in the Revolutionary War passed on the 18th day of March 1818" and that I have not nor has any person in trust for me any property or securities contracts or debts due to me nor have I any income other than what is contained in the schedule hereto annexed.

        The aforesaid Josiah Stafford is by occupation a farmer who is by no means able to pursue his said occupation rendered so by reasons of the palsy. He has three children living with him, one son Merril, aged 20 years who is not rendered incapable of laboring by any _____ whatever, one dayghter Polly, aged 18 years who is capable of contributing a part to the support of the family, one son Joel, aged 12 years.
        Schedule of property belonging to the applicant, viz,
        1 horse, beast $30.00
        1 hog $ 20.00
                Total $32.00

                                    Josiah (X) Stafford

        The said Josiah Stafford further saith that he hath received a Certificate for a pension under the Act of 1818, which he hath not now with him or he would refer to its date and number, but being advised that he cannot draw money or a pension under any certificate except _____ is made in pursuance of the Act of 1820, has made the foregoing declaration and proff. 27th November 1820.

                                    Josiah (S) Stafford
Sworn to and declared on the 27th day of November 1820, in open Court. Signed by Nelson Patterson, Thomas H. Merritt and Alexander Black, Esquires, Justices, present.

        I, German Lester, Clerk of Giles County Court, do hereby certify that the following oath and the schedula hereto annexed are truly copied from the records of the said Court and I do further certify that it is the opinion of the said Court that the total amount in value of the property exhibited in the aforesaid schedule is $32.00.

In testimony whereof I have hereunto set my hand and affixed the seal of the said Court on this 27th day of November 1820.

German Lester, Clk.

Josiah J. Stafford, Private, North Carolina Line
4 years service: Captain Garland's Company, Dobbs County Militia of North Carolina, Captain Sheppard's Company, 10th North Carolina Regiment, Captain Carney's Company, 2nd North Carolina Regiment.
Encampment: Valley Forge, Winter of 1777.

He was in the Battle of Monmouth, Moores Creek and Seige of Charlestown and other battles.

State of Tennessee]
Bedford County   ]   August Term 1835

Be it known, that at a Court of Pleas and Quarter Sessions, Justice for the County aforesaid at the Court House in the town of Shelbyville, on the 4th day of August 1835, personally appeared in open Court, Patsy Stafford, Martin W. Oakley and Jonas _. Haston(Horton ?) all of said county and upon their oaths have satisfactory proven to the court here that she, the said Patsy Stafford was the lawful wife of the late Josiah Stafford of said County, deceased, and that her said husband died on the sixteenth day of May eighteen hundred and thirty five and at the time of his death he had been placed on the Pension List Roll of the United States under the Act of Congress of the 18th March 1818 and that he is indentical Josiah Stafford mentioned in an original certificate in his possession on the day of his death which is shown to the Court here and _____ the following is a true copy.

War Department
Revolutionary Claim

I certify that in conformity with the law of the United States of the 18th March 1818, Josiah Stafford of Smith County, West Tennessee, late a Private in the service of the Revolution is inscribed on the Pension List Roll of the West Tennessee Agency at the rate of eight dollars per month to commence on the eleventh day of May one thousand eight hundred and eighteen.

Given at the War Office of the United States, this tenth day of November one thousand eight hundred and nineteen.

J.C. Calhoun
Secretary of War

And she the said Patsy Stafford further testifies that her said husband was entitled to a Pension at the rate of eight dollars per month from the first day of September 1834 to the 16th day of May 1835 which she said for services rendered the United States during the Revolutionary War and at the time of his death he resided in said Bedford County and has resided there for the most of four years past. Previously he resided in Giles County, Tennessee, Smith County, Tennessee and Bladen County, State of North Carolina.

Sworn to and subscribed the day   Patsy (X) Stafford (Seal)
and date first shown writtem   Martin W. Oakley   (Seal)
Sworn to in open Court this   Jane (X) Hooten   (Seal)
Fourth August 1835
Jas. McKisick, Clerk

Petition of Patsy Stafford

Know all men by these present that I, Patsy Stafford of the County of Bedford in the State of Tennessee, widow of the late Josiah Stafford of the said county, deceased, do hereby constitute and appoint Thomas Hooten my true and lawful attorney for me in my name to receive from the Congress of the United States for paying pension at Shelbyville   said State, the pension owed to my said husband from the 4th day of September 1834 to the 16th day of May 1835 when he died.

Witness my hand and seal this 4th day of August 1835.

Patsy (X) Stafford (Seal)
Ackn.

Which said Power of Attorney was duly acknowledged in open Court by her the said Patsy Stafford to be her ___ and deed in testimony whereof the foregoing proof made before the court here. I, James McKisick, Clerk of said Court have hereunto subscribed my name and affixed the Seal of the COurt at office in Shelbyville, this 4th day of August 1835.

Jas. McKisick, Clerk

State of tennessee]
Davidson County]
      Be it known that on the 8th day of August the subscriber, a Justice of the Peace in and for the County, personally appeared Thomas Hooten, the Attorney named in the foregoing Power of Attorney and made oath that the same was not given because of transfer and should be rescinded.
Sworn and subscribed the day and year   Thomas Hooten
list above mentioned before me
Robert Farquharson, J.P.

      Ref: GSA Report, Washington, D.C.
      Ref: Widow's Application for Pension.

* * * * * * * * * *

JOHN STONE

Name: Rank: State Served:
John Stone   PVT   Pennsylvania
Born ca 1761, died after 1828, married to Mary _____.

GSA: John Stone, S.39096, Served in Pennsylvania.
Claim No. 20.005: West Tennessee, John Stone of lawrence County in the State of Tennessee, who was a Private in the Company commanded by Lieutenant Bergh of the Regiment commanded by Colonel Hampton in the Pennsylvania Line, for the term of the war. From February 1777 to 24 March 1780.
      Inscribed on the Roll of West Tennessee at the rate of eight dollars per month, to commence on the 5th day of November 1828.
      Certificate of Pension issued the 13th of December 1828 and sent to Hon. J. Moore, House of Reps.
Arrears to 4th of March 1829 $31.16
Semi-anl allowance ending

                                  $31.00
4 March 1829   Revolutionary Claim
                                  Act March 18, 1818
                                  and May 1, 1820

Original Claim:
 District of Alabama: S.S. Circuit Court of Lawrence County, State of Alabama.
      On this 20th of September 1825, personally appeared in open Court , being a Court of Records for the fourth Circuit of the Circuit Court of the State of Alabama, having jurisdiction of sums unlimited in amount, power to fine and imprison and proceeding according to the course of the common law.
      John Stone of said County, aged sixty four years, residing in said County of Lawrence and State of Alabama, who being first duly sworn according to law doth on his oath make the following declaration in order to obtain the provision made by the Act of Congress of the 18th of March 1818 and 1st of May 1820, that he the said John Stone, enlisted for and during the war on the __ day of either January or February 1777 in the State of Pennsylvania in the Company commanded by _____ _____ as Captain name not recollected. The Lieutenant under whom this applicant enlisted was by the name of Henry Bergh in the Regiment commanded by Colonel Richard Hampton in the Line of the State of Pennsylvania on the Continental Establishment, that he continued to serve in the said Corps until 24th day of March 1781, when he was discharged from said service at Lebanon in the State of Pennsylvania where he furnished a substitute by the name of Michael Nichols who enlisted during the war. The discharge of this applicant dated the 24th of March 1781, is in the words and figures following, to wit, "This is to Certufy that the bearer, John Stone, late a Soldier in the Sixth Pennsylvania Regiment, has at his own expense engaged and

222

delivered to said Regiment, a certain Michael Nichols, enlisted for the war, in consideration of which the said John Stone is hereby discharged, the Army of the United States of America. Given at Lebanon, this twenty fourth day of March,

By Order of Colonel Richard Hampton
W. Finney, Captain, Comd. 6th Regt."

That he, this affiant, was in the Battle of Brandywine, 11th September 1777 at which time he was taken prisoner by the British and he remained a prisoner about ten months and he has no evidence now in his possession of his said service except the above discharge and an affidavit made by Matthias Henning and Valentine Shoufler which is hereunto annexed as taken in _____.

The State of Pennsylvania in the County of Lebanon, before Peter Shyker, Justice of the Peace and a certificate of the Auditor General, dated February 8th 1825, which is hereunto annexed, marked "B" and in pursuance of the Act 1st May 1820.

I do solemnly swear that I was a resident citizen of the United States on the 8th day of March 1818, and that I have not since that time by gist sale or in any manner disposed of my property or any part thereof with intent hereby to diminish it as to bring myself within the provisions of Congress entitled, "An Act to provide for certain persons engaged in the Land and Naval service of the United States in the Revolutionary War, passed on the 18th day of March 1818" and that I have not nor has any person in trust for me any property or securities contract or debts due to me, nor have I any income other than what is contained in the schedule hereunto annexed and by me subscribed, the reasons he has not made earlier for a pension were:

1st: He was unwilling to make this call upon his country so long as he could well support himself, And that he has been better able to support himself until within some short time past than at the present time and he has not until lately had in his possession, the affidavit above named and supposed some such proof of service to be necessary. The property he has disposed of June 18th of March 1818 is the following: A house and lot at four hundred dollars to William West, in payment of a debt owing to said West, for goods in the year 1818, month not recollected. Three negroes sold under a deed of trust to raise $900. for Josiah Nichols and Robert Armstrong, to pay a debt due said Nichols and Armstrong, for goods, this sale was in 1818, months not recollected, who bought them not recollected.

3rd, To forty five acres of land sold under deed of trust to William Gilchrist, and Town Lots not exceeding six of the Town of Shelbyville, Tennessee, Bedford County, names of purchasers of lots not recollected. Those lots were out lots, disposed under deed of trust for the sum of $2000. and paid to Andrew Erwin and sons in payment of a debt for goods in 1818.

4th, To the firm of Pritchett and their given names not recollected, $1600. in discharge of debt, due for goods, the property sold to raise money was 245 acres of land in 1818, sold to Mr. Brittain, given name not known.

5th, House and Lot in the town of Moulton, Lawrence County, Alabama, sold to John Brahan, to pay his a debt due for goods to the amount of $1500. in 1822.

6th, Some other articles of small amount have been disposed of to pay debts, under execution in the year 1821, to wit, a little negro girl and several beds and furniture and other household furniture.

A schedule of property now in possession:

A cow and calf, worth	$12.00
Kitchen furniture, worth	$20.00
One old Bureau, worth	$10.00
One chest, worth	$ 4.00
And a watch,	$15.00
	$61.00

John Stone

He has been engaged in selling goods in a limited way, until he failed in the year 1818, is unable to follow any hard labor, and is some times employed to attend to business for John A. Marrs and John Stone, sons-in-law of this affiant, but is unable to follow a sonstant employment of a profitable nature. The names and members of his family residing with him are his wife, Mary, about fifty five

age, she is able to do some business in cooking and managing about the house, probably enough to support herself. His daughter, Polly Tucker, aged about 35 years and her son, Jackson Tucker aged about five years, Polly Tucker is sickly and not more than able to earn her own support, and a grandchild, the mother which is dead, named Earl Bayliss about 2 years old.
Sworn to and subscribed on the 20th of September 1825 in open Court.

J. Burford, C.C.C.

State of Alabama]
Lawrence County] Circuit Court, September Term, 1825

On this 20th day of September instant, George A. Glover, in open Court, made affidavit, that he is a near neighbor of John Stone, the applicant for a pension, and that the schedule of said applicant contains a correct list of the visable property of said Stone, except some cups and saucers, and table ware, which are not worth more than $10.00. And that if said applicant has other property, it is unknown to this affiant and that he believes that the prices set by said Stone on said property, it is about its fair value.
Test: Jonathan Burford, C.C.C.   George A. Glover

I, Jonathan Burford, of the Circuit Court of Lawrence County, State of Alabama, do hereby certify that the foregoing oath or affirmation and the schedule thereto annexed a truly copied from the finds of the Court, and I do further certify that it is the opinion of the said Court that the total amount of value of the property exhibited in the foresaid schedule is sixty one dollars. In testimony whereof I have here unto set my hand and Private Seal, there being no Seal of Office, at Office the 1st day of October 1825.

(Seal)   Jonathan Burford, Clerk of
the Circuit Court of the
County of Lawrence.

NOTE: In order to obtain the balance of last payment of this pension, name and address of person paid, and possibly the date of death of John Stone, you should apply to:

    The Comptroller General
    General Accounting Office
    Records Division, Washington, D.C.

and furnish the following:

    John Stone
    Certificate No. 20005
    Issued December 13, 1828
    Rate $8.00 per month
    Commenced November 8, 1828
    Acts of March 18, 1818 and May 1, 1820
    West Tennessee Agency

NOTE: He was allowed pension, executed September 20, 1825, at which time he was aged 64 years, living in Moulton, Lawrence County, Alabama. His Pension Certificate was not issued until December 13, 1828, and he had then returned to Bedford County, Tennessee, to be with his children.
In 1825, he referred to his wife, Mary, aged about 55 years but did not give her maiden name or date of their marriage. To his daughter, Polly Tucker, aged about 35 years, and to Polly Tucker's son Jackson Tucker, aged about 5 years, and to a grandson, Earl Bayliss, aged about 2 years, whose mother is dead. The names of Earl Bayliss' parents not given.
In 1828, John Stone's daughter, Nancy Marrs and her husband, John A. Marrs, were living in Shelbyville, Bedford County, Tennessee.
John Stone, son-in-law of the Soldier, John Stone, was referred to, the Christian name of his wife was not given.

MILITARY RECORD

S - 10 - Pa.

John Stone, Rank: Private
Roll of Captain Calhoun's Company 10th Pennsylvania
Regiment commanded by Colonel Richard Hampton,

The Whole Enlistment for During the Rev. War.
Roll Dated: Sept 9, 1778 Remarks: ON Furlough

John Stone of Bedford County, Tennessee, to Alexander Greer of
Bedford County, Tennessee, for 100 acres. Dated 26 June 1809 $1000.
Situated: Both sides of Duck River, borders Thomas Talbot's north west corner to
Talbot's north east corner.
Witness: Dempsey Powel and Michael Robinson

John Stone, born 1761 in Berks County, Pennsylvania, died in 1841 in
Shelbyville, Tennessee, married Mary Magdalene Seibold who was born 1768 and
died 1842.
Children:
1. Joe
2. Wylie
3. William
4. Thomas J., born January 20, 1795, married Sallie K. Fox
5. Katie, married (1) (John) Walker, (2) William Hale
6. Lucinda, married John Stone
7. Nancy, married John A. Moores (Marrs)

Ref: GSA Report, Washington, D.C.
Ref: Bedford County, Tennessee Deed Book A, page 332
Ref: Texas Society DAR Roster Revolutionary Ancestors, Vol IV, pg
2024.

* * * * * * * * * *

JOHN TACKE

Name:	Rank:	State Served:
John Tacke	-----	---------------

Born ca 1754, died after 1840.

Ref: 1840 Bedford County, Tennessee Pension List, aged 86 years.

* * * * * * * * * *

THOMAS TALBOT

Name:	Rank:	State Served:
Thomas Talbot	PVT	---------------

Born _____, died _____, buried in Nashville, Tennessee in a private cemetery.,
married Ruth Greer.

Ruth Greer, alias Talbot, wife of Thomas Talbot, 2,625 acres, south side
of Elk River. Borders Indian Lands. (Now Lincoln County, Tennessee).
Surveyed: 10th November 1792.
Thomas Talbot, for 2,000 acres. State of North Carolina. No. 13. 10
lbs for every 100 acres. Situation: Middle District, lying on Duck River,
beginning at Thomas and Alexander Greer's north east corner, west with Thomas
and Alexander Greer's line crossing a large branch, cross fork of Lick Creek,
crossed Duck River, twice. Witness: Samuel Johnston, Esqr., etc at Fairfield.
Dated: 10 July 1788.

Ref: Bedford County, Tennessee Deed Book A, page 57.
Ref: Susie Gentry, State Historian
Ref: No GSA Report in Washington, D.C.

* * * * * * * * * *

THOMAS ROLLINS TALBOT

Name:	Rank:	State Served:
Thomas Rollins Talbot	-----	---------------

Born ca 1760, died ____ .

No GSA Report in Washington, D.C.

Thomas Rollins Talbot died in Bedford County, Tennessee, could be buried at Fairfield, Bedford County, Tennessee. No marker for his grave to be found.

Ref: Susie Gentry, State Historian.

* * * * * * * * * *

CHARLES TAYLOR

Name: Rank: State Served:
Charles Taylor   PVT   South Carolina
Born 5th August 1753 in Fairfax County, Virginia, died after 1834.

GSA: Charles Taylor, S.3760
Claim No. 7300: West Tennessee, Charles Taylor of Bedford County in the State of Tennessee, was a Private in the Company commanded by Captain Blakely of the Regiment commanded by Colonel Fletcher in the South Carolina for 16 months and 15 days.

South Carolina and Georgia Record corrected

Inscribed on the Roll of West Tennessee at the rate of 60 dollars, __ cents per annum to commence on the 4th day of March 1831.

Certificate of Pension issued the __ day of March 1833 and sent to Jas. McKisick, Shelbyville, Tennessee.

Arrears to the 4th of March $121.00
Semi-anl allowance ending 4th Sept $ 30.25
                                                         $151.25

Recorded by Daniel Boyd, Clerk   Revolutionary Claim
Book E   Vol 7   page 98   Act June 7, 1832

Declaration in order to obtain the benefit of an Act of Congress passed June 7th, 1832.

This day being the 14th day of August in the year of our Lord, one thousand eight hundred and thirty two, personally appeared in open Court before Samuel Phillips, John B. Armstrong and John L. Neill, Esquires, Gentlemen Justices of the Peace, appointed to hold the Court of Pleas and Quarter Sessions for the said County in the State aforesaid, now sitting, Charles Taylor, a resident of Bedford County in the State aforesaid, aged seventy nine years, and nine days, who after being first duly sworn according to law, doth on his oath make the following declaration in order to obtain the benefit of the Act of Congress passes June the 7th 1832.

That he entered the service of the United States under the following named Officers and served herein stated, to wit, That he volunteered in Captain Blakely's COmpany as drummer in Chesterfield District and State of South Carolina in the Winter of 1772 about the 1st of December and was marched on in order to subdue a party of Sc-fleites or Tories who were said to have embodied on the Saluda River, South Carolina under one Colonel Thomas Fletcher, he states he was marched about 50 miles in that direction when he states they met the Americans marching on to Charleston with Fletcher and about a half dozen of his men prisoners. He states that his Major's name was Hicks, and he states they were marched back home and discharged in the month of January in the year 1773.

He states that afterwards in the year 1776, he was drafted in Chesterfield District in South Carolina and served as drummer in Captain John Jones' Company and I was stationed at what was called the Ten-Mile House for two months and better, and was then discharged in writing by Colonel Culps who was our Head Commander at that place. He further states that after that he was drafted and attached to Captain McManas' Company and he states before they had orders to march, he was taken sick and shortly after was taken prisoner by the Tories and marched to their encampment below Camden on the Wateree River, where he says they kept him about one month when he effected and escaped and fled to the edge of the State of Georgia, to my brother-in-law, Benjamin Moseley's, where I remained through ____ of the Tories until Colonel Clarke marched into the State of Georgia, when I volunteered with Captain George Dooley whose Company was attached to Colonel Clarke's Troops. This he states was in the first part of May 1781. He states that he was in the Battle of Augusta and at that place he states he saw Colonels Washington and Lee at the Seige of Augusta, with Troops of Light Horse. He also states that he still remained in said Company under Captain Dooley until the close of the war and was often in actual service for over one or two months at a time. He states that in the whole of his service from first to last, he was in actual service about eighteen months. He further states that he has no documentary evidence whatever, and that he knows of no person whose testimony he can procure who can testify as to his service. He hereby relinquishes all claims to a pension or annuity except the present and declares that his name is not on the Pension Roll of any agency in the United States.

Charles Taylor

Interrogatories by the Court:

Q. 1st: Where and in what year were you born?
A.   I was born in Fairfax County in the State of Virginia on the 5th day of August 1753.
Q. 2nd: Have you any record of your age and if so where is it?
A.   I have a record of my age at home in my Prayer Book.
Q. 3rd: Where were you living when called into service? Where have you lived since the Revolutionary War and where do you now live?
A.   When I was first called into service, I lived in Chesterfield District, South Carolina, and when I was called into service last or when I volunteered, I was at my brother-in-law's, Benjamin Mosely, in Wilkes County, Georgia. Since the close of the war, I returned to South Carolina and moved from there to Rowan County and State of North Carolina and from thence to Smith County, Tennessee and moved from that to Bedford County, Tennessee where I now live.
Q. 4th: How were you called into service? Were you drafted? Did you volunteer? Or were you a substitute and if a substitute for whom?
A.   I was first a volunteer, then I was drafted twice, and the last time I volunteered until the close of the war.
Q. 5th: State the names of some of the Regular Officers who were with or the troops where you served, such Continental and Militia Regiments as you can recollect.
A.   I recollect Captain John Donaldson, also I was told that Colonel Washington and Colonel Lee who I saw in Augusta,   were   Regular Officers.
Q. 6th: Omitted.
Q. 7th: Did you ever receive a discharge and if so what has become of it?
A.   I only received a discharge signed by Captain John Jones but where it is now, I cannot tell.
Q. 8th: State the names of persons to whom you are known in your present neighborhood who can certify as to your character for veracity, and their belief of your service as a Soldier of the Revolution.
A.   The Rev. William Jenkins, Michael Fisher, Esquire, Benjamin Reaves and William Carter.

The above sworn to in open Court the day and year aforesaid.
Sworn to in open Court 14th August 1832   Charles Taylor (Seal)
Jas. McKisick, Clerk

We, William Jenkins, a Clergyman, residing in Bedford County and State of Tennessee and Michael Fisher, a resident of the same County, do hereby certify that we are well acquainted with Charles Taylor who has subscribed to the foregoing declaration in order to obtain the benefit of an Act of Congress passes 7th June 1832, that we believe him to be seventy nine years and nine days old. That he is reputed and believed in the neighborhood, where he resides to have been a Soldier of the Revolution and that we concur in that opinion. Sworn to and subscribed in open Court the 14th day of August 1832.
Sworn to in open Court 14th August 1832   William Jenkins
Jas. McKisick, Clk.   Michael Fisher

And the said Court do hereby declare their opinion after the

227

investigation of the matter and after putting the interrogatories prescribed by the War Department that the above named applicant was a Revolutionary Soldier and served as stated. And the Court further certifies that it appears to them that William Jenkins who has signed the foregoing certificate is a Clergyman of good standing in the Lutheran Church in Bedford County and that Michael Fisher who has signed the preceeding certificate, is a resident of said County of Bedford and is a credible person and that their statement is entitled to credit.

Jno. L. Neill
Samuel Phillips
John B. Armstrong

1835, Charles Taylor, aged 80 years, Private in South Carolina Line.

> Ref: GSA Report, Washington, D.C.
> Ref: 1835 Bedford County, Tennessee Pension List

* * * * * * * * * *

JOHN THEOPHILLIS THOMPSON

Name:	Rank:	State Served:
John Theophillis Thompson	Major	Maryland

Born December 7, 1759, died April 10, 1826 in Bedford County, Tennessee, married Mary Newcome. Buried in Thompson Cemetery, on Old Murray Pickle Farm. This cemetery has been destroyed and markers removed. (1974 - Eds)

No GSA Report in Washington, D.C.

NOTE: John T. Thompson, a Revolutionary Soldier, was buried in this cemetery. He had a large Box Type Vault marker on his grave. Cemetery was copied, in part, by Wayne Lentz, before it was destroyed.

Thompson History in Old Joseph Thompson Bible:
Joseph Thompson (30 Mar 1782 - 30 Mar 1824) was a son of John Theophilus Thompson (7 Dec 1759 - 10 April 1826), accepted by the DAR as a Soldier of the Revolution, was born in Frederick County, Maryland. He went from there to North Carolina and then to Bedford County, Tennessee, in the early 1800's. He was a son of Richard Thompson born in December 1735, a resident or possibly a native of Frederick County, Maryland, and of his wife Mary. His grandparents are believed to have been Sarah and John Thompson. Theophilus Thompson died in Bedford County.

On 1780, Theophilus fought under Dekalb at the Battle of Camden, South Carolina, and again in that year commanded a Company at King's Mountain and subsequently at the Battle of Cowpens in 1781. He was in the Battle of Guilford Court House.

Theophilus Thompson married Mary Newcom in North Carolina and they had three sons, Joseph, Samuel and Newcom. They may have had other children but these three are known. The family crossed the mountains in ox carts traveling in creeks to keep from being tracked by the Indians.

The information about Theophilus Thompson's Military history was obtained from DAR application of Mollie Thompson Davidson, National No. 18195. Other information as well as his Military history is contained in the Solomon Family History complied by Marion Solomon.

In Sampson County, North Carolina, on 20 January 1787, Martha Thompson , for love and affection, deeds to her beloved "Daughters" Elizabeth and Zilphia, two negro slaves. This deed is recorded in Sampson County, North Carolina, 1787 after being proven in open Court by a witness, Roger Snall, registered in Bedford County, Tennessee, 12 July 1814.

The above information shows or indicates that the Martha Thompson (3 Oct 1760 - 6 Jan 1841) who is recorded in Joseph Thompson's Bible, is the mother of his wife Elizabeth Thompson born 15 Aug 1780 and Zilphia Windrow born 18 Feb 1786 and died 18 June 1851, Zilphia probably married and outlived a Windrow. This all being true would show that Joseph Thompson's wife Elizabeth was a Thompson before she married Joseph Thompson. This Elizabeth Thompson born 15 Aug 1780 lived to be over 80 years old as she is listed in the 1860 Census but does not appear in the 1870 Census.

In the Old Joseph Thompson Bible, page 780, John: 20:17, where the page is torn there is two little stitches, x x, where Elizabeth Thompson repaired the tear.

Newton Cannon Thompson and Elizabeth Green were married by W.C.B. Thompson, a Minister of the Gospel, 17 Mar 1866.

Thompson Bible

Photocopy by Paul K. Delk
Publisher: B. Warner, Philadelphia, Pa. 1819

Record:
Joseph Thompson was born 30th March 1782 and was married 20 Dec 1804 to Elizabeth Thompson, born 15 Aug 1780.
Children:
1. Anna Thompson born 26 January 1799
2. Eliza Thompson born 29 November 1805
3. James Thompson born 6 January 1807
4. Harriet Thompson born 4 April 1809
5. Calvin Thompson born 22 March 1811
6. John A. Thompson born 27 March 1813
7. Patsey J. Thompson born 17 April 1815
8. William F. Thompson born 9 December 1817
9. Newton Cannon Thompson born 25 December 1819
10. Isabella Thompson born 30 August 1821

Martha Thompson born 3 Oct 1760 died Jan 6, 1841
Zilpha Windrow born 18 Feb 1786 died 18 June 1851

Calvin Thompson died 24 March 1852
Eliza Th ompson died 27 Sept 1811
Joseph Thompson died 30 March 1824
William Thompson died 16 Oct 1826
Harret (Thompson) Richardson died 5 May 1830
John A. Thompson died 20 June 1840
James Thompson died 26 Dec 1841 at 5 p.m.   Age 32 years, 11 months and 26 days.

Children of Newton Cannon Thompson:
1. Hattie Floyd Thompson born 28 Aug 1867, died 3 a.m. Wed., 15 Nov 1933
2. Emma Jane Thompson born 27 Feb 1869, died 7 a.m. Monday 16 Jan 1939
    Emma Jane Thompson married 28 Dec 1892 to Joshua Vernon Delk who was born 8 Jan 1863. Children:
    1. Howard Porter Delk born 19 Sept 1893
    2. Horace Cannon Delk born 26 Aug 1896
    3. Harry Hunter Delk born 16 June 1900
    4. Floyd McLean Delk born 25 Nov 1901
    5. Paul Kennedy Delk born 17 Feb 1904
    6. Allen Freed Delk born 10 Mar 1906

Deaths:
J.V. Delk died 30 Oct 1944
Emma Jane Thompson Delk died 16 Jan 1939
Harry Hunter Delk died 20 June 1901
Horace Cannon Delk died 6 Oct 1947
Floyd M. Delk died 8 Feb 1960
Howard P. Delk died 19 Sept 1964

Children of Geney Chelders, who was the colored cook for Newton Cannon Thompson and his wife Elizabeth Green Thompson:
Mary, born 1 June 1851
Daniel, born 26 Dec 1853
Nancy, born 10 Feb 1856
Nathan, born 15 Nov 1859
Malinda, born 28 Feb 1862

John Theophillus Thompson born Dec 7, 1759, died April 10, 1826, married Mary
        Newcom.
Children:
1. Samuel Thompson
2. Richard Thompson
3. Newcom Thompson, born Dec 27, 1792, died Sept 8, 1869

        Ref: Wayne Lents' Records.
        Ref: DAR National No. 18195, Mollie Thompson Davidson
        Ref: DAR Patriot Index, page 676
        Ref: Bedford County, Tennessee Deed Book D, page 442

* * * * * * * * * *

THOMAS THOMPSON

Name: Rank: State Served:
Thomas Thompson   ------   North Carolina
Born 1755 in Orange County, North Carolina, died ___, married 1776 to
Margaret ____. Came to Bedford County, Tennessee in 1806. Buried in Crowell
Chapel area, maybe buried in the Crowell Chapel Cemetery., no marker.

        From the tombstone of son John Thompson: (Crowell Chapel Cemetery)
He lived in Orange County, North Carolina. Moved to land on Cumberland River
in 1784, on to Duck River in 1806.
        He married about 1776 to Margaret ____.
Children:
John, born March 16, 1777 Orange County, North Carolina, died October 5, 1857
        in Bedford County, Tennessee, married Mary ____. Both are buried at
        Crowell Chapel Cemetery, both have markers.

No GSA Report in Washington, D.C.

No proof of Thomas Thompson being a Soldier, could have been a Patriot.

        Ref: Cemetery Records of Bedford County, Tennessee by Marsh

* * * * * * * * * *

WILLIAM TIPPER

Name: Rank: State Served:
William Tipper   PVT   North Carolina
Born 1759, died February 4, 1834 Bedford County, Tennessee

GSA: William Tipper, S.39109
Claim No. 19.015: West Tennessee, William Tipper of Bedford County in the State
of Tennessee, who was a Private in the Company commanded by Captain Dixon
of the Regiment commanded by Colonel Dixon in the North Carolina Line for the
term of one year.
        Inscribed on the Roll of West Tennessee at the rate of 8 dollars per
month, to commence on the 3 of June 1823.
        Certificate of Pension issued the 7 July 1823 and sent to S.R. Rucker,
Esq., Murfreesboro, Tennessee.
Arrears to the 4th of
Semi-anl allowance ending 4 Sept 1823 $24.50
                                                      $24.50

March 1, 1823   Revolutionary Claim
                                                      Acts March 18, 1818
                                                      and May 1, 1820

File No. 39109
        Revy. Invalid, William Tipper, Private, Revolutionary War
        Act: 18th March 1818
        Index: Vol 3   page 511
Copy of a letter from Secretary of North Carolina to L.R.R. concerning William
Tipper and Ransom Pruits.
Raleigh, 5th of April 1822.

Your letter of the 15th Ult., was received this morning states that you had lately received a letter from the War Department informing you that the Declaration of Ransom Pruits and William Tipper, _____ transmitted by you for the purpose of obtaining pensions had been forwarded to my office first since heard from, if this be a fact, I do not know how relief is to be obtained for _____ from my list of certificates given in such cases that a regular list of them that a Certificate in the case of William Tipper was made and forwarded more than a year ago, Ransom Pruits declarations _____ Gens. Sec: At this office a Certificate _____ issued for Joshua Pruits, _____ _____ S.R. Rucker, Esq.

No. 17.727: William Tipper - Declaration - Admitted on Roll 1 year.
District West Tennessee]
Bedford County Court] Jue Term, 1823

On this third day of June 1823, personally appeared in open Court in the Circuit Court of the County of Bedford, before Robert Mack, Esquire, one of the Circuit Judges of the State of Tennessee, the same being a Court of Record, William Tipper, aged sixty four years and resident in said County of Bedford, who being first duly sworn according to law, doth on his oath make the following declaration in order to obtain the benefit made by the Act of Congress of the 18th of March 1818 and of the 1st of May 1820.

That he the said William Tipper, enlisted for the term of twelve months in the year 1777 in the State of North Carolina in the Company commanded by Captain Dixon in the Regiment commanded by Colonel Dixon in the line of the North Carolina on the Continental Establishment, that he continued to serve in said Corps until the expiration of twelve months from his enlistment, when he was discharged at Salisburg in North Carolina, that he was in the Battle of the Eutaws, and that he has no other evidence now in his power of his said services, except his own oath, he having long ago lost his discharge. In persuance of the Act of the first of May 1820, I do solemnly swear that I was a resident citizen of the United States on the 18th day of March 1818 and that I have not since that time, by gift sale or in any manner dispose of my property or any part thereof, with intent thereby to diminish it as to bring myself within the provision of the Act of Congress entitled, "An Act to provide for certain persons engaged in the Land and Naval service of the United States in the Revolutionary War, passed on the 18th day of March 1818 and that I have not nor has any person in trust for me any property, securities or debts whatever, due me. And said William Tipper, further states that he is by occupation a farmer, but that on account of his age, his total business, deafness and numerous other infirmities, he cannot procure necessary assistance, but is compelled to look to the bounty of his government for a support. He is now living with his son, Kenchen Tipper, aged 35 years, who has a family and is a poor man, his wife having died since making his former declaration which was made in the County Court of Bedford on the 3rd day of January 1821, which declaration was sent on to the War Department and has never been returned.
Sworn to and delcared on in open Court this 3rd June 1823
Dan'l McKisick, Clk.   William (X) Tipper

State of Tennessee]
Bedford County   ]
I, Daniel McKisick, Clerk of the Circuit Court of Bedford County, do hereby certify, that the foregoing declaration of William Tipper is truly copied from the records of said Court. In testimony whereof I have hereunto set my hand and affixed my private seal, there being no Seal of Office, at office. This 10th day of June A.D., 1823, and _____ _____ the 47th.
Dan'l McKisick, Clk.

William Tipper, North Carolina, Private, Dixon's Company, North Carolina Regiment. Revolutionary War, appears in a Book, copied from Rolls of the Organization named above.
Date of enlistment or appointment: 12 May 1781
Terms: 12 months
Casualities: Left Service 25 May 1782
Recorded: Vol 6   page 57
        Ref: GSA Report, Washington, D.C. * * * * * * * * *

JOHN TOWSON

Name: Rank: State Served:
John Towson   -----   ---------------
Born ____, died after 1834

No GSA Report in Washington, D.C.

        Ref: 1834 P.L.W. List

* * * * * * * * * *

DAVID TUCKER

Name: Rank: State Served:
David Tucker   PVT   North Carolina
Born 1754 in Halifax County, North Carolina, died 3 January 1836 in Bedford County, Tennessee, married Sylvania ______ in 1774.

GSA: David Tucker, W.6.318, wife Sylvania, North Carolina
Claim No. 2979: West Tennessee, David Tucker of Bedford County in the State of Tennessee, who was a Private of Trust in the Company commanded by Captain Williams of the Regiment commanded by Colonel Dodd in the North Carolina Line for 13 months, Private of Infantry and Cavalry, 1777.

      Inscribed on the Roll of West Tennessee at the rate of 68 dollars, 33 cents per annum to commence on the 4th day of March 1831.

      Certificate of Pension issued 10th day of December 1832 and sent to Thomas C. Whiteside, Shelbyville, Tennessee.

Arrears to 4th Sept 1832 $102.49
Semi-anl allowance ending 4 Mar 1833 $ 34.17
                                  $136.66

Recorded by Nathan Rice, Clerk   Revolutionary Claim
Book D   Vol 9   page 161   Act June 7, 1832

Letter to H. Yoakum & 3 Auditor, 5 Dec 1838
Paid at the Treasury under the Act of the 6th April 1836
From 4 Sept 1835 to the 6th Jany 1836 the day of his death
Agt. notified 3rd Jany 1838

State of Tennessee]
Bedford County   ]   Court of Pleas and Quarter Sessions, August Term, 1832

      On this 10th day of August 1832, personally appeared in open Court before the Justices of said Court now sitting, David Tucker, a resident of Bedford County, State of Tennessee, aged seventy eight years of age, who being first duly sworn according to law doth on his oath make the following declaration in order to obtain the benefit of an Act of Congress passes the 7th June 1832 for the relief of Revolutionary Soldiers.

      He entered the service of the United States under the following named Officers and other subordinate Officers, whose names he cannot now recollect and served as herein stated.

      He volunteered as a Private Soldier for six months in the service of the United States, shortly after the Declaration of Independence on the 4th of July 1776, probably a year or so after this event. But the precise date he cannot recollect, under Captain Thomas Alston who raised a Company in the State of North Carolina in the County then called Bute, in which this applicant then and at the commencement of the war, lived. This County was afterwards divided into two counties called Franklin and Warren. Alston's Company went to Norfolk to fight the British but when it arrived there, they had left the place. The Company was then called to Wilmington by General Parsons as well as he recollects under the expectation that they would meet the enemy there, but they did not at this place. Alston's Company remained until the six months for which this applicant had volunteered expired. He was then verbally discharged by Captain Alston and went home where he remained five or six months when he again entered the service in the Militia of North Carolina in Colonel Thomas Rutledge's Regiment. In this Regiment, Frederick Wells was the Captain of the Company to which he belonged. He served under them believed five or six weeks

232

during which time this Regiment was stationed within one mile of Wilmington, Hanover County. Captain Outlaw with another Company belonging to a different Regiment was also stationed there. At the end of the five or six weeks above mentioned, he was drafted out of Well's Company for three months to march to North East River, ten or twelve miles from Wilmington to prevent the British from crossing it as a border guard. Where after remaining some time, they were met by the enemy and occassionally they shot at each other across the river. General Kennon and Captain Hardy Holmes, with their forces then retreated back to a place called Rock Fish, where they remained until the time for which they were drafted expired. During this period, three months, he was under the command of General Kennon, who was the Commander of the Drafted Regiment and in Captain Holmes' Company. As soon as he was discharged at the expiration of this term of service, he joined a Light Horse Company as a volunteer for three months, under the command of Colonel David Dodd and Captain William Williams, about this time the Tories were very troublesome in North Carolina and the above named Company to which he belonged was principally engaged in scouting in the Counties of Sampson and Duplin. They had several skirmishes with the Tories, one of which was at a place called Goshen. He states that as soon as this term of service expired, he was again drafted for three months in a Light Horse Company under the command of Colonel James Bloodwith or Bloodith and Captain Robert Merritt during which time they were engaged in scouting and endeavoring to subdue the Tories in the two last mentioned Counties and sometimes in New Hanover County but he does not recollect any particular skirmish with them.

Shortly after this three months expired, he hired a substitute by the name of Beasly to serve nine months for which he was drafted to go to Georgia. Said Beasly went there in his stead and served under the command of General Moultrie. After this term expired, he was again drafted for the same period of time and for the same service and hired another substitute whose name he does not remember. But during the eighteen months comprising these two tours, he was himself at home engaged occassionally in scouting but not in any organized Company nor for more than a few days at a time.

Soon after the expiration of the last nine months drafting for which he hired a substitute. He volunteered in a Light Horse Company under the command of Colonel Bloodwith and Captain Merrit, above mentioned for a term of three months during which they were engaged in scouting and persuing the Tories in the Counties of Duplin, Sampson and New Hanover. Shortly before this term of service expired, he was shot with a musket ball in the right thigh by the Tories in a skirmish which his Company had with him. The ball passed through his thigh and cut one of the leaders, before he recovered from the wound the Battle of Yorktown and the surrender of Cornwallis took place. This was but a short time before he recovered from his wound.

He stated that he was acquainted with Major Daniel Williams of the North Carolina Regular or Continental Line. He received no written discharge at the end of any term of his services. He has no documentary evidence of his service nor does he know of any person now living by whom he can prove it. This applicant states that he was born in Halifax County, North Carolina but the year of his birth he cannot recollect. He never could write and has no record of his age. But to the best of his recollection, he was between 21 and 22 years of age when he first entered the service as a volunteer, about thirty years ago or more. He remembers that his father told him what his age was but he does not recollect what he said it was.

This applicant lived as he has stated at the time he entered the service of his Country in Bute County, North Carolina, in that part of it was called Warren. At the close of the war, he lived in Duplin County where he continued to reside until he removed to Rutherford County, Tennessee about twenty years ago. About ten years ago, he removed to Bedford County, where he now resides. At the expiration of each term of service, he was generally discharged by his Captain.

He hereby relinguishes every claim whatever to a pension or annuity except the present and declares that his name is not on the Pension Roll of the Agency of any State. He was finally discharged shortly after he received the

wound above mentioned.
Sworn to and subscribed the day and year aforesaid

David (X) Tucker

We, Nathan Nichols, a Clergyman, residing in the County of Bedford and State of Tennessee and Jesse Scott and Jeremiah Dial and John H. Dean, residing in the same, hereby certify that we are well acquainted with David Tucker, who has sworn to and subscribed to the above declaration. That we believe him to be seventy eight years of age or there abouts. That he is reputed and believed in the neighborhood where he resides to have been a Soldier of the Revolution and we concur in that opinion. Sworn and subscribed the day and year aforesaid.
Sworn to in open Court 10th August 1832
Jas. McKisick, Clerk

Jeremiah Dial
Nathan (X) Nichols
Jesse Scott
John H. Dean

State of Tennessee]
Rutherford County]
Before me, George A. Sublett, an Acting Justice of the Peace and one of the Justices of the County Court in and for the County of Rutherford aforesaid, personally appeared, Abel Davis, aged 71 years and after being first duly sworn, deposeth and saith that he first became acquainted with David Tucker, the identical individual named in the annexed Pension Certificate, about the year 1774, that he was known said Tucker ever since he knew anybody. That deponent and said Tucker were living in Halifax County, North Carolina, that deponent did not himself see said Tucker married to Sylvania Tucker, his present widow, that said Tucker was about twelve years older than deponent, and moved into a place called Duplin sometime before his marriage. This deponent has long known the oldest son of said David Tucker and his wife Sylvania, and has understood said Elijah Tucker, him to be about sixty two years of age. Said David Tucker died a year or two since in this County, since which time his widow, the said Sylvania, who is very old, has never married. From tradition and the age of their oldest child, this deponent would suppose they were married about sixty three years ago, and further this deponent saith not.
Subscribed and sworn to before me, January 30th 1838.
Geo. A. Sublett (J.P.)
Justice of the Peace.

Abel Davis

State of Tennessee]
Rutherford County]
Before me, George A. Sublett, an Acting Justice of the Peace in and for the County aforesaid, personally appeared, Mathew Tucker, aged about fifty five years, who being first duly sworn deposeth and saith that from an Old Record, which is now lost, Elijah Tucker, the eldest son of David and Sylvania Tucker, will on the second day of June next be sisty two years of age, that is, the copy now in the possession of the family, taken from the Old Record, says "Family Records of David Tucker and Sylvania Tucker, his wife, Elijah Tucker was born 2nd day of June 1776." This deponent has always understood that said David and Sylvania were married at the house of one Hicks in Duplin County, North Carolina, by Thomas Hicks, a Justice of the Peace, sometime in the yearof our Lord, 1775. This deponent never saw or heard of any record of said marriage. He has understood that said Hicks was a man of some years at the time of their marriage and deponent believes that said Hicks has long since died. The copy of the record of ages now in the possession of the family is about twelve years old. The Old Original Record was kept in a Bible which deponent has understood was as old or older than the said Elijah. At least it was in existance from the time of his first recollection up to the family's removal from North Carolina some twenty years since, and further this deponent saith not.
Subscribed and sworn to before me, January 30, 1838.
Geo. A. Sublett (Seal)
Justice of the Peace.

Matthew Tucker

Family Account of David Tucker

1. Elijah Tucker was born June the 2nd 1776

2. Nancy Tucker was born March the 9th 1780
3. Matthew Tucker was born Aprile the 14th 1783
4. Jacob Tucker was born November the 20th 1785
5. Elizabeth Tucker was born May the 25th 1789
6. William Tucker was born October the 22nd 1792
7. David Tucker was born September the 24th 1794
8. Daniel Tucker was born June the 12th 1797
Susannah Tucker was born June the 23rd 1799
10. Lewis Tucker was born February the 15th 1802

Calvin Tucker was born May the 3rd 1810
Mary Ann Tucker was born October the 22nd 1813
       Wrote by John W. Sugg.

John Newton Tucker was born August 21 day 1824

Claim No. 2292: West Tennessee, Sylvania Tucker, widow of David Tucker, deceased, who died on the 6 January 1836 (should be 1838), of Rutherford in the State of Tennessee, who was a Private in the Company by Captain Williams of the Regiment commanded by Colonel Dodd in the North Carolina Line for 13 months, Private Infantry and 6 months, Private Cav.

       Inscribed on the Roll of West Tennessee at the rate of 68 dollars, 33 cents per annum, to commence on the 6th of January 1836 (should be 1838).

       Certificate of Pension issued the 29 day of August 1838 and sent to Thomas C. Whiteside, Shelbyville, Tennessee.

Arrears to the 4th of March 1838	$144.50
Semi-anl allowance ending 4 Sept 1838	$ 34.16
	$178.66

Recorded by D.D. Addison, Clerk   Revolutionary Claim
Book A   Vol 2   page 182   Act July 4, 1836
       Section the 3d.

Wht'd. - Oct 9th, 1838.

State of Tennessee]
Rutherford County]
       On this thirtieth day of January in the year of our Lord, one thousand eight hndred and thirty eight, personally appeared before Richard Phillips, a Justice of the Peace, and one of the Justices of the County Court of Rutherford County aforesaid, Sylvania Tucker, a resident of the County of Rutherford and State of Tennessee, aged eighty one years, who being first duly sworn according to law, doth on her oath make the following declaration, in order to obtain the benefit of the provision made by the Act of Congress passed July 4th 1836. That she is the widow of David Tucker, who was a Private in the Revolutionary War and served as by him, stated in a declaration made by him in order to obtain the benefit of the provision of an Act of Congress passed the 7th day of June 1832, entitled, "An Act Supplementory to the Act for the relief of certain surviving Officers and Soldiers of the Revolution," which said declaration she believes is now on file in the Pension Office at Washington City. That the original Pension Certificate drawn in pursuance of said declaration is herewith filed and has been in her possession ever since the death of her said husband.

       She further declares that she was married to the said David Tucker on the __ day of August in the year of our Lord one thousand seven hundred and seventy five. That her husband, the aforesaid David Tucker died on the sixth day of January in the year of our Lord, eighteen hundred and thirty six and that she has remained a widow ever since that period, as will more fully appear by proof hereto annexed. That she does not know of any person living by whom she can prove her actual marriage. That Thomas Hicks, a Justice of the Peace who performed the ceremony, was aged at the time. That she knows of no record, by which she can prove the exact time. The record of the age of her oldest son is the best record evidence she knows of. She cannot herself recollect the exact day of her marriage.
Subscribed and sworn to before me the date above written and I do further certify that said deponent is quite too infirm to attend a Court of Justice.
Richard Phillips (Seal)   Sylvania (X) Tucker
Justice of the Peace.

I, Richard Phillips. Justice as above stated, do certify that said Sylvania Tucker is a respectable woman and worthy of credit.

Jan 30, 1838
Richard Phillips (Seal)
Justice of the Peace

Red: GSA Report, Washington, D.C.
1835 Bedford County, Tennessee Pension List.

* * * * * * * * * *

SAMUEL A. TURRENTINE

Name:	Rank:	State Served:
Samuel A. Turrentine	PVT	North Carolina

Born ca 1760 in Orange County, North Carolina, died November 10, 1824 Shelbyville, Tennessee, married December 7, 1789 in Orange County, North Carolina to Sarah Wilson who was born ca 1760 and died September 6, 1835 in Bedford County, Tennessee.

No GSA Report in Washington, D.C.

Service: Private and Officer. Resided in Orange County, North Carolina.
Children:
1. Alexander
2. James, born September 27, 1794, married Sarah Thompson
3. Daniel, married Annie Thompson
4. Archaelas, born December 18, 1796, married Margaret Smith
5. Wilson, married Elvira Harris
6. Nannie, married David Thompson
7. Elizabeth, married James Thompson

> Ref: Texas Society DAR Roster Revolutionary Ancestors, Vol IV, pg 2128.

* * * * * * * * * *

JOSEPH WALKER

Name:	Rank:	State Served:
Joseph Walker	Captain	North Carolina

Born August 29, 1742 in North Carolina, died October __, 1814, married October 1777 to Mary _____ who was born March 27, 1745, died February 7, 1837. (Family says they are buried in family plot at New Hope Baptist Church Cemetery, Fairfield, Bedford County, Tennessee) No grave markers to be found.

GSA: Military Record
Joseph Walker's Company 7, Regiment North Carolina.
Appears on an abstract: (Copy, certified abstract, in possession of the State of North Carolina.
Abstract of the Muster Roll of the North Carolina Line of the Army of the United States in the Revolutionary War showing the names, alphabetically, rank, dates of Commissions and enlistments, periods of service and occurrences, of such Officers as served to the end of the war, or were reduced in the arrangement of the Army under the Resolves of Congress of the 3rd and 21st Oct 1780, and such non-commissioned Officers, musicians and Privates who enlisted for the war and continued during the same, so far as the same can be ascertained by said Rolls,

Revolutionary War
Dated: (not dated)

Joseph Walker, Captain, Walker's Company, 7th North Carolina Regiment. Revolutionary War.
Appears on a Book (Office of Army Accounts), copied from Rolls of the Organization named above.
Date of enlistment or appointment: 28 Nov 1776
Omitted Jany. '78   Vol. 6, page 76.

Children of Joseph Walker:
1. Nathaniel, born March 24, 1784, married 1806 to Mary Orrick

Early papers on this man give place of death as Wake County, North Carolina. Later paper turned in to this project gave the place of death as Bedford County, Tennessee.

> Ref: Military Record, Washington, D.C.
> Ref: DAR Patriot Index
> Ref: Colonial Records of North Carolina:
> Vol 10, page 546, 944 and 949
> Vol 11, page 595 and 623.

* * * * * * * * * *

MATTHEW WALLIS

Name:	Rank:	State Served:
Matthew Wallis	PVT	North Carolina

Born March 1, 1762 in Pennsylvania, died February 6, 1836, married Mildred _____.

GSA: Matthew Wallis, W.1519, wife Mildred. Service in North Carolina. Born in Pennsylvania.

Claim No. 7235: West Tennessee, Matthew Wallis of Bedford County in the State of West Tennessee, who was a Sergeant and Private in the Company commanded by Captain Alexander of the Regiment commanded by Colonel _____ in the North Carolina Line for 1 year, Private and 10 months, Sergeant.

Inscribed on the Roll of West tennessee at the rate of 90 dollars, ___ cents per annum to commence on the 4th day of March 1831.

Certificate of Pension issued 18 day of March 1835 and sent to John Bruce, Shelbyville, Tennessee.

Arrears to 4th of March 1833	$180.00
Semi-anl allowance ending 4 Sept	$ 45.00
	$225.00

Recorded by Daniel Boyd, Clerk	Revolutionary Claim
Book E Vol 7 page 101	Act June 7, 1832

Dead:
Paid at the Treasury under the Act of the 6 April 1838 from 4 Sept 1836 to 6 Feby 1837 the day of his death. Agent notified 20 Oct 1845. Paid as above from 4 March to 4 Sept 1836. Agt. notified 27 Nov 1840.

Declaration:
In order to obtain the benefit of the Act of Congress passed June 7, 1832.
State of Tennessee]
Bedford County   ]
On this 12 day of November 1832, personally appeared in open Court before the Worshipful James Brittain, John L. Neill, Samuel Phillips and other Esquires, Justices of the Peace, appointed to hold the Court of Pleas and Quarter Sessions of Bedford County in the State aforesaid, now sitting, Mathew Wallis, a resident of the County and State aforesaid, aged seventy years and eight months and eleven days, who being first sworn according to law, doth on his oath make the following declaration in order to obtain the benefit of the Act of Congress passed June 7, 1832.
That he entered the service of the United States under the following named Officers and served as herein stated.
That in the month of April 1779, as well as he now recollects, he entered the service of the United States as a volunteer and went into Captain William Alexander's Company. That he does not at this time recollect his Colonel's name but his General was Davidson in the Militia in the North Carolina Line. That he joined General Davidson's Army in Mecklenburg County in the State of North Carolina and marched through different parts of Mecklenburg County against the Tories.
That he served about three months during the year 1779. That

sometime in the Summer of 1779, he does not now recollect the month, he was verbally discharged by General Davidson. That during the tour, aforesaid, he was acquainted with General Davidson and Captain William Alexander and was at that time acquainted with some other Officers but the great lapse of time has erased the recollection of their names from his memory. And afterwards, about the first of January 1780, he entered the service again as a volunteer and went into Captain Samuel Flanagin's as well as he now recollects, that during the seven months, aforesaid, he marched through different parts of South Carolina. Had several skirmishes with the Tories, and some time in the Summer of 1780, he does not recollect what month, he was in the Battle of Hanging Rock in South Carolina under General Sumpter. In which battle, Captain Reace was killed, in which battle, it was said there was about three hundred of the Americans killed and the Americans retreated in order and the British kept their ground. Shortly after the Battle of the Hanging Rock, he was verbally discharged by Captain Flanagin. That during the tour, last aforesaid, he was acquainted with General Sumpter, Major Davie and Captain Flanagin, that his second tour was seven months, at the expiration of that time, he went to a place called the Waxhaw Meeting House and there waited on some of the Americans who had been badly wounded in Colonel Beauford's Defeat. That he waited on said wounded men about three weeks, but was not in any Captain's Company at that time. At the expiration of the three weeks aforesaid, he went home to Mecklenburg and about two months afterwards, he went into service again as a volunteer into Captain William Alxander's Company of Militia in the North Carolina Line. That he served under Captain Alexander about two months. That during the two months aforesaid, he marched through different parts of Mecklenburg County in North Carolina, serving against the British and Tories and at the expiration of the two months, aforesaid , he was verbally discharged by Captain Alexander.

That during the two months aforesaid, he was acquainted with Major James White and Captain William Alexander and afterwards in April 1791, he went into service again as a volunteer with Captain William Alexander's Company, again of Militia in the North Carolina Line. That Waid Hampton was his Colonel. Sumpter his General. That he served three months in Captain Alexander's Company, at the end of which time, Captain Alexander went home and then he was attached to Captain Jiles (Giles)'s Company of Militia in the North Carolina Line and served about seven months in Captain Jiles (Giles)'s Company. That at the expiration of the seven months aforesaid, he was verbally discharged by Captain Jiles (Giles). That he joined Captain Alexander's Company in April 1781 and continued in service until February 1782. Which was about ten months during all which time he served as an orderly Sergeant. That during the ten months aforesaid, he was in several small battles against the British and on the eight day of September 1781, he was in that celebrated Battle of the Eutaw Springs in which it is said that five hundred and fifty of the Americans were killed and wounded, and almost seven hundred of the British killed and wounded, in which battle, Major Rutherford was killed, that he was shot dead not more than one rod from this declarent. And Adjutant Lock was killed. That during the ten months last aforesaid, he was acquainted with General Sumpter, General Greene, Major Rutherford, Colonels Henry, Hampton, Waid Hampton, and Richard Hampton and Colonel Hill, Colonel Pope, Major Beauford, Captain Jiles (Giles), Captain Moore, and Captain Barnett. That he served in all one year ten months and three weeks. That he has no documentary evidence nor he knows of no person by whom he can prove any of his services except, as to the last ten months that he served. That as to that, he can prove it by Hugh King of Maury County and he lives about thirty miles from this County and is so old and infirm that it would be very inconvenient for him to come to this Court. But declarent has had his affidavit taken before Thomas Murdock, Esq., who is a Justice of the Peace of Bedford County. He hereby relinguishes every claim whatever to a pension or annuity except the present and declares that this name is not on the Pension Roll of the agency of any State or Territory in the United States.
Sworn to and subscribed the day and year aforesaid.
Jas. McKisick, Clerk   Matthew Wallis

Questions to be asked Matthew Wallis:

Q. 1st: Where and in what year were you born?

A. I was born, I do not recollect in what County in the State of Pennsylvania on the first of March 1762.

Q. 2nd: Have you any record of your age and if so where is it?

A. I believe I have no record of my age at this time, but I saw it about three years ago in my father's Family Bible in Mecklenburg County, North Carolina.

Q. 3rd: Where were you living when called into service? Where have you lived since the Revolutionary War and where do you now live?

A. When called into service, I lived in Mecklenburg County, State of North Carolina, I continued to live there for about twenty five years after the end of the Revolutionary War, then removed to Maury County in the State of Tennessee, lived there eight years, then removed to Bedford County in the State last aforesaid, where I now live.

Q. 4th: How were you called into service? Were you drafted? Did you volunteer or were you a substitute, for whom?

A. I always volunteered and never went into service in any other way.

Q. 5th: State the names of some of the Regular Officers who were with the troops where you served, such Continental and Militia Regiments as you can recollect and the general circumstances of your service.

A. I was acquainted with Generals Davidson, Sumpter, Greene, Colonels Waid Hampton, Henry Hampton, Richard Hampton, Pope, Hill, Majors Beauford, Rutherford, and with Captains Jiles (Giles), Barnet, Moore, Reace and the general circumstances of my services are above stated.

Q. 6th: Did you ever receive a discharge from the service and if so by whom was it given and what has become of it?

A I never received any written discharge. I was always discharged verbally.

Q. 7th: State the names of persons to whom you are known in your present neighborhood and who can testify as to your character for veracity and their belief of your service as a Soldier of the Revolution.

A. Thomas Murdock, Esquire, Colonel Aaron Boyd, James Brittain, Esq., Doctor William Cheatam Isham, Colonels James Gammel, James Stephens and Reuben Rennals and Joseph Rosson, Esquires and Ezekiel Cherry, Esquire.

Sworn to and subscribed the day and year aforesaid   Matthew Wallis

We, Joseph Rosson, Ezekiel Cherry, both residing in Bedford County in the State of tennessee, hereby certify that we are well acquainted with Mathew Wallis who has subscribed and sworn to the above declaration, that we believe him to be seventy years, eight months and eleven days of age. That he is reputed and believed in the neighborhood where he resides to have been a Soldier of the Revolution and that we concur in that opinion.

Sworn to and subscribed the day and year aforesaid.

Jas. McKisick, Clerk

Joseph Rosson
Ezek'l Cherry

And the said Court do hereby declare their opinion after the investigation of the matter and after putting the interrogatories prescribed by the War Department.

Claim No. 6557: Tennessee, Mildred Wallis, widow of Matthew Wallis (N.C.), who was a Pensioner under the Act of June 1832 and who died on the 6th February 1837, of Marshall County in the State of Tennessee who was Serg. Dragoons in the Company commanded by Captain Giles of the Regiment commanded by Colonel Hampton in the North Carolina Line for 10 months.

Inscribed on the Roll of Nashville, at the rate of 75 dollars, __ cents per annum to commence on the 6th February 1837.

Certificate of Pension issued 22nd day of February 1842 and sent to R.A. Glenn, Hurt's Cross Roads, Tennessee.

Arrears to the 4th of March 1841 $305.41

Recorded by D. Brown, Clerk   Act July 7, 1838
Book A   Vol 2   page 209

Agent notified by letter: 8 April 1842 - R.A. Glenn.

State of Tennessee]
Marshall County   ]
          Personally appeared, Mildred Ragsdale, aged 37 years past, before me, A. Laird, and after being duly sworn upon the Holy Evangelist of Almighty God, deposith and saith that in the year of eighteen hundred and twenty one, sometime in the first part of the year, she was present and saw Mathew Wallis give to his son, Mathew S. Wallis, his Family Bible and heard the said Mathew Wallis say at that time that he the said Mathew Wallis had written a true copy of the age of his children, correctly drawn from the Bible that he would retain said copy in case said Bible should get destroyed. The said Mathew S. Wallis was then preparing to move to the State of Alabama which he did shortly afterwards and that the said Mathew S. Wallis is since dead and his wife also and their children bound out and there can't be any account had of the aforesaid Bible that was giving to them by the said Mathew Wallis. She further deposeth and saith that she was well acquainted with the hand writing of the identical Mathew Wallis, deceased, and do hereby fully believes it to be the hand of the identical Mathew Wallis that wrote that identical copy of ages that has been transmitted to the War Department. That she examined the copy after it and been joined and do believe it to be in the hand writing of the said Mathew Wallis and the same copy before named and said deponent further states that she is unabled to know that she is correct in the date that she gives by the time of her marriage that took place in the year 1822.
Sworn to and subscribed before me this 31st day of July 1841.
A. Laird, J.P.   Mildred Ragsdale
for the County.

I do hereby certify that I have been well acquainted with Mildred Ragsdale, the above deponent, she is a woman of respect and credibility and that she cannot attend the Court of Records for said County by reason of being afflicted with the consumption. Given under my hand and seal this 31st day of July 1841.
                                        A. Laird, J.P. (Seal)
                                        for said County.

State of Tennessee]
Marshall County   ]
          I, Martin W. Oakley, Clerk of the COunty Court of said Marshall County, hereby certify that A. Laird is a Justice of the Peace, as above and that the foregoing signatures proporting to be his are genuine. In testimony whereof I have hereunto set my hand and office set my Seal of Office. This 4th day of August 1841.
                                        Martin W. Oakley, Clerk
                                        of said County Court.
                                        by his Deputy,
                                        John Elliott.

Bible Record of Mathew Wallis

Children:
Ezekiel Wallis, born 9th February 1786
Prudence Wallis, born 5th May 1787
Sarah Wallis, born 30th January 1789
Margret Wallis, born 1st May 1791
William Wallis, born 18th June 1796
Matthew S. Wallis, born 25 day January 1799
Mildred Wallis, 25 March 1801

State of Tennessee]
Marshall County   ]
District No. 9   ]
          On this the 2nd day of August 1839, personally appeared before the subscribers, Andrew Laird and Joseph H. Brittain, two acting Justices of the said County, Mildred Wallis, a resident of said State and County, aged seventy seven years in July past, who being sworn according to law, doth on her oath make the following declaration in order to obtain the benefit of the provision made by the Act of Congress passed July 7th 1838 entitled, "An Act granting half pay and

pensions to certain widows that she is the widow of Mathew Wallis who was a Private serving in Captain Andrew Alexander's Company who was under Major John Moore and Major Moore under Colonel Wade Hampton in the Brigade of General Thomas Sumpter of South Carolina. She further declares that she was married to the said Mathew Wallis on the 12th day of May 1785, that her husband the aforesaid Mathew Wallis died on the 6th day of February 1837. That she was not married to him prior to his leaving the service but the marriage took place previous to the 1st day of January 1794, viz, At the tome before stated. The said Mathew Wallis' name having been inscribed on the Pension List Roll of the West Tennessee Agency at the rate of $8.00 per month, she further declares that she cannot come precisely at the time the drawing commenced on account of the pension papers being mislaid, she further swears that she cannot procure any evidence now on docket and that she has not any family record by which she can show the births of children and that she has not been since married since the death of her husband the aforesaid Mathew Wallis. The said Mathew Wallis was formerly a resident of Bedford County now Marshall County.

Sworn to and subscribed before us on the 2nd day of August 2839.

Joseph H. Brittain, J.P.   Mildred (X) Wallis
Andrew Laird, J.P.

State of Tennessee]
Marshall County   ]

  We, Joseph H. Brittain and Andrew Laird, Justices of the Peace, for the said County of Marshall, do hereby certify that we are acquainted with Mildred Wallis and believe that she, from her bodily infirmities is not able to attend the Court of Records for said County of Marshall, given under our hands and seals, this the 2nd day of August 1839.

Joseph H. Brittain, J.P. (Seal)
Andrew Laird, J.P. (Seal)

State of Tennessee]
Marshall County   ]

  I, Martin W. Oakley, Clerk of the County Court of said Marshall County, do hereby certify that Joseph H. Brittain and Andrew Laird are Acting Justices of the Peace for said COunty and that the foregoing signatures purporting to be theirs, are genuine, and that full faith and credit are due all theirs.

Official Seal as such.

  In testimony whereof I have hereunto set my hand and affixed my Seal of Office in Lewisburg, this 9th day of August, A.D., 1839.

Martin W. Oakley, Clerk

  Ref: GSA Report, Washington, D.C.

* * * * * * * * * *

JACOB WILHOIT

Name: Rank: State Served:
Jacob Wilhoit   Patriot   North Carolina

Born December 22, 1751 Culpepper County, Virginia, died September 30, 1821 in Bedford County, Tennessee, married Amelia (Milly) Holt who was born April 7, 1762, died September 30, 1822 in Bedford COunty, Tennessee. Both are buried with marked graves in the Whitesell-Wilhoite Cemetery, Bedford County, Tennessee.

Tombstones:

    Jacob Wilhoite   Milly Wilhoite
    Born Dec 22, 1751 Born Apr 7, 1762
    Died Sep 30, 1821 Died Sep 30, 1822

Jacob Wilhoit came from Orange County, North Carolina and settled in 1812 on 605 acres of land located about 2½ miles west of Shelbyville on Sims Road, where he constructed a mill on Duck River called Wilhoite's or German's Mill. He, his wife Milly and some of their children are buried in the Family Graveyard on the hill back of where the old house stood.

  While we find no evidence that Jacob Wilhoit was a Soldier, the compilers did find vouchers in the Archives in Raleigh, North Carolina, showing that he supplied grain to the American Cause during the war while living in Orange County, North Carolina.

Jacob Wilhoit's wife Amelia (Milly) Holt was daughter of John and Mary (____) Holt.

Children of Jacob and Milly Wilhoit:
1. Jacob Wilhoit, Jr., born 1781 North Carolina, married December 2, 1803 in Orange County, North Carolina to Polly Powell.
2. Milly Wilhoit, born November 20, 1782 in North Carolina, died March 22, 1865, married October 12, 1803 to John Whitsell who was born November 30, 1777, died April 5, 1842 and is buried in the Whitesell-Wilhoite Cemetery in Bedford County, Tennessee. Milly Whitesell has no marker.
3. Lewis Wilhoit, born 1786(3) in North Carolina, married Frances _____, lived on Goose Creek, Bedford County, Tennessee.
4. Fannie Wilhoit, born 1784, married _____ Barnett.
5. Susan Wilhoit, married _____ Craig.
6. Hannah Wilhoit, married _____ Moore.
7. Katharine Wilhoite, born October 16, 1791, died 1851, married Flower Swift.
8. Mary Wilhoit, born 1784, married _____ Kimmons.
9. John Wilhoit, married Lizzie T. Bullock of Williamson County, Tennessee.
10. Jennie Wilhoit, married _____ Holt.
11. Cynthia Wilhoit, married Thomas Murdock.
12. Margaret Wilhoit.
13. Pierce Wilhoit]
14. Young Wilhoit] Some sources say they were also sons of Jacob Wilhoit.

Jacob Wilhoit was son of Matthias Wilhoit, born 1723 Spotsylvania County, Virginia, married 1st 1744 in Orange County, Virginia to Mary Ballenger daughter of Ed. Ballenger, married 2nd in 1774 to Hannah _____', and died 1772.

Children of Matthias Wilhoit:
1. John, born 1745 Orange County, Virginia, died June 1, 183_, married Lucy Stapp.
2. William, married October 28, 1787 to Anna Clare.
3. Tobias, born October 15, 1750 Culpepper County, Virginia, died February 7, 1838, married Mary Shirley who was born April 1, 1755.
4. Jacob, born December 22, 1751 Culpepper County, Virginia, died September 30, 1821 in Bedford County, Tennessee, married 1779 to Amelia Holt who was born April 7, 1762, died September 3, 1821 in Bedford County, Tennessee.
5. Lewis, born 1754, died 1783.
6. Joel, born 1756, married Mary Wilhoit.
7. Caty, married _____ Cook.
8. Jesse, born ca 1760.
9. Elias, born 1762 Culpepper County, Virginia, married Sarah Rebecca Huffman.
10. Absalom.
11. Johnathan, born 1766.

Ref: Vouchers paid for services during the Revolutionary War, Archives, Raleigh, North Carolina.
Ref: The Ridge Runners by Yates, Vol VIII, 1977.
Ref: Cemetery Records of Bedford County, Tennessee by Marsh

* * * * * * * * * *

JOHN WILLIAMS

Name:	Rank:	State Served:
John Williams	PVT	North Carolina

Born 16th April 1762 in Randolph County, North Carolina, died after 1840 in Bedford County, Tennessee.

In 1835, age 72, Private of Cavalry, North Carolina Line.

GSA: John Williams, S.3592, North Carolina.
Claim No. _265: West Tennessee, John Williams of Bedford County in the State of Tennessee who was a Private of Cavalry in the Company commanded by

Captain Fuller of the Regiment commanded by _____ in the North Carolina Line for 6 months from 1781.

Inscribed on the Roll of West Tennessee at the rate of 25 dollars, __ cents per annum to commence on the 4th day of March 1831.

Certificate of Pension issued the 30 day of October 1832 and sent to Samuel Anderson, Shelbyville, Tennessee.

Arrears to the 4th of Sept 1832 $37.50
Semi-anl allowance ending __ Mar 1833 $12.50
                                            $50.00

Recorded by Nathan Rice, Clerk   Revolutionary Claim
Book D   Vol 9   page 163   Act June 7, 1832

Hon. H. Maynard, Feb 7 / 00

State of Tennessee]
Bedford County   ]

August Sessions, 1832 of the Court of Pleas and Quarter Sessions of the County of Bedford and State of Tennessee.

On this 10th day of August 1832, personally appeared before the Court of Pleas and Quarter Sessions for the County of bedford now in session. Being a Court of Record, John Williams, a resident of the COunty and State aforesaid, aged 70 years, who being first duly sworn according to law, doth on his oath make the following declaration in order to obtain the benefit of the provision made by the Act of Congress passed June 7th 1832.

That he was drafted on the __ day of _____ for a tour of three months in Randolph County, North Carolina to serve in the Army of the United States during the Revolutionary War. At the period he was drafted, there was a regulation that drafted men might furnish a horse, join the Light Horse and serve two months in lieu of the thre they were drafted for. He did furnish his own horse and joined a Light Horse Company, commanded by Captain Brittain Fuller who took sick and in a short time went home, when he was commanded by Captain Jacob Williams. He was employed in ranging along the British lines through Rowan and Mecklenburg Counties and on to Charlotte. The Brittish had been to Charlotte but had left that place and went to South Carolina a short time before the American Troops got there. This applicant was in no regular battle or skirmishes. They had some firing at the Tories and thinks killed some few of them.

Applicant was discharged by General Morgan whom he knew at the expiration of the two months as he thinks some five or six days before owing to his taking sick. Some four or five months after he was discharged, the Tories became troublesome and he volunteered his service again and joined a Company commanded by Captain John Knight of Horsemen. He does not recollect whether he volunteered for any definite period but they marched through Randolph, Chatham and Guilford Counties to protect the inhabitants. He also went with a detachment to guard the members of the Assembly to Hillsborough, but he was in one engagement or battle and nothing done except some firing at the Tories during this tour. He thinks his Captain received a wound but while he was with the detachment guarding the Members of Assembly to Hillsborough after being in several upwards of two months, he was verbally discharged by his Captain.

Soon afterwards, other men were drafted from Randolph County to serve a tour of three months, the applicant took the place of James Lathom as a substitute who had been drafted and entered as before in a Company of Light Horse commanded by the said Captain John Knight. They ranged as before through Randolph, Chatham and Guilford Counties, guarding the inhabitants against the Tories. He thinks he was sent again on a detachment to guard the Members of Assembly to Hillsborough. He has a recollection of being twice in that service but cannot be certain in which tour of service he went on that duty after serving two months but he was verbally discharged by his Captain John Knight.

This applicant has lost his discharges given by General Morgan and he has no documentary evidence and he knows of no person whose testimony he can procure who can testify to his service further than the proof contained in this affidavit.

His memory is very frail from age and infirmity and he cannot state either the month, day or year he entered the service or either of the tours of duty he performed. He thinks he did not enter the service until after the Battle of Camden nor can he recollect the day, month or year of either of the times he was discharged but he recollects the war ceased soon after he was discharged the last time. And he served in all the three different tours he has described a little upwards of six months.

He was born in Randolph County, North Carolina on the 16th April 1762 according to the account given by his mother but he has not himself any register of his age, and does not know whether it is now in exexistence. He resided in Randolph County from his birth to the Revolutionary War. He lived in that County during and after the war until October 1795 when he removed to Blount County, East Tennessee, he resided in Blount County about eleven years. He then removed to Bedford County, West Tennessee where he lived about five years, then he removed to Lincoln, an adjoining County, where he lived about ten years after which he removed back to Bedford County, where he has resided ever since.

This applicant knows Colonels Washington and Lee, was with them and under their command during a part of his service. He also recollects there was a Colonel Williamson in service at the time, but he was but thinks he commanded a Regiment of Militia.

This applicant is known to Andrew Reed, Benjamin Cunningham, Robert Hastings, Elijah Williams, Edmund Green and many others in his neighborhood who he believes can testify as to his character for veracity and their belief of his services.

Sworn to and subscribed   John Williams
10th August 1832.

The said John Williams, hereby relinguishes every claim whatever to a pension or annuity except the present and declares that his name is not on the Pension Roll of the Agency of any State whatever.

Sworn to and subscribed   John Williams
this 10th August 1832
Jas. McKisick, Clk.

      Ref: GSA Report, Washington, D.C.
      Ref: 1835 Bedford County, Tennessee Pension List.

* * * * * * * * * *

JOHN WOOD

Name:	Rank:	State Served:
John Wood	PVT	North Carolina

Born December 25, 1751 in Orange County, North Carolina, died after 1834 (1834 P.L.W.). He came to Bedford County in 1814.

1835, John Woods, aged 72, Private, North Carolina

GSA: John Wood, S.1887, Service in North Carolina.

Claim No. 6349: West Tennessee, John Wood of Bedford County in the State of Tennessee who was a Private in the Company commanded by Captain Timmons of the Regiment commanded by _____ in the North Carolina Militia for 8 months and 7 days from 1776.

Inscribed on the Roll of Tennessee at the rate of 27 dollars, 43 cents per annum, to commence on the 4th day of March 1831.

Certificate of Pension issued the 28 day of February 1833 and sent to Hon. Jas. K. Polk.

Arrears to the 4th of Sept 1832	$41.14
Semi-anl allowance ending 4 March 1833	$13.71
	$54.85

Recorded by Henry H. Sylvester, Clerk	Revolutionary Claim
Book D Vol 7 page 163	Act June 7, 1832

Letter to R. Moffat, June 25, 1836
Paid at the Treasury under that Act of April 6th 1836 from 4th March to 4th Sept 1841. Agent notified June 6th, 1842.

Declaration in order to obtain the benefit of the Act of Congress passed 7th June 1832.

On this 15th day of August in the year of our Lord, one thousand eight hundred and thirty two, personally appeared in open Court, before John L. Neill, Samuel Phillips and John B. Armstrong, Esquires, Gentlemen Justices of the Peace, appointed to hold the Court of Pleas and Quarter Sessions of Bedford County in the State of Tennessee, now sitting, JOhn Wood, a resident of the COunty, State aforesaid, (a blind man) aged eighty years, seven months and twenty one days, who being first sworn according to law, doth on his oath make the following declaration, in order to obtain the benefit of the Act of Congress passed the 7th June 1832. That he entered the service of the United States under the following named Officers and served as herein stated, to wit,

That he entered the service of the United States as a volunteer in a Company of Mounted Gunmen commanded by Captain Hugh Timmon (Tinnon), he states he thinks it was the year 1776 in the Fall or Winter. He states it was in Orange County and State of North Carolina, when he first entered the service, and was marched from that County to the neighborhood of the town of Cross Creek, during the whole of this tour of duty, he states the troops he was attached to were principally engaged or employed in guarding against the depredations frequently committed on the citizens living on Deep River, Rocky River, Haw River and Capefear River, he states that on the expedition, Captain Tinnons (Timmons) Company were engaged in several Tory raids but does not recollect of any lives being lost on this side. He further states that he served on occasion a tour of three months service, and then discharged at Hillsborough in the State of North Carolina by Captain Tinnon (Timmon) in writing.

He further states that afterwards, he volunteered again in the same County in Captain Douglass' Company of Mounted Gunmen, and he thinks Colonel William McCalley was their Head Commander. He thinks they were marched very nearly the same route as mentioned in his first tour of duty but had no engagement whatever. He states that on this expedition, he served three months, and was marched back to the town of Hillsborough and discharged again in writing. The discharge was signed by Captain Douglass. He further states that after these two expeditions against the Tories and Outlaws, the Tories became so enraged against him that they threatened his life. He states he sold his land and purchased again in a Whig settlement on Little River near my father. He further states that after that he was ordered out by Captain Thomas Farmer, John Thompson who commanded the Company where he then lived, on Little River, and was attached to Captain Farmer's Company of Guards, who were guarding the forty prisoners then confined in the jail of Orange County and continued with him for the term of two months and was again discharged in writing, signed by Captain Thomas Farmer. He further states that after that when Cornwallis came to Hillsborough, he together with a great many others, joined General Butler and marched on down to Granville Old Court House. He states he was engaged with others in annoying Cornwallis' picket guards frequently. He states that Colonel Fanning of the Tories came to Hillsborough and plundered the town with a band of Tories and took the most of the citizens prisoners and marched them off down to Linley's Mill. He states that the citizens of Orange County, in the neighborhood of Hillsborough, collected together and marched on in order to rescue the prisoners taken at Hillsborough and met with Colonel Butler and Colonel Maybees and on that tour which was only about a week and a small engagement or skirmish with the Tories near Linley's Mill, but was not able to retake our prisoners. Makine in the whole a term of service, of about eight months or there abouts.

He hereby relinguishes all and every claim to a pension or annuity except the present and declares that his name is not on the Pension Roll of any Agency in the United States, and that he has no documentary evidence whatever at this time and that he knows of no person whose testimony he can procure, who can testify as to his service.

Interrogatories by the Couty:

Q. 1st: Where and what year were you born?

A. I was born in Orange County and State of North Carolina on the 25th day of December 1751.

Q. 2nd: Have you any record of your age and if so where is it?
A.   I have a record of my age at home, taken from the record in my
          father's Bible.
Q. 3rd: Where were you living when called into service? Where have you lived
          since the Revolutionary War and where do you now live?
A.   I lived in Orange County of North Carolina when I entered the service
          of the United States and remained in the same County until the close of
          the Revolutionary War, and afterwards I removed to Lawrence County in
          the State of South Carolina, I think in the year 1789 and from that I
          moved to the State of Georgia in 1792 and from that to the State of
          Tennessee in 1809 in Franklin County, I then removed to Bedford
          County, Tennessee in the year 1814, where I have lived ever since.
Q. 4th: How were you called into service? Were you a volunteer? Were you
          drafted or were you a substitute, and if a substitute, for whom?
A.   I was a volunteer during the whole of my service.
Q. 5th: State the names of some of the Regular Officers who were with you, or
          the troops where you served, such Continental and Militia Regiment as
          you can recollect, and the general circumstances of your service.
A.   I understood that Colonel Maybee was a Regular Officer who was with
          us at Linley's Mill, I also recollect Colonel Archibald Lytle, and Captain
          William Lytle. As to any Continental or Militia Regiments, I know of
          none but what I have mentioned in my declaration.
Q. 6th: Did you ever receive a discharge from the service and if so, what has
          become of it?
A.   I received three discharges and I think I lost them while I lived in the
          State of Georgia.
Q. 7th: State the names of some of your neighbors to whom you are known, who
          can testify as to your character for veracity and their belief of your
          service as a Soldier of the Revolution.
A.   The Rev. William Mullens, Thomas McGuire and William Hoozer,
          Esquires.
Sworn to and subscribed this 15th August 1832, in open Court.
Jas. McKisick, Clerk   Jno. (X) Woods

     We, William Mullens, a Clergyman, residing in the County of Bedford
and State of Tennessee, and Thomas McGuire, a resident of the same County and
State, do hereby certify that we are well acquainted with John Wood, who has
subscribed and sworn to the foregoing declaration, in order to obtain the benefit
of the Act of Congress passed 7th June 1832. That we believe him to be eighty
years, seven months and twenty one days old. That he is reputed and believed in
the neighborhood where he resides to have been a Soldier of the Revolutionary
War and that we concur in that opinion.
Sworn to in open Court this 15th day of August 1832.
Jas. McKisick, Clk.   Wm. Mullens
                                                       Thomas (X) McGuire

     An amendment to the declaration of John Woods, (A blind man) made at
August Term of Bedford County Court, 1832. In order to obtain a pension under
the Act of Congress passed 7th June 1832.
The State of Tennessee.
     On this 11th day of December in the year 1832, personally appeared
before me, the undersigned, a Justice of the Peace of Bedford County in the
State of aforesaid, John Woods, who after being duly sworn, deposeth and saith
that by reason of old age and the consequent loss of memory, he cannot state the
precise length of time he served in the War of the Revolution but according to
the best of his recollection, he served not less than the periods below, and in the
following grade (to wit), That he served on the first tour of duty mentioned in his
declaration above alluded to, not less than three months as a Private Soldier in
Captain Hugh Timmons' Company of Mounted Gunmen, on the second tour of
duty, he says he actually served three months in a Company in a Company of
Mounted Gunmen, under the command of Captain Douglass as a Private Soldier
and the third tour, he was ordered out by Captain John Thompson, (he thinks now
perhaps in the nature of a draft) and was placed in a Company of Guards, under
the command of Thomas Farmer, as stated in his declaration above alluded to,

and served as such not less than two months as a drafted soldier. And that the last tour he served, he was not less than one week, making in the whole a term of actual service of eight months and one week for which he claims a pension. And that from the great length of time since the Revolution and the consequent loss of memory, it is impossible for him to state the precise periods of the war when he served, except the first tour of duty in 1776.
Sworn to before me, and subscribed the day and year aforesaid.
Samuel Phillips, J.P.   John (X) Woods

       Ref: GSA Report, Washington, D.C.
       Ref: 1835 Bedford COunty, Tennessee Pension List.

* * * * * * * * * *

ZADOC WOOD

Name: Rank: State Served:
Zadoc (Zada) Wood   PVT   South Carolina
Born March 7, 1766 in Frederick County, Virginia, died after 1840. Possibly buried in the Friendship Cemetery near Wartrace, Bedford County, Tennessee. No tombstone to mark his grave.

GSA: Zadok Wood, S.3612, Service in South Carolina.
Claim No. 1447: West Tennessee, Zadok Wood of Bedford County in the State of West Tennessee who was a Private in the Company commanded by Captain Tensly of the Regiment commanded by Colonel Haynes in the South Carolina Line for 6 months and 21 days.
     Zadok Wood,   Records O K March 21 '04
     Inscribed on the Roll of West Tennessee at the rate of 22 dollars, 33 cents per annum, to commence on the 4th day of March 1831.
     Certificate of Pension issued the 10 day of September 1833 and sent to Charles Ready, Shelbyville.
Arrears to the 4th of September $55.82
Semi-anl allowance ending 4 March $11.16
                                                    $66.98

Recorded by Daniel Boyd, Clerk   Revolutionary Claim
Book E   Vol 7   page 10   Act June 7, 1832.

Declaration:
State of Tennessee]
Bedford County   ] Court of Pleas and Quarter Sessions, May Term 1833
     On this 9th day of May 1833, personally appeared in open Coury before Samuel Phillips, John B. Armstrong and William McGuire, Esquires, Justices of the Court of Pleas and Quarter Sessions of Bedford County and State of Tennessee, now sitting, Zadok Wood, a resident of said County and State, aged sixty seven years and two months, who being first duly sworn according to law, doth on his oath, make the following declaration, in order to obtain the benefit of the Act of Congress passed June the 7th 1832.
     That he entered the service of the United States under the following named Officers, and served as herein stated. He was drafted and entered the Militia of the State of South Carolina, as a Private Soldier, in the early part of the month of February 1782 or 1783, he cannot recollect it was near the close of the Revolutionary War, and he is positive about the month. He belonged to Captain James Tinsley's Company and the Regiment commanded by Colonel James Hayes. He does not remember the names of his other Company and Regiment Officers. He was mustered into service at Hammonds Old Store, in what was then Ninety Six District in the State of South Carolina. The day of the month, he cannot remember. General Pickens was the Commander-in Chief of the Troops to which he belonged.
     Declarent states, he marched under the command of the Officers as aforesaid, against the Cherokee Nation. The troops came to and burned, as well as he can recollect, five or six Indian Villages, at one of which, they came upon a few Indians and fired on them as they fled, two of three of whom, they killed and two or three, they took prisoners. There was no general engagement during the campaign. The whites were fired on one by two Indians from the rocks and

247

cliffs of the mountains, after which they immediately fled, and were not seen afterwards. After marching several days down the western waters, that is, down the waters of the west side of the mountains and scouring the country, burning all the Indian Towns they came to, without waiting any further resistance from them, the troops were wheeled and marched homewards, and after recrossing the mountains and reaching the white settlement, they were verbally discharged by General Pickens. Having been in service two months. It was in the month of April, they were discharged, but the day he does not remember. He is confident however, that the term he served was two months.

In the last of May or first of June following, declarent was called out again to guard Hayes' Station against the Tories. This station was situated on the waters of Little River. On this tour, he belonged to Captain William Mulwee's Company in which John Neal was First Lieutenant. He went out this time, as he did before, as a Private Militiaman. Colonel James Hayes again commanded the Regiment to which he belonged, and he was marched directly to the Fort above named. Colonel Hayes was the highest Officer in command at the Fort. Declarent was in service this time, as near as he can recollect, three weeks. He is certain it was not less than that time, and being then taken sick, he was permitted by Colonel Hayes to go home. The second day after declarent left the Fort, it was taken by the Tories under the command of William Cunningham, commonly called Devil Bill Cunningham, and Colonel Hayes together with fifteen of the men was killed.

In the month of July following, the day not recollected, declarent was again drafted and marched in defence of his country. He was mustered into service in Captain Joseph Goodman's Company at Simmon's Old Mill on Bush River in Ninety Six District. He does not remember his other Company Officers. The highest Officer in command in the detachment of troops to which he belonged, was Major Gordon. He was marched down the country towards Charleston, against the British. He, together with the other troops under Major Goodman, were stationed at Bacon's Bridge on Ashley River, twenty four or twenty five miles above Charleston for the purpose of guarding that Point. General Greene, with the main American Army was at that time, encamped six or seven miles farther down the river, and was the Commander-in-Chief of all the American Troops in that part of the Country. While declarent was stationed at Bacon's Bridge, the British was about leaving the country, and the war drawing near to a close. The Tories began to _____ _____ for quarters in large numbers, and he remembers that General Robert Cunningham and Colonel Thomas Pearson, Tory Officers, came to Major Gordon under a flag, to ask for protection and to get the Major to furnish such of their men as might come in and surrender themselves, with an escort to conduct them to General Greene. Their request was granted, and large number of them came in for several days and nights, who was _____ by the command of Major Gordon, conducted to General Greene's Encampment. Declarent was in no engagement during this campaign and then was no memorable incidents occured except as above stated. He served this tour as a Private Soldier, and after having been in service four months, was verbally discharged by Major Gordon, when he returned home. Al the times declarent served, put together, made six months and three weeks, during which time, he was in active service as a Private Soldier, and for which he claims a pension.

Declarent was born in Frederick County, Virginia, on the 7th of March 1766. He has in his possession a record of his age, which was taken from his father's Family Bible. He lived in Ninety Six District in South Carolina, at all the different periods at which he entered into service. He has already stated, he entered the service as a drafted Militiaman, and never went out in any other way. He never served with any Continental Troops, and did not personally know any of the Regular Officers. Although General Greene was his Commander-in-Chief upon his last tour, he never was immediately with Greene, but was stationed some miles from him, as already stated. After the Revolutionary War, declarent lived in Lawrence County, South Carolina until about twenty years since, when he (1807) removed to Wilson County, Tennessee, where he resided five or six years, and then removed to Bedford County (about 1814/15), where he has ever since resided. He has already stated, he never received any written discharged from the service. He is acquainted with and known to Frederick F. Bradford, The Rev'd William G. Wood, Andrew Vannoy and Thomas Couch, who reside in the same neighborhood with him, and who he believes will testify as to his character for veracity and their belief of his service as a Soldier of the Revolution. He has no documentary evidence and he knows of no person whose testimony he can procure, who can testify as to his service, except William Teague of Wilson County, Tennessee, who can prove his first tour of two months, and whose affidavit is herewith filed.

      He hereby relinguishes every claim whatever to a pension or annuity except the present, and declares that his name is not on the Pension Roll of the Agency of any State.

Sworn to and subscribed the day and year aforesaid.

Jas. McKisick, Clerk   Zadok Wood

      We, William G. Wood, a Clergyman, residing in Bedford County, Tennessee and Frederick F. Bradford, residing in the same County and State, hereby certify that we are well acquainted with Zadok Wood, who has subscribed and sworn to the following declaration, that we believe him to be sixty seven years and two months of age, that he is reputed and believed in the neighborhood where he resides to have been a Soldier of the Revolution, and we concur in that opinion.

Sworn to and subscribed the day and year aforesaid.

Jas. McKisick, Clerk   William G. Wood
                                                  Fred. F. Bradford

And the said Court hereby declares their opinion, after the investigation of the matter and after putting the interrogatories prescribed by the War Department, that the above named applicant was a Revolutionary Soldier, and served as he states. And the Court further certifies that it appears to them that William G. Wood, who had signed the preceeding certificate, is a Clergyman, resident of Bedford County, Tennessee, and that Frederick F. Bradford who had also signed the same, is a resident in the said Bedford County, Tennessee, and is a credible person, and that their statement is entitled to credit.

                                  John B. Armstrong
                                  Samuel Phillips
                                  Wm. McClure

            Ref: GSA Report, Washington, D.C.

* * * * * * * * * *

NICHOLAS WOODFIN

Name:	Rank:	State Served:
Nicholas Woodfin	-----	Virginia

Born August 2, 1759 in Greenbrier County, Virginia, died December 21, 1832 in Bedford County, Tennessee, married Hannah Ashbrook in 1786. She was born May 3, 1766 in Hampshire County, Virginia and died August 8, 1845 in Bedford County, Tennessee. Both are buried in the Woodfin Cemetery, with marked graves.

Tombstones:

Nicholas Woodfin	Mrs. Hannah Woodfin
Aug 2, 1759	Relict of N. Woodfin
Dec 21, 1832	Died Aug 8, 1845
	Age: 80 yrs.

No GSA Report in Washington, D.C.

Lived in Greenbrier County, Virginia, during Revolutionary War. Served under Captain Archibald Wood. Married 1768 in West Virginia, to Hannah Ashbrook, born May 3, 1766 and died August 9, 1845 in Bedford County, Tennessee.

Children:

1. Elizabeth, born 1786, married James McMinn
2. Sarah (Sally), born 1788, married John Naylor who died Feb 10, 1855, aged 68 years. He is buried in the Woodfin Cemetery. Sarah has no grave marker.
3. Mary, born May 3, 1790, died Oct __, 1867, married Lenciel Andrew Edwards

"Stripling", born January 19, 1783 and died May 6, 1864, both are buried
in the Woodfin Cemetery without grave markers.
4. Samuel, born 1791, married Mariah Barnhill in 1815.
5. Moses, born February 9, 1784, married (1) Margaret Rodgers, (2) Eliza G.
        Chenault.
6. Phoebe, born March 12, 1796, married Thomas Swann.
7. Rebecca, born 1800, unmarried.
8. John, born 1801, married (1) _____, (2) Frances Edgarton.
9. Jane, born April 22, 1803, unmarried.
10. Hannah, born 1805, married Thomas Haile.

Nicholas Woodfin, was a Revolutionary Soldier, serving under command
of the frountier, against the Indians, ranging from Rich's Creek to Cook's Fort.
This was very hazardous, not only from hostile Indians but from dangerous wild
animals.

Nicholas Woodfin was present when Cornwallis surrendered at Yorktown.
Nicholas Woodfin came to Rutherford County, Tennessee about 1800. He is
shown in early Census of Virginia and North Carolina. His residence during the
Revolutionary War was in Greenbrier County, (West) Virginia.
Children:
1. Sarah, born 1788/9, married John Naylor.
2. Mary, born May 3, 1790, married Lencile Andrew Edwards "Stripling".
3. Samuel, born 1791, died April 29, 1863, married Mariah Barnhill born
December 9, 1796, died March 8, 1863. Both are buried in the Woodfin Cemetery
        with grave markers.
4. Elizabeth, born 1803, married James McMinn.
5. Jane, born April 22, 1803, died March 31, 1826 and is buried beside her father
        and mother in the Woodfin Cemetery with a grave marker.
6. Hannah, born 1805, married Thomas Haile who died September 8, 1900.

Nicholas Woodfin lived at the Bedford-Rutherford County Line. The Woodfin
Cemetery is located on his land.

> Ref: Texas Society DAR Roster Revolutionary Ancestors, Vol IV, page
>   2344.
> Ref: DAR Patriot Index, page 759
> Ref: Tennessee Blue Book Roster & Soldiers, Vol 1, page 1667.
> Ref: Cemetery Records of Bedford County, Tennessee by Marsh.
> Ref: Edwards Family Records & Bible Records.

* * * * * * * * * *

AARON WOOSLEY

Name:	Rank:	State Served:
Aaron Woosley	-----	Virginia

Born ca 1753, died after 1830

GSA: Aaron Woosley, Virginia.
Claim: Aaron Woosley, inscribed on the Roll of West Tennessee at the rate of 8
dollars per month, to commence on the 25 of September 1818.
        Certificate of Pension issued the 6 of September 1818 and sent to
Alfred M. Harris, Pulaski, Tennessee.

Arrears to the 4th of September 1819	$ 90.66
Semi-anl allowance ending March 1820	$ 48.00
	$138.66

On Rolls 424

State of Tennessee   ]
Lincoln County   ]
Sixth Judicial Circuit]
        This day personally appeared Aaron Woosley, a Revolutionary Soldier,
before me Alfred M. Harris, one of the Circuit Judges of the State aforesaid for
Circuit of _____ in pursuance of an Act of the last Session of Congress, providing
a pension for poor and indigent Revolutionary Soldiers, deposeth and saith that he
is about sixty five years of age from the best information he has of his age, that

in the year 1776 or 1777 in October he enlisted in the regular service of the United States in Amelia County, State of Virginia, in a Company of Infantry commanded by Captain James Harris and after he was attached to the company commanded by Captain _____ Wells and that he enlisted for three years and served the full time of his enlistment in the Regiment commanded by Colonel Bluford and his _____ composed a part of the Virginia Line of Continental Troops commanded by General Wasaford. That after he enlisted and during the term of his services he was engaged in behalf of the United States against the common enemy in the Battle of Brandywine and Germantown and Monmouth Court House.

That he served out faithfully and the full term of his enlistment and was discharged by Colonel Bluford at Middlebrook in Pennsylvania in the year 1779 or 1780 in the Fall of the year. That this discharge he is now unable to produce having lost it by accident or through the lapse of time is destroyed. That about two months after he was discharged he again enlisted in the regular service of the United States in Amelia County, Virginia in the Company of Horsemen commanded by Captain James Gun, which belonged to the First Regiment of Light Horse commanded by Colonel White, which composed a part of the Virginia line commanded as this affiant believes, for a time, by General Stephens who was the Commander of the _____ and afterwards, taken to the south under the commande of General Wayne and then commanded by General Greene in the State of North Carolina, South Carolina and Georgia. That when he enlisted this second time he enlisted during the war and continued to serve faithfully against the common enemy in the south until the conclusion of peace in 1783, when he was regularly discharged by Colonel White in Charleston in the State of South Carolina on the 5th day of July. That during the time he served in Georgia, he received a severe wound in the shoulder by a sword, when in a skirmish with the British and Tories about five miles off shore Savannah. This affiant further states that he is in reduced circumstances and stands in need of assistance of his Country and unless he receives the Bounty Government, he will ere long he will be unable to procure even the common comforts and necessaries of life. He further states that he has never received a pension from the United States for any cause whatever, and he hereby renounces and releases his right and claim to all pensions from the United States except the one now requested for the services mentioned in these facts stated in this affidavit by any person now living within the limits of this State, nor does he know certainly of any person now living within the United States, by whom he could prove it. He is a citizen of the United States of America and resident of the County of Lincoln and the State of Tennessee. He prays to be places on the Pension Act agreeably to Act of Congress on 25th of September 1818.

Aaron (X) Woosley

Affidavits:
Alfred M. Harris, that Aaron Woosley appeared before him.
James Bright, that Alfred M. Harris was Judge of Sixth Circuit of the Courts of law.
Alfred M. Harris, that Aaron Woosley is in indigent circumstances.
Will E. Kennedy, Wm. Edmiston, Jno. Greer, Vance Greer, said that we are well acquainted with David Dodd, Jesse Dodd and Aaron Woosley.

Aaron Woosley, I do solemnly swear that I have been placed on the Pension List Roll of West Tennessee agency being number 14,879 and that I made my original declaration for a pension on the 15th day of September 1818 and that I have no particular trade or profession and my family consists of myself who am considerably disabled by means of a wound in the right shoulder by a sword received in scouting party in the State of Georgia, and my wife aged 56 years very feeble and unhealthy and one daughter named susanna aged fifteen years.
Brice Garner, Clerk of the Court of Pleas and Quarter Sessions for Lincoln County, Tennessee.

In 1830 and afterwards, Aaron Woosley was living south of Flat Creek Community in Bedford County, Tennessee and continued there until his death. Some say he is buried in Hastings Camp Ground Graveyard. No Grave marker.
Ref: GSA Report, Washington, D.C.
Ref: 1830 Census of Bedford County, Tennessee.

HOWEL DAWDY

Name:	Rank:	State Served:
Howel Dawdy (Doddy)	-----	----------------

Born ca 1746, died December 20, 1830 (now Moore County, Tennessee), married Phebe _____. They are both buried in the Dawdy Cemetery in Moore County, Tennessee.

Tombstone:

Howel Dawdy	&	Phebe, His wife
Died Dec 20, 1830		Died Dec 10, 1831
Aged: 84 years		Aged: 81 years

Service: Revolutionary Accounts, 1-1-2; 1-3-4; 1-4-2; 1-11-2.

We have little information on his service to the country during the Revolution, other than the fact that he was listed in Allen's Tennessee Soldiers in the Revolution, as residing in Washington or Sullivan County, Tennessee, 1781-83, where he was listed by the Board of Auditors of Revolutionary Accounts. Said record of payments being listed in Vol 1, page 1, Folio 2, page 3, Folio 4 and page 4, Folio 2, the latter listing shows him receiving 13 £ and 3 shillings. These Account Books are in the Archives in Raleigh, North Carolina.

Howel Dawdy was a first settler at Shelbyville in 1810 and was a First Commissioner and Ranger of the new County of Bedford. In his later years, by 1820, he and his wife Phebe had moved to adjoining Moore County, Tennessee, to be near their daughter Pheby Blyth wife of Thomas Blythe. They are all buried in the Dawdy Cemetery, on Dogtail Branch, Moore County, Tennessee.

Children:

1. Pheby, born Aug 9, 1793, died Jan 3, 1860, married Thomas Blythe who was born Mar 4, 1783 and died Aug 28, 1829. They are buried by their parents in the Dawdy Cemetery with graves marked.
2. Howel Dawdy, Jr.

    Ref: Revolutionary Accounts, Raleigh, North Carolina.

    Ref: Moore County, Tennessee Cemetery Records by Marsh

* * * * * * * * * *

JAMES MOORE

Name:	Rank:	State Served:
James Moore	Lieut.	North Carolina

Born _____, died _____.

James Moore appears as shown below in an Account stated as follows: "Major Robert Fenner, Agent for the North Carolina Line". Settled August 10, 1792, No. 5.   S. Carrell

Lt. James Moore appears in a Book of the settlement of the old money accounts of the North Carolina Line, Revolutionary War, account being dated 1782 and the last 1 July 1783. Vol 136½, page 39.   J.S. Austin.

Lieut. James Moore appears as shown below on a Record of the "Proceedings of a Board of Officers of the North Carolina Line, held by order of the honorable Brigadier General Sumner, to Regiment the Officers of said Line.

Major Henry Dixon, President

Majors	Lieutenants
John Armstrong	Wm. Bush
Reading Blount	Curtis Ivey
Thomas Donoho	Wm. Sanders
	Thomas Clarke

Captains: Ensignes:
Robt. Raiford   Wynne Dixon
Tilman Dixon   Joseph Brevard
Joseph T. Rhodes   Wm. Alexander
Anty. Sharp   Robt. Bell
Edward Yarbrough   James Scurlock."
Alexandr. Brevard

Record dated Camp Southern Army, Feby 6, 1782.

The Board proceeded and made the following arrangement, viz, First Regiment.

Name: James Moore
Rank: Lieut.
Date of Commission: July 1, 1781.
No. 9.   S. Carrell

James Moore, Lieut., Revolutionary War, appears on a statement of clothing issued to the line. Statement not dated.
No. 218388_.   Clark, Copyist.

NOTE: A note in our Revolutionary War file indicated this James Moore lived in Bedford County, Tennessee in 1830 near Moores Chapel. No absolute proof of this. Eds.

CHECKLEY: 202
CLEEK: 195
CLEVELAND: 86, 105, 194, 195
CLINTON: 15, 75
COBLE: 32, 96
COCKE: 149
COFFEY: 16, 17, 51, 152
COLDWELL: 24, 80, 127
COLE: 36, 38, 70
COLEMAN: 199
COLLINS: 75
CILVELL: 104, 105
COMMONS: 147, 153
CONJARS: 145
CONNELL (CONNEL): 91, 92
CONNELLY: 32, 34, 35
COOK: 4, 45, 47, 96, 202, 203,
    242
COOMBS: 211
COOP: 36, 37, 38, 39, 42, 61, 62
COOPER: 16, 39, 40, 41, 42, 75,
    76, 162, 184, 202
CORNWALLIS: 5, 26, 29, 37, 43,
    46, 48, 59, 79, 84, 91, 98, 100,
    108, 121, 136, 137, 150, 160,
    174, 191, 194, 209, 210, 213,
    216, 233, 245
COSBY: 3, 4
COUCH: 43, 49, 177, 178, 249
COULTER: 111
COURSEY: 42, 43, 44
COUSER (COWSER): 78, 178
COVINGTON: 21
COWDEN: 181
COX: 78, 79, 172
CRABTREE: 194
CRAIG: 7, 242
CRAWFORD: 55, 56
CRAWLEY: 28
CRENSHAW: 41
CROGER: 15
CROSS: 212, 213
CROWELL: 77
CULLEY: 101
CULPS: 226
CULVER: 45, 46, 47
CUMMINGS: 96
CUNNINGHAM: 24, 47, 48, 49,
    50, 51, 52, 54, 91, 140, 155,
    177, 201, 244, 248
CURDY: 163

DALE: 137
DAMRON: 52
DARNELL: 195
DANDRIDGE: 209
DAVENPORT: 31, 152
DAVIDSON: 5, 6, 17, 43, 49, 52,
    53, 54, 55, 63, 69, 107, 108,
    109, 126, 166, 167, 178, 228,
    230, 237, 238, 239
DAVIE: 107, 108, 109, 124, 167,
    206, 238
DAVIS: 24, 36, 38, 55, 56, 57, 65,
    78, 96, 142, 163, 166, 208,
    213, 234
DAVY: 27
DAWDY: 134, 252
DEAN: 187, 234
DEASON: 79, 80
DeBEREN: 156
DECALB: 5
DELK: 155, 158, 229
DePUGH: 150
DERAGAN: 170
DENNIS: 175, 176
DEVENEY: 32
DEWY: 204
DIAL: 57, 58, 60, 61, 62, 234
DICE: 77
DICKSON: 21, 22, 91, 92, 126,
    134, 135, 181

DILLARD: 183
DITTO: 131, 160, 161
DIXON: 83, 90, 137, 230, 231,
    252, 253
DOAK: 4
DOBBS: 165
DODDS (DODD): 232, 235, 251
DODSON: 40
DONOHOE: 83
DONALDSON: 227
DONALSON: 152
DONOHO: 252
DOOLEY: 226, 227
DORMAN: 29
DOUGAN: 58, 190
DOUGLAS (DOUGLASS): 16, 151,
    156, 245, 246
DOWEL: 52
DOWLMAN: 28
DREDEN: 113
DRAKE: 63, 64, 65, 152
DRAPER: 9, 55, 152
DRAYTON: 112
DUDLEY: 30, 70, 71, 72
DUFF: 14, 178, 179, 181
DUNCAN: 48, 49
DUNLAP: 191, 193
DUNSMORE: 91, 169
DYER: 92, 93, 165, 193, 194
DYSART: 17

EAKIN: 24, 65, 66, 67, 183
EALEY: 173
EARL (EARLS): 110, 111
EARNHART: 76, 77
EATON: 198
EDGARTON: 250
EDMISTON: 17, 251
EDMONDSON: 87
EDWARDS: 18, 51, 52, 127, 150,
    151, 213, 249, 250
ELBERT: 198
ELKINS: 68, 69
ELLEDGE: 178
ELLIOTT: 65, 124, 129, 240
EOFF: 116
ERVIN: 112
ERWIN (IRWINE): 27, 54, 151,
    178, 223
ESTILL: 102
EULESS: 203
EVANS: 90, 145
EWIN (EVIN): 166, 167
EWING: 26, 70, 71, 72, 73, 74, 91,
    92, 129, 218

FALLS: 72, 107
FANE: 74, 75, 76
FANNING: 8, 9, 98, 99, 100, 140,
    245
FARLAND: 158
FARMER: 82, 245, 246
FARQUHARSON: 222
FARRAR: 83, 84
FARRAW (FARROW): 153, 154
FENNER: 252
FERGUSON (FERGASON,
    FURGERSON, FURGUSON):
    49, 86, 99, 101, 136, 179, 187,
    197, 203
FIELDS: 140
FINNEY: 78, 223
FISHER: 76, 77, 118, 120, 214,
    227, 228
FLANAGIN: 238
FLETCHER: 226
FLOYD: 48, 78, 189
FORBES: 126
FORD: 8, 9
FOSSETT: 37, 38
FOSTER: 44, 92, 93, 94, 217

FOUNTAIN: 162   FOX: 225
FRANCIS: 194
FRAZER: 124
FREEMAN: 57, 62, 151, 194
FRIZZELL (FRIZEL): 79, 80,
    128
FUGITT: 62, 144
FULKS: 75
FULLER: 9, 17, 175, 243
FULTS: 74

GALBREATH: 182
GAMMILL (GAMMEL): 4, 239
GARDEN: 43
GARLAND: 217, 221
GARMON: 81
GARNER: 73, 251
GARNETT: 85
GARRETT: 52, 183
GASKINS: 171, 209, 210
GATES: 5, 23, 37, 51, 93, 98,
    108, 109, 167, 179, 180
GATLIN (GATLAND): 219, 220
GENTRY: 3, 32, 52, 81, 89, 90,
    110, 173, 199, 225, 226
GEORGE: 161, 162
GIBBEY: 81
GIBBS: 82, 83, 84, 85
GILBREATH: 4
GILCHRIST: 61, 223
GILES (JILES): 238, 239
GILLESPIE: 100, 140, 159, 160
GLAZE: 117, 118
GLENN: 136, 194, 239, 240
GLOVER: 224
GOLSTON: 212
GOOCH: 11
GOOD: 142
GOODMAN: 248
GOODRUM: 41
GOODWIN: 4
GORDON: 248
GORE: 78, 81, 82
GOWEN: 8, 9, 78
GRAHAM: 8, 9, 51, 107, 109,
    136, 137, 143
GRANT: 209
GRASSES: 180
GRAY: 8, 9, 85, 86, 87, 88, 89
GREEN (GREENE): 2, 15, 23,
    24, 30, 31, 41, 60, 70, 72, 79,
    84, 89, 90, 101, 121, 140,
    145, 148, 150, 151, 156, 179,
    186, 187, 194, 203, 216, 217,
    229, 238, 239, 244, 248, 251
GREER: 9, 90, 134, 163, 225,
    251
GRIFFIN: 147
GRIFFETT (GRIFETT): 68
GRIFFIS: 156
GRIMER: 104, 105
GRISSOM: 33
GUESS: 25, 26
GUILOEZAN: 97
GUN: 251
GUY: 84
GWINN (GWIN): 97, 98, 99, 100

HADLEY: 145
HAGGARD: 28, 64, 155
HAILE: 210, 250
HALBERT: 143
HALE: 39, 225
HALEY: 43, 44, 90, 91, 92
HALKHAM: 33
HALL: 13, 14, 102, 136
HALSTEAD: 170
HAMBLETON: 213
HAMMOND: 48, 149, 150